Bottom Line's
Nutrition
SECRETS

How to Tap the Incredible Healing Power of Foods, Vitamins and Minerals

by Felicia Busch

Bottom Line
Books
www.BottomLineSecrets.com

Bottom Line's Nutrition Secrets
How to Tap the Healing Power of Foods, Vitamins and Minerals

Copyright © Adaptation 2004 by Bottom Line® Books
Copyright © 2000 by Felicia Busch. All rights reserved

Published by arrangement with John Wiley & Sons, Inc.

Bottom Line® Books is a registered trademark of
Boardroom® Inc.
281 Tresser Blvd.
Stamford, CT 06901

ISBN 0–88723–303-1

10 9 8 7 6 5 4 3 2 1

Notice: This book is intended as a reference volume only, not as a medical manual. The information given here is designed to help you make informed decisions about your health. It is not intended as a substitute for any treatment that may have been prescribed by your doctor. If you suspect that you have a medical problem, we urge you to seek competent medical help.

Printed in the United States of America.

ACKNOWLEDGMENTS

Many people were responsible for the completion of this book. I owe them my heartfelt gratitude.

To Jeff Braun, my original editor at Chronimed. Without you, this book would have never happened. You are responsible for its conception and all the excitement and wonder that goes into starting such a project.

To Nancy Claridge Turner, my friend and critical editor. You guided the book through a turbulent adolescence and helped form much of the spirit of this work.

To Jeffrey Golick, my editor at John Wiley. Thank you for guiding the transformation of my ideas into an organized and thoughtful work. You were given this project late and I am still amazed at how much you accomplished in so short a time. Under your care this book grew to a level of maturity I am proud of.

To my friends and colleagues at Felicia Busch & Associates, Inc., who over the years helped refine the material presented here. Special thanks to Molly Mullroy, M.S., R.D.; Julie Mattson Ostrow, M.S., R.D.; Anne Dworak, M.P.H.; Cassie Schmidt, R.D.; Mikki Kainz Poplawski, M.S., R.D.; Paula Nessa, R.D.; Terri Loree, M.S., R.D.; Lisa Lovekin, R.D.; Sarah Becker, R.D.; and Lori Holladay, R.D.

To the countless students and interns who did considerable research online, in libraries, and at grocery and health food stores. And to the agencies that generously shared their students for field experiences, including: Regions Hospital, University of Minnesota Food Science and Nutrition Department, North Dakota State University, and the University of Minnesota Graduate School of Public Health Nutrition. Special thanks to Michelle Brooks and Jennifer Hall.

To my colleagues who have encouraged me and so generously shared their wisdom. This book was critically reviewed by colleagues who are national media spokespersons for the American Dietetic Association. This group of dedicated volunteer nutrition experts from around the country helped me to refine the nutrition facts presented and includes: Susan Adams, M.S., R.D.; Tammy Baker, M.S., R.D.; Leslie Bonci, M.P.H., R.D.; Connie Diekman, Med., R.D., F.A.D.A.; Gail Frank, Dr.P.H., R.D.; JoAnn Hattner, M.P.H., R.D., C.S.P.; Janet L. Helm,

M.S., R.D.; Edith Howard Hogan, R.D.; Cindy Moore, M.S., R.D.; Jackie A. Newgent, R.D., C.D.N.; Betty Nowlin, M.P.H., R.D.; Diane Quagliani, M.B.A., R.D.; Sheah Rarback, M.S., R.D., F.A.D.A.; Cynthia A. Thomson, Ph.D., R.D.; Elizabeth M. Ward, M.S., R.D.; and Althea Zanecosky, M.S., R.D.

Special thanks to my husband Kevin, for your patience when deadlines were coming and for your willingness to free up time for me to write. To my sons Matthew, Ryan, and Daniel, I owe you much time and attention you missed while I was busy working on the book. Get ready to collect! ❦

—*Felicia Busch, M.P.H., R.D., F.A.D.A*

ABOUT THE AUTHOR

FELICIA BUSCH, M.P.H., R.D., F.A.D.A., is a noted nutrition expert. She writes for a variety of consumer and professional newsletters, magazines, and newspapers, and is a frequent guest on radio and TV. A popular speaker, Ms. Busch is a spokesperson for the American Diabetic Association.

AUTHOR'S DEDICATION

FOR MY SISTER IVY,
WHO INSPIRES ME WITH HER COURAGEOUS
BATTLE AGAINST CANCER

INTRODUCTION

It's not acceptable anymore to only pursue a "healthful diet." The recent explosion of scientific information related to how we nourish our bodies has forever altered the role of food. The dramatic change in the foods we eat, shop for, and design has created a new cornucopia of choices. Such choices are often more frustrating than freeing. My goal in writing this book is to help cut through the clutter and share the most exciting and reputable nutrition information available today. Yes, you need to choose a healthy balance of foods. You may also need to take supplements. This book will show you how to put it all together.

Two years of research went into the recommendations offered here. The expertise of top researchers, specialists, and nutrition scientists is included. You decide which information applies to your particular set of circumstances. Nutrition is the interconnected science of a host of nutrients and other factors that don't neatly fit into separate chapters. *Here's how we did it…*

Chapter 1 gets personal. Who you are and how you live will impact your nutritional needs. You'll need to dig into your family history to trace your medical roots and learn how your ancestry may impact your health. Quizzes and checklists will help you put into perspective your risk for the common chronic diseases of our day.

Chapters 2 and 3 cover the old and new basics of nutrition. Calories, carbohydrate, protein, fat, fiber, and water will always be essential nutrients. Nutrient thieves that steal precious components from food are exposed. These chapters are right up front on purpose. Food comes first in the pursuit of health; supplements are just that—something to consider after you've done all you can to eat right.

The secrets of eating styles from around the world and across the ages are explored in *Chapter 4*. You'll find nutrition plans ranging from Ayurvedic to Zen macrobiotic and dietary guidelines from around the globe. These models will help steer you to the right food fit for your unique circumstances and needs.

Chapters 5 through 8 delve into the nitty-gritty facts about vitamins, minerals, alternative supplements, and herbal products. Learn what they can and can't do to improve (or harm) your health. Where possible, specific amounts and formulations are recommended.

The information in *Chapter 9* sums up the wealth of information we have on how nutrition causes, treats, or cures a variety of the most common disorders and diseases.

One book can't possibly provide every answer. In fact, not all the right questions have even been asked yet in the field of food and nutrition. The final chapter will help you become a better nutrition consumer—of both products and services. You'll learn how to spot the quacks and ways to identify junk science.

Sprinkled throughout the volume are signposts to guide you. *They include…*

NUTRITION HOW TO'S: Specific steps you can take to make changes.

GO FIGURE: The math behind nutrition formulas, measurement units, and calculations.

HANDY HOTLINES: Where to call for more information or help with particular issues.

LINK UPS: Our recommended web sites for more depth on a topic or to keep abreast of new research.

SELECTED STUDIES: There was not room to include all the key or important studies on any topic. Some of the most recent research is highlighted for you. Reading any of these studies (online or in the library) will present you with a whole list of related reference articles at the end of each publication for further exploration.

Much nutrition information is confusing and conflicting. I've tried to translate the science of nutrition into easily understandable key concepts and recommendations. Now I see an even greater challenge. Keeping up to date with the explosion of new information and research is a daunting task. Use the Handy Hotlines and Link Ups to keep current and connected.

I hope this book will inspire you to look more carefully at how you eat and to make those small changes that can add up to huge health benefits. When you do that, you'll be taking a giant leap toward optimal health and happiness. 🍂

CONTENTS

Acknowledgments   iii
Introduction   v

PART I

UNDERSTANDING THE NEW NUTRITION

1. The New Nutrition   3
Nutrition for a Better Healthspan   4
How Do You Measure Up?   5
Keep a Diary of What You Eat   7
It's a Family Affair   10
Determine Your Nutritional Health   11
Think You Are a Super Taster?   13
Major Health Risks of Poor Nutrition   15
Rate Your Risk for Heart Disease   17
Body Mass Index: How Do You
    Shape Up?   20
What Are Your Risks for Osteoporosis?   23
Rate Your Risk for Stroke   24

**2. You Are What You Eat:
    A Nutrition Primer**   27
Are You in the Know About H$_2$O?   27
Calories: A Control Issue   30
How Many Calories Do You
    Really Burn?   32
Carbohydrates: Keep Them Complex   33
Protein: Your Handyman   34
Focus on Fat   34
Rate Your Fat Habits   37

Fiber   39
Nutrition How To's for Your Fiber Fix   40

3. Foods in the News
The Good News—From Avocados to
    Zucchini   42
Amazing Avocados   43
Beans, Beans, They're Good for
    Your Heart   43
What's the Beef over Beef?   45
Biotech Benefits   46
Pick Some Blueberries   47
Bran Will Keep You Regular   48
Broccoli—Crown Jewel of Nutrition   49
Brown Rice Is Best   49
Canola from Canada   50
Capsaicin—It's Hot   51
Carrots—Encapsulated Carotene   52
Cheese—Choose Carefully   52
Chicken Choices   54
Chocolate—Food or Drug?   54
Couscous—Moroccan Mainstay   55
Get Unstuck with Cranberries   55
Eggs Are Okay   57
Fishing for Health   58
Flaxseed Each Day Keeps the
    Doctor Away?   60
Garlic—Crushed Hopes?   60
Grape Juice—No Wine Here   62
Grapefruit—Red Is Richer   62
Honey—The Bitter Truth   63

Irradiation—If It's Good Enough for
   Astronauts… 64
Jicama—Root Vegetable or Bean? 65
Kiwi—Packed with Power 65
Lentils—Healthy Legumes 66
Melons—Sweet and Nutritious 67
Mushrooms—Better Cooked Than Raw 67
Nuts to You 68
Oats—For Your Health 69
Olive Oil—What a Fat! 70
Papaya—Delicious Health Treat 71
Pasta—It's Primo! 72
Pick a Peck of Peppers 72
Psyllium—It's Husky 73
Salads—Go for the Dark Greens 73
Soft Drinks Edge Out Milk 74
Joy of Soy 74
Strawberries—Nutritious Delight 75
Sweet Potatoes, Please 76
Time for Tea? 76
Tomatoes Catch Up 78
Vegetables—Can It 78
Wheat Germ—WOW! 80
Wine—Health Aid or Health Hazard? 80
Yogurt—A Cultured Taste 81
Zucchini—What a Squash! 81
The Bad News—Nutrient Thieves 82
Alcohol Effects 83
Caffeine—Trouble Brewing? 83
Fake Foods 84

PART II

GETTING WHAT YOU NEED

4. Eating Style Options 87
Make Mealtime Quality Time 87
Teen Eating Machines 88
Nutrition How To's for Feeding Teens 88
Older Adults 89
How to Eat Well When You're
   Not Motivated 89
Dietary Guidelines Around the World 89
Girth of a Nation 90
Food Guide Pyramid 92

The Challenge in Following
   Nutrition Guidelines 93
The Tumbling Pyramid: How
   Americans Really Eat 94
Eating Styles 95
Ayurvedic Diet 96
Homeopathy 97
Macrobiotics 97
Mediterranean Diet 99
Traditional Chinese Medicine (TCM) 100
Vegetarian Eating—Nuts About
   Veggies 102
Vegetarian Pyramid 103
Nutrient-Based Eating Styles 103
The Young and the Meatless 104
High Protein Usually Means
   High Fat 104
Moderate Low-Fat Eating 105
High-Carbohydrate, Very
   Low-Fat Diets 105
Choose Your Own Style 106
It's All About You 106

5. Vitamins 108
Vitamin-Mineral Revelations 109
Animal, Vegetable, or Mineral? 110
From A to Zinc 110
Alphabet Soup of Standards 111
More Is Not Always Better 112
Nutrients in a Nutshell 112
Fat-Soluble Nutrients 113
Vitamin A 114
Vitamin D 115
Vitamin E 118
Vitamin K 119
Water-Soluble Vitamins 120
Thiamin (Vitamin B-1) 120
Riboflavin (Vitamin B-2) 121
Niacin (Vitamin B-3) 121
Pyridoxine (Vitamin B-6) 122
Cobalamin (Vitamin B-12) 123
Folate 123
Biotin 125
Pantothenic Acid (Vitamin B-5) 126
Vitamin C 126

Vitamin-Like Compounds   128
Choline   128
Carnitine   129
Inositol   129
Taurine   129
Pills in Food Form   130
What Vitamins Do You Need for
    Special Situations?   132

6. Minerals   133
Colloidal Confusion   133
Major Minerals   134
Calcium   134
Magnesium   135
Phosphorus   136
Electrolytes   136
Chloride   136
Potassium   137
Sodium   137
The Great Sodium Debate   138
Salt Sense   138
Where's the Salt in Your Favorite
    Fast Foods?   139
Trace Elements   140
Iron   140
Chromium   141
Copper   141
Fluoride   142
Iodine   142
Selenium   143
Manganese   144
Molybdenum   144
Zinc   144
Mineral Needs for Special Situations 146
Supplement Scenarios   147

7. Alternative Supplements   148
Amino Acids   149
Arginine   149
L-tryptophan   150
PABA   150
SAM-e   150
Enzymes   151
CoQ-10   151
Ergogenic Aids   151

Chromium Picolinate   152
The Truth About Sports Beverages   153
The Creatine Craze   154
Hormones   155
DHEA   155
Melatonin Mania   156
Other Common Alternatives   156
Bee Pollen   156
Chitosan   157
Cholestin   157
GBL   158
Glucosamine   158
Royal Jelly   159
Lecithin   159
Laetrile   159
Fish Oil Capsules   159
Pycogenol   159
Shark Cartilage   160
Spirulina   160

8. Herbal Products   162
Herb Appeal   162
Nightmare on Herb Street   164
Herbs Throughout the Ages   165
How You Buy Herbs   166
Botanicals Available Over-the-Counter 167
Buying Better Botanicals   169
Common Myths About Herbs   169
Quality Products   171
Safety Classifications   171
Herb Hunter's Guide   172
Astragalus   172
Black Cohosh   173
Cat's Claw Bark   173
Chamomile   174
Echinacea   174
Evening Primrose Oil   175
Feverfew   176
Ginger   176
Ginkgo Biloba   177
Ginseng   178
Hawthorn   179
Horse Chestnut Seed Extract   179
Kava   179
Licorice   180

St. John's Wort — 180
Saw Palmetto — 181
Valerian — 182
Herbal Tea Time — 182
Beware of Diet Teas — 183
Professional Help — 183
Warning: Herbs That Can Be Harmful — 184
Weeding Through Herbal Research — 185
Future Focus — 187

PART III

HEALING AND HYPE

9. Eating to Heal — 191
The Connection Between Diet
    and Disease — 191
Alzheimer's Disease — 192
Anemia — 193
Arthritis — 195
Asthma — 197
Attention Deficit Hyperactivity
    Disorder — 198
Cancer — 199
Cataracts — 201
Diabetes — 203
Epilepsy — 205
Fibromyalgia Syndrome — 206
Food Allergies, Sensitivities, and
    Intolerances — 207
Heart Disease — 209
The Cholesterol Connection — 210
HDL (Good) and LDL (Bad)
    Cholesterol — 210
Triglycerides — 211
Lp (a) — 211
High Blood Pressure — 213
HIV/AIDS — 214
Inflammatory Bowel Disease — 216
Macular Degeneration — 217
Menopause — 218
Migraines and Headaches — 220
Obesity — 221
Warning: Pitfalls of Popular
    Diet Programs — 222
Osteoporosis — 223

Premenstrual Syndrome (PMS) — 226
Ulcers — 227

**10. Evaluating Nutrition Products
    and Purveyors** — 229
Sizing Up Research — 230
The Power of Placebo — 230
Sensationalized Science — 230
Don't Swallow Half-Baked
    Nutrition Claims — 232
Junk Science — 234
Supplement Savvy — 234
The Claim Game — 236
What Your Dietary Supplement
    Label Must Tell You — 237
How To Read A Supplement Label — 238
Supplement Profiteers — 239
Protecting Your Investment — 240
Alternative to What? — 241
Expert Evaluation — 242
Who's Who in Nutrition — 243
Registered Dietitian (RD) — 243
Nutritionist — 243
Certified Nutritional
    Consultant (CNC) — 243
Alternative Systems of Practice — 244
Surfing the Net — 244
How to Duck the Quacks — 245
Nutty Nutritionists — 246
Web Fraud — 247
Why Bogus Therapies Seem to Work — 247
If You Can't Beat 'Em—Join 'Em — 248

APPENDICES

Glossary: A Mouthful of Nutrition
    Diction — 251
Ingredient Lists: What Am I Eating? — 254
Federal Nutrients Standards — 257

INDEX — 261

PART I

UNDERSTANDING
THE NEW NUTRITION

THE NEW NUTRITION

You hold the power and responsibility to shape your own health through the miracle of food. With the right foods, you can increase your lifespan, improve your appearance and lift your mood.

We are at a scientific crossroads in human history. We know more than ever imagined about how food can prevent devastating disease or heal genetically inherited weaknesses. What you eat has the awesome ability to change your destiny. Whether you are 22 or 92, seize your opportunity now.

In a lifetime, you will eat eighty thousand meals or the equivalent of seventy tons of food and drink. The most recent National Health and Nutrition Examination Survey (NHANES) reports that 80 percent of women and 70 percent of men ate less than two-thirds of the Recommended Dietary Allowances (RDAs) for one or more nutrients. At least one-third of the elderly in the United States are nutritionally deficient, and the problem will grow as our population ages.

Why are we eating ourselves into early death and disability? In less than one hundred years we have transformed our society from the farm to the factory, and now we're speeding down the information superhighway from our padded office chairs. These changes have impacted both our food and physical activity habits.

Why don't Americans consume enough nutrients from foods? *Most of us…*

- Don't eat enough calories to get adequate vitamin/mineral intakes
- Eat a limited variety of food without enough fruits, vegetables, and grains
- Choose too many processed foods
- Take incomplete or haphazardly chosen supplements

Food used to be simple. You or your neighbors grew most of it. Labels were not required because it was easy to tell a bushel of corn from a bucket of berries. Food preparation and cooking were done at home. People ate what was in season and stored extra for the winter months.

Today, grocery store shelves are stuffed with packaged, processed extras. You have to search to find foods that used to be staples. Even "fresh" foods like produce are often several weeks old when they reach your local market. We're also depending on others to select and prepare our foods. Fast-food drive-through lanes and restaurant eat-in and take-out service are replacing the family dining table. A 1999 report from the United States Department of Agriculture's (USDA's) Economic Research Service found that meals eaten away from home—which include one of every three for the average American—are much less nutritious than home-prepared foods. Eating out typically means taking in about 25 percent less fiber, calcium, and iron than you'd get from foods prepared at home. That's a lot of missed nutrition when you consider that in the 1990s we ate almost twice as many meals away from home compared to the 1980s.

Most of us can't—or don't want to—go back to the good old days. With today's food choices you can eat better. More important, optimal nutrition can help you feel good, age more gracefully, and live longer.

Nutrition for a Better Healthspan

It's the dawn of a new era in nutrition. New nutrition includes more than just meeting basic calorie, vitamin, and mineral needs. Nutrition today requires an understanding of new food attributes that can prevent or delay the onset of chronic disease. There needs to be a new awareness of claims for food and supplements that often far outpace the scientific research to back them up.

Never before in human history have people been able to live as long as we can. But with these extra years come a greater chance of developing chronic disease. Disabling diseases can keep you from enjoying a longer life or erode the quality of those extra years. About ten years ago a front-page newspaper headline startled many people. It read: Eat Right, Don't Drink, Don't Smoke, Exercise Every Day and You'll Live Six Months Longer. "Why bother!" was a common response. Is maintaining healthful habits worth a lousy six months? Unfortunately, the real conclusion of that story was buried. The research report found that people who have healthful lifestyles enjoy a tremendously superior quality of life in their last years. Those who drink, smoke, don't exercise, and make poor food choices often spend their final years in misery, hooked up to machines in long-term care facilities unable to care for themselves. Today's technology can keep almost anyone's body alive indefinitely. It's your spirit, zest for life, and ability to function that make the real difference as you age.

The compelling evidence proves that what you eat has a direct effect on your health and potential to enjoy life. Take charge of your health now. Whether this is your first look at nutrition or you're already quite knowledgeable, plan a strategy that fits your lifestyle on a long-term basis. This book will help you. You'll discover simple ways to make small changes that significantly impact how you look and feel—both now and in the future.

Don't Settle for Being Average

No one likes to think of themselves as average. Indeed, the whole "nutrition revolution" is aimed toward more personalized, customized eating options. Nutrient requirements for the *average* American may not be optimal for *you*. Many factors affect your health and well-being. Some of those you have control over, like diet and exercise. At the moment, genetic factors such as family history remain outside of your direct control. Amazingly, this may change for the youngest, and for future generations of Americans today.

A great place to start is by comparing yourself to both the average and ideal American. In Chapter 4 you will learn about new-age and age-old eating styles that may prove a better match for your unique lifestyle. As you complete this chapter, you will develop a comprehensive picture of your health and potential health risks. Analyzing what you're doing right now will give you a sense of where to make improvements.

Here's the latest data on the "average" U.S. man and woman (aged 25 to 50), compared to today's ideals. Obviously, you can't change your height, but your food intake and exercise output are within your control. Where do you fit?

Fewer Calories = Fatter Americans. How can the "ideal" man and woman have higher fat and calorie intakes than the average person? The key is calories—or lack of them. Americans today eat fewer calories than they should to have a healthful food intake. At the same time, there are more overweight people in our country than ever before. In 1980 approximately 25 percent of Americans were overweight, according to government statistics. In 2000, it ballooned to 64 percent, says the National Center for Health Statistics.

Fewer calories and fatter people? If you haven't figured it out, the missing puzzle piece is exercise, or rather the lack of exercise. For many, extra pounds pile up because of small, but consistent, imbalances. Just fifty extra calories a day adds up to five pounds a year. In ten years your weight would slowly swell to fifty extra pounds. Of course, these calculations don't take into account that calorie needs decrease with age.

If you're part of the minority who maintain an outwardly normal weight, don't feel smug yet. A normal weight may look good on the outside but doesn't provide a clue to your internal health. The self-assessments in this chapter will.

Deprivation—that's what many people think is required to be healthy. Instead of focusing on what you need to eliminate

HOW DO YOU MEASURE UP?

	Average U.S. Man	Ideal U.S. Man	Me	Ideal U.S. Woman	Average U.S. Woman
Height	5' 10"	5' 10"	_____	5' 4"	5' 4"
Weight	175	166	_____	125	142
Average Daily Intake					
Calories	2,153	2,708	_____	2,094	1,769
Protein	90 g	60 g	_____	46 g	65 g
Carbohydrate	404 g	393 g	_____	304 g	229 g
Fat	83 g	90 g	_____	70 g	64 g
Fiber	19 g	27 g	_____	20 g	13 g
Cholesterol	203 mg	< 300 mg	_____	< 300 mg	208 mg

Sources: United States Recommended Dietary Allowances, National Health and Nutrition Examination Survey III from your lifestyle, try a new approach. Look at what you're missing and figure out how to add in those things. You have two options for getting started. If you're a person who's highly motivated and ready to take action now—go get a sharp pencil or two—it's time to do some planning. As you read through this chapter, take time to fill in the quizzes and questionnaires right in the chapter to help keep you on track.

On the other hand, if you tend to get bogged down or sidetracked, I encourage you to skim the fill-in-the-blank parts and finish reading the entire book before you begin.

For the Record

Dig out whatever medical records you have on hand. *Find out the following before you start…*

- Blood pressure (systolic/diastolic)
- Total cholesterol
- High-density lipoprotein (HDL) and low-density lipoprotein (LDL) cholesterol
- Electrocardiogram results, if you've ever had this test

Also, ask your doctor if you've ever had atrial fibrillation (irregular heartbeat in the upper chambers of your heart).

Rate Your Plate

Keep track of everything you eat and drink for the next three days. Research shows this is the best way to determine how you eat. Write it all down. If you need a form to get started, use the one on page 8. A blank checkbook register works better because you can carry it around in your pocket or purse. This task may take some time, but the valuable information you gain will be worth it.

NUTRITION HOW TO:
Make copies of the form on page 8 or transfer the headings into a check register. Don't depend on your memory at the end of the day. As soon as you finish eating anything, write it down. If possible include at least one weekend day—especially if your eating changes dramatically on weekends.

It's human nature not to 'fess up to every single thing you eat or drink—but do it anyway. Remember, this record is for you. So don't try to fool yourself. Eat the way you usually do. That will give you the best snapshot of your own style of normal eating. You'll be able to compare and contrast your eating style with today's nutrition recommendations.

Sample Food Record

Write down everything—get picky! Keep track of all beverages, including water, coffee, and diet soft drinks. You're counting more than calories here. Be sure to list seasonings, condiments, and extras. Don't forget the three french fries you snatched from your kid's Happy Meal or the piece of candy from your coworker's desk. They all add up, so write them down. Be as precise as you can about serving sizes. Look on food packages for clues, such as the total weight of a product. Be especially careful estimating fats such as oils, margarine, and salad dressings. If you eat at quick service or other restaurants, ask if they have nutrition information available on their products. The key is to get as much detail as possible about all that you eat and drink. The quality of your personal food analysis is only as good as the quality of your record keeping.

Next, use your completed food journal as a guide to help answer the following

KEEP A DIARY OF WHAT YOU EAT

How Much	Food or Drink	Time	With Whom/ Where	Accompanying Activity
1/4 cup	100% bran cereal	7:11 a.m.	Kevin, Matthew,	Helping Matthew
1/2 cup	1% milk		Ryan, and	practice spelling
			Daniel	words
1/2 large	Banana	7:23		
6 small	Jelly Beans	7:40	Alone in the car	Driving to work
1/2 cup	Water	9:00	Paula at the	Talking
			water fountain	
2 slices	Extra-thick whole-grain bread	11:50	Julie and Mikki at company cafeteria	Talking, looking at photos
2 thin slices (about 1 ounce)	extra-lean ham			
2 tsp.	Dijon mustard			
small piece	iceberg lettuce			
1 1/2 cups	Tossed salad made with romaine lettuce, mushrooms, shredded carrot	1225 pm.		
3 Tbs.	light ranch dressing			
12 oz.	bottled water plain	2:00	Alone at my desk	Making my to-do list

questions. Your answers focus on important areas that don't show up on a nutrient analysis summary. What you write here will give you a quick way to tune in to your eating style and habits.

Access the free web site on page 9 so you can enter your food journal into a computerized program that provides detailed feedback on specific nutrients. If you don't have access to a computer, use any of the popular food composition books (*Bowes & Church's Food Values of Portions Commonly Used*, J. B. Lippincott Co., or *The Most Complete Food Counter*, Pocket Books) and look everything up. This method takes a lot longer, but you'll get similar results. If you go to library for a nutrient composition book, ask if they have any computers online; it will be much faster and more fun. You'll need to know your current height

YOUR PERSONAL FOOD RECORD

How Much	Food or Drink	Time	With Whom/ Where	Accompanying Activity

LINK UP to *http://www.nutrition. about.com/msub8.htm* for a complete resource to analyze your daily food intake. Provided by Rick Hall, R.D., from About.com.

and weight and will be asked to estimate your activity level. Simply key in the basic kind of food on your list and up will pop a detailed selection from which to choose your specific item and amount.

You'll learn what you're doing right and where there's room to make small improvements for big gains in your overall health. In just a few days you can have a clearer understanding of your eating style. This do-it-yourself nutrition analysis won't be nearly as precise as a professionally supervised analysis. So don't hesitate to consult a professional, especially if you are pregnant, have health problems, are at risk for chronic disease, or are following a restricted diet.

Personal Nutritional Survey

Who purchases the food in your home? _____

Who prepares it? _____

How many meals do you eat each day? _____

How many snacks? _____

Do you ever skip meals? Which ones? _____

Do you eat alone? How often? _____

What else are you doing while you eat? (working, watching TV, driving, etc.) _____

_____

Do you avoid any foods for health or personal choice reasons? Which ones? _____

_____

How many times each week do you eat foods prepared away from home? _____

What restaurants do you go to most often? _____

List any medications (over-the-counter or prescribed) you regularly take: _____

_____

List each supplement, how much you regularly take, and what benefit you are seeking: _____

_____

Do you eat when you're not hungry? When or why? _____

Do you eat too much of any type of food? Which ones? _____

Are there foods you don't eat enough of? Which ones? _____

How often do you consume soft drinks and alcoholic beverages? Which ones? _____

_____

(See Chapter 10 for information on how to choose a qualified nutrition professional.)

It's a Family Affair

Now that we've covered the basic information about your current eating habits, it's time to explore the other factors that impact your health and nutritional status. While you have little control over most of the following concerns, it's important to know your family history as you plan your nutrition strategy.

Nutrition is a balance between environmental and genetic factors. Almost every chronic disease that has a nutrition component also has a genetic component. Studies of families, especially those with twins who are separated at birth, provide strong evidence that genetics affects the development of chronic disease. Sometimes, as with obesity, a family history greatly increases your risk of the same disease. On the other hand, many cancers are the result of environmental conditions, not your genetic makeup.

To help determine your chances of developing a chronic disease, talk with your family. Find out who developed health problems, at what age, and with what outcome. Note clusters of related ailments—heart disease, types of cancer, and so on. Then talk to your doctor. Ask for guidance in evaluating the information you have collected. One case of cancer in your extended family may be just bad luck. But if you find several, then your own personal risk increases. This is especially true if the relatives were in your immediate family or were affected at a young age. If that's your situation, a genetic counselor or specialist might be the most appropriate person to review your history. They might suggest additional tests to more clearly judge your personal risk. For example,

> **LINK UP** to *http://www.lifelinks.mb. ca* for other sample forms and information on how to complete your family medical history.

there is a new homocysteine test for heart disease, or perhaps you need a baseline mammogram earlier than age 40.

Shore Up Your Immune System

In the 1990s at least ten top-selling books on nutrition had "immunity" in their titles. You may know that immunity is important to your health, but just what does it have to do with the food you eat? In addition to immunizations to build immunity, it's now becoming clearer that what you eat can make a big difference in how your body fights off disease and protects itself.

It's hard not to use military adjectives when talking about your immune system. It's mission is to protect and defend your entire body. There are two main branches of your immune system. In the first group are the defenders who provide general service. Defenders fight off everything they encounter to protect you from harm. Your skin, hair, sweat, body oils, saliva, and tears are part of the defense. These immune protectors get physical and set up invasion barriers to protect your internal organs and tissues.

NUTRITION HOW TO:
- Take inventory of your medical history, lifestyle, and current eating habits.
- Analyze your food records and complete your personal nutrition survey.

DETERMINE YOUR NUTRITIONAL HEALTH

The warning signs of poor nutritional health are often overlooked. Use this checklist to find out if you are at nutritional risk. Read the statements and circle the numbers in the yes column that apply.

For each yes answer you score the number in the box. Total your score to determine your nutritional health.

	YES
I have an illness or condition that made me change the kind and/or amount of food I eat.	2
I eat fewer than two meals per day.	3
I eat few fruits or vegetables or milk products.	2
I drink three or more servings of beer, liquor, or wine almost every day.	2
I have tooth or mouth problems that make it hard for me to eat.	2
I don't always have enough money to buy the food I need.	4
I eat alone most of the time.	1
I take three or more different prescribed or over-the-counter drugs a day.	1
Without wanting to, I have lost or gained ten pounds in the last six months.	2
I'm not always physically able to shop, cook, and/or feed myself.	2

TOTAL = _____

0–2   Good! Recheck your nutritional score in six months.

3–5   You are at moderate nutritional risk. See what can be done to improve your eating habits and lifestyle. Recheck your nutritional score in three months.

6 or more   You are at high nutritional risk. Take this checklist the next time you see your doctor, dietitian, or health care provider. Talk with them about any problems you may have.

Remember that warning signs suggest risk but do not diagnose any medical condition.

Source: Nutrition Screening Initiative

The selective service immune protectors are more highly trained. They launch antibodies that destroy just one type of invader. Then they go on the attack. Together, these specialists are equipped to combat more than 100 billion types of enemies, and they have very long memories. If you've ever been attacked by a particular germ before, they remember and launch an immediate attack.

Having a decreased level of even a single nutrient can weaken your natural resistance to disease. Sometimes your immune system can get shell-shocked. Your defenders spin out of control and start attacking your own body tissues. Lupus is a form of arthritis that is caused by an immune system gone bad. A variety of factors help strengthen and protect immunity. Eating a healthful diet that contains a variety of specific nutrients that can enhance your immune system is essential. A strong immune system can help you stave off many of the health problems we've looked at—in spite of your family history.

Dietary Evolution

Computers are helping humans gain insights that may help solve today's diet-related health problems. University of Arkansas anthropologist Peter Ungar has found a way to use computer-mapping techniques to chart the landscape of teeth and learn how the human diet might have evolved. Precise computer-calculated numbers chart the grooves in tooth surfaces and indicate how food and liquid might accumulate or drain over the teeth. Human dental fossils mapped with GRASS (Geographical Resources Analysis Support System) help to show what humans evolved to eat. "We didn't evolve to eat cheeseburgers and milkshakes, that's for sure," says Ungar. Human ancestors consumed fewer grains and more

LINK UP to *http://www.sciam.com* for the *Scientific American* web site, and search for "Food for Thought," William R. Leonard's article on diet and human evolution.

fruits and vegetables, getting more protein, vitamins, minerals, and fiber than people in today's affluent societies eat. As humans grew grains, developed alcohol, cultivated sugar, and mined salt, dietary changes began to evolve so fast that our anatomy could not adapt. This relatively rapid change in eating habits has increased many chronic diseases such as cancer, diabetes, high blood pressure, and heart disease.

Impact of Food versus Family Genetics

What you eat—and what you avoid eating—can change the odds for or against your long-term health. Optimal nutrition can also help ward off conditions including heart disease, cancer, adult-onset diabetes, hypertension, and osteoporosis.

Your nutritional needs are unique—different from anyone else's. Yet all food follows a similar pathway in each of our bodies. Metabolism is responsible for the digestion, absorption, distribution, transformation, storage, and excretion of nutrients. Metabolism causes lots of extreme variations in nutrient needs in people born with flaws in their metabolic system. Faulty genes are to blame for nutrition-related disorders that range from lactose intolerance and inherited high blood cholesterol to cystic fibrosis. These types of genetic diseases are called inborn errors of metabolism. Essential enzymes that are missing at birth affect individual nutrient needs. Some of these disorders can be treated by avoiding or restricting particular foods. Others require supplementation of nutrients, sometimes in huge amounts, for improvement.

More subtle genetic variations are now being uncovered.

A 1998 *Nutrition Reviews* article reports that genetic diversity causes widely different needs for the nutrient folic acid. Researchers estimate that from 8 to 18 percent of people worldwide have a genetic mutation that raises how much homocysteine is in their blood. High levels of this amino acid mean a higher risk for heart disease, stroke, and blood vessel disease. How much folic acid and vitamins B-6 and B-12 you need to keep homocysteine levels normal can double or triple if you have the mutated version of this gene.

The challenge of nutrition research today is to identify these minor genetic traits that need customized dietary planning. It's time to move beyond the one-size-fits-all approach. Of the many environmental factors that can tip the odds in your favor or tilt them against you, food may be the most important. Fortunately, it is one of the few variables that you can do something about. It's estimated that good nutrition can reduce the incidence of colon cancer by 75 percent, breast cancer by 50 percent, and cancers in general by up to 40 percent. Dr. John Potter, head of a panel on diet and prevention appointed by the World Cancer Research Fund and the American Institute for Cancer Research, says that even those who have a strong predisposition for a certain disease locked into their genes still have their health risks altered by environmental conditions.

The simple fact that your personal genetic code is unique means that not all people will benefit equally from improving their eating habits. This explains why some people

---

GO FIGURE: THINK YOU ARE A SUPER TASTER? Sensitivity to bitter taste is an inherited trait. Because many plant poisons have a bitter taste, the ability to identify and reject bitter substances was an evolutionary advantage. Research suggests that these "super tasters" tend to reject foods such as broccoli, grapefruit, and soy. Try this test to see if you are a super taster.

Using a hole punch, punch a hole in the middle of a one-inch square of wax paper. Place the hole on the tip of your tongue. Swab some blue food coloring on the exposed part of the tongue. Using a magnifying glass and a flashlight, count the number of pinkish circles (fungiform papillae). Super tasters will have dozens of papillae; nontasters will have only five or six.

---

who "do everything right" develop fatal diseases in their 30s and 40s. Remember the extremely untimely deaths of athletes Florence Griffith Joyner and Jim Fixx? On the other hand, almost everyone knows of someone who makes poor food choices, never exercises, smokes, and lives a century or more—like cigar-puffing comedian George Burns.

You can't change who your birth parents are, and for the moment you're stuck with whatever random combination of genes you received from them. Here's a quick summary of the more common conditions that may have a genetic link and how to evaluate your likelihood of developing them. For more specifics on how to improve your odds of preventing or managing one of these chronic conditions, see Chapter 9.

Food Allergies

Eight foods cause 90 percent of all allergic reactions. They are peanuts, tree nuts, shellfish, fish, eggs, soy, wheat, and milk.

Allergic symptoms such as hives, tingling lips, and breathing difficulties begin within minutes to one hour after contact with the food. You don't have to eat something to develop an allergic reaction. Schoolchildren allergic to milk can have a reaction if milk is accidentally splashed on their skin. Flying in an airplane can cause someone with a peanut allergy to react. Peanuts don't even have to be served on the flight—the peanut dust in dirty air filters is enough to trigger a reaction.

A severe food allergy is a serious, life-threatening condition. If you find that hard to believe, it's probably because so many people think they are allergic to particular foods. A recent survey showed that up to 25 percent of adults believe they have a food allergy—and scientists estimate that between 6 and 7 million Americans suffer from true food allergies, including up to 5 percent of all children. Fortunately, most children outgrow their allergies, but nut allergies are usually lifelong.

Although anyone can develop a food allergy, often it's an inherited trait. Children with one allergic parent have about twice the risk of food allergy than children without allergic parents. If both parents are allergic, a child is four times more likely to develop a food allergy than if neither parent is allergic. Most studies show that what a mother eats when she is pregnant has little, if any, effect on sensitizing her child to food allergy. For that reason, it's not recommended to avoid foods during pregnancy that you can otherwise eat and enjoy without symptoms. One exception may be peanut products. It's suggested that women who have allergies or have a close family member with allergies avoid peanuts and peanut-containing products during pregnancy.

On the other hand, breast milk is more likely to protect your baby if allergies run in your family. For most infants, breast-feeding has a protective effect against food allergy. Babies fed infant formula are more likely to develop food allergies as infants. It's believed that allergy-susceptible infants who are breast-fed may be sensitized to the tiny amounts of food allergens in their mothers' breast milk. If you or your spouse is allergic, it might be reasonable to avoid highly allergic foods such as nuts and shellfish for as long as you breast-feed your infant.

If you suspect you may be allergic to one or more foods, see a board-certified allergist. Allergists are the only professionals qualified to diagnose and treat most allergies.

You've already collected most of the medical history you need to schedule an appointment. *Here are the steps commonly used to diagnose a food allergy…*

1. Review the symptoms you experience and figure out your family history for allergies.

2. Evaluate your food records to note if any particular foods seem to trigger reactions.

3. Have a physical examination to rule out other health problems that may be causing your symptoms.

4. Get a skin test: small amounts of suspect food components are injected into your skin to evaluate skin and blood antibody reactions.

5. Go on an elimination and challenge diet supervised by your allergist. First you eliminate the suspect food for several days. Then at the doctor's office you eat that food and are observed for reactions.

It's important to verify allergies to food so that you don't mistakenly eliminate wholesome foods from your diet without cause. For more information on the difference between food allergy and food intolerance, see Chapter 9.

LINK UP to *http://www.foodallergy. org* for further information on food allergies. The Food Allergy Anaphylaxis Network also provides a wealth of resources to help people cope with food allergies.

Major Health Risks That Are Related to Poor Nutrition

Cancer

According to the American Cancer Society (ACS), as many as 30 percent of the 555,000 cancer deaths in 2002 were related to nutrition—more than the 155,000 tobacco-related annual deaths and the 14,100 deaths related to excess alcohol. Several cancers, including many forms of breast and colon cancer, are primarily genetic in origin. But more often cancer develops from the interaction between your genetic code and your environment— which includes what you eat. Although you may inherit a gene for a certain type of cancer, it usually takes some kind of environmental event (smoking, high-fat diet, chemical exposure) to stimulate the growth of precancerous cells. Your genes may load the gun, but it's your food choices and environment that pull the trigger.

Not all cancers have similar roots. Most research suggests that a low-fat diet aids in the prevention of cancer. But women on severe fat-restricted diets (15 percent of calories or less) actually produce more dense breast tissue over time, and dense tissue more frequently

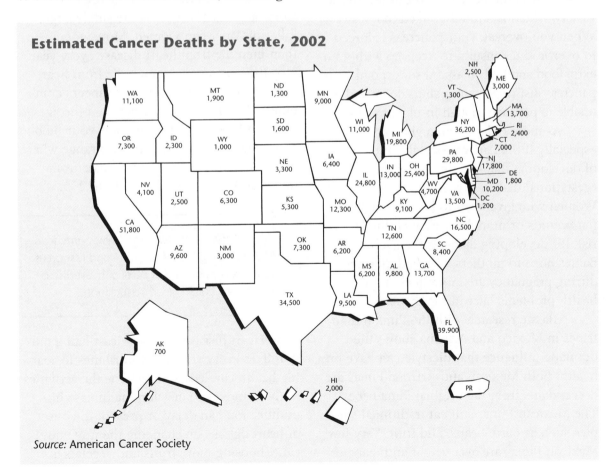

Estimated Cancer Deaths by State, 2002

Source: American Cancer Society

15

develops into cancerous lumps. Don't get frustrated over these contradictory positions. Remember there are few absolutes.

Diabetes

Both types of diabetes, Type 1 (starts in childhood; always requires insulin) and Type 2 (adult-onset; sometimes requires insulin), have genetic links proven by research on families and twins. There are 625,000 new diabetics diagnosed each year. That's a 10 percent increase in the last decade. More than 80 percent of diabetics die with some form of heart or cardiovascular disease. Adult-onset isn't such an accurate description now that more teens and young adults are developing Type 2 diabetes. More than 80 percent of all diabetes is the adult-onset variety, which is strongly linked to obesity. When you overeat, your pancreas is forced to overproduce insulin to keep up with your extra food and body mass. At some point your pancreas just wears out or shuts down and is unable to produce enough insulin any more.

As more older women give birth, especially if they are overweight, the rate of developing diabetes during pregnancy (gestational diabetes) rises dramatically. Women who give birth to babies weighing ten pounds or more have a much higher risk for developing diabetes themselves. Babies born to mothers who had diabetes during pregnancy are more likely to have health problems later in life themselves.

Classic research with the Pima Indian tribes in Mexico and Arizona shows the dramatic influence that lifestyle can have on health. Both Mexican and Arizona Pimas are descendants from the original Pima tribe. The Mexican Pimas still eat traditional staples such as corn, beans, and fruit. Very few Mexican Pimas are overweight and diabetes

is rare. Pimas who live in Arizona eat a typical American diet that is high in both sugar and fat. Many Pimas from Arizona are overweight. As a result, it's normal for these Pimas to develop diabetes by the time they are 55.

Heart Disease

Fewer Americans are dying each year from heart disease, but the number of people with first heart attacks has held steady or even increased since 1987. In a study reported in the September 1998 *New England Journal of Medicine*, Wayne Rosamond from the University of North Carolina says the decrease in deaths is most likely due to better treatment for people once they have a heart attack, not from prevention.

Don't skip this section if you're female. Coronary heart disease is the single largest killer of American women. More women than men die from heart disease every year. Two times as many women die from heart disease than from all types of cancers combined. If you're a woman between the ages of 45 and 64, it's critical to have your blood cholesterol tested. That's the age range where most women's cholesterol increases from under 200 to an average of 217 to 235.

LINK UP to *http://www.american heart.org* for information and resources on the prevention and control of heart disease from the American Heart Association.

Heart disease claims at least half a million lives every year and contributes to soaring health care costs. It restricts the activities of thousands who develop the disease in midlife. You can delay or prevent the onset of heart disease by changing the way you eat. Choosing more fruits and vegetables

RATE YOUR RISK FOR HEART DISEASE

1. Record the point score for your age and sex.

Men	Age	Women
−1	30–34	−9
0	35–39	−4
1	40–44	0
2	45–49	3
3	50–54	6
4	55–59	7
5	60–64	8
6	65–69	8
7	70–74	8

2. Find the point score for your LDL cholesterol level.

Men	LDL	Women
−3	below 100	−2
0	100–159	0
1	160–189	2
2	190 or higher	2

3. Find the point score for your HDL cholesterol level.

Men	HDL	Women
2	below 35	5
1	35–44	2
0	45–49	1
0	50–59	0
−1	60 or higher	−2

4. Find the point score for your blood pressure.

If your systolic and diastolic pressures are in different categories, use the point score from the higher category. For example: 115/82 = 0 points for both men and women.

Men	Systolic/Diastolic	Women
0	below 120/below 80	−3
0	120–129/80–84	0
1	130–139/85–89	0
2	140–159/90–99	2
3	160 or higher/100 or higher	3

5. Find your point score for other risk factors.

Men	Risk Factor	Women	
2	Do you have diabetes?	4	
2	Do you smoke?	2	_____

Total up your points. _____

NOTE: Be sure to subtract negative points.

Your risk of getting heart disease in the next ten years is:

Men	Total Score	Women
1%	less than –2	1%
2%	–2	1%
2%	–1	2%
3%	0	2%
4%	1	2%
4%	2	3%
6%	3	3%
7%	4	4%
9%	5	5%
11%	6	6%
14%	7	7%
18%	8	8%
22%	9	9%
27%	10	11%
33%	11	13%
40%	12	15%
47%	13	17%
56%	14	20%
	15	24%
	16	27%
	17 or more	32%

6. Compare your risk with others.

Age	Average-Risk Men	Low-Risk Men	Low-Risk Women	Average-Risk Women
30–34	3%	2%	Less than 1%	Less than 1%
35–39	5%	3%	Less than 1%	Less than 1%
40–44	7%	4%	2%	2%
45–49	11%	5%	4%	3%
50–54	14%	8%	6%	5%
55–59	16%	12%	7%	7%
60–64	21%	12%	9%	8%
65–69	25%	13%	11%	8%
70–74	30%	14%	14%	8%

Source: Adapted from Framingham Heart Study Data in *Circulation*, 1998

NOTE: The people in the Framingham study were mostly white, middle-class men who lived in a Boston suburb. If you aren't white or middle class, your risks could be higher or lower. Since not many women over 55 were included in this study, the risks for older women are probably much higher than these numbers indicate. Other risk factors that are too hard to measure, such as family history, levels of exercise, and obesity, were not included, but probably show up in other areas, such as blood pressure or having diabetes. Remember, there are no perfect studies or evaluation methods.

can lower both cholesterol and blood pressure. Food modifications alone cannot overcome the ill effects of smoking, high blood pressure, being overweight, and not exercising, but they can help you live better and longer.

The checklists in this chapter will help determine your probable risk for heart diseases compared to others your age. They're a combination of scientifically tested ratings. If you're under 30 or over 74, there isn't enough research to predict your age-related risk.

Compare Your Risk

Okay, so how do you compare with the average person your age? Use the chart above to see if your risk rate is better or worse than others your same age.

MIX AND MATCH YOUR TEN A DAY

Fruit or Vegetable	Servings
12 oz. glass fruit juice	2
8 oz. glass vegetable juice	2
1/2 cup canned or frozen fruit	1
1 large piece fresh fruit	2
Lettuce and tomato (on a sandwich)	1
1/2 cup cooked or raw vegetables	1
Large dinner salad (2 cups lettuce)	2
Vegetable-topped pizza (1 slice)	1
Fruit juice Popsicle	1
Fresh fruit (to top frozen yogurt)	1

NOTE: "Low-risk" people don't smoke or have diabetes. Their blood pressure is 130/85 or lower. Their LDL is 100 to 129 and their HDL is 45 or more for men and 55 or more for women.

High Blood Pressure

Almost half of all people with high blood pressure have a parent with high blood pressure, too. About 10 percent of our population has blood pressure that increases when they eat too much sodium. Since more African Americans than Caucasians have this sensitivity, it may be linked to genes.

Environmental factors, including diet and smoking, are estimated to influence half your risk of developing this silent killer. Eating ten servings of fruits and vegetables is as effective as prescription drugs in lowering high blood pressure. Before you roll your eyes and wonder how you could possibly eat ten servings every day, take a look at the "Mix and Match" chart on page 19.

Obesity

The majority of the adult U.S. population—at least 97 million adults—are overweight or obese. The rate of obesity has risen from 25 percent of adults in 1980 to 64 percent in 2000. These alarming statistics are even worse for low-income populations, especially for poorer women.

It's not just Americans who are getting fatter. According to the World Health Organization Consultation of Obesity, in 1998 the global projections on obesity for the next

BODY MASS INDEX: HOW DO YOU SHAPE UP?

Your body mass index (BMI) is a way to judge your body weight in relation to your height. The National Institutes of Health (NIH) says BMI is the best initial rule of thumb for judging if you weigh too much. If you are amazingly fit and well muscled or under 5 feet tall or younger than 18 or over 70, this test won't work for you. For the rest, it's just what the NIH said—an initial way to consider the health of your shape.

Calculate Your Body Mass Index (BMI)

$$BMI = \frac{(W \times 705) \div H}{H}$$

W = Your weight in pounds.

H = Your height in inches.

19 or less: Underweight, may suggest malnutrition or serious disease.

20–24: Healthy weight.

25–27: Overweight.

28–30: Overweight, with moderate health risk especially if you have a weight-related health problem or a family history of high blood pressure, heart disease, and/or diabetes.

over 30: Obese, with severe health risk for weight-related problems above, plus osteoarthritis, stroke, and some forms of cancer.

decade are so serious that action is urgently required. Obesity is today's most neglected public health problem.

Willpower and self-control have little to do with the ability to maintain a healthy weight. At least six factors influence your weight—behavior, environment, health status, culture, income level, and genetics. Most people who are overweight had at least one overweight parent. If both your parents were overweight, it's highly likely you will be overweight or constantly struggling to maintain a healthy weight. Metabolism may be partly determined by your genetic makeup. Some people are also genetically prone to store extra fat on certain parts of their bodies. If you're not overweight but have thick thighs or chubby cheeks, blame your ancestors.

Research hasn't shed much light as to why some people tend to gain weight so easily, while others never stray from their ideal weight. Medical researchers are making strides in identifying the causes of obesity. On the other hand, most common solutions for weight management fail miserably.

The Excessive Fat and Consumption Trends in Obesity Risk (X-FACTOR) survey says only 30 percent of obese adults report that a doctor has encouraged them to diet for health reasons. Even a minor loss of 5 to 10 percent body weight can dramatically improve health for those who are overweight. If you weigh 200 pounds (and if 150 is your ideal weight), losing just 10 to 20 pounds could lower your high blood pressure, send your cholesterol level back to normal, or allow you to stop medication to control your blood sugar levels.

Do You Have a Hazardous Waist?

Need an easier way to check if your body is up to par? Just wrap a tape measure around your middle near your belly button. A waist measurement of 35 inches or more in women and 41 inches or more in men means you probably have too much tummy fat. Abdominal fat is a more serious threat to your health than fat stored elsewhere. Almost all your vital organs are housed between your shoulders and waist, and extra fat here changes hormone levels, alters insulin production, and makes your organs work extra hard. Fat pads on your hips, thighs, or rear end don't have the same dramatic health effects.

LINK UP to *www.consumer.gov/weight loss/bmi.htm* or *www.halls.md/body-mass-index/bmi.htm* for handy calculators of your body mass index.

SELECTED STUDIES

Women overweight in the abdominal area are at increased risk for coronary heart disease. An eight-year study followed 44,702 women, aged 40 to 60. Women with a waist-to-hip measurement ratio of .88 or more were 3.25 times more likely to have coronary heart disease than women with a ratio of .72 (*Journal of the American Medical Association,* vol. 280, 1998). Waist-to-hip ratio is determined by dividing your waist measurement by your hip measurement (e.g., 32 ÷ 4 = .8). This research shows that regardless of BMI, the risk for heart disease skyrockets for women with too much tummy fat.

Body fat isn't all bad. It's like a soft polar fleece wrap that keeps your body temperature constant and protects vital organs. Without enough fat, brain development in children decreases and sex hormones don't work well. Teenage girls who are too lean often have delayed puberty. Too little body fat for too long can lead to permanent infertility in young women. Overzealous parents who impose fat restrictions on children under the

LINK UP to *http://www.shapeup.org* to access former surgeon general C. Everett Koop's web site on weight control. Be sure to visit the cyberkitchen and the fitness center.

LINK UP to *http://www.caloriecontrol. org* for overall diet and fitness information from the Calorie Control Council.

LINK UP to *http://www.nof.org* to get the cutting-edge reports on new research and treatments for osteoporosis from the National Osteoporosis Foundation.

age of 2 can irreversibly stunt the growth of their children's bodies and minds.

Osteoporosis

The woman in the doctor's waiting room may be 35 years old, but her bones are like a 47-year-old woman's. She looks and feels like a healthy young woman, but she's suffering from osteoporosis. What you eat as a teenager has a direct impact on the strength and density of your bones as you age. Other factors play a role, but foods rich in calcium are key to the prevention of osteoporosis.

Short women with northern European ancestors have a higher rate of osteoporosis than any other group. Osteoporosis is a disease that gradually weakens your bones and often leads to painful fractures, including hip fractures. For many people with osteoporosis, a broken hip results in a fall, not the other way around.

Early diagnosis of bone loss is important because you lose more bone as you age. Osteoporosis is a silent risk factor. You don't feel anything as a result of your weakened bones—until you break your hip, back, or wrist. Bone fractures resulting from osteoporosis are not only disabling, they can be life-threatening. According to C. Conrad Johnston, Jr., M.D.,

vice president of the National Osteoporosis Foundation, "Twenty percent of people die in the year following a hip fracture."

Osteoporosis Risk

What are your chances of developing brittle bones? See the risk factor chart on page 23. Five or more high-risk answers increase the likelihood of osteoporosis.

The more checks you have in the high-risk categories, the greater your overall risk for developing osteoporosis. You can improve more than half of the risk categories with permanent lifestyle changes.

If your answers to these questions show you have a high risk for osteoporosis, ask your doctor to order a bone density test. This is the only sure way to determine the strength of your skeleton and estimate your risk for fracture. The tests (there are several methods) are all painless and easy. Your bone density, after it has been measured or calculated, is compared to age-matched normal samples of bone.

SELECTED STUDIES

Researchers studying the ongoing bone mineral density and risk of fractures in 207 mother-daughter pairs have shown a strong genetic link for osteoporosis. There is a strong correlation between the height, weight, and body composition of these mother-daughter pairs that may contribute to the inheritance of bone density (*Journal of Bone and Mineral Research*, January 1999). Osteoporosis prevention and early intervention is critical for women with a positive family history of this disease.

WHAT ARE YOUR RISKS FOR OSTEOPOROSIS?

Five or more "High Risk" answers increase your odds of getting osteoporosis

Risk Factors	High Risk	Low Risk
Sex	Women	Men
Race	White or Asian	All others
Age	Over 45	Under 45
Weight	Thin, underweight, or frail	Normal or overweight
Exercise	No regular exercise or only swimming	Regularly exercise, especially weight-bearing activities like walking, bicycling, aerobics, and tennis
Smoking	Yes	No
Alcohol consumption	Drink 2 or more alcoholic beverages per day	Don't drink alcohol or drink 1 or fewer per day
Calcium intake (1,200 mg day = 4 cups milk)	No	Yes
Family history of osteoporosis	Yes	No

HANDY HOTLINE: To find a bone density testing center near you, a service of the National Osteoporosis Foundation Action Line, call 1-800-464-6700.

Stroke

Strokes strike lightning fast without warning —just a split-second feeling that something has gone very wrong. The problems that cause stroke, however, are years in the making. Eating lots of fruits and vegetables, controlling your weight, and drinking skim or low-fat milk may reduce your risk from this killer.

A stroke is like a heart attack in your brain. Blood vessels in your brain can develop plaque and clots just like those in your heart and other parts of your body. When a major blood vessel to the brain is blocked, the part of your brain nourished by that blood vessel dies. Though it's not included in the following risk assessment, women who use oral contraceptives are much more likely to have a stroke than those who don't use birth control pills.

Recent study findings have suggested that risks for stroke or heart attack rise in the hours following a high-fat meal. That's because an overload of fat affects the ability of arteries to dilate in response to changes in blood flow during digestion. For that reason it's important to pay attention to how you eat over time but also to what you eat in a single day or a single meal.

RATE YOUR RISK FOR STROKE

You need to be 54 or older to take this quiz.

1. Record the point score for your age.

Age	Points
54–56	0
57–59	1
60–62	2
63–65	3
66–68	4
69–71	5
72–74	6
75–77	7
78–80	8
81–83	9
84–86	10

2. Record your point score for your systolic blood pressure.

NOTE: If you take medicine for high blood pressure, be sure to use your systolic blood pressure while on medication.

Systolic BP for Men	Points	Systolic BP for Women
95–105	0	95–104
106–116	1	105–114
117–126	2	115–124
127–137	3	125–134
138–148	4	135–144
149–159	5	145–154
160–170	6	155–164
171–181	7	165–174
182–191	8	175–184
192–202	9	185–194
203–213	10	195–204

3. Find your total point score for other risk factors.

Men's Points for Yes	Risk Factors	Women's Points for Yes
2	Do you have diabetes?	3
3	Do you smoke?	3
6	Have you ever had an electrocardiogram that shows you have an enlarged heart muscle (left ventricular hypertrophy)?	4
3	Have you had one or more of any of the following?	2

- Heart attack
- Chest pain during physical activity
- Severe leg pain on exertion that results from an inadequate blood supply (intermittent claudication)
- The symptoms of a heart attack, but no increase in the enzymes that show muscle damage
- Congestive heart failure symptoms including breathlessness and severely swollen ankles caused by your heart's failure to pump enough blood and oxygen

4. Find your point score if you take medication to lower your blood pressure.

NOTE: If you do not take medication, your score is 0.

Men who take medications for high blood pressure score 2 points.

Women use the chart below:

Women's Systolic Blood Pressure on Medication	Points
95–104	0
105–124	1
125–134	2
135–154	3
155–164	4
165–184	5
185–204	6

5. Add your total points to find your risk.

Men	Points	Women
3%	1	1%
3%	2	1%
4%	3	2%
4%	4	2%
5%	5	2%
5%	6	3%
6%	7	4%
7%	8	4%
8%	9	5%
10%	10	6%
11%	11	8%
13%	12	9%
15%	13	11%
17%	14	13%
20%	15	16%
22%	16	19%
26%	17	23%
29%	18	27%
33%	19	32%
37%	20	37%
42%	21	43%
47%	22	50%
52%	23	57%
57%	24	64%
63%	25	71%
68%	26	78%
74%	27	84%
79%	28	
84%	29	
88%	30	

6. Compare your risk for stroke with others.

Men	Age	Women
3%	55–59	6%
5%	60–64	8%
7%	65–69	11%
11%	70–74	14%
16%	75–79	18%
24%	80–84	22%

Source: Adapted from Framingham Heart Study Data published in *Circulation,* 1998

NOTE: The people in the Framingham study on stroke were mostly white, middle-class men who lived in a Boston suburb. If you aren't white or middle class, your risks could be higher or lower. Since not many women over 55 were included in this study, the risks for older women are probably much higher than these numbers indicate. Other risk factors that are too hard to measure, such as family history, levels of exercise, and obesity, were not included, but probably show up in other areas, such as blood pressure or having diabetes. Remember, there is no perfect study.

The next few chapters showcase why eating healthful foods is such a smart thing to do. You'll find out how it's the balance of nutrients in foods that make some eating styles better than others. Once you understand the complexities of the nutrients in the foods you eat, it's easier to appreciate why balance, variety, and moderation are keys to improving your odds for a long and enjoyable life. ☙

LINK UP to *http://www.nof.org* to get the cutting-edge reports on new research and treatments for osteoporosis from the National Osteoporosis Foundation.

2

YOU ARE WHAT YOU EAT: A NUTRITION PRIMER

ew nutrition is a process, not specific actions. New nutrition is an attitude about food that is positive and enthusiastic. New nutrition is more than getting the minimum you need to avoid deficiency. It's the enjoyment of choosing, preparing and eating wholesome foods that taste good and are satisfying. Your food choices should concentrate on foods that are your best health investment. New nutrition includes foods that provide emotional comfort, too, so don't eliminate your favorites. Learn to appreciate them in moderation if they have too much or too little of what you need.

Eat foods as close to their natural state as possible. A fresh apple is more nutritious than applesauce. Applesauce is a better choice than apple pie. Savor the flavor and sensations of the foods you eat. Slow down and make eating an event instead of a chore. Enjoy the process of learning about the new nutrition—it tastes great! Remember, it's your total eating habits over time that matter most. Your choices of individual foods should be made with this in mind.

Are You in the Know About H$_2$O?

Why start a chapter on food with a discussion of water? Water is the basis of life. Your body is nearly two-thirds water, making it the most important nutrient. You can survive for long periods of time without calories, protein, carbohydrate, fat, vitamins, and minerals. Without water, you won't last more than a few days.

It's estimated that two-thirds of Americans fall at least 1 quart shy of getting their daily half-gallon requirement of water. You typically lose two to three quarts of water each day through breathing, sweat, urine and elimination.

Do you make the common mistake of waiting until you're thirsty before taking a drink of water? Thirst isn't an early signal of water needs; it's a warning sign that you're dehydrated and need to drink—and fast. By the time you feel thirsty you have already lost about 1 percent of your total body water. Some subtle signs of dehydration include dry lips, dark-colored urine, muscle or joint soreness, headaches, crankiness, fatigue, and constipation. More serious complications caused by extreme dehydration

27

BODY OF WATER

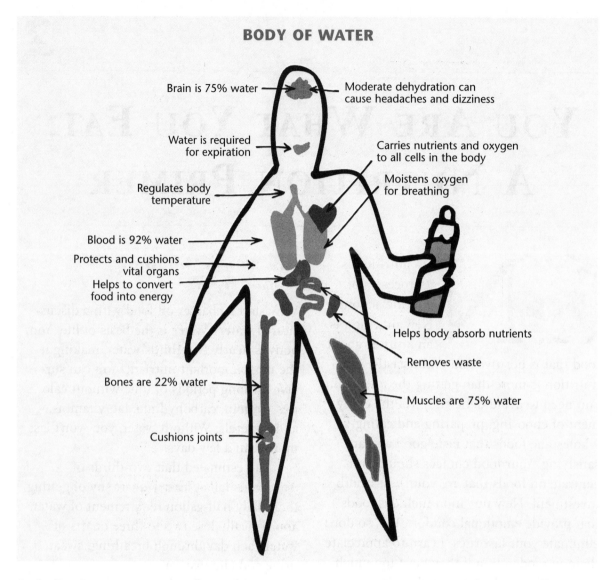

Brain is 75% water

Moderate dehydration can cause headaches and dizziness

Water is required for expiration

Carries nutrients and oxygen to all cells in the body

Moistens oxygen for breathing

Regulates body temperature

Blood is 92% water

Protects and cushions vital organs

Helps to convert food into energy

Helps body absorb nutrients

Removes waste

Bones are 22% water

Muscles are 75% water

Cushions joints

include seizures, permanent brain damage, or even death.

In addition to water, milk, juice, and soup count toward your daily fluid intake because of their high water content. But don't include alcohol, coffee, nonherbal tea, and soft drinks that contain caffeine, as they may have a mild diuretic effect. Caffeine can hold back water from the tissues that need it. Since your body is nearly two-thirds water, it is important to stay ahead of dehydration. If you are out in hot, humid weather or are exercising vigorously, you need to replace 150 percent of the amount of water lost to keep hydrated. If you lose 1 pound of sweat during a workout (16 ounces), you need 24 ounces of fluid to rehydrate. *The*

GO FIGURE: It's been estimated that you can use only 54 percent of the water from a diet cola. Bladder cancer risk drops 7 percent for every 8 ounces of water you drink.

NUTRITION ACTIONS TO DRINK MORE WATER:

- Take water breaks instead of coffee breaks.
- Choose water instead of soft drinks or coffee.
- Drink water before meals and snacks.
- Drink water before, during, and after any physical activity.
- Keep a bottle of water on your desk to sip from throughout the work day.
- Alternate sparkling or plain bottled water with alcoholic drinks at parties and social gatherings.

message is crystal clear: Drink plenty of water every day.

The critical role of water in maintaining personal health has made the safety of public drinking water a national issue. Disease from untreated water is virtually nonexistent in the United States, but natural disasters such as floods, earthquakes, or accidental contamination of wells or municipal water supplies can be devastating. Beginning in 1999, all local water utilities were required to send citizens a report on the safety of the local tap water. At a minimum your report should tell you where your water comes from, levels of pollutants, and if these levels violate Environmental Protection Agency (EPA) regulations. Most important, the report should include a plan to correct any problems. Some water quality reports are incomplete or indecipherable. If you don't understand your report, get help.

HANDY HOTLINE: Call the EPA's water hotline at 1-800-426-4791.

LINK UP to *http://www.epa.gov/safewater* for more information on how to find out the rating of your local water supply from the Environmental Protection Agency.

Is Bottled Better?

Water is classified as "bottled water" or "drinking water" if it meets all applicable federal and state standards, is sealed in a sanitary container, and is sold for human consumption. Bottled water, of which Americans consumed five billion gallons in 2002—the same amount that spills from Niagara Falls in two hours—cannot contain sweeteners or chemical additives (other than flavors, extracts, or essences) and must be free of calories, caffeine and sugar. Flavors, extracts, and essences—derived from spices or fruit—can be added to bottled water, but these additions must comprise less than 1 percent (by weight) of the final product. Beverages containing more than the 1-percent flavor limit are classified as soft drinks, not bottled water. In addition, bottled water may be sodium-free or contain very low amounts of sodium. Some bottled waters contain natural or added carbonation.

Recently, the safety of bottled water has been called into question. The National Resources Defense Council (NRDC) released a study in March 1999 that concluded some bottled water is not necessarily cleaner or safer than most tap water. However, only a small fraction of the 103 brands tested had problems. Many of the brands that failed the NRDC tests were grocery-store gallon jugs and very small local bottlers. However, most U.S. bottlers voluntarily belong to the International Bottled Water Association (IBWA) that requires more stringent testing and regulatory levels than federal or state rules. In addition, members of the IBWA, who produce about 85 percent of the bottled water sold in the United States, must meet strict industry standards established by the association. These standards, contained in the

LINK UP to *http://www.bottledwater. org/public/ibwp_facts_reg.htm* if you want all the details on bottled water regulations from the International Bottled Water Association.

NUTRITION ACTION: Since disasters usually happen without warning, keep a few days' supply of bottled water stored for emergencies. Estimate ½ gallon per person each day for drinking water and an additional ½ gallon for cooking, washing, and first aid.

IBWA "Model Code," exceed the FDA regulations currently in place for bottled water. According to the Centers for Disease Control and Prevention (CDC), bottled water, which the FDA regulates, has never been responsible for an outbreak of waterborne illness.

Calories: A Control Issue

Your body uses the energy from the foods you eat to support basic bodily functions and physical activity. This energy comes in the form of calories. Your calorie needs change many times over the course of a lifetime. Infants and teens need the most calories per pound to help meet increased demands during growth spurts. Pregnant women also have increased need for calories, especially during the later months of pregnancy and if they breast-feed their baby. People who are active, do manual labor for a living, or exercise frequently need more calories than people who aren't physically active. Calorie needs

GO FIGURE: COUNTING CALORIES

3,500 calories	= 454 grams	= 1 pound
1 gram	= ⅟₂₈ ounce	= the weight of 1 small paper clip
1 gram protein	= 4 calories	= ⅓ small egg white
1 gram carbohydrate	= 4 calories	= 1½ teaspoons apple juice
1 gram fat	= 9 calories	= scant ¼ teaspoon olive oil
1 gram alcohol	= 7 calories	= 1 ounce beer, 1 tablespoon wine, or ½ teaspoon 100-proof distilled spirit

One ounce of beer has more than the 7 calories that alcohol provides—it also contains calories from carbohydrates. The energy or calorie content of a food depends on the combination of nutrients it has. In theory, it takes 3,500 extra or unused calories to equal 1 pound. If you eat an extra 500 calories a day for a week, you should gain 1 pound if your activities remain constant. Too many calories above what you need for energy will make you fat.

also shrink some with age. Regardless of how many calories you need, your need for important nutrients doesn't shrink. That's why it's harder for inactive people to get enough nutrients from food.

Just look around—about two in three Americans are overweight. At any given time one in four men and almost half of all women are trying to lose weight. The solution isn't lower-calorie diets. We already eat fewer calories in the United States than almost ever before in our country's more than two-hundred-year history. The typical American woman doesn't eat enough calories to get the minimum levels of nutrients needed for health. Researchers at the USDA discovered it's next to impossible to eat enough nutritious foods on limited-calorie diets. In *Ideas for Better Eating: Menus and Recipes to Make Use of the Dietary Guideline from the USDA* (1981), top nutritionists tried to create meal plans that would meet the USDA Dietary Guidelines and RDAs at varying calorie levels. The bottom level was to be 1,200 calories. It couldn't be done— even by the experts. It takes a minimum of 1,600 calories worth of nutritious food to meet the recommended minimum levels of vitamins and minerals. A 1,600-calorie intake doesn't allow for many extras like alcohol, soft drinks, and candy.

The solution? Activity. We just don't move enough. Modern conveniences have pushed physical activity out of our lives.

LINK UP to *www.surgeongeneral. gov* for the first ever surgeon general's report on physical activity and health that includes recommendations for regular moderate physical activity from the Center for Disease Control.

How many phone extensions and remote control devices do you have in your home? Have you ever driven by a health club and watched people circle the parking lot for ten or more minutes trying to find a close spot? Heaven forbid we have to walk more than a few steps to enter the building for an aerobics class. If you want to have a healthful eating style, you need to burn enough calories to be able to eat a reasonable amount of food.

HANDY HOTLINE: For the Center for Disease Control's nutrition and physical activity information line is 1-888-232-4674 (CDC-4NRG).

Calories and Common Sense Still Count

Calories are more than a system to determine how fattening a particular food is. A calorie is a unit of energy that you either use or store. You add calories by eating food. You subtract calories by what you do—breathing, walking, talking, even digesting food! The balance between what you eat and what you do determines how much you weigh and your level of health.

Too often we think of balancing the calorie equation by cutting back on food intake. It's time to refocus on the other side of the equation—the output or expenditure of calories. Back in the 1950s, renowned nutritionist Dr. Jean Mayer suggested that Americans were gaining weight not because we were eating too much, but because we weren't moving enough. Other experts thought he was way off base. Today, there is mounting evidence that Dr. Mayer was right. Small differences in how much we work our bodies may be a primary cause of obesity.

The Burning Truth

Not all activities burn calories at the same rate. Exercising harder or faster for a given activity will only slightly increase the calories you expend. A better way to use up more calories is to exercise longer at the same intensity. Lighter people burn fewer calories doing the same activities as heavier people.

If you keep your food intake constant and decrease your daily physical activity by 500 calories, you would gain a pound in one week (7 days x 500 calories = 3,500 calories = 1 pound). But research from the University of Vermont shows that it's not quite that simple. Excess calories from fat are more fattening than extra carbohydrate calories. Your body has a limited capacity to change carbohydrate into body fat, but the sky is almost the limit when it comes to storing fat calories. If you eat 100 excess calories from fat, 97 of them will be converted to body fat. If your 100 surplus calories came from carbohydrate, only 77 would turn to fat. The rest would be used for energy.

On the activity side of the equation, there are discrepancies, too. The less lean muscle tissue you have, the fewer calories you need to maintain your weight. If two people weigh exactly the same, but have different proportions of muscle and fat, they will need different amounts of calories to perform the same activities. A well-muscled person needs more calories per pound than someone who has a high proportion of

HOW MANY CALORIES DO YOU REALLY BURN?

For Every 20 Minutes of Continuous Activity	125 Pounds	150 Pounds	175 Pounds
Light housework (washing dishes, folding clothes, cooking)	35	45	50
Raking leaves, gardening	60	75	85
Heavy housework (scrubbing floors, vacuuming, carpentry)	65	80	95
Cycling (6 mph)	65	80	95
Walking (3 mph)	85	110	125
Mowing the lawn (push mower)	110	135	160
Aerobic exercise (dance, kick boxing)	125	150	180
Swimming (continuous laps)	140	165	190
Cross-country skiing	195	235	270
Climbing stairs	235	280	335
Jogging (7 mph)	255	310	360

body fat. When you diet (cut calories) to lose weight, at least 25 to 30 percent of the weight you shed isn't fat but water, muscle, bone, and other lean tissue. That's true regardless of what type of food plan you choose. The less muscle in your body, the lower your metabolic rate—and the harder it will be to lose fat and keep it off.

There is no single, easy way to accurately calculate your calorie needs. How much energy you spend in a given task or activity can vary considerably. The amount of energy you expend doing the same work (mowing the lawn, shoveling snow) changes day to day.

GO FIGURE YOUR CALORIE NEEDS: A quick estimate of your energy needs is:

- 1,600 calories—many women and older adults
- 2,200 calories—children, teenage girls, active women, most men
- 2,800 calories—teenage boys, active men

NOTE: Pregnant or breast-feeding women usually require more calories than those listed for women or active women.

LINK UP to *http://www.health status.com/calorieburn.htm* to calculate your individual calorie requirements at the HealthStatus assessment site.

Carbohydrates: Keep Them Complex

There are two types of carbohydrates: simple and complex. Both types are found almost exclusively in plant foods—fruits, vegetables and whole grains. Simple carbohydrates are sometimes called simple sugars, and are usually the kind in snacks foods, cakes and cookies. The more important complex carbohydrates are also called starches.

Complex carbohydrates are the premium grade of fuel for your body's energy needs. That's because carbohydrates are easily stored in your muscles. These complex carbohydrates break down more slowly than simple sugars and release their available glucose over time. Most nutritionists agree you should eat more complex carbohydrates and less fat and simple carbohydrates.

Did you ever try this experiment in high school science class? Put a small piece of unsalted soda cracker on your tongue. Keep in it your mouth, without chewing, for several minutes. All of a sudden you will begin to notice a sweet taste. That's because carbohydrate digestion has already started in your mouth. Salivary enzymes change the long chains of complex carbohydrates into shorter glucose (or sugar) chains. While they digest rapidly, complex carbohydrates take longer to break down than simple carbohydrates and give you a greater feeling of fullness when you eat.

Simple carbohydrates are (as the name suggests) much less complex, and that makes them easier to be digested and utilized as a quick source of energy. Foods that are high in simple sugars usually have few, if any, naturally occurring vitamins or minerals. Examples of simple carbohydrates include white sugar, brown sugar, honey, soft drinks, hard candy, and various sugars that are added to many processed foods. Fruit juice, because it does not contain the fiber found in fresh fruit, also acts like a simple carbohydrate. Simple sugars become a problem when you eat too many of them instead of more nutritious foods.

Diets rich in complex carbohydrates can increase your brain level of the amino acid tryptophan, which is converted to serotonin, a calm-down, feel-good chemical. Some people, especially women, may tend to crave carbohydrate foods for the anti-depressant effect that high levels of serotonin provide.

Protein: Your Handyman

Protein is your body's do-it-yourself handyman. Protein helps to build and maintain just about everything in your body. From muscles to membranes and blood vessels to bones, protein helps make it and keep it in good repair. Different proteins have different jobs. Keratin helps form hair, nails, and the outer layer of your skin. Actin, myosin, and myoglobin form the meaty part of muscle. The "globin" (GLOW-bin) part of hemoglobin is the protein that fills the rubbery inside of your bones, including the marrow.

Proteins are made up of structural units called amino acids, of which there are twenty-two. Nine of these amino acids you can only get from foods. They are called the essential amino acids (leucine, lysine, isoleucine, tryptophan, threonine, methionine, valine, phenylalanine, and histidine). Your body makes the other thirteen amino acids when needed. All twenty-two amino acids link together to form chains. It's like playing Scrabble; you work with the letters you have to build onto base words. Similarly, you need to eat foods containing just the right essential amino acid to fill each link in the body's amino acid chain to make it complete.

Amino acids can be found in many foods, but animal foods have the highest and most complete assortment. Beans, lentils, and grain products also have some protein, but vegetable foods have less total

amino acids and fewer combinations of the essential ones. Vegetarians may remember the days when they were advised to eat "complementary proteins." We now know that you don't have to combine foods at mealtime to make complete proteins. Eating an assortment of non-meat protein foods over the course of a day does just fine.

Most Americans eat more protein than they need. Although it's important to get enough protein, too much can be hard on your kidneys and make them work overtime. Too little protein isn't desirable either. Skimping on protein can leave you sluggish and prone to infection. Protein is an energizing nutrient. If you've been seriously ill, injured, or have had major surgery, your body needs extra protein, calories, and other nutrients for repair and recovery. If your handyman doesn't have the right tools, he can't do the job.

Focus on Fat

A St. Paul firefighter, on the verge of retirement, was required to attend my nutrition class as part of on-the-job continuing education. The topic was how to lower blood cholesterol levels. He was clearly not interested (this was in the 1970s). He alternated muttering snide comments and snoring during the presentation. At the end of class he blurted out, "Miss, I don't believe anything you just said. My old uncle Joe had a farm, and every day for breakfast he ate a half dozen fried eggs, bacon, and sausage and poured real cream in his coffee. For lunch and supper his wife served fried meat and poured gravy over the whole plate. They ate pies and used butter on everything. His diet was loaded with fat and he lived to be 99 and died peacefully in his sleep." It was a dietitian's dream-come-true to respond to him. "What you said makes perfect sense," I began. "I'll bet your uncle Joe led a heart-healthy lifestyle. He lived at a time when farmers did hard labor for ten or more hours a day. [Remember this nephew was at retirement age in the 1970s.] They didn't have the benefit of air-conditioned tractors and labor-saving devices in the early 1900s. It wasn't unusual for farmers to burn 10,000 or more calories a day. College football players in training easily eat that much today. If you need 10,000 calories to meet energy needs, you can eat as much as 333 grams of fat a day and still be on a low-fat diet. Just think of all the other nutritious foods you could consume with the remaining 6,000+ calories!"

For years the message has been to eat less fat. Now the reality is beginning to look considerably more complicated. The controversy over fat has leapt out of the frying pan and into the fire. For more than a decade we have been fixated on types of fat and fat grams. Some people are drastically cutting back on fat and at the same time eating more calories and gaining weight. Fat was named the culprit for practically

WHERE'S THE FAT?
TOP SOURCES OF FAT IN AMERICAN DIETS

For Men	For Women
Mixed dishes and combination foods in which meat, poultry, or fish are primary ingredients	Mixed dishes and combination foods in which meat, poultry, or fish are primary ingredients
Mixed dishes and combination foods in which grains are primary ingredients	Mixed dishes and combination foods in which grains are primary ingredients
Beef, not in mixtures	Table fats like butter or margarine
Hot dogs, sausages, and luncheon meats	Beef, not in mixtures
Table fats like butter or margarine	Milk, other than nonfat
Milk, other than nonfat	Hot dogs, sausages, and luncheon meats
Salad dressings	Salad dressings
Fried potatoes and potato chips	Cookies, cakes, and pies
Cookies, cakes, and pies	Cheese, not in mixtures
Cheese, not in mixtures	Bread

Source: Continuing Survey of Food Intakes by Individuals, 1989–1991

every chronic disease. Now scientists are taking a closer look. Maybe fat isn't so bad. After all, it's an essential nutrient needed for good health from cradle to grave.

Fats are really combinations of many different fatty acids, and each one differently affects how your body works. With nine calories per gram, fat is the most concentrated energy source in food. Fat is critical for growth in children, is required for healthy skin, helps hormone-like substances regulate body processes, and is essential for the absorption of fat-soluble vitamins.

The average American male consumes 101 grams of fat each day, while the typical woman has 65 grams, according to the USDA Center for Nutrition Policy and Promotion. Although that represents a decline in the amount of fat that comes from total calories —down from men's 139 and women's 83 daily fat grams in 1965—the sad fact is that most Americans continue to consume more calories each day. Eating more calories without increasing physical activity is not the ideal way to decrease the percentage of calories from fat, unless exercise is increased.

Have you ever felt that just thinking about fatty foods makes you fat? Your instincts may not be off base. A study at Purdue University tested the effects of tasting high-fat foods on blood fat levels. Two varieties of cream cheese were the variables. One cream cheese was full-fat and the other fat-free. The people in the test were asked to hold some cream cheese in their mouth and not swallow. They actually had to spit it out. The level of triglycerides in the blood was measured both before and right after their taste. Those who had the full-fat cream cheese had significantly elevated triglyceride levels compared to those who had the fake, fat-free stuff.

Types of Fat

People really started thinking about the fat in their diets in 1960s and 1970s, when experts started to recognize the connection between fat and diseases such as heart disease and cancer. Dietary cholesterol was viewed as the first heart-hurting villain, not fat. Then, saturated fat was deemed the bad guy. As a result, many consumers started reading the ingredient lists for products they routinely bought. They learned that "animal" fats were bad and "vegetable" fats were good. Until that time, many of the newer convenience products like cake and baking mixes contained lard.

When consumers found lard and other animal fats in their favorite products, they resisted. As a result of major consumer backlash, most food companies quickly dropped saturated fats and replaced them with hydrogenated vegetable oils. Fast-food restaurants also made the switch from cooking french fries in beef tallow to frying in hydrogenated vegetable oils. While "hydrogenated vegetable oils" may sound better than lard, they may be worse for your overall health. That's because hydrogenated fats not only raise levels of harmful cholesterol (LDL), these fats can reduce the amount of the protective, "good" cholesterol (HDL) at a greater rate than saturated fats.

Fats are combinations of different fatty acids. Foods that contain fat may have combinations of three or four different fatty acids. You may have heard that olive oil is a monounsaturated fat. It really is a combination of monounsaturated, polyunsaturated, and saturated fatty acids. Olive oil's most predominant fatty acid, however, is monounsaturated.

RATE YOUR FAT HABITS

Circle the answer that best corresponds to your usual eating habits, then tally your score to see how your fat intake rates.

Do you:	Rarely	Sometimes	Often
Drink 1% or skim milk?	0	5	10
Add butter or margarine to bread, potatoes, or vegetables?	10	5	0
Use nonstick pans or cooking sprays instead of oils or solid fats?	0	5	10
Usually snack on regular chips, cookies, crackers, cheese, or nuts?	10	5	0
Use more than 1 tablespoon of regular (or 2 tablespoons of low-fat) salad dressing at a time?	10	5	0
Eat regular hot dogs, luncheon meat, or sausage more than once a week?	10	5	0
Remove extra fat from meat and skin from chicken before eating? OR If you don't eat meat, do you use reduced-fat cheeses and nut butters?	0	5	10
Balance high-fat foods with low-fat choices during the day?	0	5	10
Choose meals that include french fries when you eat out?	10	5	0
Eat pastries and doughnuts for breakfast or snacks?	10	5	0

Scoring

- **0–45** It's time for some changes. Look for reduced-fat versions of your high-fat favorites.

- **50–80** You're on your way but need a little fine-tuning. Review your food records and make notes of where you can cut the fat.

- **85–100** Keep up the good work. Don't get obsessive about fat—remember, it is good for you in moderation.

FAT EFFECTS: THE GOOD, THE BAD, AND THE UGLY

	Trans	Poly-Saturated	Mono-Unsaturated	Unsaturated
HDL Cholesterol (GOOD)	Lowers (X)	Raises	Lowers (X)	Neutral
LDL Cholesterol (BAD)	Raises (X)	Raises (X)	Lowers	Neutral
Total Cholesterol (UGLY)	Raises (X)	Raises (X)	Lowers	Neutral

X = Undesirable Effect

Monounsaturated

Because monounsaturated fats aren't damaged by oxidation, they are less likely to increase cholesterol buildup in your arteries. *Mono* is the Latin word for "one." That means monounsaturated fatty acids have one double bond. The more bonds a fatty acid has, the more saturated or stable it is. Monounsaturated fats tend to break down more readily than saturated fats. They are best used for salad dressing, stir-frying, and sautéing. Because most monounsaturated fats come from nuts, seeds, or olives, they add distinct flavors to foods. Some of the most common sources of monounsaturated fat include olives and olive oil, canola oil, peanuts and peanut oil, walnuts, sesame seed oil, and avocados.

SELECTED STUDIES

A Swedish study of more than 61,000 women between the ages of 40 and 76 collected data on eating habits and other risks for breast cancer. Researchers found that replacing other types of fat with monounsaturated fat—specifically, the use of canola and olive oils—cut these women's risk of breast cancer by 45 percent (*Archives of Internal Medicine,* January 1998). In similar case-control studies, researchers in Greece, Spain and Italy produced similar results. While these studies focused on the cancer-protective properties of olive oil, some speculate that the protective benefit lies with monounsaturated fats as a whole category of food, rather than specifically with olive oil.

Polyunsaturated

This fat is liquid at room temperature; its structure has two or more double bonds, thus giving the name "polyunsaturated" (*poly* means "many"). Research suggests that these fats lower blood cholesterol if they are substituted for other fats in a low-fat diet. Most polyunsaturated oils are odorless and can withstand high temperatures. They work well for deep-fat and pan frying, general baking, and cooking. Best sources include corn, cottonseed, soybean, safflower, and sunflower oils.

Saturated

This fat is usually solid at room temperature and has no double bonds in its structure. Research suggests that particular saturated fatty acids can increase blood cholesterol by raising levels of "bad" LDL cholesterol, which can clog arterial walls, increasing risk of a heart attack or stroke. Saturated fats also raise the good (HDL) cholesterol, and that is a positive benefit. However, LDLs increase at a higher rate from saturated fats, which is

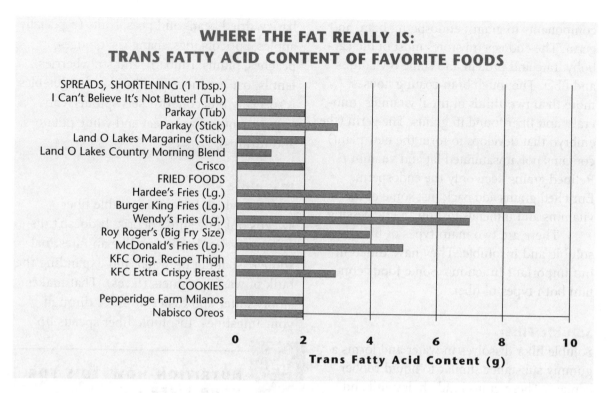

WHERE THE FAT REALLY IS:
TRANS FATTY ACID CONTENT OF FAVORITE FOODS

Trans Fatty Acid Content (g)

why most experts recommend limiting saturated fats to 7 to 10 percent of total calories. Look for the grams of saturated fat on the nutrition facts label of the food you buy. The primary sources of saturated fat include animal foods such as meat and cheese, snack foods, and coconut and palm tree oils.

Trans

Trans fats are processed by taking a less expensive unsaturated fat (like oil) and adding hydrogen to its chemical makeup to give it a richer taste and more solid consistency. Research suggests that these fats increase blood cholesterol—sometimes more than pure saturated fats—and should therefore be limited. You'll find trans fats in almost all restaurant-fried foods (although some are switching to healthier oils) and most commercial cookies, cakes, frostings, crackers, snack foods, and chips. Margarine, while it suffered the brunt of the criticism about trans

fatty acids, is not a major source compared to the other foods mentioned.

Fiber

Fiber is the part of a plant that cannot be digested by human enzymes. Fiber is found in most plant foods—vegetables, fruits, whole grains, and legumes. Because fiber is not digested, it provides no calories or energy. It does provide bulk that helps move waste quickly through your intestinal tract. *This benefits you in two ways:* Fiber-rich foods fill you up faster, so you're less likely to consume more calories. And fiber can also help lower cholesterol because some forms can actually block fats and cholesterol in the intestines before they reach your bloodstream.

Whole grains, such as wheat, oats, barley, rye, and brown rice, retain all the parts of the grain kernel after milling. There are three components to grains: endosperm, bran, and germ. The endosperm stores most of the carbohydrate and protein and some B vitamins and fiber. The tough bran coating houses more than two-thirds of the B vitamins, minerals, and fiber found in grains. The germ (the embryo that develops to form the new plant) contains polyunsaturated fat and vitamin E. Refined grains keep only the endosperm. Enriched grains add back just some of the vitamins and minerals lost during processing.

There are two main types of fiber—soluble and insoluble. They have different but important functions. Some foods contain both types of fiber.

Soluble Fiber

Soluble fiber dissolves in water and forms a gummy substance similar to liquid rubber cement. These gums bind cholesterol and carbohydrates in your intestines, and that decreases blood sugar and circulating cholesterol. The best sources of soluble fiber include barley, dried beans and peas, fruits (especially apples, apricots, figs, mangoes, oranges, peaches, plums, rhubarb, and strawberries), lentils, oat products, psyllium, and vegetables (especially broccoli, brussels sprouts, cabbage, carrots, okra, sweet and white potatoes, and turnips).

Insoluble Fiber

Nature's whisk broom, insoluble fiber sweeps out unwanted debris. It doesn't dissolve in water, but it acts like an intestinal sponge, soaking up water and expanding the bulk of waste products (feces). That makes stools softer and easier to move through your intestines. Insoluble fiber speeds up

GO FIGURE YOUR FIBER NEEDS: Most experts recommend you aim for 1 gram of fiber for every 100 calories you eat. That translates to 25 grams of fiber for 2,500 calories, and 30 grams for 3,000 calories. Even if you eat less than 2,500 calories, 25 grams a day is considered the minimum.

Use a different formula to calculate fiber needs for children. "Age + 5" is the rule to follow. A 2-year-old should have no more than 7 grams of fiber and a 10-year-old up to 15 grams daily. Children should not have fiber-added products or fiber supplements. Too much fiber in the diets of growing children can decrease appetite and increase nutrient losses.

NUTRITION HOW TO'S FOR YOUR FIBER FIX:

Befriend Beans—Rich in fiber and protein, try packaged instant beans, reduced-fat refried canned beans, or other canned beans. Build meals around bean dishes and add to salads and soups.

Go for Grains—Look for 100 percent whole-wheat or whole-grain bread and check fiber grams on food labels.

Feast on Fruit—Eat a piece of fruit instead of drinking juice or eat dried fruit as a snack.

Put Away Your Peeler—Eat the skins of potatoes and other fruits and vegetables; just be sure to wash them well first.

Boost Breakfast—Mix a high-fiber cereal (more than 5 grams of fiber a serving) with your regular brand and top with fruit.

Skip the Chips—Eat crackers with 2 grams of fiber per ounce instead of chips and serve with a chickpea dip such as hummus instead of cream-based dips.

the time waste is in your digestive tract and helps to prevent constipation, hemorrhoids, and diverticulosis. Soft but bulky stools that move quickly also decrease your chance of developing rectal and colon cancer. Hard stools can injure the delicate walls of your large intestine. Since waste material contains what your body doesn't want or need, a speedy exit is desirable. The longer waste stays in you, the more direct contact you have with harmful bacteria and toxins. The best sources of insoluble fiber include bran cereals, brown rice, corn and popcorn, fruits (especially apples, berries, pears), vegetables (especially asparagus, beets, carrots, kale, okra, peas, sweet and white potatoes, spinach), 100 percent whole-grain breads, and pastas.

Since both types of fiber require water for processing, it's essential to stay well hydrated. If you increase your fiber intake, you need to drink more water, too. Increasing physical activity is also recommended as you increase fiber because it helps stimulate muscle tone necessary for speedy elimination.

Most people aren't willing to count calories, add up fiber grams, or figure percentages every day. It takes too much time and effort. Yes, the basics in this chapter are important, but strapping a calculator to your wrist isn't the way to make food decisions. Change your view of food. Instead of seeing how many calories or fat grams are in a particular food, look for the benefits. Choose foods based on their positive attributes, such as colorful produce that's bursting with flavor and nutrients or hearty whole-grain breads. Eat like a gourmet and savor every bite. There's more to food than its nutritional value; it's an essential part of the social side of life. Try to make meals an event instead of a mad dash. It does take more planning time to have optimal nutrition, but it's worth it physically and emotionally. Don't get bogged down in the numbers; they're only a reference point—use them that way. ❦

3

FOODS IN THE NEWS

hat does food have to do with health and happiness? More than we ever imagined. Hidden within foods are hundreds of compounds that take the food-health connection to an exciting new level. Mother Nature planned a clever way to protect her luscious bounty. Smelly sulfur compounds in onion and garlic act as a natural insect repellent. Other plant chemicals, or phytochemicals, protect vegetation from the ravages of weather, harmful bacteria and viruses. When you eat foods that contain these plant-protecting compounds, they begin to protect you, too. Instead of providing insect resistance, they work to halt the forces that zap health in humans, such as cancer and heart disease, and may even slow the aging process. Foods from animals can also play a role in maintaining and promoting health. Their special mix of nutrients provides some of the richest combinations of protein and minerals.

Foods are not perfect. Eat too much of anything and it will probably make you sick. That's why the habitual nutrition advice of balance, variety, and moderation has never gone out of style. When it was first discovered that ingredients in foods can cause cancer, the reaction was to identify and remove all carcinogens from food. But that's not possible—too much of anything could probably cause cancer. Today's advice is to eat a greater variety of foods and to be active enough so you can consume plenty of foods and thereby have access to the huge variety of compounds that can promote health and longevity.

The Good News—From Avocados to Zucchini

There is no one miracle food that has everything you need. For that we should be thankful, because variety is the spice of life. In fact, if you rely on the same repeated repertoire of foods, you probably don't have a nutritious diet. Some food surveys show that many Americans eat a grand total of about twenty different foods. That's not only boring; it's bound to be unhealthy. Variety is a key component of new nutrition. Here's a sampling of some recent findings about the healing power of food—and some recipes to whet your appetite.

Amazing Avocados

With more than five hundred varieties to choose from, it's stunning to think that most Americans are familiar with only two types of this fruit. Haas avocados from California are small in size and have a thick bumpy skin that ripens to an eggplant-like color. Bite-for-bite, they have more than twice the fat and calories of the second variety, the Florida avocado, which is much larger and has a brighter, smoother green skin. Still, both types of avocado have mostly monounsaturated fat, which can lower cholesterol. A 3-ounce serving contains about 9.7 grams of fat and 2.5 grams of fiber. However, the Haas avocado contains up to one-third of its fat from saturated fat. Avocados are also a great source of folate (meeting 31 percent of the recommended intake in those 3 ounces) and a decent source of potassium, vitamins B-6 and C, niacin, magnesium, and potassium.

Buying Basics: Buy fruit that feel heavy for their size, and avoid rock-hard avocados. Choose very soft fruit only if you plan to eat it the same day.

Peak Season: Florida avocados peak from mid-June to mid-March. Haas avocados peak from February to October. Both varieties are usually available year round.

Preparation Tips: Avocados are usually eaten raw since cooking can cause a bitter flavor.

To prepare, slice in half lengthwise and remove the pit. Scoop out or slice the soft green flesh. The light green color will quickly oxidize and turn brown when exposed to air. Prevent browning by rubbing slices with lime or lemon juice or by adding lime or lemon juice to fresh mashed avocado.

Storage Solutions: You can freeze avocado mashed with lime or lemon juice up to six months if you seal it in an airtight container. Sliced or whole avocados do not freeze well. Store unripe avocados on the countertop inside an open paper bag.

Recipes:
EASY GUACAMOLE
1 large ripe avocado, mashed
½ cup prepared salsa
1 clove crushed garlic (or ½ tsp. garlic powder)
¼ fresh lime, squeezed, or 1 Tbsp. lime juice

Pour lime juice immediately over mashed avocado to prevent browning. Gently stir in salsa and garlic. Serve chilled.

Beans, Beans, They're Good For Your Heart

Beans are a cornerstone in the diets of more than 300 million people worldwide. The typical American eats only about 8 pounds per year. That's unfortunate, since beans are among the best foods available. A one-cup serving contains about half the recommended amount of folic acid, which is believed to protect against heart disease, prevent birth defects, and form red blood cells and the genetic material within each cell.

Beans also contain nearly 30 percent of the daily iron requirement and about 25 percent of magnesium and copper requirements. And beans are an excellent source of fiber—especially soluble fiber that helps lower cholesterol and heart disease risk. One study found that a half-cup of beans daily helped reduce cholesterol levels by 10 percent. This fiber also helps stabilize blood sugar levels.

Yes, there are unpleasant side effects associated with bean consumption—flatulence or gas. On average, most people pass gas about fifteen to twenty times every day.

A variety of foods besides dried beans can cause gas, such as bran, broccoli, and cabbage.

SELECTED STUDIES

A 2001 study in *Archives of Internal Medicine* found that people who ate beans four times a week were 22 percent less likely to have heart disease than those who ate them once a week. They also had lower blood pressure and total cholesterol, and were less likely to be diagnosed with high blood pressure and diabetes.

NUTRITION HOW TO'S: FEND OFF FLATULENCE

Try these tips to help reduce potentially embarrassing emissions.

- Soak beans before cooking and be sure to use fresh water for cooking.

- Build your bean intake slowly. Give the bacteria in your digestive tract time to adjust to processing those complex carbohydrates.

- Consider a gas-reducing aid (like Beano) that helps break down the complex carbohydrates in beans before they can ferment in your colon.

Buying Basics: Dried beans, also called legumes, are found in more than 13,000 known varieties. Look for whole, firm dried beans—and check bags for expiration dates. Canned and frozen beans are also available.

Peak Season: Available year round in all varieties. Fresh legumes are available in summer months.

Preparation Tips: Legumes can be eaten fresh, sprouted, dried, roasted, or ground into flour. Dried beans can be soaked overnight in the refrigerator. Be sure to drain and rinse well before cooking—this will help remove compounds that can cause gas.

The California Dry Bean Advisory Board offers the following method for gas-free beans. In a 5-quart saucepan, place 1 pound of beans in 10 or more cups of boiling water; boil for 2–3 minutes, cover, and set aside overnight. By morning, 75 to 90 percent of the indigestible sugars will have dissolved into the soaking water. Drain and then rinse the beans thoroughly before cooking them. Fresh beans do not need to be soaked, but should be slow cooked for several hours.

Storage Solutions: Store dried beans in an airtight container for up to one year. Keep some canned beans on your pantry shelf for those times you can't soak and cook ahead.

Recipe:
ZESTY BLACK BEAN SALAD

1 lb. black beans
Water to cover beans 3" in saucepan
1 red pepper, chopped
1 green pepper, chopped
½ cup green onions, chopped
2 roma tomatoes, chopped
¼ cup frozen corn
1 small jalapeño pepper, finely minced
1 garlic clove, finely minced
¼ cup extra virgin olive oil
¼ cup lime juice
¼ tsp. salt
¼ tsp. pepper
Dash cayenne pepper
¼ tsp. teaspoon cilantro

Cook beans in water until tender, rinse, and drain. Combine all vegetables with cooked beans. Whisk together oil, lime juice, salt, peppers, and cilantro. Pour over bean-vegetable mixture and toss until well coated. Chill before serving.

What's the Beef over Beef?

Beef has gotten a bad reputation in recent years for its high fat and cholesterol, and because ground and lunchmeats may carry food-borne illnesses like *E. coli* and *listeria*. Lean portions of meat can help prevent nutrient deficiencies, boost your immune system, and build stronger blood.

Moderation is the key. Researchers for the American Council on Science and Health (ACSH) investigated claims that vegetarian diets are better for you because they eliminate meat. According to Dr. Ruth Kava, ACSH director of nutrition, "The mere fact that a diet is meatless does not guarantee that it is healthful. And although eliminating meat is a way to reduce saturated fat and increase plant foods in the diet, it is not the only way. Balance, moderation, and variety are the keys to a healthy eating plan."

The researchers found that vegetarians tend to make more healthful lifestyle choices, such as regular exercise; they maintain a desirable weight; and they don't smoke, abuse alcohol, or use illegal drugs. Current thinking is that it's not the absence of meat but the presence of lots of whole grains, fruits, and vegetables that make an eating style healthful.

Lean cuts of beef are typically high in B vitamins, zinc and iron, and certain cuts are also rich in conjugated linoleic acid (CLA), which studies show can inhibit malignant melanomas as well as colorectal, breast and lung cancer cell lines.

SELECTED STUDIES

A clinical trial at three different research centers that compared the effects of lean red meat and lean white meat on blood cholesterol levels was the third study to conclude that lean red meat, as part of a healthful diet, can help lower blood cholesterol levels. The study included 191 men and women who followed a basic low-fat diet. The half who used lean red meat had similar reductions in low-density lipoprotein cholesterol (LDL—the bad stuff) and elevations in high-density lipoprotein cholesterol levels (HDL—the good stuff) (*Archives of Internal Medicine,* June 1999). If you enjoy red meat, there's no reason to ban it from your diet; just choose lean cuts like round and loin.

Buying Basics: Beef is available in many different cuts. Stick to USDA Grade Choices or Select beef for the leanest cuts. They have the least amount of fat marbling throughout the meat. Choose from what's known as the "skinny six" cuts—eye of round, top round sirloin, bottom round, top loin, and tenderloin. The most tender cuts come from the rib and loin. Tougher cuts come from the rump and shoulder. Choose meat that looks evenly red and not does not seem to be dried out.

Peak Season: Available year round.

Preparation Tips: Remove all visible fat prior to cooking. Choose your cooking method to match your cut of beef. Marinate tougher cuts to make them tender, or do it the old-fashioned way and pound with a meat mallet to break down the tough connective tissue. Drain cooked ground beef crumbles to remove excess fat. Pour cooked ground beef into a colander and rinse with hot water. Use immediately or freeze in one-pound packages for later.

Storage Solutions: Use fresh ground beef within one day of purchase or freeze immediately. To freeze beef, first seal in an airtight plastic bag, then seal the bag in foil or freezer wrap. Label with the date and type of meat. For best quality, use frozen meats within six months.

Recipe:
HERBED TENDERLOIN STEAKS

2 4-oz. beef tenderloin steaks

¼ tsp. dried basil

¼ tsp. dried rosemary

¼ tsp. dried oregano

Dash of salt

⅛ tsp. black pepper

1 garlic clove, minced

Combine all seasonings together. Moisten surface of steaks lightly with water. Sprinkle seasonings evenly over all surfaces of the steaks. Rub well into meat.

Refrigerate seasoned steaks in refrigerator for up to four hours to enhance the flavor, or cook immediately. Grill or broil using a medium temperature until desired doneness.

Biotech Benefits

Do you eat cheese? If so, you benefit from advances in biotechnology. More than half of the rennet used in cheese making is produced through a biotech fermentation process that eliminates the "old-fashioned" method. Rapid-rise yeast products that speed up bread making were developed in England by rearranging and duplicating certain yeast genes. Imagine French fries that absorb less fat, crops designed to resist bugs without insecticides, and plants rich in nitrogen without the use of chemical fertilizers. This isn't science fiction. Each of these ideas is being developed right now. Some, like insect-resistant crops, are already a reality.

Early humans were hunters and gatherers who ate only what they found or could successfully hunt. Eventually they learned how to grow certain plants as crops. For ten thousand years people have been using genetic science to improve crops and create new food products. Selecting seeds, baking bread, brewing beer, fermenting fruit into wine and making cheese are all examples of harnessing biology to make and modify plants and food products. Some of these methods have become quite sophisticated over time.

Traditional plant crossbreeding, which actually began in the 19th century, helps improve on the random cross-pollination naturally provided by birds, bees, and other insects. It typically takes ten to twelve years to sort out and breed a plant that has the characteristics desired in a new variety. The International Food Information Council (IFIC) describes it this way: "When two whole plants are crossed, each having some 100,000 genes or so, all the genes from both plants get jumbled together. Since breeders' want only one or a few, this presents a big headache. It's like wanting to add a certain French word to the English dictionary and having to combine the entire French and English dictionaries—just to add that single word."

Modern biotechnology is much more selective. Crop breeders can actually identify and select the precise genetic trait they want and move it into another plant. It's like having a tool that can instantly find a needle in a haystack. The prime benefits of biotechnology are a more healthful environment and less reliance on harmful chemicals. *Some examples...*

- Better-tasting, vine-ripened tomatoes year-round. Most tomatoes are picked while green and then chemically ripened with ethylene gas to turn red. Biotechnology eliminates the need for chemical gassing.

- Pesticide and insecticide reduction through plants bred to ward off destructive insects and resist harmful bacteria and viruses. Farmers who use seed that produces resistant plants can cut back or even eliminate their use of chemical herbicides, pesticides and insecticides. That results in less toxic exposure to farm workers, the soil and water.

- Improved nutrient content of foods to help reduce world hunger and malnutrition. For example, increasing the levels of lysine in rice can reduce the number of children in China who develop blindness as a result of lysine amino acid deficiency. Africans who rely on sweet potato crops for survival lose over half of their crop each year to feathery mottle virus. Biotechnology has bred a sweet potato resistant to this disease that not only dramatically increases production but also reduces the use of chemicals.

- Biotechnology is expected to positively impact food production by allowing for heartier crops that can withstand drought and flooding or better tolerate extremes of heat and cold. Almost half of the $12 billion American farmers spend on fertilizer each year evaporates or washes away. High nitrogen-absorbing plant varieties may be able to reduce the need for fertilizers and help protect our environment.

SELECTED STUDIES

The Food and Drug Administration has ruled that there is no evidence to suggest that bio-engineered foods are unsafe. However, the agency has proposed mandatory rules that would tighten their scrutiny. In 2001, the agency required that developers of bioengineered foods submit a scientific and regulatory assessment of the products at least 120 days before they are marketed.

Pick Some Blueberries

Blueberries are a perfect example of a fruit with hidden qualities. A quick look at the nutritional analysis doesn't show much to get excited about—except their rich vitamin C content, that provides one-third of your daily requirement in just one cup. But the health benefits of eating blueberries may extend to preventing cancer and retarding the effects of aging—particularly loss of memory and motor skills. Anthocyanins and other natural compounds are the key. These chemicals are responsible for the intense blue color of the berries.

SELECTED STUDIES

According to research done at the Jean Mayer USDA Human Nutrition Research Center on Aging at Tufts University, blueberries have the highest antioxidant capacity of forty tested fruits and vegetables (*Journal of Agricultural and Food Chemistry,* 1998). Choose deep blue or wild blueberries because they have the highest concentration of ellagic acid, the active ingredient in this fruit.

A 2001 study by Clemson University researchers found that blueberries might help inhibit the growth of tumors that cause breast and cervical tumors. And Japanese researchers found that regular blueberry eaters were less likely to have vision deterioration than folks who don't often eat blueberries. In both studies, the high antioxidant properties of blueberries were cited.

Buying Basics: Choose firm, sweet-smelling whole berries with no sign of mold or mildew. Berries should appear plump and have a deep indigo-blue color. Wild blueberries are much smaller than cultivated blueberries.

Peak Season: May to October.

Preparation Tips: Pick off all stems, and remove bruised or moldy fruit. For best flavor, bring refrigerated berries to room temperature before serving.

Storage Solutions: Store berries loosely covered in the refrigerator. Use fresh berries within two weeks but preferably as soon as possible. Wash just prior to use. Discard shriveled or moldy berries.

To quick freeze for storage, place berries on a paper towel-lined baking sheet; freeze for one hour, then seal in an airtight container. Frozen blueberries will keep up to six months.

Recipe:
WILD BLUEBERRY SMOOTHIE

6 oz. blueberries (fresh or frozen)

6 oz. plain yogurt

1 Tbsp. honey

½ cup ice (3 ice cubes)

Blend well at high speed and serve immediately.

Bran Will Keep You Regular

Bran is the outer layer of a grain kernel where most of its fiber and nutrients are stored. Bran is the most concentrated way to get a dose of insoluble fiber. And why is insoluble fiber so important? First, fiber is filling and that's good news if you're trying to control your calorie intake. Fiber has an amazing capacity to absorb and hold lots of water. This action fools your gut into thinking you've eaten more than you have and your stomach stops sending hunger signals to your brain. High fiber foods create bulk that stimulates your intestines to contract and move elimination along. This increased speed means that waste matter doesn't stagnate in your colon and cause trouble. A softer, bulkier stool that passes quickly helps prevent hemorrhoids, bowel diseases and even cancer.

Buying Basics: You don't need to swallow bran like a foul-tasting medicine. Search for breakfast cereals with added bran that taste good. Compare the sodium, sugar and fat content, and choose the one that fits you best.

Peak Season: Available year round.

Preparation Tips: There's no rule that you have to eat cereal only in the morning with milk. Add bran cereal to yogurt or mix a couple of tablespoons with your favorite cookie or bread recipe. Coat fish or chicken with a mixture of flour and crushed bran cereal. Try substituting whole bran in place of breadcrumbs for meatloaf.

Storage Solutions: Most bran cereals stay fresh for a few months after opening. To slow down spoilage, transfer cereal to an airtight container or refrigerate the box.

Recipe:
HEAVY-DUTY BRAN MUFFINS

1½ cups bran (plain wheat bran, not a cereal)

½ cup boiling water

1 egg

3 oz. honey

1¼ cups buttermilk

¼ cup oil

1¼ cups whole-wheat flour

1¼ teaspoons baking soda

½ cup raisins

Preheat oven to 375 degrees F. Spray muffin tins with cooking spray or line with paper baking cups. In a large bowl, mix the bran and boiling water, and let it stand. In a medium bowl, beat together the egg, honey, buttermilk, and oil. Add this mixture to the bowl with the bran and water. Stir the flour and baking soda together, and combine into the bran mixture, add the raisins, and stir again. Fill the muffin tins and bake for about 15 minutes. Let stand for a few minutes, then remove and let cool slightly before serving.

Broccoli—Crown Jewel of Nutrition

Little was known about this vegetable until the 1920s, when the first commercially grown broccoli was grown and harvested in Brooklyn, New York. In 1923, the D'Arrigo Brothers Company made a trial planting of Italian sprouting broccoli in California. A few crates were sent to Boston, and by 1925 the broccoli market was established. Over the last 25 years, broccoli consumption has increased nearly 1,000 percent!

Broccoli is a good source of vitamin A, potassium, folacin, iron and fiber. It also contains important phytochemicals, including beta-carotene, indoles and isothiocyanates. Sulfurophanes, which belong to the isothiocyanates family, are found in high amounts in cruciferous vegetables such as broccoli. Unlike conventional antioxidants, which function by directly neutralizing oxidants produced by the body, these compounds help to protect the body by increasing the rate of detoxification and elimination of foreign substances.

Buying Basics: Choose broccoli that is tightly formed, deep-green with firm stalks. A yellowish-green color means the broccoli is past its prime.

Peak Season: Available year round.

Preparation tips: Trim the ends and peel the stalks of the individual broccoli. Rinse with cold water before using. Broccoli can be eaten cooked or raw.

Storage Solutions: Refrigerate the broccoli in a perforated plastic bag for up to 4 days. Frozen broccoli will maintain quality for several months in a tightly sealed bag.

Recipe:
BROCCOLI WITH ORANGE SAUCE

    1 lb. broccoli florets
    ½ cup chicken broth
    ½ cup orange juice
    2 tsp. cornstarch
    ½ tsp. basil
    ½ tsp. sugar
    ¼ tsp. salt
    ¼ tsp. pepper
    1 orange, peeled and thinly sliced

Steam broccoli 5 minutes until tender but crisp. While broccoli is steaming, stir together broth and juice in small saucepan over medium-high heat. Add cornstarch and stir until dissolved. Stir in basil, sugar, salt, and pepper. Bring mixture to a boil, then reduce heat and simmer until sauce begins to thicken and bubble. Cook 1 minute more. Stir in sliced orange and cooked broccoli. Toss gently to coat with sauce and serve immediately.

Brown Rice Is Best

All rice grains are covered with an inedible husk that has to be removed before eating. Underneath this hull lies another layer—a very nutritious coating, which is left on for brown rice or removed to create white rice. This nutritious, high-fiber bran coating gives brown rice its light tan color, nutlike flavor and chewy texture.

Rice naturally contains thiamin, niacin and iron. However, during the milling process, the quantities of these nutrients are reduced. To bring the nutritional value of the milled product up to that of whole-grain brown, white rice is enriched with thiamin, niacin and iron and is additionally fortified with folic acid. The enrichment mixture is applied to rice as a coating. Therefore, never wash or rinse white rice before or after cooking. You would be washing away the added enrichment and other water-soluble vitamins and minerals. Imported white rice is not necessarily fortified. While some nutrients are added back to white rice, brown rice provides much more fiber—1.8 grams per half cup compared to .3 grams per half cup in white rice.

Buying Basics: As is the case for white rice, brown rice is available in three sizes: short-, medium-, and long-grain. When cooked, long-grain rice produces light, dry grains that separate easily. Short-grain rice has fat, almost round grains that have higher starch content than either the long- or medium-grain varieties, or the grains stick together when cooked. Medium-grain rice, as could be expected from its name, has a size and character between the other two. Instant brown rice is also available.

Peak Season: Brown rice is available in most food markets year round. Natural food stores carry the largest variety of brown rice.

Preparation Tips: A cup of raw brown rice makes about 2½ cups cooked brown rice. To prepare a smaller or larger amount, just use the formula 1 part rice to 1½ parts water. For increased flavor, use vegetable stock instead of water or add a few favorite herbs to the cooking water. Brown rice needs a little longer to cook than white rice does— it takes about 45 minutes to develop its nutlike flavor.

Storage Solutions: It's best to keep brown rice in the refrigerator. Since brown rice contains the whole kernel of grain, it is more perishable. Prepare a double batch of brown rice and freeze the extra in a heavy-duty food storage bag. Defrost in the microwave on nights when you don't have time to prepare from scratch. Cooked brown rice will keep from three to five days in the refrigerator.

Recipe:
BROWN RICE AND CHICKEN SALAD

1 cup brown rice

1½ cups water

½ lb. cooked chicken breast, diced

1 stalk celery, chopped

1 green pepper, chopped

¼ cup sliced black olives

¼ cup fresh parsley, chopped

⅓ cup olive oil

⅓ cup white wine vinegar

10 cherry tomatoes, halved

Cook rice in a covered pot with water until liquid is absorbed and rice is fluffy (about 40–45 minutes). Remove from heat. Toss all ingredients together, but save cherry tomatoes to garnish top. May be served warm or chilled.

Canola from Canada
The term canola combines two words, Canadian and oil. Canola is a genetic variation of rapeseed developed specifically for its nutritional qualities by Canadian plant breeders. Canola contains the lowest level of saturated fatty acids of any vegetable oil and is high in monounsaturated fatty acids. Like all vegetable oils, canola oil is cholesterol-free.

Buying Basics: Look for oil that is 100% canola oil; some manufacturers add other oils to canola to make blends.

Peak Season: Available year round.

Preparation Tips: When a recipe calls for canola oil, try using less than suggested. It may be a "good" fat, but it still contains fat calories.

Storage Solutions: Store the oil in the pantry for best results, and keep it away from light and heat. If your oil starts to smell "off" throw it out. Most oils will keep for up to six months.

Recipe:
SASSY SALAD DRESSING

½ cup canola oil

½ cup balsamic vinegar

2 Tbsp. orange juice

2 tsp. soy sauce

1 tsp. dry mustard

1 tsp. curry powder

1 clove garlic, crushed

Combine all ingredients in a small glass jar or cruet with lid. Shake well. Refrigerate and use within one week.

Capsaicin—It's Hot

The fiery heat you feel from hot peppers is from a pungent compound called *capsaicin* (cap-SAY-shun). Hot peppers are a natural and instant decongestant and expectorant— they make your eyes and nose run.

Capsaicin (also called Substance P), most concentrated in the white membranes of the pepper, is released by your body when you eat hot peppers. It's a chemical that sends pain and itch signals to the brain. There is some evidence that capsaicin may lower cholesterol, help prevent stomach ulcers and even ease arthritis pain (capsaicin is an ingredient in *Zostrix*, a pain-relief cream also used to relieve shingles).

Buying Basics: Hot peppers range between one and ten inches in length depending on the variety. Fresh peppers may have smooth or wrinkly skins and are red or green in color. Choose fresh peppers with bright, deep colors that are free of bruises or blemishes. Buy only the amount of ground or dried cayenne pepper that you can use in six months.

Peak Season: Available year round. Peak season is May through November for fresh peppers.

Preparation Tips: Red peppers are typically spicier than green peppers. Use caution when handling hot peppers as they can irritate your skin and cause painful burning if they come in contact with your eyes. If possible wear gloves while working with hot peppers. The seeds contain most of the capsaicin, and most recipes don't call for using the seeds or veins of the peppers. Drink milk, not water, to cool the taste buds.

Storage Solutions: Store fresh peppers in a paper bag in the refrigerator. Chopped fresh peppers can be frozen in heavy-duty plastic freezer bags for up to three months. Keep dried pepper in a cool, dry place, and use within six months from date of purchase.

Recipe:
CAYENNE PEPPER RUB

1 tsp. ground cayenne pepper

1 tsp. coarse ground black pepper

2 Tbsp. paprika

1 tsp. celery salt

1 tsp. chili powder

½ tsp. dry mustard

Combine all ingredients and mix well. Use to season meat or poultry. Store any unused rub in a sealed container in the freezer.

Carrots—Encapsulated Carotene

Unlike most other vegetables, carrots are more nutritious when they are consumed cooked rather than raw. Because raw carrots have tough cellular walls, your body is able to convert less than 25 percent of the beta carotene into vitamin A. Cooking partially dissolves cellulose-thickened cell walls, freeing up nutrients by breaking down the cell membranes. When you eat cooked carrots as part of a meal that also provides some fat, you can absorb more than half of the available carotene.

Buying Basics: Choose carrots that are long and narrow, for best flavor. Avoid carrots that are bendable or have cracks. Carrots with attached greens should be fresh looking and not wilted.

Peak Season: Available year round.

Preparation Tips: Most carrots can be rinsed and rubbed and don't require peeling. If skins are thick or very dirty, peel off a thin layer. Packaged baby carrots are pre-washed, but a quick rinse under cold water will perk them up a bit. Carrots can be sliced, shredded, or cut into "coin" shapes.

Storage Solutions: Store carrots in a plastic bag in the crisper inside the refrigerator. When buying carrots with the green tops, remove the greens before storing them.

Recipes:
CARROT MANGO SALSA
½ cup grated carrot
1 medium mango, peeled and grated
1 tsp. minced fresh ginger
1 clove garlic, minced
2 Tbsp. red wine vinegar
2 Tbsp. firmly packed, light brown sugar
2 Tbsp. chopped cilantro or parsley
1 Tbsp. lime juice

In small bowl, combine all ingredients. Cover; chill at least 1 hour to blend flavors.

CRANBERRY CARROT SAUTÉ
1 pound carrots, peeled and cut into 2 ½-x½-inch sticks
1 tsp. salt, divided
1 Tbsp. brown sugar
1 tsp. cinnamon
¾ tsp. dry mustard
¼ cup orange juice
1 Tbsp. butter or margarine
½ cup dried cranberries
⅓ cup pecans, coarsely chopped

Place carrots and ½ tsp. salt in a large saucepan, cover with water, and bring to a boil. Reduce heat and cook 10 minutes or until carrots are fork tender and drain. Combine brown sugar, cinnamon, mustard, orange juice, and remaining salt in a small mixing bowl. Melt butter in a large skillet, and add carrots and orange juice mixture. Cook 2 to 3 minutes, and then gently toss in cranberries and pecans.

Cheese—Choose Carefully

Americans are consuming more cheese than ever before. Between 1990 and 2000, per capita consumption of cheese increased by more than 21 percent. Cheese contains a high concentration of essential nutrients, in particular protein and calcium, as well as other nutrients such as phosphorus, zinc, vitamin A, riboflavin, and vitamin B-12. The type of milk used and the manufacturing process (e.g., manner of coagulation, length of aging) influence the nutrient content of specific cheeses. Unfortunately, most cheeses are high in fat. Look for reduced-fat varieties of cheeses when possible.

Cheese has several health attributes. Obviously there's the calcium content. In addition, certain cheeses such as cheddar, Swiss, blue, Monterey Jack, and processed American cheese, among others, have been demonstrated to reduce the risk of dental caries. How this works is not completely understood; several theories have been suggested. Consuming cheese may stimulate the flow of saliva, which has properties that reduce caries. Milk proteins in cheese have been demonstrated to neutralize plaque acids through their buffering capacity. Cheese appears to prevent acid demineralization and enhance remineralization of tooth enamel. To help reduce tooth decay, health professionals recommend eating cheese immediately after meals or as a between-meal snack on those occasions when it's impossible to brush your teeth.

Buying Basics: There are four basic types of cheese products sold.

Natural cheese, which starts with fresh milk, is produced by separating milk solids from milk and curdling it with a bacteria culture. The curd is then separated from the whey and aged to produce a variety of cheeses. The length of aging, or ripening, determines whether the cheese is mild, medium, or sharp. The longer the aging, the richer the flavor and the higher the cost.

Pasteurized processed cheese starts with a blend of fresh and aged natural cheeses. They are shredded, mixed and heated to blend and develop a uniform flavor, body, and texture. The blend may be one or more varieties of natural cheese and may contain pimentos, fruits, vegetables, or meats. A smoked flavor may be added also.

When the word "food" is added to pasteurized processed cheese, the term identifies it as a product that contains less cheese and more nonfat dry milk or whey solids and water. It has a lower milk fat content and more moisture than process cheese.

Cheese food is milder in flavor, soft and spreads easily. It melts quickly because of the higher moisture content. It may contain other ingredients and have a smoked flavor too.

Pasteurized processed cheese spread is made like processed cheese food but is higher in moisture and has a lower milk fat content. It is more spreadable than most cheese and may contain flavoring.

Many cheeses, particularly aged cheeses such as Cheddar and Swiss, contain little or no lactose. For this reason, cheese is an important source of calcium and many other nutrients found in milk for individuals who have difficulty digesting lactose or milk sugar.

Peak Season: Available year round.

Preparation Tips: The less fat a cheese contains, the harder it is to use with good results in cooking. Typical cheeses have about 70 percent fat, which provides the rich and creamy smoothness that is so appealing.

When the fat is reduced, cheese becomes less pliable and more difficult to melt. Serve non-fat cheese "as is" in salads or on sandwiches. For best flavor, bring cheese to room temperature before serving.

Storage Solutions: Because of their high moisture content, reduced-fat and fat-free cheese turn moldy more quickly than their full-fat counterparts. Keep all cheeses well wrapped and in the refrigerator. If dry cheeses like Parmesan or Romano develop mold on the surface, it is safe to cut away the moldy part if you remove at least ¾ inch around the mold. Never eat soft cheese that has developed mold or white spots.

Recipe:
CHEESY CHILI RICE

 1 cup long-grain white rice (uncooked)
 1 small can chopped chilies
 ½ cup Monterey jack cheese
  (sliced or grated)
 2 cans beef consommé or broth

Spread rice in an ovenproof glass-baking dish. Top with chilies and cheese. Pour the soup over the rice and bake at 400 degrees F for 1 hour.

Chicken Choices

It's surprising to learn that chicken is not always a healthier choice than "red meat." A piece of dark-meat chicken with the skin on can be higher in total and saturated fat than some popular beef cuts. Chicken also contains the same amount of cholesterol per ounce as beef—that's because cholesterol is found throughout the meat—not just in the fat. Your best bet is skinless chicken breast if you're aiming for a low-fat selection. But beware, you can quickly lose the low-fat advantage if you smother that chicken breast in a fatty sauce or gravy or serve it fried.

Buying Basics: Choose chicken that looks plump and firm with skin that is moist and not dry or shriveled (if skin is still on). Free-range chickens are becoming increasingly popular; the meat tends to be a little tougher but many say it is more flavorful. Free-range chickens are allowed to roam around a bit, but they have no nutritional advantage.

Peak Season: Available year round.

Preparation Tips: No matter how you cook chicken, make sure to cook it thoroughly. The meat juices should be white and not pink. One of the reasons for the popularity of chicken is its versatility. When choosing cooking methods and recipes, think flavor, without adding fat. Try a variety of herbs, spices, marinades and sauces.

Storage Solutions: Chicken is highly perishable and should always be stored in the coldest part of the refrigerator—the back. Use chicken within two to three days of purchase. If you freeze chicken, be sure to wash it first, then wrap securely and label with the purchase date. Frozen chicken parts will keep up to nine months.

Recipe:
PASTA STIR-FRY WITH CHICKEN

 1 Tbsp. sesame oil
 1 tsp. garlic, minced
 2 green onions (scallions)
 1 stalk celery
 1 carrot
 ½ tsp. crushed red pepper
 ½ cup sherry
 ¼ cup low-sodium soy sauce
 2 Tbsp. cornstarch
 ¼ cup water
 ¾ lb. chicken breast, cooked
 ½ lb. vermicelli
 ½ cup water chestnuts, sliced

Chop scallions, celery, carrots, and meat for stir-frying. Stir-fry vegetables (except water chestnuts) in sesame oil until crisp-tender. Mix sherry, soy sauce, cornstarch, and water. Heat to thicken and add water chestnuts. Cook vermicelli. Toss meat and vegetables with the pasta and sauce. Chill.

Chocolate—Food or Drug?

Researchers have wondered for a long time what in chocolate generates such a craving. Is it the fat in chocolate, the sugar, the caffeine? *Anandamide*, a chemical in chocolate, is a naturally occurring substance produced by brain cells that mimics the mental effects of marijuana.

Buying Basics: There is a great variety of chocolate products on the market including:

Baking chocolate: Comes in both semisweet and unsweetened varieties and is sold in blocks, chunks, or chips.

Cocoa powder: Primarily used for baking, can be plain or sweetened.

Semi-sweet chocolate: Solid form of chocolate that has added sugar.

Unsweetened chocolate: Solid form of chocolate that contains up to 75 percent cocoa solids and has no added sugar or dairy products. Unsweetened chocolate is too bitter to eat plain.

White chocolate: Is not really chocolate since it's not made from the bean of the cocoa plant. It is made from cocoa butter and has added milk, sugar, and vanilla and is similar in texture to real chocolate.

Peak Season: Available year round.

Preparation Tips: Take care not to melt chocolate at high temperatures or you will lose flavor. For best results, break chocolate into small pieces and heat gently in an uncovered double boiler, stirring constantly.

Storage Solutions: Chocolate is best stored at room temperature either tightly wrapped or in an airtight container. It can also be stored in the refrigerator or freezer, but this may cause a whitish film of cocoa butter to rise and coat the surface. This separation does not affect the flavor of chocolate but does alter the appearance. Never store chocolate in a warm place.

Couscous—Moroccan Mainstay

Couscous is a type of pasta originating in North Africa. It consists of small grains of which semolina is the main ingredient. Couscous is used as the main ingredient in many dishes in much the same way as rice. The raw pieces are roughly the size of coarse sugar grains. American couscous is precooked, dried pasta prepared from 100 percent Durum Wheat Semolina, available in fine, medium and blended granulations.

Buying Basics: Couscous is a staple in most grocery stores; look for it in the pasta or rice section. Avoid couscous "mixes" that have lots of added salt or sugar.

Peak Season: Available year round.

Preparation Tips: Quick-cooking couscous is prepared by steeping it in boiling water or broth for 5 minutes. It can be served as a plain side dish or partnered with fruit, vegetables, or meat.

Storage Solutions: Keep in an airtight container in a cool, dry place.

Recipe:
SOUTHWESTERN COUSCOUS
1 cup vegetable or chicken broth
¼ cup chopped onion
1 4-oz. can diced green chili
    peppers
¼ tsp. ground turmeric
⅛ tsp. black pepper
⅔ cup couscous (uncooked)

In a small saucepan combine all ingredients, except couscous, and bring to a roiling boil. Remove from heat and stir in couscous. Let stand, covered, for five minutes. Fluff with a fork before serving.

Get Unstuck with Cranberries
Drinking cranberry juice is a common home remedy for urinary tract infections. Not until the late 1990s did anyone figure out why cranberry juice is so effective. It was thought to acidify the urine, but new research says that what really happens is

that specific compounds in cranberries inhibit *E. coli* bacterial cells from sticking in the urinary tract; they also have a similar effect in preventing ulcers by keeping ulcer-causing bacteria from sticking to stomach walls.

Cranberries may have other health benefits: Preliminary research suggests that as part of a healthy diet, cranberries may decrease total cholesterol and LDL and improve blood flow. And like blueberries, they may also inhibit some cancerous tumors. Some experts think that polyphenolic compounds in cranberries may help to protect against degenerative diseases such as Alzheimer's and Parkinson's as well as the memory and coordination losses associated with aging.

SELECTED STUDIES

Dr. Amy Howell of Rutgers University in New Jersey estimates that the amount of condensed tannins in a 10-ounce glass of cranberry juice taken on a daily basis could help prevent urinary tract infections (*New England Journal of Medicine,* October 1998). The National Kidney Foundation suggests drinking one glass of cranberry juice daily to maintain urinary health.

Buying Basics: Choose firm, round, dark red berries. It's impossible to find or drink 100 percent cranberry juice—it's too bitter. Look for 100 percent juice blends that contain some cranberry juice or choose a frozen cranberry juice cocktail with the least amount of added sugar.

Peak Season: August through December. Canned and juice available year round.

Preparation Tips: Cranberries are great baked in muffins and breads. Their intense flavor adds zest to relishes and sauces. Cranberry relish is a traditional garnish to turkey dinner and is used in many winter holiday recipes. Rinse fresh cranberries gently under cold water and drain. Discard any bruised or damaged fruit.

Storage Solutions: Refrigerate cranberries in a plastic bag for up to a month. Freeze unused cranberries in an airtight plastic bag or container in the freezer up to six months.

Recipes:
CRANBERRY HERB TEA

    8 oz. cranberry juice cocktail
    3 oz. water
    1 orange and spice tea bag
    Fresh lemon slice (optional)

In a large mug heat cranberry juice cocktail and water until boiling. Add tea bag and steep 3 minutes. Garnish with lemon slice.

CRANBERRY SALSA

    1 16-oz. can whole cranberries
    ¼ cup jalapeño peppers, finely
        chopped
    1 green onion, sliced (scallion)
    1 tsp. cilantro
    1 tsp. cumin
    1 tsp. lime juice

Combine all ingredients and chill before serving. Will keep in refrigerator for up to one week.

Dates Deserve Your Attention

Dates grow in thick clusters on giant date palm trees. The date palm, native to the Middle East, was mentioned in the Bible as the "tree of life," and the word "date" comes from the Greek *daktulos,* which means "finger." Dates bunches can weigh as much as 40 pounds, and large trees will yield more than 1,000 dates each year. Most dates are cultivated in Tunisia and California. The most well known varieties are Deglet Noor and Hawaii. In many countries dates are added to salads, couscous dishes, and curries, but in North America they're most commonly used in baked desserts and confections. Because dates are very high in simple carbohydrates, they can actually be converted into sugar. Fresh dates are much lower in calories than dried dates. All dates are high in iron and potassium and also contain folate, vitamin A, and the B vitamins. Dates are beneficial for anemia, constipation, and fatigue.

Buying Basics: Dates are classified into three categories—soft, semi soft, and dry—according to the softness of the fruit. Dry varieties are not the same as "dried" dates (which have been deliberately dehydrated). "Dry" dates are fresh dates that simply contain relatively little moisture when ripe. Dates vary in length from one to two inches depending on the variety. When ripe, dates can be golden or deep brown in color. Choose fresh dates that are plump and soft with smooth, shiny skins. Avoid shriveled or moldy dates or those that appear to have tiny crystals on them.

Peak Season: Dried dates are available year round. Fresh dates peak from late summer through mid-fall.

Preparation Tips: If dates are clumped together in a solid mass, microwave them at half power for 45 seconds. Let stand one minute before separating. Keep a cup of very hot water near when chopping dates. Dip your knife blade in occasionally to help prevent sticking. If dried dates seem excessively dry, you can plump them by soaking them in hot water or juice for about 15 minutes.

Storage Solutions: Store fresh dates in a plastic bag in the refrigerator for up to two weeks. Store dried dates in a cool, dry place for six to 12 months.

Recipe:
SPORTS POWER BARS

2 cups quick cooking oats
¾ cup pecans, chopped
⅓ cup light stick margarine
½ cup firmly packed dark brown sugar
¼ cup honey
¾ cup dried cherries
¼ cup chopped dried dates
1 cup honey graham cereal squares

Preheat oven to 350 degrees F. Pour uncooked oatmeal and chopped pecans into baking pan with sides. Bake 10 minutes or until golden brown and fragrant (stir every 5 minutes because the mixture on the edges will brown first). Set aside when done.

Combine margarine, brown sugar, and honey in large saucepan. Cook over medium heat until mixture boils. Pour oat mixture, cherries, dates, and cereal squares into honey mixture. Stir until well blended. Coat an 8-inch square baking pan with vegetable spray and pour in mixture. With lightly floured hands, press firmly into pan. Bake for 10–12 minutes. Let cool and cut into bars.

Eggs Are Okay

It's the amount of cholesterol in your blood, not in your omelet, that contributes to risk for heart disease. Mounting scientific research shows that cholesterol from food has just a slight impact on blood cholesterol levels in most healthy people. "There's no connection between cholesterol in food and cholesterol in the blood," says world-renowned nutrition and fat expert Dr. Ancel Keys. Still, an egg yolk has 219 milligrams of cholesterol—about two-thirds of the total recommended amount. But eggs are a great source of protein—an egg white has 3.5 grams with only 17 calories. A yolk contains 26 percent of vitamin B-12 and 12 percent of folate (and all that cholesterol).

SELECTED STUDIES

Harvard researchers have debunked the myth that you should reduce egg consumption if you want to lower blood cholesterol and prevent coronary heart disease. In two large prospective cohort studies of men and women, they found no overall association between egg consumption and risk of heart disease or stroke (*Journal of the American Medical Association,* April 1999). These findings suggest that eating an average of one egg per day (seven eggs per week) won't increase the risk of heart disease or stroke for healthy adults who do not have diabetes.

Buying Basics: Choose eggs that have uncracked, smooth, and round outsides. Choose eggs that have clearly labeled expiration or sell by dates. There is no nutritional difference between brown shell eggs and those with white shells. It is the breed of chicken that determines the color of the shell. Pasteurized eggs are now available as whole fresh eggs in the shell and are the best choice for eggs that you intend to not cook completely.

Peak Season: Available year round.

Preparation Tips: To significantly lower the cholesterol level in a recipe substitute two egg whites for one whole egg. (Although when you substitute egg whites the total fat content will only be lowered one gram per egg.)

Eggs can be poached, fried, scrambled, soft- and hard-cooked, as well as microwaved. If you must use a recipe that calls for raw or not fully cooked eggs, choose only pasteurized eggs.

Storage Solutions: Store eggs in the refrigerator inside the original carton since this keeps excess heat and humidity out. Never put eggs in the molded rack inside the refrigerator door; this exposes the eggs to warm air whenever the door is opened. If refrigerated correctly, the eggs can be kept safely for several weeks—but not past the stamped expiration date.

Recipe:
EGGCHILADA

    2 eggs
    1 large whole-wheat flour tortilla
    2 Tbsp. salsa
    1 Tbsp. shredded cheddar cheese

Beat eggs and cook in non-stick skillet over medium heat. Fold in salsa and cheese. Spread fully cooked mixture down center of tortilla. Roll tortilla around eggs. Garnish with extra salsa if desired.

Fishing for Health

Two or three servings of fish every week is good for your health. The average North American has just one serving of fish weekly. For optimal benefits choose cold-water fish including mackerel, herring, sardines, salmon, and trout. Even though these fish have more fat than others, they're packed with healthful omega-3 fatty acids, which have a protective effect against heart disease and may help improve skin conditions such as psoriasis. *Other benefits of eating seafood rich in omega-3 include…*

- Promoting proper development of brain, nerve, and eye tissue during pregnancy and infancy.

NUTRITION HOW TO'S: BUYING FISH

- Find a local fish or grocery store that gets regular shipments of high-quality fresh and/or flash-frozen fish.

- Look for signs of freshness, including bright clear eyes, reddish gills, and shiny scales that stick to the fish's skin.

- Take a whiff; there shouldn't be a strong "fishy" odor when raw or cooked. A strong smell indicates decay or bacterial contamination.

- Ask what's freshest and buy it if you're not committed to a certain variety.

- Choose smaller rather than larger fish—they've had less exposure to chemical pollutants.

- Lowering the risk of heartbeat abnormalities that may result in sudden heart attack or death.

- Prolonging life after a heart attack by improving heart function and reducing damage from heart disease.

- Modestly lowering blood pressure, thereby reducing the risk of heart attack and stroke.

- Improving symptoms of inflammatory diseases such as arthritis.

Use fish as a substitute for other fatty foods you consume, such as processed or fat-riddled meats and fried foods. Usually these foods have more total fat and much more saturated fat than fish. For information on fish oil capsules, see page 159.

Unfortunately, you do need to be concerned about contaminants fish pick up from polluted waters. Eating raw fish or shellfish puts you at risk for food-borne diseases, especially parasites, or in the case of mollusks, bacteria or viruses.

Buying Basics: Choose firm, moist steaks or fillets with shiny scales. If the head is still attached choose fish with firm, clear—not cloudy eyes. If the fish smells "fishy" do not buy it, this means the fish is no longer fresh.

Peak Season: Available year round. Ask which varieties are the freshest catch of the day.

Preparation Tips: When you cook lean fish such as cod, perch, or haddock, avoid direct heat. Instead poach, steam, or bake with vegetables.

Fish with a higher fat content like salmon, tuna, or mackerel can be cooked with dry-heat methods including grilling, baking, or broiling. The general rule of thumb for cooking fish is 10 minutes for every inch of the thickest part of the fish.

Storage Solutions: It is best if you cook the fish the same day you purchase it, but the fish can be left in the refrigerator. Store overnight in a plastic bag placed on a bowl of ice. Most lean fish can be frozen for up to six months and a fattier fish up to three months.

Recipes:
GRILLED FISH

1 lb. fish fillets
¼ cup lemon juice
1 Tbsp. fresh parsley, chopped
1 tsp. fresh dill weed
¼ tsp. salt
¼ tsp. black pepper
¼ tsp. paprika
1 onion, thinly sliced

Use heavy aluminum foil cut into large squares. Place equal portions of the fish fillets on each piece of foil. Add lemon juice, parsley, dill, salt and pepper into a bowl. Stir to blend well. Pour this mixture over the fish, sprinkle with paprika, and top with the onion slices. Fold the foil around the mixture and seal, leaving a little space for the food to expand while cooking. Place on hot grill and cook for 5–7 minutes per side. Fish should flake easily when done.

Flaxseed Each Day
Keeps the Doctor Away?

Flax is a blue-flowering crop with oil-rich, tiny seeds that range in color from light to reddish brown. The Babylonians cultivated flaxseed as early as 3000 B.C. for linen textiles, and in 650 B.C. Hippocrates used flaxseed for the relief of intestinal discomfort. Today it's common in products such as multigrain cereals and snack foods. Flax adds a pleasant, nutty flavor to foods. With the rise in popularity of bread shops, it is possible to buy fresh bread that contains flaxseed (check the ingredient list).

Over half the fat in flax comes from healthful omega-3 and omega-6 fatty acids. Flax is also a good source of both soluble and insoluble fiber. It has 75 times more lignin than any other plant food. It is found mostly at food co-ops; be sure to ask for milled flaxseed. You can also grind flax at home in a mini-food processor. The seeds must be broken to reap the benefits.

Studies show that consumption of flaxseed improves bowel regularity and maintains blood glucose levels. Flaxseed appears to protect against certain types of cancer, particularly hormone-sensitive cancers such as breast, endometrium, and prostate. New research also suggests that alpha-linolenic acid, an omega-3 fatty acid that is abundant in flaxseed, offers protective effects against both coronary heart disease and stroke. Omega-3 has been shown

NUTRITION HOW TO'S: WAYS TO ADD FLAX

- Add flaxseed to baked goods.
- Sprinkle some broken flaxseed over yogurt, cereal, and salads.

to also protect against hypertension and inflammatory and autoimmune disorders.

Buying Basics: Larger grocery stores sell a variety of items that contain flaxseed. You may have to search co-ops or health food stores to find plain flax.

Peak Season: Available year round.

Preparation Tips: Try grinding your own flaxseed at home in a small coffee bean grinder. You won't gain health benefits by consuming flaxseed whole. Flaxseed can be added to a variety of foods including bread, casseroles, and salads.

Storage Solutions: Flaxseed should be stored in an airtight container in the refrigerator for up to two months.

Garlic—Crushed Hopes?

Garlic advocates make some potent claims. Hundreds of studies on garlic have been completed in recent years to test its therapeutic effects on a range of conditions—from heart disease to cancer. The trouble is that many of these studies aren't very good. Some had no control group, the study participants who have a "placebo" dummy product used as a comparison. Other studies had too few people to draw conclusions.

Garlic, along with onions, leeks, and shallots, are part of the lily family. It's been a staple food and medicine for thousands of years. Egyptian slaves who built the pyramids ate garlic to increase their stamina. Garlic has been used both inside and outside the body to treat everything from viruses to vampires. Garlic was commonly used in both world wars to help ward off infection on the battlefields. The word garlic comes from the Anglo-Saxon "*gar-leac*," or spear plant.

The chemical that gives garlic its strong smell is *allicin* (from the Celtic language meaning "hot" or "burning"). This unstable compound is released only when the garlic clove is bruised, chewed, or crushed. Allicin breaks down into other sulfur-containing compounds. Some scientists believe that the allicin is the beneficial ingredient in garlic; others disagree. The Center for Science in the Public Interest (CSPI) tested various garlic supplements and concluded that people should consume fresh garlic or garlic powder instead of garlic pills or capsules. One-third teaspoon of garlic powder contains as much or more allicin than some best-selling supplements. One fresh garlic clove is equivalent to one-third teaspoon of garlic powder.

SELECTED STUDIES

A government review of many garlic studies had generally optimistic findings. In 37 studies, researchers found that garlic (or supplements) has a protective cardiovascular effect, primarily by lowering cholesterol and triglycerides, a type of blood fat associated with increased risk of heart disease. In 27 other studies, the findings were mixed, and in 12 others, no benefit was seen from garlic.

Other studies suggest, but do not prove, that frequent garlic consumption may be associated with decreased odds of laryngeal, gastric, colorectal, and endometrial cancers. But again, those studies were too small to make definitive conclusions. Garlic is known to have antioxidant properties, but the extent of their benefits is still under investigation.

Meanwhile, a study at the University of California at Irvine showed allicin is unlikely to survive in the digestive tract and would be destroyed within minutes of entering your bloodstream (*Journal of Agricultural Food Chemistry*, January 1997). If that's true, it's highly improbable that allicin can accomplish anything at the cellular level. Of course, some compound other than allicin might have the beneficial effects—but no one has found it yet.

The good news is that garlic can't hurt. *The American Herbal Products Association's Botanical Safety Handbook* rates garlic, also considered an herbal medicine, class 2c for safety (not to be used while breast-feeding). The worst it will do is cause digestive upset in sensitive persons.

Buying Basics: Choose firm, plump garlic bulbs with dry skins. Avoid garlic heads that have mold, have been broken apart or appear dried out.

Peak Season: Available year round.

Preparation Tips: The vast majority of recipes call for peeled garlic. Crushing, chopping, pressuring, or pureeing garlic releases more healthful essential oils and gives a more pungent flavor to foods. Cooked garlic has a more mellow flavor than raw garlic.

Storage Solutions: Store fresh garlic in an open container, away from other foods in a cool dark place—but not in the refrigerator. Unpeeled garlic can be kept up to 8 weeks. Once broken from the bulb, garlic cloves will stay fresh for three to 10 days.

Recipe:
GARLIC SPREAD

1 clove garlic, peeled
¼ cup fresh basil (1 tsp. dried basil)
⅓ cup green onion, chopped
1 cup low-fat cottage cheese
½ cup feta cheese, crumbled (2 oz.)

Combine all ingredients in small food processor until finely chopped. Chill before serving. Tastes great spread on bread, bagels, or on top of potatoes or vegetables.

Grape Juice—No Wine Here

If you want the reported benefits of drinking wine, without the alcohol, grape juice is the choice for you. Grape juice was originally invented as a nonalcoholic substitute for ceremonial wine during prohibition. It contains the same flavonoids as red wine. But you need to drink more grape juice to get the same levels. According to grape juice researcher John Foltz from the University of Wisconsin at Madison, it takes a 12-ounce glass of 100 percent pure grape juice (not grape drink) to provide the same benefits found in four to five ounces of wine. Keep in mind that 100 percent grape juice is a concentrated source of energy providing 20 calories per ounce, so a 12-ounce glass has 240 calories.

Buying Basics: Choose 100 percent juice (white or purple), not juice drink or juice cocktails to get maximum health benefits.

Peak Season: Available year round.

Preparation Tips: Grape juice can be added to cooked dishes. Try using white grape juice to poach dried fruit, chicken, or fish. Grape juice can be used in place of water to make gelatin.

Storage Solutions: Once bottled juice has been opened it should be stored in the refrigerator for best taste. Keep frozen juice concentrate frozen until ready to mix. Store all juices with a tight-fitting cover or lid to prevent loss of nutrients.

Recipes:
HOT SPICED GRAPE JUICE

½ gallon purple grape juice
4 whole cardamom pods
2 cinnamon sticks
1 tsp. nutmeg

Combine all ingredients in a large saucepan. Bring to a boil, and then reduce heat to simmer for 20 minutes. Remove whole spices and serve immediately.

BELIEVE-IT-OR-NOT BBQ SAUCE

6 oz. can 100% frozen concentrated grape juice
1 cup catsup
¼ cup water
2 Tbsp. Worcestershire sauce
1 medium tomato, chopped fine
2 Tbsp. onion, minced
1 Tbsp. horseradish
1 tsp. dry mustard

Combine all ingredients in a saucepan. Simmer 10 minutes over medium heat to blend flavors. Use as a basting sauce for meats or vegetables.

Grapefruit—Red Is Richer

There are lots of myths about this tart, tropical treat. It doesn't burn calories or melt fat away. The grapefruit diet isn't magical. It's low in calories, requires exercise, and replaces the usual variety of fruits with lots of grapefruit. One half grapefruit (about four ounces) contains 80 percent of your recommended daily vitamin C in about 40 calories, and contains nearly one gram of fiber to fill you up.

If you like grapefruit, choose the red or pink varieties, which contain more lycopene than white varieties. This is true for most deep-colored fruits and vegetables. Lycopene may reduce the risk of certain cancers.

But pill takers beware; grapefruit can interfere with some medications and increase the dose you absorb. Naringin in grapefruit juice turns off an enzyme in your small intestine that works to metabolize certain drugs. When a drug is not absorbed at the normal rate, more or less of it gets into your bloodstream. This makes the dose different than the amount prescribed and changes the drug's effect. The drugs that most frequently react with naringin include calcium channel blockers that control high blood pressure; Seldane, an allergy medication; and Halcion, an anti-anxiety drug.

Buying Basics: Choose grapefruits that feel heavy for their size. Avoid fruits with soft spots or bruises. However, most grapefruit do have irregularly colored skin and this does not affect taste.

Peak Season: Arizona and California grapefruits are available January through August. Florida and Texas grapefruits peak October through June.

Preparation Tips: Grapefruit is juiciest when rolled between palm and countertop before peeling or slicing. To peel, use an orange peeler or your fingertips. Grapefruit may also be cut in half, served in wedges, or scooped out with a spoon.

Storage Solutions: All citrus fruit can be kept at room temperature for up to a week and refrigerated for several weeks.

Recipe:
BROILED GRAPEFRUIT WITH PORT WINE
  2 grapefruit
  2 Tbsp. port wine

Preheat broiler. Cut grapefruit into halves. Trim a thin section of the uncut end of each half so the grapefruit can sit without wobbling. Section the grapefruit. Place grapefruit in a baking pan, and sprinkle with wine. Place pan about 2 inches from the broiler, and broil about 5 minutes. Watch carefully to prevent burning. Cool before eating.

Honey—The Bitter Truth
Honey, like all other sugars, is a sweetener. It provides calories but little in the way of nutrients. Of course, beekeepers and honey producers vehemently deny this fact. One tablespoon of honey provides 64 calories— all in simple carbohydrates with no real nutritional value. Meanwhile, a tablespoon of sugar has 45 calories. You'd have to eat one and a half cups of honey to get even 10 percent of any nutrient other than carbohydrates. That much honey has 1,500 calories and provides more than 140 percent of your total carbohydrate needs for the day.

If you use less honey than sugar to sweeten your coffee or tea (it has a higher sweetening power than white sugar), you've eaten fewer empty calories and that's good. However, honey is sticky sweet and, if not brushed off your teeth, it can promote tooth decay faster than other sugars, including white and brown sugars. Never feed babies younger than one year of age any form of honey, including honey graham crackers or other products made with honey. Honey can contain deadly spores that can cause infant botulism.

Honey's unique composition of sugar and high acidity makes it useful for treating minor burns and scrapes. Antimicrobial agents in honey, such as propolis found in nectar, can halt the growth of certain bacteria, yeast and molds. The high sugar content helps pull water out of cuts and sores. Since germs need water to grow and multiply, they don't fare as well when honey is used to dry them up. Sometimes honey can be used to help constipation because its water-drawing action can move needed fluid into your bowels.

Buying Basics: Alfalfa and clover honey are the most common varieties, but also look for blackberry, heather, and acacia. Honey can be purchased as a liquid or in a crystalline from. Most commercial honey is heated to prevent crystal and yeast formation.

Peak Season: Available year round.

Preparation Tips: When substituting honey for granulated sugar in recipes, keep in mind that because of its high fructose content, honey has more sweetening power than sugar. Not all products will work well with honey since it also has a much higher water volume than white sugar. Start by substituting just one quarter the sugar in a recipe with honey. When making either cakes or cookies, mix the honey with the fat or the liquid before adding. Then mix it thoroughly with the other ingredients. If this is not done, a soggy layer will form on the top of the baked product. Reduce oven temperature by 25 degrees F to prevent over-browning.

Storage Solutions: Honey should always be stored at room temperature and out of sunlight—a pantry shelf is ideal. Do not refrigerate honey since cool temperatures will speed up crystallization.

If your honey becomes grainy or difficult to pour, simply warm the honey slowly in a heatproof container in a pan of warm water to reverse the crystallization process.

Recipe:
HONEYED RED FRUIT

½ pint fresh strawberries, sliced
2 blood oranges
½ pint fresh raspberries
½ lemon
3 Tbsp. honey
4 mint leaves

Peel oranges, and cut three slices from the middle of each fruit. Squeeze the remaining fruit for juice. Add the orange juice to lemon juice and honey and mix well. Arrange sliced oranges, strawberries, and raspberries in bowls. Drizzle honey mixture over the top and garnish with mint leaf.

Irradiation—If It's Good Enough for Astronauts...

Since the 1970s, U.S. and Soviet astronauts have been enjoying irradiated foods in space. And now, students in the national school lunch program can eat meat that's been irradiated at school cafeterias. This technology that rids food of parasites and bacteria, including *E. coli* and *salmonella,* by exposing it to low levels of gamma rays or electrons is controversial.

Food irradiation technology in the United States began as part of the "Atoms for Peace" program established by President Eisenhower. Food irradiation is a food safety tool. Ionized energy (gamma rays, electron beams, or X-rays) is applied to foods to eliminate harmful bacteria without the use of heat. Sometimes irradiation is called "cold pasteurization." More than forty types of foods have been approved for irradiation around the world.

Irradiation doesn't make food radioactive. The energy levels used during irradiation are far too low to induce radiation. The process is similar to light passing through a glass window. Food is moved through an energy field and never touches the energy source. Irradiation damages food nutrients far less than basic cooking or microwaving.

Federal regulations require that most irradiated foods be identified with the radura (RAH-dur-ah) symbol accompanied by the words "treated with irradiation" or "treated by irradiation." Currently meat, poultry, fruits, vegetables, grains, spices, seasonings and dry enzymes used in food production have been approved for irradiation.

SELECTED STUDIES
What's the benefit of irradiated meat? Food irradiation has been identified as a safe technology to reduce the risk of food-borne illness that may result from the production process, reports the *Journal of the American Dietetic Association* in 2000. Low doses of radiation can kill more than 99 percent of salmonella in poultry but offers only a "negligible loss of nutrients or sensory qualities in food, since it does not substantially raise the temperature of the food during processing."

Jicama—Root Vegetable or Bean?
The jicama (HEE-ka-mah) is a tuberous vegetable that looks like a large beige turnip but is a member of the bean family. It's also called the Mexican yam bean. Its crunchy texture is similar to water chestnuts, but it has a sweet, nutty flavor. Jicama is low in calories and fat, a good source of vitamin C, and contains some potassium, iron, and calcium as well.

Buying Basics: Choose smooth, rounded jicama with unblemished skins. There should be a slight give when you press the skin to indicate juiciness. Avoid any that have dry or discolored flesh.

Peak Season: Available year round.

Preparation Tips: Halve or quarter the jicama and then remove the thin skin with a paring knife or vegetable peeler. Jicama does not discolor when exposed to air. Jicama does not lose its crunchiness when cooked, so it makes a great addition to stir-fry dishes, casseroles, and soups.

Storage Solutions: Uncut jicama will keep in a cool, dark place for several weeks. Once cut, store jicama in the refrigerator.

Recipe:
TROPICAL COLESLAW
  3 cups shredded cabbage
  1 medium jicama, peeled and shredded
  1 mango, chopped
  2 green onions (scallions), chopped
  1 lime, juiced
  ¼ cup poppy seed dressing

Combine cabbage, jicama, mango, and onion. Sprinkle with lime juice and poppy seed dressing and stir to combine.

Kiwi—Packed with Power
According to recent studies, kiwifruit is the most nutrient dense of all the major fruits. You may already know that kiwifruit is packed with more vitamin C than oranges. Kiwi is also a good source of the phytochemical lutein that helps reduce the risk of cancer, heart disease, and may help prevent cataracts and macular degeneration—a leading cause of blindness. Potassium from fruits and vegetables helps the heart work more efficiently and is significant in controlling blood pressure—the "silent killer." Potassium controls heart activity and maintains fluid balance. A single serving of kiwifruit outranks bananas as the top low-sodium, high-potassium fruit.

Buying Basics: Select kiwifruits that are unblemished and firm but not rock hard. The flesh should yield to gentle pressure, similar to that of a ripe peach. Avoid those that are shriveled, moldy, or have soft spots.

Availability: California kiwifruit are available from October through May. The New Zealand season is exactly opposite—April through November, which provides for fresh kiwifruit year round.

Preparation Tips: This small, oval fruit has a thin brownish-green skin with a fuzzy surface. The flesh, which is a distinctive green, with tiny purplish seeds surrounding a white core, may be eaten raw or cooked.

Storage Solutions: Store unripe kiwis at room temperature until skin indents slightly when touched. Place kiwifruit in a paper bag with an apple or banana to speed ripening. Ripe kiwis can be kept in the refrigerator for up to three weeks.

Recipe:
SPICY KIWI SALSA

> 4 kiwifruit, peeled and finely diced
> 1 tsp. red jalapeño or other fresh hot red pepper, minced
> 1 Tbsp. tequila
> 1 Tbsp. orange juice
> 1 Tbsp. mint, chopped
> Pinch salt

Combine ingredients and chill 30 minutes to 1 hour.

Lentils—Healthy Legumes

The lentil is a cousin of the bean, and both are a part of the legume family. Lentils come from the Latin language for the word "lens." Lentils are packed with nutrients, fiber, complex carbohydrates, and folic acid.

Lentils are a low-calorie, low-fat, and cholesterol-free food, and they are inexpensive. Lentils provide more folic acid than any other unfortified food. Lentils are also an important source of iron, especially for women, whose iron needs are greater than men's. Eating lentils with foods rich in vitamin C, like tomatoes, green peppers, broccoli, and citrus fruits or juices, helps the body absorb iron more efficiently.

Lentils also contain soluble fiber, which acts as a scrub brush that cleans the digestive system. This type of fiber also decreases serum glucose and cholesterol and decreases insulin requirements for people with diabetes.

Buying Basics: The size and appearance of lentils varies depending on the variety. The outer seed coat can be mottled or speckled, and ranges in color from reddish-brown to grayish-brown to green. The inner coat, or cotyledon, can be red or yellow.

The two main varieties in the U.S. are brewer lentils and Red Chief. Brewer lentils are green or brown in color. Red chief are quick cooking since the outer skin has been removed. Lentils are sold prepackaged and in loose bins. If you buy them prepackaged, look for well-sealed or uniform boxes.

Peak Season: Available year round.

Preparation Tips: Sort lentils by removing any debris and discarding discolored or shriveled beans. Red lentils cook quickly and are often used in soups or dips, because they tend to lose their shape and become mushy. The brown or green lentils hold their shape the best and are excellent in salads. Lentils require from 30–45 minutes cooking, and most require no presoaking. Don't add salt to lentils while cooking (it will make them tough).

Storage Solutions: Lentils can be kept indefinitely in a cool, dry place. After long storage, the color may fade slightly, but the taste will not be noticeably altered.

Recipe:
BBQ LENTILS

    1 cup lentils
    2½ cups water
    ¼ cup molasses
    1 Tbsp. brown sugar
    2 tsp. vinegar
    ¼ cup catsup
    ½ tsp. dry mustard
    1 tsp. Worcestershire sauce
    1 8-oz. can tomato sauce
    1 Tbsp. onion, minced

    Add lentils to water and bring to a boil, then lower heat and simmer gently for 30 minutes or until tender but whole. Add remaining ingredients to the cooked lentils and transfer to an ovenproof dish. Bake at 350 degrees F for 45 minutes.

Melons—Sweet and Nutritious

Melon varieties differ nutritionally depending on the type. They do, however, have one thing in common—they are all 90 percent or more water, have a sweet, juicy pulp, and are very nutritious. A six-ounce serving of cantaloupe has 100 percent or more of the recommended amounts of both vitamins A and C. A two-cup serving of watermelon has more iron than any other fruit serving. A six-ounce portion of honeydew contains 410 milligrams of potassium.

Buying Basics: Melons picked before they are mature will never ripen and reach full flavor. Melons should be symmetrical in shape and the blossom end should give when pressed with your fingertip. Avoid melons with lumps or spots or those that are rock-hard. Another hint for freshness is that melons should have a pleasantly sweet aroma. In addition to the basic melons, look for Crenshaw, Persian and Casaba melons.

Peak Season: Cantaloupes peak between June and November. Honeydew melons are available year round. The best time for watermelons is July through October.

Preparation Tips: Always rinse whole melons before slicing to remove any surface dirt or bacteria. Most melons can be sliced in half, removing the seeds with a spoon. Watermelon seeds form in concentric circles and are best avoided by cutting into circular slices. Use a cookie cutter to remove center seeds.

Storage Solutions: All varieties of melon should be kept refrigerated in a plastic bag or wrap and kept no longer than five to seven days. When you store melons, do not remove the seeds, even if you cut the fruit. Wait until you are ready to serve since the seeds help keep the surface of the fruit moist.

Recipe:
TROPICAL SUNRISE

    4 oz. 100% grapefruit juice
    ¼ cup watermelon chunks
    ¼ cup pineapple chunks
    ¼ cup cantaloupe chunks
    ⅓ cup vanilla yogurt
    Put all ingredients in a blender. Blend for a few seconds on high speed or until ingredients are thoroughly combined. Pour into a large glass. Serve chilled.

Mushrooms—Better Cooked Than Raw

If you like raw mushrooms in your salad—go ahead, but don't go overboard. You're better off with cooked mushrooms in terms of nutrition and health. First, for the same volume, you get double or triple the nutrients from cooked mushrooms. Cooking removes much of the water and concentrates nutrients and flavor. In addition, raw mushrooms contain toxic compounds called hydrazines that are eliminated when mushrooms are cooked or dried. It's not really known just how harmful hydrazines are in humans but you're better off without them.

Buying Basics: Button mushrooms are standard fare in most grocery stores. Be adventurous—try special varieties including shitake, chanterelle, enoki, oyster, or Portobello. Look for clear, not mottled, color in mushrooms. Avoid those with dark brown spots.

Peak Season: Available year round.

Preparation Tips: Never wash mushrooms; they absorb water like a sponge and that dilutes flavor. Use a soft vegetable brush to gently wipe away dirt. A damp paper towel works well too. Chop or slice just before using to prevent oxidation that turns the surfaces brown.

Storage Solutions: Mushrooms like it cool and moist but also need circulating air. Store them in an open paper bag in the refrigerator —but not the crisper (not enough air movement). Mushrooms stored in plastic bags or trays tend to turn slimy more quickly.

Recipe:
GRILLED PORTOBELLO MUSHROOMS

    2 Portobello mushrooms
    2 Tbsp. canola oil
    2 Tbsp. onion, chopped
    2 cloves garlic, minced
    4 Tbsp. balsamic vinegar

Clean mushrooms and remove stems. Place caps on a plate with the gills up. In a small bowl combine the oil, onion, garlic, and vinegar. Pour this mixture evenly over the mushroom caps and let stand for one hour. Grill over high heat for 5–10 minutes. Serve immediately.

Nuts to You
It might seem nutty at first, but evidence is building that fat-filled nuts may be beneficial in reducing blood cholesterol levels and protecting against heart disease. While all nuts contain fat—and plenty of it—in many types, up to 85 percent of the fat is polyunsaturated and monounsaturated. It is thought that these unsaturated fats may help to lower "bad" LDL cholesterol and Type 2 diabetes.

Granted, if you add nuts to your diet, be sure to cut back on fat elsewhere. Recent studies suggest that walnuts, in particular, may help raise "good" HDL cholesterol— along with providing a good source of magnesium and folate and no sodium. Almonds are a rich source of monounsaturated fats and are also high in magnesium (as well as riboflavin and iron). And chestnuts are virtually fat-free and yield a surprising amount of vitamin C.

A study by Harvard researchers published in November 2002 found that women who frequently ate nuts or peanut butter dramatically reduced their risk of Type 2 diabetes—and the more they had, the better their protection. Women who ate five ounces of nuts per week had a 30 percent reduced risk compared to never or rarely consuming nuts. Women who ate a tablespoon of peanut butter five times a week had a 20 percent reduced risk. Again, those monounsaturated fats are credited—by helping to improve glucose and insulin stability.

But these benefits are obtained only if you replace foods high in saturated fats (such as fried foods and fatty meats) with nuts. You can't just add them into your diet. Nuts are an excellent source of fiber, vitamin E, magnesium, zinc, selenium, copper, potassium, phosphorus, biotin, riboflavin, niacin, and iron. Some nuts are also good sources of folate. In addition to vitamins and minerals, nuts also contain beneficial plant chemicals that help protect you from a variety of chronic diseases.

Buying Basics: Be sure to check the freshness date when you buy shelled nuts. Choose whole nuts that are not discolored, shriveled, or moldy. Dry roasted nuts do not have much less fat than oil roasted—usually just one less gram per serving.

Peak Season: Fall and winter are the best time to buy most whole nut varieties. Shelled and roasted varieties are available year round.

Preparation Tips: The best way to open shelled nuts is with a nutcracker or pliers. Roast chestnuts over an open fire in an old-fashioned corn popper, or baked in a covered-shallow pan at 450 degrees F for 30 minutes.

Storage Solutions: Nuts will go rancid quickly due to their high fat content. Shelled nuts should be kept frozen or in the refrigerator. Unshelled nuts can be kept in a cool, dry place for a few months.

Recipe:
TRAIL MIX

 1 cup cashew pieces
 1 cup smoked almonds
 1 cup broken banana chips
 1 cup dried dates, chopped
 1 cup dried pineapple chunks
 ¼ cup flaked coconut

Combine all ingredients and store in an airtight container.

Oats—For Your Health

More than forty scientific studies show that eating oatmeal daily may help lower blood cholesterol. In fact, the U.S. Food and Drug Administration granted the first food-specific health claim for use on oatmeal: Soluble fiber from oatmeal, as part of a diet low in saturated fat and cholesterol, may reduce the risk of heart disease. Oats can help to lower LDL (the "bad" cholesterol) blood cholesterol levels. Though most of its cholesterol-lowering power comes from the soluble fiber beta-glucan, recent research suggests that other components of oats—such as the protein and natural antioxidants—may also contribute to heart health. Emerging research suggests that oatmeal may help maintain healthy blood pressure levels and may help promote healthy blood flow. Oatmeal, as a source of fiber, may also help to slow the rate of digestion, which may help to maintain healthy blood sugar levels, as well as curb appetite.

Buying Basics: Old-fashioned oats are whole oat groats that are rolled to flatten them. They contain all parts of the oat grain including the bran, endosperm and germ portion. Quick oats are made the same way but are simply cut into slightly smaller pieces so they cook faster. Instant oats use the exact same oats; only they are rolled a little bit thinner and cut finer so that they cook very quickly. However, instant oatmeal often has added sugars and other flavoring ingredients.

Peak Season: Available year round.

Preparation Tips: For best results, always follow label recommendations as brands and formulations vary considerably.

Storage Solutions: Keep oats in a dark, dry location in a well-sealed container to keep bugs out. If you live in a humid climate, it's best to store oats in the refrigerator. Oats will keep up to one year if properly stored. Oat groats and bran have a shorter shelf life and can be kept up to six months if refrigerated.

Recipe:

OLD-FASHIONED OATMEAL PORRIDGE

½ cup steel-cut oats

2½ cups water

½ tsp. salt

½ cup dried fruit—any combination
    e.g. apricots, dates, blueberries, cherries

Slowly pour oats into boiling salted water. Cover and simmer 30 minutes. Add more or less water to reach desired consistency. Stir in dried fruit a few minutes before cooking is complete.

Olive Oil—What a Fat!

All oils—olive or otherwise—contain the same amount of calories (120) and fat grams (14) per tablespoon. When you replace the saturated fats in your diet with monounsaturated fats, such as those found in olive oil, you might reap health benefits. To gain improvements such as lower blood cholesterol and added protection against heart disease, you can't just add olive oil to your diet. You also have to cut back on other fats and oils.

Still, olive oil is the cornerstone of the so-called "Mediterranean Diet," which has been studied extensively in recent years. Researchers wanted to know why people living in Italy and other countries surrounding the Mediterranean Sea had low incidences of heart disease and other conditions, even though their overall dietary fat was high. They found that olive oil, which is packed with heart-healthy monounsaturated fats, was the likely reason.

Olive oil also helps the body to better absorb and use lycopene (a cancer-fighting ingredient in tomatoes) than other oils—which may further explain its health-promoting powers. In 2000, researchers discovered that tomato/olive oil combination generated increased plasma antioxidant activity by around 20 percent compared to other oils.

Light or extra-light olive oil does not mean light in calories! Instead light refers to the very subtle flavor of this oil. Light olive oil is "all-purpose" oil that can be used in everyday cooking without affecting flavor. All olive oils are classified by the amount of acidity, flavor, color and aroma they impart. The European Economic Communities (EEC) set the standards. Olive oil is more expensive than most vegetable oils. That's because olive oil manufacturing is more labor intensive from harvest to production. Most olive oil producers don't use cheaper, speedier modern processes such as heat extraction and chemical solvents. The higher price of certain olive oils reflects both quality and flavor.

Although olive oil does not require refrigeration, it does lose quality when exposed to heat and light. Many food experts prefer to keep olive oil refrigerated. While chilling may cause some clouding, it doesn't affect the oil's flavor or quality. Any cloudiness will disappear when the oil is returned to room temperature.

Buying Basics: Buy only small amounts of olive oil at a time to preserve freshness and quality.

Peak Season: Available year round.

Preparation Tips: Olive oil can be strongly flavored and is not suitable for most baking. Use the rich flavor of olive oil to best advantage in marinades, sauces and salad dressings. Try dipping crusty bread into olive oil instead of butter or margarine.

Storage Solutions: Cooking oils may spoil or become rancid when exposed to heat, light, or oxygen. Keep small quantities in an airtight container in the pantry or cupboard or store in the refrigerator. Stored this way the oil should keep for up to six months.

Recipe:
OLIVE OIL FOR DIPPING

    1 cup olive oil

    ¼ cup red wine

    1 clove garlic

    ½ tsp. salt

    ¼ tsp. black pepper, coarse ground

Steep crushed garlic clove in olive oil for about 1 hour. Remove garlic. Add vinegar, salt and pepper to taste. Mix well to combine oil and vinegar. Serve as a dip with a selection of fresh raw vegetables or bread.

Papaya—Delicious Health Treat

The papaya, also known as "paw paw fruit," can grow from seed to a 20-foot, fruit-bearing tree in less than 18 months. Papaya is the only food containing Papain, a powerful enzyme that digests proteins. In digesting proteins, Papain frees the amino acids for quick absorption. Papaya is high in vitamin C—just a single half of a papaya has 150 percent of the daily vitamin C requirement. Papaya is also a good source of fiber and an excellent source of folate.

Buying Basics: Papayas can range widely in size from less than a pound to more than 10 pounds. The most common variety is Solo or Hawaiian and is about six inches long. Mexican papayas are much larger than Hawaiian types and may weigh up to 10 pounds and be more than 15 inches long. The flesh may be yellow, orange, or pink. The flavor is less intense than the Hawaiian papaya but is still delicious. Ripe papaya should yield to gentle pressure. A deep-colored, blotchy skin often indicates good flavor.

Peak Season: Available year round.

Preparation Tips: Ripe papayas are best eaten raw. Green or unripe papayas can be cooked and eaten as a vegetable. Halve papayas and remove seeds. The skin can be removed, if desired, with a vegetable peeler.

Storage Solutions: Ripe fruit should be refrigerated and used as soon as possible. Store unripe fruit at room temperature and check frequently—they ripen quickly.

Recipe:
PAPAYA CHUTNEY

    1 ripe papaya

    ¼ cup white wine vinegar

    ¼ cup lemon juice

    1 Tbsp. cilantro, chopped

    1 Tbsp. olive oil

    1 Tbsp. honey

    ¾ tsp. ground ginger

    ⅛ tsp. chili powder

    ¼ tsp. cinnamon

Cut papaya in half and scoop out centers. Chop papaya finely. Heat all ingredients to boiling in 10-inch skillet; reduce heat. Cover and simmer 40 minutes, stirring occasionally. Serve warm or cold.

Pasta—It's Primo!

Popular legend has it that Marco Polo introduced pasta to Italy following his exploration of the Far East in the late 13th century; however, historians can trace pasta back as far as the fourth century B.C., where an Etruscan tomb showed a group of natives making what appears to be pasta. The Chinese were making a noodle-like food as early as 3000 B.C. American dry pasta is made with semolina, which is produced by grinding kernels of durum wheat. Sometimes other hard wheats are also used. The semolina is mixed with water until it forms dough. The dough is kneaded until it reaches the correct consistency, and then it is pushed, or extruded, through a die—a metal disc with holes in it. The size and shape of the holes in the die determine what the shape of the pasta will be. Then it is sent through large dryers that circulate hot, moist air to slowly dry the pasta.

Buying Basics: Pasta comes in more than 600 shapes in Italy, but in the U.S. only about 150 varieties are available. Choose any type of pasta you'd like, and you'll never get bored. Special flavored pasta is also available—wheat, spinach, lobster, chili, mushroom, and sesame to name a few. Some pastas work best with certain sauces or flavors.

Peak Season: Available year round.

Preparation Tips: Boil four to six quarts of water for one pound of dry pasta. (You can reduce the water depending on how much pasta you are cooking.) Stir in pasta and return the water to a boil. Stir the pasta occasionally during cooking. Follow the package directions for cooking times.

If the pasta is to be used as part of a dish that requires further cooking, undercook the pasta by one-third of the cooking time specified on the package The only time you should rinse pasta after draining is when you are going to use it in a cold dish. In those cases, rinse the pasta under cold water to stop the cooking process, and drain well.

Storage Solutions: Store all varieties of pasta in airtight containers away from light and heat. Keep leftover cooked pasta in the refrigerator for up to three days. When it's time to reheat, simply put it in a colander and then place it directly into boiling water for one minute.

Recipe:
LEMON BASIL PASTA

½ lb. dry pasta

2 lemons, juiced with rinds grated

¼ cup lemon juice

½ cup olive oil

1 tomato, cored and chopped

¼ cup fresh basil leaves, chopped

1 tsp. dried basil

½ cup Parmesan cheese, grated

½ tsp. salt

½ tsp. black pepper

Cook pasta, drain, and toss with lemon juice, rind and olive oil while warm. Combine with all other ingredients and chill thoroughly.

Pick a Peck of Peppers

Peppers, both sweet and hot, were first cultivated in Central and South America some 2,000 years ago. Columbus introduced them to Europe after his first voyage to the New World. Portuguese traders eventually brought them to India and Southeast Asia.

Today the sweet pepper is a mainstay of many European and Middle Eastern cuisines.

Buying Basics: Choose peppers that are firm and brightly colored with smooth skin. Although red peppers start out as green while on the plant, they don't change color after picking. So if you want them red, buy them red. Yellow and dark purple peppers are a special variety.

Peak Season: Available year round. Peak season is May through September.

Preparation Tips: Wash the peppers well, and remove the seeds and stem with a paring knife.

Storage Solutions: Store peppers in the refrigerator loosely wrapped in plastic for up to two weeks.

Recipe:
PASTA WITH RED PEPPER SAUCE

¼ cup olive oil
1 yellow onion, divided
1 red pepper, divided
¼ bunch fresh basil
½ tsp. salt
½ tsp. pepper
½ cup chicken broth
¾ lb. bow tie pasta, dry
¼ cup cilantro, chopped

Slice onions and peppers and place half in pan; toss with olive oil. Sauté until onions brown, stirring every 5 minutes. Add basil, salt, and pepper. Cook 10 more minutes. Puree remaining pepper/onion mix with cilantro. Add chicken broth if needed to make sauce consistency similar to tomato sauce. Cook pasta, cool, and toss with sauce and pepper strips. Chill.

Psyllium—It's Husky

Psyllium contributes dietary fiber, which has been shown to lower blood lipid levels and reduce the risk of heart disease. In one study, people consuming seven grams of psyllium each day lowered their overall cholesterol levels from 4 to 11 percent and dropped their serum LDL cholesterol concentrations from 6 to 18 percent. Other studies have suggested, but not conclusively proven, that psyllium may also help prevent cancers affecting the digestive tract.

Plantain plants from India are the source of psyllium husks. It's the husk portion that is known for its high-soluble fiber content and that is used in food and some over-the-counter laxatives. Soluble fiber, along with a low-fat diet, can lower blood cholesterol. Psyllium husk has 14 times more soluble fiber than oat bran.

Buying Basics: It's difficult to find plain psyllium in most grocery stores, though it's easy to locate as an ingredient in many cold cereals and pastas. Shop co-ops or a health food store to find psyllium grain.

Peak Season: Available year round.

Preparation Tips: Add 1–2 teaspoons of psyllium to smoothies, bread doughs, and cookie batters.

Storage Solutions: Like other whole grains, psyllium should be stored in a cool, dry place for no more than six months.

Salads—Go for the Dark Greens

Lettuce may be the most popular salad green, but unfortunately it is just about the least nutritious. You have to look to the darker colored salad greens to find more than just filler. Generally the darker the lettuce leaf the higher the nutritional value.

There are three main types of lettuce —and they all come in an array of shapes and hues. Cabbage lettuce has a round head with tightly packed leaves that grow from a center core. Cos lettuce is a crisp, long-leaved lettuce with leaves that grow out from a stem rather than a core. Finally, loose-leaf lettuce is a catchall term for several varieties that have short curly leaves and stems.

Buying Basics: Look for well-proportioned heads that have deep, rich color. Avoid lettuce that appears wilted or has brown streaks or spots.

Peak Season: Iceberg lettuce is available year round. Other varieties are more plentiful in the spring and summer months.

Preparation Tips: Always wash head lettuce before serving. Discard outer leaves as they have the greatest exposure to dirt, grit and agricultural chemicals. Bagged lettuce or salads have already been pre-washed and require no further preparation.

Storage Solutions: If you buy lettuce wrapped in cellophane, keep it in the original wrap until ready to use. Most leaf lettuce and Boston or Bibb lettuce keep only a few days in the refrigerator. Romaine lettuce is heartier and will store refrigerated for up to ten days.

Recipe:
FIELD GREEN SALAD

    8 oz. mixed baby salad greens
    ¼ cup walnuts or pecans, chopped
    2 oz. feta cheese, crumbled
    2 green apples, cored and diced
    Prepared raspberry vinaigrette salad
       dressing

Wash and pat dry greens. Arrange on plates and top with nuts, cheese and apples. Dress with vinaigrette.

NUTRITION HOW TO: For the lunch hour meal (which now averages twenty-four minutes), add low-fat cheese to sandwiches and salads, eat a cup of low-fat yogurt, or drink a glass of milk. Most convenience and grocery stores sell milk in containers for immediate, single-serving consumption.

Soft Drinks Edge Out Milk

Twenty years ago, teenagers drank two times more milk than soft drinks. Now they drink twice as much soda as milk. This intake of soft drinks significantly lowers intake levels for calcium and other key nutrients. Teen girls who regularly consume soft drinks take in 20 percent less calcium than non-drinkers. This lower calcium intake contributes to broken bones now and osteoporosis later. Obesity has risen in tandem with soft-drink consumption, which for many teens accounts for 15 to 20 percent of their daily calories.

Recipe:

Make your own substitute for carbonated soft drinks by combining six ounces of juice with six ounces of sparkling water. You get half the sugar and calories and still have a flavorful carbonated beverage.

Joy of Soy

More than 500 scientific studies have investigated the disease-fighting potential of soy. Most have found that people who consume a diet high in soy have historically had lower incidence of heart disease, cancer and other chronic diseases. *One reason:* Soy is the basis of many vegetarian diets (and vegans typically practice an overall healthier lifestyle). But soy products also are the only food that contains *genistein* (JEN-iss-tyne).

This compound helps stop the growth of tumors and can lower cholesterol in those with high levels in their blood.

Soybeans also contain a unique group of phytochemicals called isoflavones, which are commonly called phytoestrogens. Much of the interest in soy estrogens and how they might relieve menopausal symptoms began with a single report published in the January 1998 *Obstetrics and Gynecology Journal*. Since then, numerous studies have linked regular consumption of soy with lower rates of heart disease, cancer, osteoporosis, diabetes and menopausal complications.

According to the FDA, studies have shown that soy protein can reduce the risk of coronary heart disease when it's part of a diet low in saturated fat and cholesterol. Foods containing at least 6.25 grams of soy protein per serving can carry labels claiming a heart health benefit. Soy protein differs from other vegetable proteins because it changes how the liver processes cholesterol. To gain heart health benefits, you need to eat at least 25 grams of soy protein a day.

Soy protein comes from soybeans, one of the major sources of protein worldwide. Soy may be added to many different types of foods and beverages. It is used to make tofu, some types of noodles, and meat substitutes such as soy burgers. Soymilk is frequently prescribed for babies allergic to other types of milk.

Buying Basics: Experiment with the variety of soy products available to find some you like. If soymilk isn't to your liking, try tofu or other products.

Peak Season: Available year round.

Preparation Tips: Use soymilk cup for cup in any recipe using milk. Fresh or frozen soybeans, otherwise known as edamame, are a good substitute for green peas or as a snack straight from the pod.

Storage Solutions: For best quality, keep all soy foods refrigerated unless they are packed in shelf-stable containers.

Recipe:
HERBED EDAMAME

2 cups edamame beans, cooked and shelled
1 Tbsp. olive oil
1/2 Tbsp. fresh parsley, chopped
1/2 Tbsp. fresh tarragon, chopped
1/2 Tbsp. fresh chervil, chopped
1 Tbsp. fresh chives, chopped
Salt and black pepper to taste

Toss edamame beans with remaining ingredients over medium heat for about one minute. *Variation:* If you don't have all of the herbs called for, use more of the ones you do have. Even one fresh herb adds delightful flavor to edamame. Avoid using dried herbs in this recipe.

Strawberries—Nutritious Delight
These bright, ruby red delights are actually a member of the rose family and have been growing in the wild for centuries. Strawberries are a super source of vitamin C—with even more of this nutrient than an orange. They also provide a healthy dose of potassium and fiber. Strawberries are one of a handful of fruits that contain the phytochemical ellagic acid, which is thought to reduce the risk of many types of cancer. A final distinction—strawberries are the only fruit that has its seeds on the outside rather than on the inside.

Buying Basics: Choose bright-colored, plump strawberries that are not bruised or discolored. Strawberries do not ripen after picking.

Small fruit tend to be the sweetest. Avoid berries that are packed in containers with juice stains or if they are wrapped tightly in plastic.

Peak Season: Available year round but are most abundant and flavorful in April, May, and June.

Preparation Tips: Rinse thoroughly, remove hull, and slice for maximum juice.

Storage Solutions: Do not wash before storing. Remove the bruised or discolored berries for they will rot the other berries if they come into contact. Place berries in a single layer on a paper towel in a moisture-proof container. They will last two to three days.

Recipe:
STRAWBERRY SMOOTHIE

2 cups ice cubes
1 cup skim milk
⅓ cup plain or vanilla yogurt
⅔ cup strawberries
1½ tsp. sugar
1 tsp. vanilla extract

Pour all of the ingredients into the blender. Blend for 45 to 60 seconds until smooth. Pour into a glass and enjoy.

Sweet Potatoes, Please
These roots of gold deserve more attention. The sweet potato is the richest vegetable source of vitamin A—providing 250 percent of the recommended amount in a single potato—and is loaded with beta-carotene; sweet potatoes and yams are one of the few good sources of vitamin E that are not loaded with fat. With just 117 calories, you'll also get 3.5 grams of fiber and nearly as much vitamin C as a half-grapefruit.

Buying Basics: Look for sweet potatoes that have smooth skins and no bruises.

Peak Season: Available year round since they are cured for long-term storage. Fresh, uncured sweet potatoes are available from August to October.

Preparation Tips: Always scrub skins with a vegetable brush under cool water to remove dirt. Place sweet potatoes on aluminum foil when baking since they produce sticky syrup as they heat.

Storage Solutions: Cold, moist conditions can damage sweet potatoes so keep in a cool pantry and not the refrigerator.

Recipe:
MASHED SWEET POTATOES

2 lbs. sweet potatoes (about 6 small)
¾ cup buttermilk
½ tsp. orange peel, grated
½ tsp. salt
¼ tsp. pepper

Peel sweet potatoes and cut into chunks. Boil uncovered until fork tender, about 20 minutes. Drain liquid and add remaining ingredients. Mash with potato masher or whip with electric mixer until desired consistency.

Time for Tea?
Tea drinking originated in China nearly five thousand years ago and spread throughout Asia and the world, becoming firmly entrenched in many cultures. After water, tea is the second most consumed beverage worldwide. Tea has long been held in high esteem for its soothing and medicinal qualities. New scientific evidence suggests that drinking tea may reduce the risk of heart

disease and cancer, lower blood pressure, and even help prevent tooth decay.

Researchers at Kyushu University in Japan have identified four components in tea that help mop up the bacteria in your mouth that promote tooth decay. Tannin, catechin, caffeine, and tocopherol in tea help increase the acid resistance of tooth enamel.

It takes just three minutes of brewing for tea to release its health-promoting compounds. Tea is high in polyphenols—a type of antioxidant—and may be beneficial in reducing cancer risk. Polyphenols in tea make up 30 percent of tea's dry weight. In fact, tea bags are better than large loose tea leaves because the tiny pulverized leaves provide greater surface area in contact with hot water and can release more polyphenols.

Differences among green, black and oolong teas result from the degree of processing and the level of contact with oxygen. Green tea is not exposed to oxygen, and after processing most closely resembles the chemical composition of the fresh tea leaf. This lack of oxidation may explain why regular consumption of green tea has been linked to a lower risk of cancer in scores of studies. Black tea is exposed to the air for up to three hours. Oolong tea has a shorter period of oxidation, and falls between green and black tea in health benefits.

SELECTED STUDIES

- The antioxidant activity of 22 common vegetables and green and black tea were measured. Investigators found that green and black tea were much more effective antioxidants against a common free radical than all of the vegetables tested, including broccoli, carrots, and garlic (*Journal of Agricultural and Food Chemistry*, December 1996).

- Drinking at least one cup of tea daily could reduce the risk of heart attack by 44 percent, according to research presented at the Society of Medicine Conference in London in July 1999. A more recent study, published in August 2002, found drinking a cup of green tea daily could also lower cancer risk.

Buying Basics: Tea can be purchased loose, in tea bags, or in bulk. Tea bags should always be individually wrapped to preserve volatile oils.

Peak Season: Available year round.

Preparation Tips: Tea aficionados suggest using a ceramic teapot with a fitted lid for best tea brewing. Rinse teapot with warm water and then add one teaspoon of tea or tea bag. In a separate teakettle bring water to a full boil, eight ounces per teaspoon of tea or tea bag. Pour boiling water over tea and let steep with the lid on for 3–5 minutes.

Storage Solutions: Store all types of tea in a cool, dark cupboard for up to one month. Loose tea should be kept in a tightly sealed glass container. Tea will not spoil but loses much of its aroma and flavor when kept too long. If you can't smell the flavor anymore it's time to throw it out.

Recipe:
GREEN TEA POACHED SALMON
    4 cups green tea
    2 tsp. ginger, grated
    2 tsp. garlic, minced
    2 tsp. white onion, minced
    1½ lbs. salmon

In a deep skillet, simmer green tea, ginger, onion and garlic for 10 minutes. Place salmon gently into the poaching liquid. Adjust heat to a gentle simmer, and cook 8–10 minutes until fish is firm to the touch.

Tomatoes Catch Up

For centuries tomatoes were thought to be toxic, capable of causing everything from appendicitis to cancer to mental illness. Today tomatoes are one of America's favorite foods. We eat more tomatoes, both fresh and processed, than nearly any other fruit or vegetable. That's good news because tomatoes contain the red pigment lycopene, a fantastic phytochemical that has been shown to inhibit lung, breast, and endometrial cancer cells. Research has also indicated that the lycopene in tomatoes can help older people stay active longer.

But perhaps the most compelling evidence is the role of tomatoes against prostate cancer. Numerous studies show that men who consume tomatoes—whether whole, cooked, or in sauces—had a significantly lower risk of prostate cancer than men who don't eat tomatoes.

Lycopene can withstand exposure to high heat, so canned tomatoes and tomato sauce are rich sources. If you cook your fresh tomatoes just a bit, it causes the cell walls to burst and even more lycopene is released for your body to absorb.

Did you know that salsa has replaced catsup as the most consumed condiment in the United States? That's good news because it's easy to down a serving or two of tomatoes in the form of salsa.

Buying Basics: Choose tomatoes with a fruity smell, unripe tomatoes have no scent. Look for firm, smooth, deep red tomatoes without bruises or soft spots.

Peak Season: Available year round, but peak season is mid to late summer.

Preparation Tips: Always rinse thoroughly before preparation. To peel a tomato easily, drop it into boiling water for one to two minutes. Next, dunk in a bowl of ice water and then cut out a small cone around the stem and remove. The skin should now slip off easily.

Storage Solutions: Keep tomatoes at room temperature, never in the refrigerator. To speed ripening, place tomatoes in a brown paper bag for several days.

Recipe:
TOMATO JUBILEE

    1 green pepper
    1 yellow pepper
    4 tomatoes
    ½ red onion
    1 cucumber
    Dressing:
    1 cup light Italian dressing
    1 tsp. celery seed
    1 cup parsley, chopped
    1 tsp. dried tarragon

Slice and/or chop all vegetables into bite-sized pieces. Whisk dressing ingredients together and toss gently with vegetables. Serve chilled.

Vegetables—Can It

Fresh is best when it comes to choosing vegetables, right? Not necessarily, according to research from the human nutrition researchers at the University of Illinois. Processed vegetables lose some vitamin C when heated, but it is nearly the same amount that fresh vegetables lose when they're cooked. (The vitamin loss occurs at 275 degrees F.) Most fresh vegetables are picked several weeks before they arrive at your local produce counter. Nutrient losses during shipping and storage can be equal to or greater than what is lost during cooking. The nutritional value of fresh produce decreases with time.

NUTRITION HOW TO: If you're serious about not wasting nutrients, start storing leftover liquid from canned vegetables. Keep a pitcher in your freezer to collect the broth. Keep adding new broth on top of the frozen portion until you have enough to use as soup stock. Simply thaw and use this nutrient gold mine the next time you make soup. If sodium is a concern, buy low-sodium canned vegetables.

According to the University of Minnesota Extension Service, nearly half of some vitamins may be lost within a few day of harvesting unless fresh produce is quickly cooled or preserved. Within one to two weeks, even refrigerated produce will continue to lose up to half or more of some vitamins.

Food companies choose top-quality varieties of produce for processing—top quality means high in nutrients. Varieties grown for canning and freezing start out with more vitamins and minerals than the typical fresh produce shipped to your local supermarket.

If you're going to cook your vegetables, it doesn't matter much which form you choose—fresh, frozen, or canned—just eat them. Choose raw vegetables from local sources when possible. If you're cutting back on sodium, choose fresh and plain varieties of frozen vegetables. You can also drain canned vegetables, but you'll be pouring off some beneficial nutrients along with the extra sodium.

Buying Basics: Avoid dented or bulging cans or cans with labels that appear faded or streaked. For top quality, choose Grade A (Fancy) vegetables; they are most succulent and tender with uniform size, color, and shape. Grade B (Extra Standard) are high in quality but slightly less uniform in size and color. They may have a few blemishes and are a bit more mature with slightly different taste. Their cost is lower and they're good for casseroles and gelatin salads.

Grade C (Standard) are fairly good quality but not uniform in color and flavor and are more mature than other grades. They are the least expensive, and best suited for soups and stews. All grades are perfectly wholesome and nutritious. The difference in the standards is how closely each one comes to the "ideal" qualities for that specific product.

Peak Season: Available year round.

Preparation Tips: To prepare canned vegetables, drain the liquid into a saucepan and bring it to a boil. Then, add the vegetables, heat through for about two minutes without boiling, and serve. For frozen, follow package instructions.

Storage Solutions: Store cans in a cool place where the temperature is between 55 and 70 degrees F (67 degrees F is ideal). Vegetables in cans stored at 85 degrees F lose twice as much vitamin content as those stored at 67 degrees F. Save leftover canned vegetable juices in the freezer and use as vegetable stock in other recipes or to make soup.

Recipe:
SUMMER SUCCOTASH
    1 tsp. olive oil
    ½ red onion, diced
    1 medium red pepper, seeded and
        diced
    1 clove garlic, minced
    1 can yellow corn
    1 can lima beans
    ½ cup fat-free, reduced-sodium
        chicken broth
    Salt and pepper to taste

Heat olive oil in a nonstick skillet over medium heat. Add the onion, peppers and garlic and cook until softened, stirring occasionally. Do not brown. Add the corn and beans and stir well, then stir in the chicken broth. Cook until the vegetables are heated through. Season with salt and pepper as desired.

Wheat Germ—WOW!

Wheat germ is one of the standard staples of the "health food" revolution. And it deserves its reputation as a powerhouse of nutrition. Technically wheat germ is the embryo of a kernel of wheat. The germ is the part of the grain removed when whole wheat flour is processed into white flour. This heart of the wheat kernel is a concentrated source of several essential nutrients including vitamin E, folate, phosphorous, thiamin, zinc, and magnesium. Wheat germ adds a delicious taste and healthy crunch to virtually any recipe, and it's an easy way to add extra nutrition.

Buying Basics: Due to wheat germ's high fat content, it goes rancid quickly. The best way to buy it is prepackaged in jars. Fresh wheat germ should smell like toasted nuts and should not have a musty aroma.

Peak Season: Available year round.

Preparation Tips: Wheat germ can replace up to one-half cup of flour in recipes for muffins, breads, pancakes, and many other baked goods. Wheat germ tends to absorb extra moisture, so you may need to add one or two extra tablespoons of liquid for every ½ cup of wheat germ you add to a recipe.

Storage Solutions: Keep wheat germ in a tightly sealed container in the refrigerator.

Wine—Health Aid or Health Hazard?

While moderate alcohol drinking has been shown to reduce heart disease risk, wine drinkers have a lower risk of developing certain cancers than people who consume equal amounts of beer or hard liquor. That's because grapes (especially red grapes) have a substance called reversatrol that inhibits the damaging effects of aging-related diseases. Besides cancer and heart disease, studies show that as few as one to four glasses of wine a month can reduce the risk for macular degeneration (loss of central vision) by 20 percent.

SELECTED STUDIES

There have been more than 60 studies linking moderate alcohol consumption to reduced risk of heart disease—many of them focusing on wine's reported benefits. But in January 2001, the American Heart Association said the benefits might be overstated. While one to two glasses a day may be helpful, most experts agree there are better ways to reduce disease risks, such as eating a low-fat diet and exercising regularly. While it shows a protective effect against some cancers, some studies have linked drinking with an increased risk of breast cancer.

Buying Basics: Volumes of material have been written on how to buy wine. Let's keep it simple. Most white wines are intended for drinking within two to three years after the vintage date. Many red wines are good or even improve with age. Pinot Noir and Zinfandel wines can age well too. When pairing wine with meals, you won't go wrong with white wine for light meats and vegetarian foods and red wines for dark meats.

Peak Season: Available year round.

Preparation Tips: The alcohol content of wine decreases with exposure to heat. A slow cooking roast will have very little alcohol, but much flavor left from any added wine. A wine sauce that is not cooked and poured over food will still retain all of the alcohol. Never serve any food prepared with wine or other spirits to someone who is avoiding alcohol. Contrary to popular folklore—the alcohol does remain.

Storage Solutions: The kitchen is probably the worst place to keep wine. Store in a cool, dry place away from heat and light.

Recipe:
EASY WINE MARINADE

> 1 cup dry red or white wine
>
> 2 Tbsp. soy sauce
>
> 1 small onion, grated
>
> 1 celery stalk, thinly sliced
>
> 2 garlic cloves, finely minced

Mix together all ingredients. For use with meat, cover all sides thoroughly and marinate for several hours in the refrigerator, turning occasionally.

Yogurt—A Cultured Taste

Yogurt is a dairy product made by culturing cream and/or milk with live and active cultures. The cultures in yogurt are living organisms. Yogurt that's produced in the U.S. is made with two specific live and active cultures—*Lactobacillus bulgaricus* (L. bulgaricus) and *Streptococcus thermophilus* (S. thermophilus). These metabolize some of the milk sugar (lactose) in the milk into lactic acid. This action helps change the consistency of liquid milk into yogurt. L. bulgaricus and S. thermophilus are required by U.S. Food and Drug Administration (FDA) standards for a product to be called yogurt. Other cultures may be added but are not required.

Buying Basics: Because live and active cultures make yogurt what it is, check yogurt labels for these vital ingredients before you buy. Some yogurts have extremely low levels of cultures and others are heat-treated or pasteurized after culturing, destroying the cultures and their properties. Choose a yogurt that is either low fat or fat free.

Peak Season: Available year round.

Preparation Tips: Enjoy yogurt plain or with fruit, wheat germ, or granola. It can also be used as a low-fat substitute for sour cream or cream in some recipes.

Storage Solutions: Store the yogurt in its original container in the refrigerator. Yogurt should be eaten within several days of the "sell by" date in order to take full advantage of the amount of live and active cultures present in the yogurt at the time of manufacture.

Recipe:
GRAPEFRUIT YOGURT SALAD DRESSING

> 1 whole grapefruit, peeled and sectioned
>
> 1 8-oz. container nonfat vanilla yogurt
>
> 2 tsp. poppy seeds
>
> 1 tsp. dry mustard

Place all ingredients in a blender. Blend for a few seconds on high speed or until ingredients are thoroughly combined. Serve on tossed salad greens or over vegetables.

Zucchini—What a Squash!

Although not as nutrient-packed as squash and pumpkin, this summer squash contains a decent amount of the antioxidant beta-carotene. The edible yellow-orange blossoms contain trace amounts of vitamin C and potassium, too. Zucchini is perhaps best known for its versatility—you can put it in anything from soups and salads to breads, muffins, and pancakes. And at only 14 calories per half-cup cup serving, it's certainly not going to pack on the pounds. Don't peel your zucchini, since the skin is where the bulk of its nutrients are found.

Buying Basics: The smaller the better is the best rule of thumb to choose zucchini with good flavor. Skin should be smooth and unblemished.

Peak Season: Available year round, but peak season is late spring and early summer.

Preparation Tips: Rinse well before preparation to remove dirt. Small, thin-skinned zucchini do not need to be peeled.

Storage Solutions: Zucchini are quite perishable once picked. Use within a few days or store in the refrigerator for up to one week in a plastic bag.

Recipe:
ZUCCHINI STIR FRY

> 3 lbs. fresh zucchini, sliced into
> 　　1-inch pieces
> ¼ cup almonds, sliced
> 2 Tbsp. sesame oil
> ¼ cup Parmesan cheese
> ¼ cup fresh parsley, chopped
> 2 cloves garlic, minced
> 1 tsp. dried oregano
> 1 tsp. rosemary, crushed
> 1 fresh tomato, chopped
> Salt and pepper to taste

Heat oil in a wok or skillet. Add zucchini and stir-fry until golden brown. Combine remaining ingredients and add to wok. Remove from heat and serve.

The Bad News— Nutrient Thieves

Nutrients are always team players; they all work together. Optimal intakes of all vitamins, minerals, and other essential nutrients are the foundation of good nutrition. But even if you eat right, there are nutrient thieves waiting to rob you of those precious goods and compromise your health. Here are some of the most common nutrient busters that you should watch out for.

- *Alcohol* destroys a variety of nutrients it comes in contact with, even though it may offer other health benefits.
- *Antacids* can deplete your stores of vitamin D (though some add calcium).
- *Caffeine* overload speeds up metabolism and pumps vitamins and minerals through your system too fast for optimal absorption.
- *Cooking* with high temperatures, rough food handling, cutting and chopping food, and cooking foods in lots of water can all speed up nutrient losses.
- *Diuretics* pull water and water-soluble vitamins out in urine. You can also lose electrolytes such as potassium and magnesium.
- *Excess fiber* isn't recommended for the very young and very old. It blocks the absorption of some vitamins B and D and some minerals.
- *Oil-based laxatives* can leach vitamins A, D, E, and K from your gut. Overuse of any laxative can speed how fast food moves through your system, and that limits nutrient absorption.
- *Pollution* from smog, car exhaust, and chemical run-off into water increases free radicals in your system. Free radicals speed up cell damage.

- *Smoking* increases free radical action, and that raises your need for vitamin C. But taking supplements is not a solution because too much vitamin C increases the nicotine output in your urine, and that will increase how much nicotine you need to satisfy your addiction. Instead, eat more citrus fruits and juices and other foods high in vitamin C.
- *Stress* increases free radical activity in your system.

Alcohol Effects

Alcohol consumption is an important issue for each person to consider. Alcohol has a tremendous ability to eat away at your nutritional and overall health. A social drinker who weighs 150 pounds and has normal liver function metabolizes seven to 14 grams of alcohol (six to 12 ounces of beer) in one hour. If you drink slightly less than the amount of alcohol your liver can metabolize, your blood alcohol content will remain low. When the rate of alcohol exceeds your liver's metabolic capacity, your blood alcohol will rise and symptoms of intoxication appear.

Women cannot metabolize as much alcohol as men because their stomachs have lower levels of a key alcohol-metabolizing enzyme, alcohol dehydrogenase. Women also are much quicker to develop alcohol-related health problems, such as cirrhosis of the liver, than men with the same drinking history. Alcohol is toxic to the cells that line both the esophagus and the stomach, and heavy drinking increases the risk of cancer

GO FIGURE:
1 drink of alcohol = 4 oz. of wine, 12 oz. of beer, or 1½ oz. of hard liquor.

at these sites. Large quantities of alcohol can lead to high blood pressure and scar tissue formation in the heart muscle. This can lead to fat infiltration into the heart muscle and cause an enlarged heart.

Moderate alcohol consumption, on the other hand, may have some beneficial effects. "Moderate" is defined by the U.S. Dietary Guidelines as no more than one drink per day for women and two drinks per day for men. (And no, you can't save them up and have a six-pack while watching the game on Sunday and still be a moderate drinker.) Various research shows that a small amount of alcohol daily can have the beneficial effect of lowering the risk for heart disease. Many frail elderly people find that a small alcoholic drink before dinner may help stimulate their appetite. That also works for others, too, so if you're trying to lose weight, remember that alcohol before meals will make you want to eat more. As with all things, alcohol—if you choose to drink in moderation—is okay.

Caffeine—Trouble Brewing?

It's America's favorite drug. Caffeine is a mild stimulant that can fight fatigue, improve your mood, and even boost mental and physical performance. Studies have shown that as little as 32 mg of caffeine—the amount in one-third cup of coffee—helps people pay better attention to a long, repetitious series of tones or pictures. It's true that caffeine can enhance how you perform monotonous tasks like keyboarding, listening to a boring speaker, or prolonged driving. Too much caffeine over time, though, is addictive. If you want to cut back, do it gradually to help prevent mood swings and irritability.

For years, researchers have tried to understand caffeine's relationship to chronic

CAFFEINE IN COMMON FOODS AND MEDICATIONS

Average Caffeine (mg)

Coffee

Espresso, 2 oz.	120
Regular, brewed 6 oz.	105
Instant, 6 oz.	55

Tea

Black, 6 oz.	36
Oolong, 6 oz.	35
Green, 6 oz.	30

Soft Drinks

Surge 12 oz.	72
Mountain Dew 12 oz.	55
Coke, varieties 12 oz.	35–50
Sunkist Orange 12 oz.	42
Pepsi 12 oz.	38

Chocolate

Unsweetened baking chocolate, 1 oz.	58
Milk chocolate candy bar, 1.5 oz. average	11

Pain Relievers

Aspirin-Free Excedrin, Excedrin Extra Strength, 1 caplet	65
Vanquish, 1 caplet	33

Stimulants

No Doz Maximum Strength 1 caplet	200
Vivarin, 1 tablet or 1 caplet	200

Source: Manufacturers' data

disease. No strong positive association has ever been proven because it's hard to look at just caffeine intake. For example, many heavy coffee drinkers also smoke, consume lots of alcohol, and tend to have high-fat diets. Coffee has also changed over time. Odds are you're not familiar with cafestol and kahweol. They are two substances found in the oils of coffee grounds. As long as you drink instant coffee or use a drip filter (as do most home coffeemakers), you won't be exposed to this twosome that's believed to raise LDL (bad) cholesterol and triglycerides. Some researchers think that the popularity of drip coffeemakers since 1975 (instead of perked or brewed coffee) explains why more recent studies show no higher risk of heart disease in coffee drinkers. Since caffeine is a drug usually found in foods and beverages with little redeeming nutrient value, it makes sense to limit your consumption.

Fake Foods

Foods without fat or calories that taste great—that's what the American consumer seems to want. According to a 1996 survey done by the Calorie Control Council, 88 percent of adults said they consume low-fat, reduced-fat, or fat-free foods and beverages. But fat substitutes and reduced-fat foods do not make up for poor eating habits.

Sugar and fat substitutes have failed miserably. They were supposed to let us have our cake and eat it, too. That's the problem. We want to drink a diet pop with a chocolate candy bar. With fat-free cookies, the whole package sometimes becomes one serving instead of two or three cookies. Don't fool yourself—these "substitutes" usually aren't substituting for anything. ❦

PART II

GETTING WHAT YOU NEED

4

EATING STYLE OPTIONS

 In this section we will look at age-related differences that affect nutritional needs. We'll also compare and contrast a variety of eating styles from around the world and across the centuries. Almost any system of food choices can be adapted to provide optimal nutrition for your own individual needs. The challenge is in learning enough about a particular system to understand the subtleties. Food and food choices are deeply rooted in cultural systems. Within a given culture, values and food choices seem reasonable and make sense in that context. What seems to be logical, sensible, important, and reasonable in one culture may seem dumb, irrational, or unimportant to an outsider. For these reasons, be cautious about making moral judgments on alternative eating styles.

Throughout life, people everywhere need the same nutrients, though in different amounts at different times. Some health concerns are lifelong, and others are particularly important at specific stages of life. For example, we know that coronary heart disease develops slowly over time and learning healthful eating habits in childhood can decrease risk as an adult. Teens and pregnant women need extra amounts of particular nutrients, including calcium and calories, to foster the extra growth their bodies require.

It's a Small, Small World

Children are not miniature adults. What may be the ideal food choices for you are probably not right for young children. Obviously kids don't need the same quantity of food as adults. Quality of food should also be a consideration. Many cultures do have specific recommendations for feeding children. There is no doubt that growing bodies and minds have unique dietary needs, particularly for energy, fat, and calcium.

Make Mealtime Quality Time

Several recent studies suggest that dining as a family offers many health benefits. A 1999 study at Cincinnati Children's Hospital Medical Center found that families who have at least five dinners together each week have better-adjusted teens—those less likely to use drugs, become depressed, or have problems with the law.

Meanwhile, a year later, Harvard researchers reviewed the diet of 16,000 teens and learned that those who ate most dinner meals with their families had healthier diets. And a Lou Harris survey of 2,000 high school seniors found that those who ate dinner with their parents or siblings at least four times a week actually scored higher on academic tests than those who ate family dinners fewer times per week.

Eating with others promotes positive connections. It's a pattern that should start as soon as infants are able to eat solid foods. Mealtime is a primary setting for developing social skills and awareness. Preschoolers gain a sense of manners and consideration for others by passing foods and not taking second helpings until everyone has been served. These eating and social skills can transfer to other everyday activities. Not learning these skills can have serious consequences.

Eating meals together is often the only opportunity for parents and children to stay in tune with each other. Schedule conflicts can make that a challenge. *To get back into the habit of family meals...*

- Establish fun traditions, for example, Sunday brunch.

- Look beyond dinner—breakfast, weekend lunches, and snack time count, too.

- Assign everyone a role in getting family meals on the table.

Teen Eating Machines

Adolescence is a time of turbulent changes, both psychological and physical. *A variety of hormones trigger four major physical changes...*

LINK UP to *http://www.kidsfood. com* for fun sites for kids to explore foods and nutrition on their own.

- Growth rate increases.

- Height and weight increase.

- Body composition changes.

- Sexual maturity is achieved.

There is a wide variation in growth rate from teenager to teenager. Most girls begin their growth spurt two or more years before boys their same age. Girls gain proportionately more fat than boys, so that by age 20 they have about twice as much body fat as males.

Needs for almost every nutrient increase during these years of tremendous growth. Girls need more nutrients at a younger age to support optimal growth and development. Boys need more nutrients and calories and continue to need more food as adults to maintain their larger muscle mass.

NUTRITION HOW TO'S FOR FEEDING TEENS:

You don't have control over everything teenagers eat, but you can indirectly influence what they eat at home. Here are some ideas to help teens develop healthful food habits.

- Provide quick-to-fix breakfast foods such as cereal, muffins, bagels, yogurt, or leftovers from last night's dinner (macaroni and cheese, pizza, etc.).

- If your teen skips breakfast or isn't hungry, offer foods for the backpack to be eaten later (fresh fruit, canned fruit or vegetable juices, a sandwich, etc.).

- Anticipate when your teen will be hungry and stock the refrigerator with nutritious snack foods.

- Teach teens to cook so they have the basic skills for kitchen independence.

- Arrange mealtimes that don't conflict with activities important to your teen.

Like many adults, teens tend to consume iron, calcium, magnesium, vitamin A, and vitamin B-6 at levels that fall short of their needs for these nutrients.

Older Adults

Age has its privileges—and its aches and pains. However, symptoms once attributed to "old age" are often the result of poor eating habits. Beginning at age 30, flavor and aroma perceptions begin to decline. At age 70 these decreases become more noticeable, and they decline significantly at age 80. In fact, people over 60 may need two to eight times higher concentrations of salt or sugar to achieve the same taste sensations as a young adult. These sensory losses are not just part of normal aging, but also develop from diseases and certain medications that alter taste and smell.

Ready for some more bad news? Somewhere between the ages of 40 and 50 your calorie needs decrease by up to 10 percent every ten years. That translates into about 100 calories less per day per decade. Yet you still need almost every key nutrient in the same amounts as younger people, and there are some essential nutrients whose requirements actually increase with age (vitamins B-6, B-12, D, E, and the minerals chromium and zinc). These nutrients aid in digestion, nutrient absorption, nerve functioning, help to balance blood sugar levels, and strengthen your immune system.

How to Eat Well When You're Not Motivated

- Plan to eat with a friend as often as possible—even cook and shop together. Eating with others often improves your appetite.

- Buy precut fruits, vegetables, and prepared salads to keep on hand when you don't feel like washing and chopping.

- Enhance the aroma of foods by adding peppers, garlic, onions, lemon, or mint.

- Use herb blends and spices to add more flavor to bland foods. The nerve that carries herb and spice sensations seems to be less affected by aging than other flavor-carrying nerves.

- At mealtimes, eat the most nutritious foods first, when you are hungrier.

- Chew your food well. The longer food is in your mouth and mixing with saliva, the more time your taste buds have to send those flavor sensations to your brain.

- Alternate bites of different foods on your plate. Your taste buds can get "tired" of one food, and the flavor intensity decreases if you eat one thing at a time.

- If you seem to "fill up" after just a few bites, try eating six smaller meals rather than three large ones.

Dietary Guidelines Around the World

If you want to be healthy, eat like a healthy person. But which healthy person should you imitate? Nutrition needs to be personalized for your unique circumstances. One starting point to consider is your ethnic heritage. As much as we have in common as human beings, there are also subtle variations that make each of us unique. If we all have very similar heart and circulatory systems, then why are some groups of people more prone to heart disease or high blood pressure? Many people intolerant to milk never develop osteoporosis, even though they don't get nearly the recommended amount of calcium. Part of this mystery can be explained by natural adaptation.

GIRTH OF A NATION

Compare the average weight of both men and women (based on a height of 5'4") from around the world. These dramatic differences may be even more profound today, since the data for this study was collected more than a decade ago.

Country or Region	Weight in Pounds*
United States of America	160
Southern Europe	152
Eastern Europe	151
Western and Central Europe	145
Northern Europe	145
South and Central America	141
Africa	136
Asia	123

* Combined average weights of men and women.

Source: Adapted from INTERSALT data from *Obesity,* 1992

Think about the first time you sat face to face with a computer. Many people were resistant to this new technology. It was difficult to use, you didn't understand how it worked, and it took a lot of practice to get things right. Once you had some training, actually read the instruction manual, or pleaded with someone to show you what to do, things clicked. This same process is important for understanding eating patterns from around the world. For example, here's a country-by-country snapshot of nutrition issues deemed important for good health. Most North American, Asian, and European countries have used dietary guidelines for many years. As rates of obesity and chronic disease increase in developing countries, they too are adopting national nutrition guidelines. These recommendations take into account varying nutritional priorities, food supplies, and cultural eating patterns of each country. Obviously there will be differences and similarities. Most important is what they have in common. *Worldwide consensus shows that all people should...*

- Eat a variety of foods.
- Maintain a healthy weight and active lifestyle.
- Eat a diet low in fat, especially saturated fat.
- Limit sodium and sugar.
- Avoid alcohol, or drink in moderation.

Cultural Diversity in Dietary Guidelines

Here's a quick view of dietary guidelines from around the world, highlighting each country's unique aspects.

Australia has a special guideline to encourage and support breast-feeding. Special guidelines for children and teens stress that low-fat diets are not appropriate for young children. Aussie children are encouraged to drink water when they are thirsty.

Canada recommends no more than 5 percent of total calories come from alcohol, or be no less than two drinks daily. Caffeine consumption should be kept to the equivalent of four or fewer cups of coffee daily. Fluoridation of all community water supplies is a national priority.

Denmark has just a few guidelines—short and to the point. Don't eat too much. Eat coarse foods. Eat more bread, corn, potatoes, vegetables, and fruit. Eat less fat,

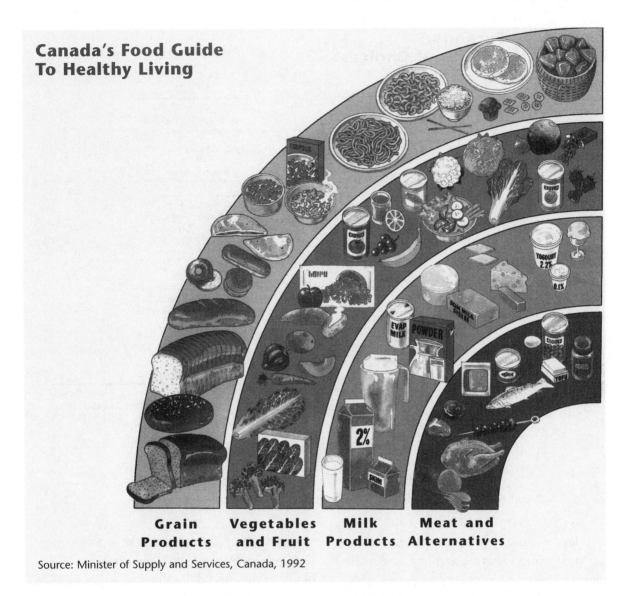

Canada's Food Guide To Healthy Living

| Grain Products | Vegetables and Fruit | Milk Products | Meat and Alternatives |

Source: Minister of Supply and Services, Canada, 1992

fatty meats, whole-milk dairy products, and sugar.

France wants its citizens to eat three meals a day and include more vegetable proteins.

Germany promotes eating small meals more often to help people keep calories under control. German nutritionists also advise to prepare foods safely.

Hungary gets specific on milk consumption and suggests drinking half a liter (about 2 cups) of low-fat milk daily. Four or five meals a day is recommended for hungry Hungarians, but none too rich or too light. Alcohol is forbidden for children and pregnant women.

Israel wins for the best graphic description of its dietary guidelines. It prefers a figure-eight-shaped cup or chalice filled with fruits and vegetables and topped off with water. A belt cinches in the waist or stem of the glass and represents a small fat intake. Grains are the large bottom portion of the cup.

Food Guide Pyramid:
A Guide to Daily Food Choices

KEY
These symbols show fats and added sugars in food.
- ● Fat (naturally occurring and added)
- ▼ Sugars (added)

Fats & Sweets
USE SPARINGLY

Milk, Yogurt, & Cheese Group
2–3 SERVINGS

Meat, Poultry, Fish, Dry Beans, Eggs, & Nuts Group
2–3 SERVINGS

Vegetable Group
3–5 SERVINGS

Fruit Group
2–4 SERVINGS

Bread, Cereal, Rice, & Pasta Group
6–11 SERVINGS

Source: U.S. Department of Agriculture and the U.S. Department of Health and Human Services

Japan is the only country to take a stab at defining variety. Eat thirty foodstuffs a day and eat staples, main dishes, and side dishes together. Its sodium limit of 10,000 mg a day is more than four times higher than the U.S. sodium guidelines. The Japanese could inspire the world with their final guideline: Happy eating makes for happy family life; sit down and eat together and talk; treasure favorite family foods and home cooking.

Korea is the only country to mention taking good care of your teeth as an important part of nutrition. The recommended fat intake of 20 percent of calories is the lowest in the world. Koreans also take a philosophical approach to eating: Keep harmony between diet and daily life and enjoy meals.

The Netherlands' nutrition policymakers prefer a technically precise position. Percentages and target intakes of nutrients abound. The sodium guideline is 8,000 mg a day. One guideline is the caution to realize that current alcohol consumption is far too high in many cases.

New Zealand's basic guidelines are short and to the point. What they lack in length, they make up for by including six additional sets of guidelines. Infants and toddlers, children, teens, older people, pregnant women, and breast-feeding women each have individualized standard recommendations.

Norway's National Nutrition Council has a great motto: Food plus Joy equals Health.

The Philippines proclaims basic guidelines with no frills. Eat clean and safe food, practice a healthful lifestyle, and promote breast-feeding and proper weaning.

South Africa is the most recent country to adopt nutrition guidelines. Because there is a transition from rural, traditional eating patterns to a more Western lifestyle, it's understandable that the recommendations mimic those of most industrialized countries. One notable exception is the recommendation to drink lots of clean, safe water. South Africa is also working on adapting guidelines for children under 5 and people with special dietary needs.

Thailand's guidelines almost mimic U.S. recommendations. They do suggest that the people of Thailand recognize and eat well-prepared food that is free of microorganisms and food contaminants. From the Japanese they have borrowed the motto: A happy family is when family members eat together and enjoy treasured family recipes and good home cooking.

The United Kingdom's National Food Guide uses a plate of food rather than a pyramid for its graphic. It resembles a divided plate similar to a school lunch tray. One-third contains fruits and vegetables, one-third is grains, and the final third includes dairy products and meat, fish, and alternatives. Fats and sweets are given just a sliver of the last section of the plate.

The United States has not yet integrated the science and social aspects of nutrition into its guidelines. No "enjoy your meals" or "treasure family foods" mottoes for us. We don't even encourage breast-feeding our babies. Water is still a forgotten nutrient in the United States. Remember that dietary guidelines apply to your total way of eating, not just one food, one meal, or even one day. It's your food choices over time that impact your health.

The Challenge in Following Nutrition Guidelines

Archaeologists and historians have unearthed details of how our ancient ancestors foraged, hunted, and harvested food. It is clear that regional weather patterns have had a major influence on staple foods worldwide. For example, tropical regions with abundant rainfall are ideally suited for growth of fruits, which are prominent in the diets of local people. Cereal grains are another example. Rice is a staple in Southeast Asia because the climate is ideally suited for its growth. South America's staple grain is corn. In North America, wheat grows well and is widely consumed. The extremely rugged terrain of many Nordic countries and their proximity to the sea results in a strong reliance on the ocean for food.

Importing and exporting of foods worldwide has transformed and expanded the variety of foods available to many people. This unprecedented year-round availability of so many foods should have led to major health improvements worldwide. And it has. People today are (on the whole) taller and stronger, and live longer than their ancestors. World food trade has also hastened the spread of poor eating habits to cultures and countries that can least afford them. It's great to be able to bring home fresh berries and bananas from the grocery store in the midst of a Midwest blizzard. But

The Tumbling Pyramid: How Americans Really Eat

This tumbling pyramid is closer to reality than the recommended (and balanced) food guide pyramid. *The lesson:* most of us need to eat more from the middle of the pyramid and trim back on the fats, oils, and sweets.

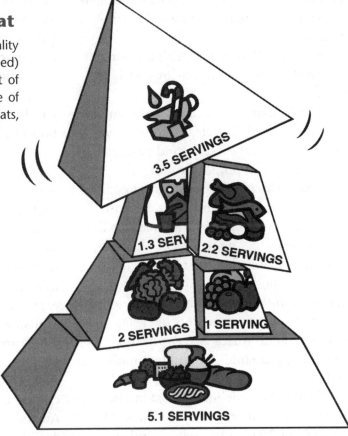

3.5 SERVINGS

1.3 SER

2.2 SERVINGS

2 SERVINGS

1 SERVING

5.1 SERVINGS

Source: Eating in America Today, Edition II: A Dietary Pattern and Intake Report

it's a shame—and dangerous—that soft drinks and empty-calorie snack foods are for sale in poverty-stricken Third World countries.

It's important to understand that changing your eating style might fend off heart disease or cancer. It's quite another step to do something about it. Food is more than just something to eat. Food choices and eating styles reflect wide-ranging cultural, social, and psychological factors.

Traditional American food patterns are changing in a number of ways. More women are working. We increasingly rely on food technology. Household size is smaller and more people live alone. Fewer people have time to cook or prepare meals. The average

time spent in meal preparation today is less than 15 minutes for dinner. Compare that to over an hour just fifteen years ago. Even the definition of cooking has changed. Cooking today is defined by actually touching food with your hands when you prepare it. Heating a frozen dinner isn't considered cooking, but opening a prepared bagged salad and mixing in croutons and cheese is! A lot of meal preparation in the United States is really meal assembly. You divide up a packaged tossed salad mix, microwave a frozen entree, open a package of dinner rolls, and yell "dinner's ready." Often it's children and teens, not the adults, who assume the main role in choosing and preparing meals.

Packaged cake mixes were one of the first convenience items that consumers liked. Just crack an egg or two, add some milk or water, and you had a "homemade" cake. Major food companies were so delighted with sales they invented new and improved cake mixes. All you had to add was water. Sales nose-dived and the new mixes were taken off the market. Why? If you didn't get to crack an egg, it didn't feel like cooking.

Obsessed Eating

There are additional concerns, beyond meeting basic nutritional goals. The incidence rate for eating disorder diseases, especially among young women and girls, is soaring. Self-induced anorexia (severe undereating) and bulimia (compulsive overeating, then purging) are psychological and physical disorders found only in highly developed countries with a preoccupation for thinness. Bulimia and anorexia share similarities even though each is a different disorder. Both are defined by an intense preoccupation with food and body weight, and can be life-threatening. Now a third type of disordered eating has been identified.

Orthorexia (or-tho-REX-ee-ah) is the newest eating disorder to add to the list of modern ailments. Orthorexia is a long-term psychological obsession that results in the systematic elimination of specific foods or entire food groups believed to be harmful to one's health—in short, making healthy eating an obsession. "Whereas anorexics or bulimics focus on the quantity of food, orthorexics fixate on quality," says Steve Bratman, M.D., a Colorado physician who coined this new term in 1997. Orthorexics

fool themselves into believing they have to eat the way they do. They think their strict control over food prevents cravings, fatigue, and a whole host of other symptoms. Women are far more likely to fall into this trap than men. Obsession over food is a way of life for many women. *Here are some common examples of crossing the line between disciplined dieter and eating extremist...*

Allergy Activists spend hours at the grocery store and on the phone to food manufacturers asking questions about foods and food additives they think cause allergic reactions. These people have never seen an allergist or had any testing done to verify the presence of true food allergies. Be careful not to confuse these folks with people who have true food allergies. The main difference is that allergy activists are usually "allergic" to foods that can't possibly cause allergic reactions.

Fat Phobics are experts at detecting the slightest trace of fat in a food. Their goal is a no-fat diet. Such a diet is not only impossible, it is also unhealthy.

Sugar Sleuths scour food labels for any trace of sugar. Although most sugar is an empty-calorie food, there are naturally occurring sugars in nutritious foods like fruit, juice, and milk products.

Eating Styles

A healthful way of eating can take many forms. No one food provides all the nutrients required for optimal health. Foods can be combined in many different ways to make up a lifestyle approach that provides all the nutrients you need. As you evaluate the different eating styles and philosophies summarized here, use the following questions as a guide to help you determine if they are right for you:

- Are a variety of nutritious foods from every nutrient category included?
- Are foods eaten in balanced amounts?
- Are recommended fat, sugar, and sodium levels modest?
- Will this way of eating fit my lifestyle?
- Will the foods be easy to find and prepare?

Ayurvedic Diet

This five thousand-year-old system of medicine from India is the oldest recorded healing therapy still in existence today. *Ayurveda* (ah-yoor-VAY-dah) is a Sanskrit word that means "the science or knowledge of life." As such it embraces every aspect of who you are and what you do. An Ayurvedic doctor will tell you what your dosha (body/personality) type is and then customize a plan of foods, herbs, exercise, and other lifestyle habits that will produce health and harmony for you. Ayurveda is based on an immense system of classifications.

Ayurveda emphasizes oneness with nature, longevity, and enlightenment and has a strong nutritional component. In

AYURVEDIC COMBINATIONS

Style	Climate	Age	Meal Frequency	Foods	Tastes	Avoid	Added Nutrients
Anti-Vata	cold, dry, windy climates such as high deserts or high plains	old age	frequent regular meals	warm, heavy, moistening, strengthening	sweet, sour, salty	fast, instant, and junk foods, beans	vitamins A, D, E, C, zinc, and calcium
Anti-Pitta	hot tropical or desert climates such as the U.S. South	middle age	three meals a day, don't eat late dinner	cool, slightly dry, a little heavy	sweet, bitter, astringent	mild foods, alcohol, nuts, oil, spices, animal products	vitamins B and K, calcium, and iron
Anti-Kapha	damp, cold regions like the U.S. Midwest Northeast, and Northwest	youth and child-hood	three meals a day, but eat less in morning and evening, avoid breakfast	warm, light, dry	pungent, bitter, astringent	oils, dairy foods, animal products, sweeteners	spices, herbs, and enzymes instead of vitamins and minerals except vitamin B

Ayurveda, the physical body is believed to be made of the same elements found in nature: akash (space), vayu (air), tejas (fire), jala (water), and prithvi (earth). These elements are further organized into a combination of three different humors or personalities. These body humors include kapha (calm, steady, good-natured), vata (spiritual and creative), and pitta (impulsive and strong-willed). Ayurveda also classifies foods and medicinal herbs into six major tastes—sweet, salty, sour, pungent, astringent, and bitter—and six major qualities—oily, heavy, light, dry, hot, and cold. Climate and age are also factored into your dietary regimen. It's impossible to explain such a complex system in a few pages. Use this chart for a simplistic overview of the combinations.

Tastes and qualities have more to do with how a food affects the body than with its actual flavor and texture. For example, milk is considered sweet, oily, heavy, and cold, while spinach is astringent, light, and hot. A proper Ayurvedic meal includes a variety of foods representing different tastes and qualities. It is essential that the correct method of preparation is used, amounts of food are appropriate, and the emotional attitude of both the food preparer and eater are harmonious. As a health system, Ayurveda attempts to use good nutrition, along with many other lifestyle approaches, to bring the body into balance and maintain it there. This approach is based on the belief that improper diet is the cause of most disease.

Homeopathy

Homeopathy is a relative newcomer, dating back to the late 1700s when Samuel Hahnemann, a German physician, began this new system of care. At the time, homeopathy was a welcome change from bloodletting, leeching, purging, and other medical procedures of the day. The word homeopathy means "like treats like." It's based on giving minute amounts of herbs, minerals, and other substances that would cause the very disease you're trying to cure. Treatment with such small doses is believed to stimulate your own natural defense system and encourage self-healing—much like getting a flu vaccine. The doses used are so small they are unlikely to have any bad effects, but there's no proof they help either. Homeopathy seeks to take advantage of your natural healing power. The complete range of symptoms is considered: emotions, brain, and body.

Homeopaths are the first to admit that they can't explain the mechanism that makes homeopathic medicine work. It's difficult to discuss homeopathy objectively. The bases of this medical practice are very thin and routinely exaggerated. Only scanty scientific evidence is available to prove that homeopathy has any health benefits. Because homeopathic remedies were actually less dangerous than those used earlier, many medical practitioners adopted them. At the turn of the twentieth century, popularity declined. There is no specific diet or set of nutritional recommendations used in homeopathy. If you are diagnosed with a particular problem, part of the healing antidote prescribed for you may come with diet restrictions to avoid certain foods or food ingredients. For example, you might be told to avoid coffee or all caffeine-containing products.

Macrobiotics

The original macrobiotic diet was developed by Yukikazu Sakurazawa in 1913. This self-taught Japanese pioneer believed that an ideal food plan was based on grains and the Asian system of balance, yin and yang.

KUSHI'S MACROBIOTIC EATING PLAN

Food Group	Proportion of Debt	Varieties
Whole grains	50–60%	barley, buckwheat, millet, oats, rice, and wheat noodles: ramen, saifun, soba, somen, udon
Vegetables	20–25%	bok choy, burdock, collard greens, daikon, kale, lotus root, watercress
Seaweed and beans	5–10%	seaweeds: arame, dulse, hiziki, kombu, nori, wakame beans: adzuki, natto, soybeans, tempeh, tofu
Soups	5–10%	miso

Note: If you live in a very cold climate, some white-flesh fish is included; if you live in a tropical climate, some fruits are allowed.

Meat, eggs, dairy products, sugar, caffeine, alcohol, and processed foods were forbidden. Sakurazawa's favorite student, Michio Kushi, brought macrobiotics to America "as a healing response to the devastation of World War II." Today, Kushi and his wife, Aveline, run the Kushi Institute in Becket, Massachusetts, where they work with practitioners and individuals to teach their updated macrobiotic system of eating. Kushi's macrobiotics is different from the "hippie" Zen macrobiotic of the 1960s (which was a severe diet that claimed brown rice was the perfect—and therefore the only—food to eat).

If you choose a macrobiotic eating style, here's what you need to know...

You'll feel worse before you feel better. Common adjustment symptoms include fatigue, mild aches and pains, fever, chills, coughing, perspiration, frequent urination, skin discharges, skin rashes, unusual body odor, diarrhea and/or constipation, reduction in sexual desire, irritability, and temporary loss of menstrual cycle in women. Advocates suggest these effects happen because your body is purging toxins. Once you've gotten rid of them, you'll supposedly feel better. However, not everyone does.

You will need to eat a wide variety of foods. Permitted foods are so limited in macrobiotics that it is essential to eat a little of practically everything that is allowed. That's the best way to ensure you get as many nutrients from food as possible.

You should take supplements. Even though supplements are not advised, it's practically impossible to get enough B-12 from the allowed foods. Better yet would be a complete multivitamin-mineral supplement. Be sure it includes vitamin C, vitamin E, calcium, magnesium, and iron.

This diet is not for kids. A population study in the Netherlands found that children under 2 fed macrobiotic diets had retarded growth, fat and muscle loss, and slow motor development. Pregnant women

LINK UP to *http://www.kushi institute.org* for the online connection to the Kushi Institute.

may also risk the health of their developing baby if their nutrient levels fall too low.

Mediterranean Diet

During World War II, heart disease rates plummeted in countries with shortages of meat and dairy products. When world-renowned researcher Dr. Ancel Keys and his wife traveled around Europe and Africa in the 1950s measuring blood cholesterol levels, they noticed that affluent people, who were eating more meat and dairy, were more likely to have high cholesterol and suffer heart attacks than poor people. Keys assembled a research team that looked at the diets, lifestyles, and blood cholesterol levels of more than 12,000 healthy middle-age men in Finland, Greece, Italy, Japan, the Netherlands, the United States, and Yugoslavia. The participants in the Seven Countries Study ranged from 2,000 U.S. and 750 Italian railroad workers to 500 faculty members of the University of Belgrade to 1,000 residents of two fishing villages in Japan.

After five, ten, fifteen, and twenty years, Keys counted how many people had—or had died of—heart disease. After ten years, the 775 men from Finland fared the worst: 28 percent had developed heart disease. The Finns were eating more saturated fat (mostly from cheese and butter) than almost anyone else—24 percent of their calories. That's double what Americans now eat. The Japanese residents of the fishing villages of Tanushimaru and Ushibuka ate the least fat (9 percent of calories) and saturated fat (3 percent of calories). Only 5 percent of them had developed heart disease. That was far better than the Finns, but it wasn't the best. That honor went to the 655 men from the Greek island of Crete. After ten years, 2 percent of them had developed heart disease, and none of

them had died. Amazingly, the Greeks were eating about as much total fat as the artery-clogged Finns. Their intake of saturated fat was far lower (about 8 percent of calories), but it wasn't as low as that of the mostly rice-and-vegetable Japanese diet.

The Mediterranean diet, back in the 1950s and 1960s, was dominated by olive oil and whole-grain bread. These two foods alone accounted for 50 to more than 60 percent of total calories. The diet was also rich in beans, fresh fruits, and vegetables. Meat, sugar, and most dairy products were consumed in very small amounts. It's also important to keep in mind that the lifestyle and physical activity patterns in this culture decades ago were vastly different than U.S. lifestyles are today.

There are several explanations on how olive oil seems to prevent heart disease. Much of the research has focused on the fact that olive oil is an excellent source of monounsaturated fats, "which appears to raise blood levels of HDL" (the good cholesterol), explains researcher Scott Grundy of the University of Texas Health Sciences Center in Dallas. Meanwhile, low-fat, high-carbohydrate diets can lower HDL. But, on a low-fat, high-carbohydrate diet, your LDL will fall far faster, and your ratio of total cholesterol to HDL will actually improve.

However, newer research indicates that olive oil is also a great source of vitamin E, also believed to protect heart disease by preventing cholesterol plaques from sticking on artery walls and hardening—the atherosclerosis that causes heart attacks. A study by Italian researchers published in the *American Journal of Clinical Nutrition* in August 2000 found that women who consumed more vitamin E were less likely to get early signs of cardiovascular disease than those getting lower amounts. Most of the healthy women got their E supplies from olive oil, legumes, and vegetables.

The Greeks and Japanese were not only less likely candidates for heart disease, they also were (and are) less likely to get breast, colon, and prostate cancer. What's more, a recent study from Spain found that women who consumed the most olive oil were one-third less likely to develop breast cancer than women who ate the least olive oil. It's not clear whether it's the olive oil or the fruits and vegetables in the Mediterranean diet that are protective. Either way, both the Mediterranean and low-fat diets seem to lower the risk of cancer.

Weight gain is the most controversial part of the Mediterranean diet. Keep in mind that while the Greeks consumed large amounts of olive oil, they also led very active lifestyles, burning 3,500 to 5,000 calories a day. A tablespoon of olive oil (like other cooking oils) contains 120 calories, so most experts suggest using olive oil as a replacement to other fats—not in addition to them. It's amazing that most people assume olive oil in any amount has health benefits. At the end of a nutrition seminar for senior citizens several years ago, a woman came up to me and said, "My husband and I have been using olive oil for six months now to lower cholesterol. We put it in our juice each morning, I fry all our meats with it, and we use about a gallon a month. Isn't that great!" she exclaimed. This unfortunate woman had read in the paper that olive oil lowered cholesterol and assumed that the more she ate, the lower her cholesterol would go. The real reason she wanted to talk to me was that both she and her husband had gained about fifteen pounds each—and they didn't know why!

The Mediterranean diet is far more than using olive oil instead of salad dressing and margarine. You've got to substitute the oil for foods like meat, poultry, cheese, and pastries. That's the only way to keep your saturated fat as low as it was in the Mediterranean diet. It's a fairly simple eating style. The focus is on dry beans, vegetables, fruits, grains, olive oil, nuts, minimal amounts of meat, and wine in moderation. Each of these simple foods provides major nutritional benefits. Because beans are eaten daily, the Mediterranean diet is high in soluble fiber. It is unlikely that the Mediterranean diet would meet current dietary recommendations for calcium and possibly iron. And there's no avoiding the fact that these folks who lived a generation ago had very different exercise and activity patterns than today's Americans.

Traditional Chinese Medicine (TCM)

TCM is a comprehensive health system that includes diet, herbs, exercise, traditional Asian martial arts, and massage. The fundamental principle of health is the invisible energy force called qi (CHEE). These energy forces flow through your body along a series of channels called meridians. In addition to qi, your body consists of the material components of moisture and blood and the immaterial parts called spirit and essence. The balance of five elements—qi, moisture, blood, spirit, and essence—is essential for optimal health.

Traditional Chinese Medicine relies on herbs, acupuncture, nutrition, body work, and exercise to balance your body's energy. Further divisions are made for networks of organs: the kidneys, heart, lungs, liver, and spleen. These systems are responsible for regulating and distributing the five elements.

TRADITIONAL CHINESE MEDICINE CATEGORIES

Flavor of Food	Effects and Properties
Sour	Acts on liver; astringent and stops abnormal discharges
Bitter	Affects the heart; removes excess heat, eliminates dampness, removes toxic substances, corrects the direction of qi, purges pathogenic fire
Spicy	Directed to the lungs; disperses and promotes qi circulation
Salty	Acts on kidneys; reduces hard lumps or masses in the body
Sweet	Works on spleen; nourishes, invigorates, regulates qi and blood, relieves spasms and pain
Bland	Targets stomach and spleen; promotes urination, strengthens spleen, eliminates dampness

Season	Effects and Recommended Foods
Autumn	Dry weather; eat yin foods to moisten the lungs such as honey, sesame, dairy, apples, bananas, grapes, water chestnuts, pears, oranges, tangerines, radishes, kelp, and lotus root
Winter	Cold weather; eat warm/hot foods such as lamb, ginger, pepper, onion, Chinese green onion, garlic, and green leafy vegetables
Spring	Liver is in hyperfunctioning state, digestion and spleen functions are suppressed. Choose sweet, hot, and sour flavors to nourish the spleen, such as Chinese dates, honey, malt sugar, and carrots
Summer	Weaker digestion; eat light foods that are easily digested such as watermelon and a variety of vegetables

A practitioner of TCM will spend considerable time examining your body for imbalances in these systems. A pulse check can last many minutes while you are checked for pulse quality, rhythm, and strength. Your tongue and ears will also be closely inspected for signs of disturbance. When these data are combined with information about your medical and family history and usual lifestyle, a personalized healing program will be developed for you.

Acupuncture is perhaps the most controversial aspect of TCM. Acupuncture needles are quite different from the needles you've been stuck with for vaccines or injections. The tiny stainless steel needles are so thin, you might not even notice they've been placed in strategic areas to rechannel your circulation. Each of the five organ networks has a corresponding set of energy points known as "meridians." Depending on your specific health problem, the needles may be placed for just a few minutes or up to an hour.

Vegetarian Eating—Nuts About Veggies

If you think that vegetarians eat a lot of weird food, think again. Macaroni and cheese, peanut butter and jelly sandwiches, tomato soup, breakfast cereal, and eggs are all food options for some vegetarians.

Vegetarians are less likely to develop chronic degenerative conditions that plague the rest of the American population—diabetes, high blood pressure, heart disease, and obesity—because these conditions are often affected by dietary saturated fats, and animal foods are typically highest in saturated fats. Meanwhile, plant food sources usually are rich in polyunsaturated and monounsaturated fats, which are not only "heart-healthy," but they can better regulate blood glucose and insulin levels to help prevent diabetes. Although just leaving out animal foods does not undo all the "wrongs" of the typical American diet. Without sufficient knowledge of nutrient needs, going on a vegetarian diet because it seems politically correct or the right thing to do could lead to vitamin and mineral deficiencies.

Protein isn't a problem. Plant sources alone can provide plenty of protein. In fact, like most Americans, vegans (the strictest of all types of vegetarian eaters who shun ALL animal foods, including eggs and milk) tend not to be deficient in protein. A cup and a half of pasta alone contains 11 grams of protein. Add in 1 cup of broccoli and one-half cup of tomato sauce, and the protein tally jumps to

19 grams. For years, vegetarians were counseled to eat complementary proteins—two or more foods that contain different combinations of the complete proteins found in meat (whole-grain bread and peanut butter is one example). Today we know there's no need to eat complementary foods together, so long as you follow a varied diet each day.

One of the biggest pluses of eating a plant-based diet is that plant foods help keep fat content low. But you don't have to go completely vegetarian to enjoy the health benefits of a vegetarian lifestyle. Small changes in the proportions of foods from plants and animals will give the same results. Cut back on portion sizes of meat and fill the gap with extra vegetables, grains, or legumes.

Of the approximately five million Americans who consistently eat a vegetarian diet, 90 percent consume eggs and cheese and drink milk. People who eat fish and white meats are not really vegetarians. *Each type has a different name, depending on what foods they include:* ovo (eats eggs), lacto (eats dairy products), lacto-ovo (eats eggs and dairy products). Vegans are vegetarians who do not use other animal products and by-products such as eggs, dairy products, honey, leather, fur, silk, wool, cosmetics, and soaps derived from animal products, according to the Vegetarian Resource Group. People choose a vegan lifestyle for different reasons. Some have moral opposition to use of animal products; others feel it's better for our world environment not to rely on animal resources. Some believe a plant-based diet is more healthful than one that includes animal foods. *Vegan diets require a real commitment of time:* time to learn about food and nutrition, time to plan menus, and time to prepare foods.

Vegetarian Pyramid

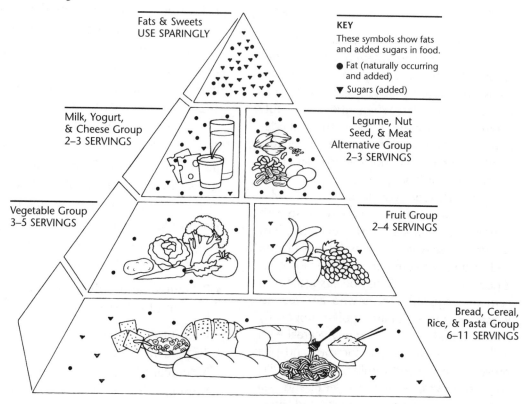

Source: U.S. Department of Agriculture and the U.S. Department of Health and Human Services

WHERE CAN YOU GET VEGETARIAN FOODS?

Source	Percentage That Offer Complete Vegetarian Meals
Worksite Cafeterias	17%
Hospital Cafeterias	23%
Universities	27%
Restaurants	40%
Secondary Schools	80%
Contract Foodservice Management Companies	90%
Correctional Feeding (prisons)	100%

Source: *Food Industry Newsletter,* May 4, 1998

LINK UP to *http://www.vrg.org* for information on vegetarian nutrition and recipes from the Vegetarian Resource Group.

Nutrient-Based Eating Styles

40-30-30, 55-15-30, and 65-15-15. No, these are not good picks for the lottery, they are number sequences that represent some popular combinations of the proportion of carbohydrate to protein to fat in an "ideal" diet. There is no perfect, one-size-fits-all recommendation for how to choose food by the numbers.

THE YOUNG AND THE MEATLESS

French fries and soft drinks aren't exactly what come to mind when you think vegetarian. But that's what some vegetarian teens—the fastest-growing segment of U.S. vegetarians—order when they eat out. Parents' concerns about the nutritional adequacy of a teen vegetarian diet are often justified, according to Cyndi Reeser, chair of the vegetarian nutrition practice group of the American Dietetic Association. "Teens who adopt a vegetarian eating pattern do so with strong convictions and few nutrient resources," says Reeser. Low intakes of iron and calcium are common in all teenage girls. Zinc and vitamin B-12 may be of special concern for vegetarian teens who are vegans. Reeser recommends parents offer support by stocking foods with teen appeal: cereal with milk or soy milk, bagels, hummus and pita bread, bean dip and tortillas, low-fat tortilla chips and salsa, ready-to-eat lentil and pea soups, veggie burgers, yogurt, and dried fruit and nut mixes. A daily multivitamin and mineral supplement may also be a good option.

Offer to give your teen a nutrition consultation with a registered dietitian and ask if you can sit in on the session, suggests Reeser. Vegetarian teens most at risk are those who eat a limited variety of foods, skip meals frequently, avoid entire categories of foods, or are preoccupied with thinness and body image.

High Protein Usually Means High Fat

Men love high-protein diets. These eating plans grant permission to chow down on beefy steaks and drink beer. Minnesota Vikings football coach Dennis Green's high-protein diet gained such local acclaim that Minnesota grocery stores started stocking pork rinds. Customers were demanding the never-before-stocked snack item because "Denny eats it." Pork rinds were big on Green's "high-protein diet," and he loved sharing how much he enjoyed eating these grease-laden globs of pig skin.

The American College of Sports Medicine, the American Dietetic Association, the Women's Sports Foundation, and the Cooper Institute for Aerobics Research have released a joint statement saying that high-protein plans are the answer neither for weight loss nor for athletic performance and can cause harm. *Here are their reasons…*

- Protein should only make up 10 to 15 percent of calories per day.

- High-protein plans usually recommend 40 percent of calories from carbohydrates, 30 percent from protein, and 30 percent from fat; this provides a diet inadequate in some major nutrients, particularly carbohydrates.

- Although some people manage to lose weight on a high-protein plan, it is only because they eat so few calories.

The health and diet aisle of your local bookstore is chock full of titles such as *Protein Power, The Zone, Healthy for Life, The 5 Day Miracle Diet,* and *Dr. Atkins' New Diet Revolution,* all featuring protein-powered diets. Such diets have a decidedly familiar ring. They are making a comeback from their heyday in the 1970s. But these "new" high-protein diets are the same old bad news. Following such an eating plan can result in an immediate and dramatic loss of body fluid. It's rewarding to see the pounds drops quickly at first, and most dieters think they've lost a lot of body fat, not just water. The buildup of ketones caused by high-protein diets can cause fatigue, weakness, headache, irritability, bad breath, dehydration, and kidney trouble. Ketogenic diets are especially dangerous for older people or those with untreated diabetes. *Here's a quick rundown on the current popular high-protein fad diets...*

- *Dr. Atkins' New Diet Revolution:* The original high-protein diet is relatively high-fat with low carbohydrate levels ranging from a meager 15 gm (1 serving of fruit, bread, rice, or pasta) to a barely adequate 60 gm a day for beginning dieters.

  But at the American Heart Association's Scientific Sessions 2002, Duke researcher Eric Westman, MD, presented research finding that people who spent six months on the Atkins diet lost more weight and had better cholesterol readings than the typical low-fat, higher-carb diets recommended by the American Heart Association, Weight Watchers and others. However, it should be noted the study included only 120 dieters and was funded by the Atkins Foundation.

- *The 5 Day Miracle Diet,* by Adelle Puhn, is a bit more generous with carbohydrates but not much. Women are advised to eat starchy vegetables, potatoes, or beans only on alternate days—either for lunch or dinner but not both. What about pasta? Not more than twice a week and only at dinner.

- The diet in Barry Sears's *The Zone* is referred to as "40-30-30" by those in the know, where the 40 represents a goal of 40 percent of total calories from protein, plus 30 percent from carbohydrates, and 30 percent from fat. This is still considerably more protein (two to three times) and less carbohydrate than most nutritionists recommend. However, you're unlikely to experience a buildup of ketones on this diet.

So what's the alternative? It may not be a hot new trend, but eating plenty of fruits, vegetables, and whole grains along with moderate amounts of lean meats and low-fat dairy foods, coupled with regular physical activity, is the safest bet for keeping off unwanted pounds.

Moderate Low-Fat Eating

Americans are eating fewer calories from fat, but that may not be all good news. Many people are just replacing high-fat diets with diets heavy in processed carbohydrates— low-fat chips, cookies, and other snack foods. What you need to do is eat more fruits and vegetables containing beneficial nutrients. Today's focus on the 30 percent of calories from fat has failed to help most people make better food choices. Fat is just one factor to review on a food label. If a food is fat-free but also devoid of any other nutrients, it offers no positive benefit. The proliferation of fat-free and low-fat products has offered more opportunity to eat poorly.

High-Carbohydrate, Very Low-Fat Diets

With 15 percent of calories from fat, these diets are very difficult to follow because variety and amounts of many foods and food groups are severely restricted. The Pritikin diet is perhaps the best example of severe fat restriction. There is no dispute that for some, this combination of foods can actually stop or reverse symptoms of heart disease. This eating style is great for these folks, but not to be recommended as an overall healthful diet. Why? Studies in progress are helping to explain why not everyone reduces their risk for heart disease by going on low-fat diets. The answers aren't all in yet. According to nutrition and obesity expert C. Wayne

Calloway, M.D., one-fourth of the U.S. population develops insulin resistance on these high-carbohydrate diets—a condition that frequently leads to diabetes. "The trend for the future is more targeted dietary prescriptions for individuals, not one-size-fits-all diets," says Calloway.

Choose Your Own Style

Considering all the data you collected in Chapter 1 and what you understand so far, it's time to plan your own eating style. To implement any broad guidelines may seem overwhelming. You need to make healthful choices that fit your lifestyle so you can do the things you want to do. Here are some simple, action-oriented tips to provide easy and manageable ways to help change your behavior and integrate basic dietary guidelines into your life.

It's All About You

Be Realistic—Make small changes over time in what you eat and the level of activity you do. After all, small steps work better than giant leaps.

- Park your car in the farthest spot. You'll walk more and burn extra calories.

- For lower-fat chili or tacos, put cooked ground beef in a strainer and rinse briefly with hot water. Drain well and continue with your recipe.

- To cut calories and fat, use a cooking spray instead of oil to sauté foods.

- Check the vending machine for lower-fat goodies like pretzels, bagels, low-fat yogurt, fresh fruit, and skim milk.

- Shopping on the run? Choose products that say "low," "high," or "reduced" on the label—these terms are easy to see and mean what they say.

Be Adventurous—Expand your tastes to enjoy a variety of foods.

- Try a fruit or vegetable you haven't had before. Make it a monthly goal.

- Enjoy a meal at a Thai, Indian, or Japanese restaurant.

- Prepare one new recipe each month from a favorite magazine or newspaper article.

- Dig into a different grain: couscous, bulgur, or quinoa, for instance.

- Pick up a food you don't normally buy each time you shop.

- Try imaginative low-fat snacks such as fruit kabobs or air-popped popcorn seasoned lightly with herbs or grated cheese.

- Strive to eat the number of servings recommended from each of the food groups in the Food Guide Pyramid.

- Choose an entree that is grilled or broiled when eating out.

Be Flexible—Go ahead and balance what you eat and the physical activity you do over several days. No need to worry about just one meal or one day.

- Eat a lighter breakfast and lunch to plan for "pizza with the works" for dinner.

- Don't pack on extra pounds during vacations. Work in plenty of walking, biking, hiking, or active games to balance out special vacation meals.

- Did you splurge on a "soup to nuts" special occasion meal? No problem. Eat lighter and move more for a few days afterward.

- No need to track every food you eat. But for foods you eat often, check the percent DV (daily value) column on food labels and balance high-fat choices with lower-fat ones.
- Enjoy a walk with a friend or family member before dinner.

Be Sensible—Enjoy all foods, just don't overdo it.

- Slow down! It takes twenty minutes for your brain to send the signal that you've had enough to eat.
- When served oversized portions in restaurants, eat half and take the rest home to enjoy the next day.
- Have only one helping and enjoy every bite.
- Make your ice-cream cone a single, not a double, dip.
- Serve your snacks on a plate to control the amount you eat rather than eating straight out of the bag.

Be Active—Walk the dog, don't just watch the dog walk.

- Set your goal at thirty minutes of moderate activity most days. In ten-minute increments, it's easier.
- Take a brisk ten-minute walk on your lunch break. You'll feel good and have more energy, too.
- Hop off the bus a few blocks early and walk briskly the rest of the way.
- Keep active around the house: sweep the garage, scrub the floors, vacuum the rugs, or trim the shrubs. It all helps you get fit—and the house will look great, too.
- Try a fun new activity. How about ballroom dancing, Roller-Blading, ice skating, or line dancing?
- Get energized. Take a brisk ten-minute walk in the morning, at lunch, and after dinner to total thirty minutes a day.
- Climb the stairs instead of riding the elevator. You'll be more fit without adding additional time to your fitness routine. 🍃

5

VITAMINS

If you eat a balanced diet, you don't need supplements. This has been the on-the-record advice of most health professionals for decades (although privately, many join the half of all Americans in taking daily supplements). But substantial evidence shows that intakes greater than the Recommended Dietary Allowances (RDAs) of specific vitamins and minerals may reduce the risk of particular diseases—and those amounts can usually be achieved only with supplements. The evaluation of your diet from Chapter 1 will help you determine which supplements are needed for optimal health. An appropriate intake of the right vitamins and minerals will help you feel and look your best no matter what your age. You may be able to significantly reduce the risk of chronic, crippling diseases that steal your energy, enjoyment, and enthusiasm for life. Supplements are not magic bullets, nor will they neutralize the impact of a high-fat, low-fiber diet of overly processed foods. Don't rely on supplements as a nutritional shortcut—you won't come out a winner.

Recent scientific studies have begun to focus on intake levels above the amount needed to prevent nutritional deficiencies in an effort to optimize health. Examples include studies that report that particular nutrients have "antioxidant" effects that protect against heart disease, certain cancers, and cataracts. They're called antioxidants because they prevent damage from a process known as oxidation, which technically is a chemical reaction that occurs when a substance is exposed to oxygen. In your body, oxidation occurs as part of the natural aging process, as well as exposure to environmental pollutants ranging from pesticides to smog and other pollutants. When not controlled, oxidation damages cells and speeds up the aging process and increases risk of diseases often thought to be age-related—including heart disease and cancer.

The vitamins broadly classified as "antioxidants" include beta-carotene, a form of vitamin A, as well as vitamins C and E and the mineral selenium. However, other nutrients also have antioxidant properties and are often recommended in supplement form: Niacin supplements used alone and in combination with other medications can lower blood cholesterol. Calcium in amounts higher than those usually achieved through diet alone can slow the development of osteoporosis by keeping bone mass strong and may also lower blood pressure in some people.

Despite these dramatic findings, there's little official governmental acknowledgment that supplements are recommended for use except by a small number of groups including:

- Newborns routinely given a single dose of vitamin K to prevent abnormal bleeding.

- Pregnant and breast-feeding women's increased needs for most nutrients.

- Women of childbearing age who benefit from folate supplements.

- Women with heavy menstrual periods who may need iron supplementation.

- Those on very low-calorie diets who simply don't eat enough to get essential nutrients.

- Vegans (vegetarians who eat no animal products) who often don't eat enough foods rich in calcium, iron, zinc, and vitamin B-12.

- People with chronic illnesses that affect how they absorb nutrients.

One reason is because current dietary guidelines—including the Recommended Daily Allowances—are focused on using vitamins and minerals to prevent nutritional deficiencies that may cause some diseases. Granted, many of the deficiency diseases (like scurvy) and night blindness are not common in the U.S., but they do exist in other parts of the world.

Eating nutrient-rich foods is clearly the preferred way to consume vitamins and minerals because healthy foods also contain phytochemicals, fiber, and other health-boosting substances not found in pills. But anyone eating fewer than 1,500 calories a day simply can't eat enough food to meet even the minimum standards for some nutrients. And to be realistic, you may not eat the right combination of foods to meet minimum intake standards and may not be close to preventive amounts.

DEPLORABLE DIETS

The U.S. Committee on Dietary Allowances estimates that many Americans consume 30 percent or more of their calories from foods that provide few, if any, vitamins or minerals. A 1998 study of the dietary sources of nutrients in U.S. adults reports similar results:

Food Category	Percent of Total Calories
Cakes, cookies, quick breads, and doughnuts	5.5
Soft drinks/sodas	4.1
Salad dressings/mayonnaise	3.1
Margarine	3.0
Sugars/syrups/jams	2.8
Alcoholic beverages	2.5
Potato chips/corn chips/popcorn	2.1
Oils	1.0
Fruit drinks (not juice)	1.0

Source: Journal of the American Dietetic Association, 1998

Vitamin-Mineral Revelations

Vitamin and mineral knowledge is in its infancy. In 1906, the first vitamin, vitamin A, was discovered and extracted into pill form. Initially, research focused on finding the smallest amount of a nutrient that would prevent common deficiency diseases like scurvy (which results from vitamin C deficiency) and beriberi (prompted by thiamin deficiency). Then, as more nutrients were identified—in alphabetical order—how they interacted became important. Today we're on the threshold of a whole new era identifying more unique categories of nutrients and learning how they optimize health and thwart disease.

Animal, Vegetable, or Mineral?

Vitamins are chemical compounds containing carbon, which is necessary for growth, health, metabolism, and physical well being. Vitamins are found in plant and animal foods. Some vitamins are essential parts of enzymes—the molecules that help complete chemical reactions. Other vitamins form parts of hormones—substances that promote and protect overall health and reproduction.

Plants make almost all of their own vitamins. Animals can create their own vitamins, too. For example, cats and dogs manufacture vitamin C. Humans must obtain vitamins from foods, produce them in their skin or liver, or make them with intestinal bacteria. For example, vitamin D can be synthesized by skin when exposed to sunlight;

vitamin K and biotin are made from bacteria in the colon; and niacin is converted from the amino acid tryptophan in your gut.

There are facts we know about vitamins and minerals...

- Vitamins and minerals don't provide calories or energy.

- All necessary vitamins and minerals can be found in food.

- All vitamins are organic since they contain the element carbon.

- All minerals are inorganic since they do not contain carbon.

- If you don't consume a particular vitamin or mineral, a deficiency will result over time.

- For most vitamins and minerals, the best form or most available source is the food we eat.

From A to Zinc

It's not surprising if vitamins and minerals seem a little foreign. Unlike most common things we measure, nutrients are tallied using the metric system of grams, milligrams, and micrograms. These are very tiny measurements—one gram is about the weight of a

GO FIGURE:
NUTRIENT MEASURES AND CONVERSIONS:

5 grams	= 1 teaspoon		
14 grams	= ½ ounce	= 1 tablespoon	= 3 teaspoons
28 grams	= 1 ounce	= 2 tablespoons	
10,000 micrograms	= 1,000 milligrams	= 1 gram	
1 IU of vitamin A	= .3 mcg retinol	= .6 mcg beta-carotene	
1 mg alpha-tocopherol acetate	= 1 IU		

small paper clip. In fact, your total vitamin and mineral needs for a day would barely add up to one-eighth teaspoon. To make it even more complex, some nutrients are measured in more than one way. For example, vitamin A is counted in retinol equivalents (REs), international units (IUs), and beta-carotene equivalencies. In this book the most common unit of measure is used whenever possible, so that it's easier for you to compare food and supplement labels.

Alphabet Soup of Standards

To confuse matters more, there are a variety of scientific standards, none of them adequate, to help sort out how much of a particular nutrient is desirable. Sometimes government and other standards complement each other; occasionally they conflict. Policymakers and health organizations need to carefully review and update their recommendations on supplement use to provide consumers with credible and consistent information. This takes time, so sometimes information gets out in the media long before enough science is available to make a clear recommendation. We've included all of the government's recommended nutrient charts in one of the appendices of this book.

Recommended Dietary Allowances (RDAs) were once the gold standard of nutrient recommendations. The RDAs tell us how much of each nutrient the population as a whole needs to prevent deficiency states. But even its creators admit that the numbers are not as meaningful as you might hope. The RDAs were designed by the National Academy of Sciences in 1941 for the War Department. They were used as a guide to feed U.S. soldiers, and the basic concepts haven't changed much in the last fifty years. If you ate close to 100 percent of the RDAs for the nutrients listed, chances were good

you had a balanced diet; that is, if you were a healthy person to start with. If you consume the RDA for vitamin C (60 mg), for instance, you will have a very low risk of scurvy.

Adequate Intakes (AIs) are the "best guesses" of experts when not enough science is available to make a formal RDA. Based on a combination of research and observation, they offer a range of intakes that should keep most people healthy.

Daily Values (DVs and %DVs) were invented when the food label was redesigned in 1992. Many people are understandably confused by these new standards. If you are healthy and fit and eat exactly 2,000 calories a day, then the DVs are tailored with you in mind. Since most of us don't eat exactly a 2,000-calorie diet, you may need more or less than 100 percent of the DVs.

Dietary Reference Intakes (DRIs) are the new kids on the block and are being promoted as a major leap forward in nutrition science. It's no longer feasible to have a single reference number for each nutrient. DRIs take a broader perspective, examining each nutrient's role in decreasing your risk of developing chronic diseases. They also set an upper level of intake to protect you from the risk of toxicity. The new goal is more than protection against deficiency; it aims at lowering your risk of major chronic diseases. Currently DRIs are available for B vitamins and vitamins and minerals involved in bone health such as calcium and magnesium. It is expected that in the near future, DRIs will be developed for all nutrients.

Tolerable Upper Intake Levels (ULs) are the maximum amount of a nutrient that won't hurt you, if you are a healthy person to begin with. ULs are not intended to be a recommended level of intake but a marker for reasonable safety for those who want to "push the envelope" to the maximum safe levels. For most nutrients, this number refers to total intake from food, fortified food, and nutritional supplements.

More Is Not Always Better

A megadose of a nutrient is typically any amount greater than ten times the RDA. At this level nutrients act differently in your body. Megadoses of some nutrients have significant drug-like effects. The most frequent side effects from excess supplemental doses are vague. They can include common symptoms such as headache, weakness, fatigue, nausea and vomiting, but can also cause serious effects such as nerve damage. Often these are the same early symptoms of many other illnesses, including vitamin deficiency. If you notice any early warning signs, be sure to tell your health care provider you are taking supplements. It's a good idea to compile a list of all the supplements you're taking and share this with your doctor at every visit.

Fortified foods have nutrients added to them during processing. Federal law requires manufacturers to add specific nutrients to certain foods. For example, milk processors add vitamins A and D. Food companies can choose to selectively add almost any nutrient to increase the appeal of a food. For instance, orange juice and rice both come in calcium-fortified versions. Getting nutrients from fortified foods is similar to taking a supplement. There is no guarantee that the form of the nutrient added contains all the known and unknown benefits of eating a real food source.

Nutrients in a Nutshell

With so many gaps in knowledge and differences between individual needs, it's difficult to weed through the tangle of data that continues to grow around vitamins and minerals. The following vitamin profiles offer a framework for determining if you would benefit from an increased intake. Chapter 6 does the same for minerals.

This section will dispel myths and accurately summarize the facts and current findings on each vitamin, detailing several important aspects such as…

- Up-to-date information. A quick review of interesting facts, current knowledge, and research trends.

- A brief description of each nutrient and why you need it.

- Recommendations for optimal intake. These levels may be higher than the current RDA or DV, based on the analysis of scientific studies, review papers, and interviews with leading experts. The unit of measure (IU, mg, mcg, etc.) listed is the most common way each vitamin is sold.

- Natural food sources. These are foods that provide at least 25 percent of the RDA in just one serving. If you are low in any particular nutrient, scan this list for quick, concentrated food ideas.

- Fortified foods. You should eat foods that are naturally high in nutrients. If you can't or won't, try foods that have those particular nutrients added during processing. Eating a fortified food is a second-rate choice; taking a supplement is third on the list.

- Minimum toxic doses. This is the smallest amount of a nutrient that can cause side effects ranging from annoying to life-threatening.

- Selected studies. These are quick glimpses of highlights from current research related to a particular nutrient, not a comprehensive list of studies. Journal or report citations are provided if you want to look them up yourself. When you look up one of these studies, check the reference list the authors provide if you want to do more digging.

Vitamins don't have glamorous or exciting names. The first one was named fat-soluble A and the second, water-soluble B. When riboflavin was discovered in 1926, it was found dissolvable in water and was called water-soluble B-2. So the original B vitamin became B-1. Things really got jumbled when someone figured out that B-1 was two vitamins—thiamin and niacin. Thiamin kept the B-1 name, and since B-2 was already taken, niacin was dubbed B-3. And so the story goes. Why isn't there a vitamin B-4 or B-9? Over-zealous researchers sometimes named a compound a vitamin and then later realized their mistake. It was too messy to continually reassign numbers. Eventually vitamin researchers wisened up and started giving names instead of numbers to their discoveries.

Fat-Soluble Nutrients

Fat-soluble vitamins include vitamins A, D, E, and K. They are unique because they are found and stored in fatty tissue. You must eat some fat so these nutrients can be absorbed from foods. Because these vitamins are held in fatty tissue, you don't need to replenish them every day—you can "save them up" over time. However, fat-soluble vitamins have a much greater potential for being toxic, since storage in body fat is almost unlimited. It's almost impossible to overdose on fat-soluble vitamins from food sources, but taken in supplement form, some can cause serious effects. Most experts

TOXIC TALK

Both one-time overdoses or prolonged over-consumption can cause health impairments. Toxic doses of vitamins and minerals rarely result from eating too much food; oversupplementation is the culprit. *There are three types of vitamin/mineral toxicity...*

- Acute or sudden toxicity occurs from one very big dose or from several huge doses over a few days. You get sick right away.

- Chronic toxicity develops after weeks or months of habitually taking extreme levels of a nutrient. For example, megadoses (amounts ten times or more the RDA) of vitamin B-6 can cause nerve disorders and skin rashes. Permanent damage may occur with some forms of chronic toxicity. Most people who develop toxic reactions to supplements don't have a clue it's their vitamin or mineral intake that's causing the problem. What commonly happens is you go through an expensive and exhaustive series of tests. Finally, you remember to tell your doctor that you take supplements. If you're lucky, your symptoms go away shortly after you stop them.

- Teratogenic toxicity refers to harmful changes in a baby's development that occur during pregnancy. Pregnant women risk miscarriage or severe birth defects if they take large amounts of certain supplements, such as vitamin A.

recommend against taking vitamins A, D, and K in supplement form other than what is found in "safe" multivitamin formulas. However, since vitamin E has been found to offer protection against heart disease and some cancers, it's often recommended to those prone to these diseases—usually in doses no more than 400 IUs daily.

Vitamin A

Vitamins are not the simple structures scientists once thought they were. Continuing research shows that many nutrients, like vitamin A, are a family of compounds. The three main types of vitamin A are carotenoids, retinol, and retinal. The carotenoids (ka-ROT-en-oids) are a group of more than 500 individual carotenes, the most popular member being beta-carotene. You can see them in the natural coloring of foods: the red in a pepper, the orange in a carrot, and the yellow in squash. Some vitamin A is masked so it can be found in a few leafy green vegetables as well. The only adverse effect of eating too many carotenoids over time is that your skin may take on a light orange glow. That's because the fat in skin cells store excesses of vitamin A. If you cut back on your intake, the unusual color will disappear within two to six weeks.

Retinol and retinal are found in animal foods. They are ready to be used by the body as is. That's why they are sometimes referred to as preformed vitamin A. Your overall intake is the sum total of all types of vitamin A you consume.

Until recently only preformed vitamin A was typically found in supplement tablets. Now we know that beta-carotene and other carotenoids such as *lycopene* (LYE-co-peen) and *lutein* (LEW-tea-in) do more than just change into vitamin A. They also act as antioxidants. Lutein (from dark green leafy vegetables) has been shown to reduce the risk of cataracts. Tomatoes, watermelon, and grapefruit contain lycopene, which may protect men from prostate cancer.

Xerophthalmia (zeer-OH-thal-ME-ah) is the deficiency disease that results from too little vitamin A, and while still a health problem in many underdeveloped countries, it is rare in the U.S. and other Western nations. When the mucous (moisture) membranes in the eye dry out, small particles of dirt settle there. Bacteria can enter the vulnerable eye through the scratches caused by these dirt particles. White blood cells, which help fight infection, start attacking bacteria in the scratches and cause lesions. As the lesions grow, blindness can result. Other signs of vitamin A deficiency include respiratory infection, stunted growth, and extremely dry skin (keratinization).

Recent research suggests that optimal intakes of vitamin A may strengthen the immune system and fend off certain cancers. Vitamin A helps protect body surfaces designed to keep infection and disease out. These special surfaces include your skin—one reason why vitamin A is an important ingredient in many skin creams and the moist lining of your mouth, throat, and digestive tract. Vitamin A's influence on immunity may be one of the ways it helps prevent the initiation or growth of cancer cells.

Why you need it: Vitamin A is critical for normal growth and healthy development. It's especially key in stimulating night and color vision. That's because vitamin A helps maintain the protective layers of the skin, including the eyes. Vitamin A combines with a special protein in your eye that improves night vision.

For optimal health: 5,000 IU/day of vitamin A for men; 4,000 IU for women (6,500 IU if nursing).

Best natural food sources: Carrot, pumpkin, cantaloupe, kale, mango, peppers, squash, sweet potato, and turnip greens.

Fortified foods: low-fat and skim milk, margarine, and ready-to-eat cereals.

Minimum toxic dose: 6,500 IU or 15 to 30 mg or more/day of vitamin A may cause blurred vision, diarrhea, headaches, irritability, muscle weakness, skin scaling or peeling, and vomiting. In growing children excess vitamin A can cause premature bone closures that result in deformities. Too much vitamin A is also known to cause stunted growth in children and excess doses in supplement form can cause nerve damage. During pregnancy, vitamin A toxicity causes a variety of birth defects.

SELECTED STUDIES

- A hot topic of study is the role of vitamin A and HIV. Some findings have showed that supplemental vitamin A has little protective effect in HIV patients. But one promising 2001 study in the journal *Nutrition* found that HIV-infected babies with lower blood levels of vitamin A had an increased risk of dying from the disease—suggestion that the nutrient, given in supplemental form, may help boost immunity or offer protection to HIV patients.

- People who eat at restaurants at least once a week consume fewer carotenoids than people who eat at home *(American Journal of Public Health,* February 1997). That's because most restaurant meals lack deep yellow and orange vegetables rich in vitamin A. If you eat out frequently, be sure to eat lots of vitamin A–rich foods at home and for snacks.

- Almost 23,000 pregnant women consuming various levels of vitamin A were contacted after the birth of their children. Women who had combined food and supplement intakes of 15,000 IUs of preformed vitamin A had a 3.5 times increased risk for birth defects compared to women who typically consumed just 5,000 IU. Those women who took 10,000 IU or more of vitamin A from supplements alone had a 4.8 times higher rate of infants born with a birth defect *(New England Journal of Medicine,* November 1995). If you might get pregnant, don't take extra amounts of vitamin A from supplements beyond what's in a daily multivitamin tablet.

- An increased intake of beta-carotene by healthy, breast-feeding women increases the supply of beta-carotene available to their infants *(American Journal of Clinical Nutrition,* February 1998). This is one more study that proves breast milk is the best milk for babies.

Vitamin D

A stroll in the park, tending your garden, or watching the kids splash in the pool are some of the more pleasant ways to obtain vitamin D. Since you make your own vitamin D when you're in the sun, it's sometimes called the sunshine vitamin.

Vitamin D comes in three forms: Calciferol (cal-SIFF-er-all), *cholecalciferol* (KO-lee-cal-SIFF-er-all), and *ergocalciferol* (UR-go-cal-SIFF-er-all). All can be made by exposing your skin to a sufficient amount of sunlight or artificial ultraviolet radiation. Vitamin D is also found in fortified milk and other dairy products. Vitamin D helps calcium be absorbed into the body. Without enough vitamin D, your body adapts by absorbing only 10 to 15 percent of all the calcium you take in. Too little vitamin D can speed up the development of the crippling bone disease osteoporosis. Occasionally, a vitamin D deficiency may cause slow, progressive hearing loss. If the bones in the inner ear become too weak or porous, they will not properly transmit sound waves. Sometimes this special type of hearing loss can be improved with an adequate intake of vitamin D.

Concern over sun-damaged skin and skin cancer has resulted in the increased use of sunscreens and sun-avoidance. If you shy away from the sun, you may not get enough vitamin D. There are many factors to consider when evaluating how reasonable it is to bask in the warmth of the sun in order to make your own vitamin D...

- Where you live. Check your latitude on the map on the next page. If you live in the southernmost half of the United States, chances are good that with regular outdoor time you can make and store plenty of vitamin D. If you live in the north, you should rely more on food sources of vitamin D.

- Season. In many northern climates it is impossible to have sufficient sun exposure in late fall, winter, and early spring due to the earth's distance from the sun.

- Sun protection. Sunscreens, clothing, hats, and other protective items block exposure to sunlight necessary to make vitamin D. Your skin must be exposed (the more the better) and free of any protective sunscreen for the sun to perform its magic. If you regularly apply sunscreen with a sun protection factor (SPF) of 8 or more, you won't make enough vitamin D from sun exposure.

- Mobility. If you stay indoors frequently or have extensive restrictions on activity (such as those in nursing homes or confined to bed), you probably aren't outdoors enough to soak up needed rays.

- Skin tone. Individuals with dark skin pigmentation have a higher melanin content and require a much longer exposure time (thirty to forty minutes, three to four times a week) than people with light skin tones (fifteen to twenty minutes, three to four times a week).

- Age. If you're over 70, your ability to make vitamin D from sun exposure is reduced by half. For instance, a fair-skinned child who plays outdoors year-round would probably not need a supplement of vitamin D, whereas a homebound elderly woman would require fortified foods or pills to prevent potential weakening of bone tissue.

Vitamin D isn't just for bones anymore. Newer research is finding that this nutrient may help protect against colon cancer. Although in early stages of research, investigators reported in the May 17, 2002 issue of *Science* that the nutrient may help detoxify cancer-causing agents released during digestion of high-fat foods.

This nutrient also helps regulate how much calcium stays in your blood, which plays a key role in the transmission of nerve impulses for muscle contraction. Perhaps the most important muscle that needs calcium to work effectively is your heart.

If you regularly rely on laxatives (all types) or antacids with aluminum or magnesium (these lower calcium absorption), be aware because these products can lower the amount of vitamin D you absorb from foods. The cholesterol-lowering drug cholestyramine (Questran) also disrupts absorption and metabolism of vitamin D. Fat substitutes like Olean and the fat-blocking drug Xenical also limit the amount of fat-soluble nutrients your body is able to absorb. If you regularly consume any of these, you should take a multivitamin supplement.

Why you need it: Vitamin D is essential for helping calcium get into your bones. Without proper levels of vitamin D, you can't absorb enough calcium no matter how much you take in. This nutrient also helps maintain proper heart function.

For optimal health: 400 to 600 IU or 5 to 10 mcg/day of vitamin D. Diabetics and

WHERE'S THE SUNSHINE? EXPOSE YOURSELF TO VITAMIN D

Sunlight too weak for vitamin D synthesis from November through February

Portland

42°

40°

Boise

Minneapolis

Chicago

Boston

Philadelphia

Columbus

Sacramento

Denver

Topeka

Sunlight adequate year-round

Sunlight too weak for vitamin D synthesis during January and February

To manufacture your own Vitamin D, you must be in the sun without sunscreen.

people who are exposed to high levels of toxic chemicals at work or air pollution where they live may need the higher optimal amounts.

Best natural food sources: Tuna, salmon, and sardines.

Fortified foods: Milk, margarine, and butter.

Minimum toxic dose: 1,000 IU or 25 mcg/day of vitamin D or more may cause constipation; headaches; nausea; high blood pressure; seizures; growth retardation; calcium deposits in the heart, blood vessels, and kidneys.

SELECTED STUDIES

- Elderly people at risk for falls and fractures might benefit from vitamin D supplementation, researchers said in an April 2002 article in the *American Journal of Clinical Nutrition.* That's because vitamin D deficiency leads to muscle weakness, and as a result, disability. Several weeks or months of vitamin D supplementation will typically correct such deficiencies.

- An eight-year study of 556 older men and women with osteoporosis found that those with low to moderate intakes (averaging 200 IU) and blood levels of vitamin D were three times more likely to have their symptoms worsen over time compared to those who had intakes of closer to 400 IU of vitamin D daily *(Annals of Internal Medicine,* September 1996). People with osteoporosis should carefully monitor the amount of vitamin D they consume to prevent pain and fractures.

• Another study showed what effects skin thickness, age, body fat, and sunlight can have on your blood levels of vitamin D (*American Journal of Clinical Nutrition*, 1993). The more risk factors you have, the harder it is for you to make or absorb vitamin D.

Vitamin E

If all the hype about vitamin E were true, you could live well past 100 and have the sex drive and youthful appearance of a teen-ager. Vitamin E is no fountain of youth, but it does provide significant health benefits. Working as an antioxidant, vitamin E protects various tissues from destruction by damage-causing cells called "free radicals." Optimal intakes of vitamin E have also been linked to reduction of heart disease and cancer.

Unfortunately, vitamin E is one nutrient that is difficult to obtain in optimal amounts from moderate-calorie foods. It takes almost a pound of vegetables such as spinach, sweet potatoes, or peas to provide just 20 to 30 IU of vitamin E—and most therapeutic doses are at least 10 times those amounts. Oils, nuts, and seeds are more concentrated sources of vitamin E, but they also contribute hefty amounts of fat grams and calories. Antacids decrease vitamin E absorption. If you habitually take antacids, you will need supplemental vitamin E.

NUTRITION HOW TO: Vitamin E is the only nutrient where the "natural" form is preferable over synthetic versions. Ignore the product label and read the ingredient list. Look for d-alpha-tocopherol. If you see dl-alpha-tocopherol, it's the synthetic version. The extra "l" makes all the difference. An easy way to remember what to avoid is dl = don't like.

Why you need it: Vitamin E protects vitamin A and essential fatty acids from oxidation; prevents breakdown of body tissues. Vitamin E may also decrease heart attack risk by preventing fats from sticking to artery walls, and may also improve immunity.

For optimal health: 50 to 400 IU/day of vitamin E from foods or the natural form of the vitamin.

Best natural food sources: Almonds, hazelnuts (filberts), peanut butter, rice bran oil, shrimp, sunflower seeds, wheat germ, and wheat germ oil.

Fortified foods: Ready-to-eat cereals.

Minimum toxic dose: 800 to 1,000 IU/day of vitamin E or more may cause breast tenderness, depression, diarrhea, double vision, fatigue, intestinal cramping, mood swings, and weak muscles. High doses can also interfere with the effectiveness of anticoagulant (blood-thinning) medicines that are prescribed to prevent blood clotting. Continued high intakes deplete vitamin A stores.

SELECTED STUDIES

• An ongoing study by Harvard researchers of 87,000 nurses first found in 1993 that women who took vitamin E supplements of 100 IU a day for at least two years had a 40 percent reduced risk of nonfatal heart attacks and deaths from coronary heart disease, prompting researchers to begin studying the role of vitamin E as a protector against heart disease. This led to dozens of findings suggesting some protective effects, including a 16-nation report in European countries with different mortality rates that concluded that high blood levels of vitamin E were the "most significant determinants of coronary heart disease." In fact, vitamin E blood levels predicted coronary events more accurately than high cholesterol, high blood pressure, or smoking, those researchers said.

- The same Harvard study now speculates vitamin E may help protect against Parkinson's disease. Studying the same nurses, as well as 47,000 men, the researchers noted that those who took vitamin E supplements had much lower risks of the degenerative disease.

- Vitamin E may also protect against Alzheimer's and other aging-related diseases. A study, reported in the *American Journal of Clinical Nutrition* in 1997, found that vitamin E has the ability to stabilize free radicals that break down and degenerate cells, restricting blood flow.

Vitamin K

You don't hear much about vitamin K, but it is important. Most notably it helps your blood to clot and helps form bone tissue. Extra amounts of vitamin K are frequently needed by those on long-term antibiotic therapy and anyone who does not metabolize fat normally.

If you've ever had a baby, you might remember that almost all newborns are given an injection of vitamin K shortly before they leave the hospital. That's because newborns have not yet developed normal, healthy bacteria in their digestive tract that help produce one of the three forms of vitamin K called K-2 (*menaquione*).

There are two other types of this nutrient. Vitamin K-1 (*phylloquinone*) is found in foods and is also made by bacteria in your gut. K-3 (*menadione*) is a synthetic form of vitamin K found in the liver and is the most active form of the three. Most Americans consume more than the RDA of vitamin K. That makes deficiency quite rare.

Some calcium supplements also contain vitamin K.

Why you need it: Vitamin K controls blood clotting, maintains bone, and helps heal bone fractures.

For optimal health: 80 to 200 mcg/day of vitamin K.

Best natural food sources: Asparagus, broccoli, brussels sprouts, cabbage, collard greens, endive, green apples, kale, red leaf lettuce, Swiss chard, and watercress.

Fortified foods: No food is fortified at 25 percent of the RDA.

Minimum toxic dose: Not known. May cause impaired liver function in those with advanced liver disease; jaundice and brain damage in infants. Large intakes of vitamin K can interact with the prescription drug *warfarin* (Coumadin).

SELECTED STUDIES

- Women who consume low levels of vitamin K have a greater risk of hip fractures than women who consume high or moderate levels of this nutrient (*American Journal of Clinical Nutrition,* January 1999). A single large salad of dark green leafy vegetables can provide all the extra vitamin K you need.

- A meta-analysis of six controlled clinical trials was evaluated to determine the safest and most effective method of administering vitamin K to infants to prevent hemorrhagic disease. No link with childhood cancer, as had been suggested by other research, was found (*Canadian Medical Association Journal,* February 1996). There is no compelling reason to change the current practice of administering vitamin K to newborns.

Water-Soluble Vitamins

The eight B vitamins plus vitamin C make up the water-soluble nutrients. Unlike fat-soluble nutrients, these can't go into long-term storage—which means that excess amounts are removed from your body in sweat and urine. That's good news because this makes it hard to "overdose" on these nutrients. But it also means that it's easy to lose water-soluble nutrients before you even open your mouth to put them in. That's because exposure to light, air, or heat during storage, processing, or cooking diminishes availability. It's important to carefully handle and prepare foods that contain B and C vitamins so you don't end up washing these nutrients down the drain or pouring them out with the cooking water.

Thiamin (Vitamin B-1)

Unless you eat lots of raw fish or rely on overly processed foods, chances are you're getting plenty of *thiamin* (THYE-ah-min). However, if you regularly sashay up to the sushi bar, beware that lurking in your un-cooked fish is thiaminase, an enzyme that inactivates the nutrient thiamin. Cooking will deactivate this pesky thiamin destroyer.

The thiamin deficiency disease *beriberi* (Sri Lankan for "I can't, I can't") is most commonly seen where white rice is a staple food. Symptoms of depression and weakness show up as quickly as ten days without thiamin in the diet. Other symptoms include weight loss, loss of appetite, irritability, tingling skin, and deep muscle pain.

U.S. grain products are enriched with thiamin. Don't wash or rinse pasta or rice before cooking or you'll cause thiamin to leach out into the water. If you happen to buy imported rice, it's usually not enriched and should be washed to sift out impurities. If you buy imported, unenriched white rice, be sure to eat plenty of other enriched grains.

Alcoholics have an increased risk for thiamin deficiency, since alcohol significantly diminishes the ability to absorb and use thiamin. Alcohol-related thiamin deficiency leads to a cluster of symptoms including mental confusion, memory loss, and poor muscle control over arms and legs.

Why you need it: Thiamin helps the body release energy from carbohydrate foods during metabolism, helps nervous system functioning, and keeps mucous membranes healthy.

For optimal health: 1.5 mg/day of thiamin (those on high-carbohydrate diets may need more).

Best natural food sources: Pork, wheat germ, oatmeal, eggs, sunflower seeds.

Fortified foods: Bread, pasta, rice, ready-to-eat cereals, and oatmeals.

Minimum toxic dose: 300 mg/day of thiamin or more may cause drowsiness or a hypersensitive reaction resembling anaphylactic shock.

SELECTED STUDIES

- A study in the March 2000 issue of *Ophthalmology* found that thiamin, along with other B vitamins, may play a more important role than previously believed in preventing the most common form of cataracts.

- Thiamin deficiency may occur in many people with congestive heart failure who are taking diuretic medications. Diuretics that inhibit sodium and chloride reabsorption may lead to deficiencies that in turn contribute to an increased risk of heart failure (*Journal of the American Dietetic Association,* May 1995). If you take diuretics regularly for heart problems, have your thiamin levels checked at least once a year.

Riboflavin (Vitamin B-2)

Luminous yellow-green color patterns that shimmer in milk whey, liver, and eggs are what first attracted scientists to investigate what was later called *riboflavin* (RYE-boe-flay-vin). View your eggs or milk at just the right angle and you, too, can see the glorious rainbow of colors.

If you eat lots of overly refined foods, you may not get enough riboflavin. The most common symptoms of riboflavin deficiency include inflammation of the mouth and tongue. Small cracks and fissures at the corners of your mouth may also be a telltale sign that you're not eating right.

Unlike most other water-soluble nutrients, riboflavin is not overly sensitive to high temperatures. The riboflavin in milk can easily withstand pasteurization temperatures. On the other hand, riboflavin is very fragile when exposed to light. That's why milk is packed in paper or plastic containers (not glass). Opaque milk cartons help shield riboflavin from light at the grocery store and in your refrigerator.

Why you need it: Riboflavin helps the release of energy from protein, carbohydrate, and fat during metabolism. It promotes normal growth and helps convert the amino acid tryptophan to niacin.

For optimal health: 1.8 mg/day of riboflavin.

Best natural food sources: Low-fat or nonfat milk and yogurt, and buttermilk. (*Note:* the lower the fat content, the higher the riboflavin content of dairy products.)

Fortified foods: Bread, pasta, and ready-to-eat cereals.

Minimum toxic dose: 1 gm/day of riboflavin or more may cause dark urine, nausea, or vomiting.

SELECTED STUDIES

- A study of fifty-four people with severe migraines were given either 400 mg of riboflavin daily or a placebo. After three months the riboflavin takers had 37 percent fewer migraines (*Neurology,* February 1998). Tell your doctor if you plan to increase your intake of riboflavin to control migraine headaches. There is no information on the long-term effects of high levels of riboflavin.

- Riboflavin deficiency in people with rheumatoid arthritis appears to be linked with continuing inflammation of the joints (*Annals of Rheumatic Disease,* November 1996). People with severe, inflammatory rheumatoid arthritis should evaluate the amount of riboflavin in their diet. If levels are low, higher intakes may help reduce symptoms.

Niacin (Vitamin B-3)

Niacin (NYE-a-sin) can be formed in the body from tryptophan, an essential amino acid. Tryptophan is found in meat, poultry, fish, and eggs.

During the depression years, these foods were scarce. Dementia (loss or decrease in mental function), diarrhea, and dermatitis are the three Ds of niacin deficiency, also known as pellagra. When corn became a staple food in the early 1700s in Europe, pellagra reached epidemic proportions. Reliance on corn foods in the southeastern United States in the early 1900s sparked our own pellagra epidemic. That's because the niacin in corn is bound to a protein molecule that prevents absorption. In 1941 the federal grain enrichment program was developed as a response to the devastation caused by pellagra. Today, many corn-based products like tortillas are soaked in lime water, which releases the niacin and makes it usable. Our higher standard of living and the increased availability of protein-rich foods has all but eliminated pellagra.

Niacin can lower blood cholesterol levels in some people, but usually when taken in very high amounts. Remember that megadoses of a vitamin change the way that these nutrients work in your body. Niacin in megadose amounts acts like many cholesterol-lowering drugs. A common side effect from niacin therapy is skin flushing. Time-release niacin supplements were developed to help reduce this effect, but these slow-absorbing formulas have been found to be more toxic to the liver. If you have liver disease, gout, peptic ulcers, or a high intake of alcohol, regular and time-release niacin supplements are not recommended.

Why you need it: Niacin helps the release of energy from protein, carbohydrate, and fat during metabolism; maintains normal function of skin, nerves, and digestive system.

For optimal health: 20 mg/day of niacin.

Best natural food sources: Chicken, lamb, pork, veal, mackerel, mullet, salmon, swordfish.

Fortified foods: Breads, pasta, and cereal.

Minimum toxic dose: Amounts as low as 50 mg/day of niacin can produce flushing if taken on an empty stomach. 500 mg or more may cause high blood sugar, itching, irregular heart rhythm, nausea, and ulcers. Blurred vision, eye and eyelid swelling, and loss of eyebrows and eyelashes are also common side effects of too much niacin.

SELECTED STUDIES

A study of the side effects of niacin drug therapy when used to lower cholesterol showed a variety of problems. Heart palpitations; worsening of diabetic control; and accelerated peptic ulcer, gout, and hepatitis disease were common (*Coronary Artery Disease,* April 1996). Niacin therapy should be used only in people with significantly high blood cholesterol levels. Don't take niacin in large amounts without medical guidance.

Pyridoxine (Vitamin B-6)

Pyridoxine (peer-i-DOX-een) is needed to process amino acids—the building blocks of all proteins and some hormones. It helps make the hormones serotonin, melatonin, and dopamine, and aids in the formation of several neurotransmitters, which is why it's considered an essential nutrient in the regulation of mental processes and possibly mood.

This is evident in its use to treat premenstrual syndrome (PMS) and autism. The PMS connection first came in the early 1980s, and it didn't take long—just until 1983—to see the first descriptions of toxicity described in the *New England Journal of Medicine* (see Selected Studies). Even today, many physicians and clinics that specialize in treating PMS routinely prescribe between 800 and 2,000 mg of B-6 per day.

In one of the longest "streaks" in research, a consecutive string of 18 studies starting in the early 1960s found that B-6 provided positive results as a treatment for autistic children, because it formulates brain cells. Another important function of B-6 is protein metabolism. It helps cells figure out which amino acids to break down for energy and which to convert into other amino acids. It's also crucial in making key nervous system regulators or neurotransmitters. It's the link between B-6 and neurotransmitters that started the PMS research.

Why you need it: Vitamin B-6 helps use protein to build body tissue, aids in metabolism of fat, maintains chemical balance of body fluids, and regulates water excretion.

The higher your protein intake, the higher your need is for vitamin B-6.

> *For optimal health:* 2 mg/day of B-6.
> *Best natural food sources:* Bananas, plantain, and chicken.
> *Fortified foods:* Ready-to-eat cereals and oatmeal.

> *Minimum toxic dose:* 200 mg/day of vitamin B-6 or more over time may cause physiological dependence, which leads to undesirable higher needs. 500 mg or more may cause nerve disorders, pain, numbness, sun-induced skin rash, or weakness in limbs. May cause depression when large amounts are taken with oral contraceptives.

SELECTED STUDIES

- In 1999, the American College of Physicians issued a study examining research dating back to 1966 and found that B-6, in doses more than 50 mg, does relieve overall premenstrual and depressive symptoms (although most of the earlier studies failed to meet some methodologic criteria).

- A study published in 1983 first identified the syndrome caused by megadoses of pyridoxine, vitamin B-6. Seven individuals taking 2 gm or more of the supplement daily had difficulty walking, numb feet, numbness and clumsiness in the hands, and severely impaired sensation of touch and temperature in both upper and lower limbs. All improved after withdrawal of the supplement (*New England Journal of Medicine*, August 1983). Two gm of B-6 is a huge increase over normal needs for this nutrient.

Cobalamin (Vitamin B-12)

Cobalamin (ko-BALL-ah-men) can sometimes be a true miracle cure. Picture an elderly woman admitted to the hospital with symptoms of senility. She is frail, but is able to care for herself, carry on intelligent conversations, and answer common questions. Gradually her mental abilities fade to the point that Alzheimer's or senility are considered. After ruling out these and other serious problems, a simple injection of vitamin B-12 leads to sudden, dramatic improvements. She's up, walking the halls of her hospital wing, smiling, and is back to normal.

Getting enough vitamin B-12 can be a problem for many older adults because aging bodies don't secrete the amount of stomach acid necessary for absorption of the vitamin. A B-12 deficiency can cause serious neuralgic problems. Low levels may also increase susceptibility to heart attack and stroke. Folic acid and B-12 work together. If there is too much folic acid, a deficiency of B-12 can be hidden from routine blood analyses.

Vegans and other vegetarians who eat almost no animal foods may develop a deficiency in vitamin B-12 over time. Have your blood level of vitamin B-12 checked about every five years if you don't eat meat, fish, poultry, eggs, and milk.

> *Why you need it:* Vitamin B-12 is essential for new tissue growth and red blood cells and may help fight certain cancers, cardiovascular disease, depression, and mental dysfunction. It also helps the body use fatty acids and some amino acids.

> *Optimal intake:* 2 to 6 mcg/day of B-12.
> *Best natural food sources:* Meat, fish, poultry, eggs, and milk.
> *Fortified foods:* Cereals and breads.
> *Minimum toxic level:* None known.

Folate

Folate (FOE-late), *folic* (FOLL-ick) *acid*, *folacin* (FOE-la-cin)—whatever you choose to call it—has earned the honor of contributing the most striking public health improvement of any vitamin this decade—it is now a cornerstone in prenatal nutrition. Optimal amounts of folic acid during conception and early fetal development drastically reduce the chances of having a baby born with a devastating neural tube defect (NTD) like spina bifida. In fact, up to 70 percent of birth defects of the brain and spine and many cases of Down's syndrome can be prevented by maintaining adequate folate levels before and during pregnancy. In October 2002, Swedish researchers found that women deficient in folate had a 50 percent increased risk of having an early miscarriage. Before the link with folate was discovered, about 2,500 babies were born with NTDs in the United States each year. When more women start consuming the new recommended folate levels, those numbers are expected to drop by half.

Now folate may shine in the spotlight again. Evidence is mounting that optimal levels of folate (along with B-6 and B-12) help reduce heart disease by controlling the amount of the amino acid *homocysteine* (ho-mo-SIS-teen). Normally, homocysteine is converted into other amino acids. If this conversion does not take place fast enough, bloodstream levels of homocysteine become too high and can damage artery walls, which propels the buildup of atherosclerotic plaque. Preliminary research suggests it may help reduce the risk of some cancers and dementia associated with Alzheimer's disease.

Unfortunately, as many as 88 percent of all Americans fall short when it comes to meeting the DV for this nutrient. Many foods are good sources of folic acid, but you need to eat at least five to nine servings of fruits and vegetables a day to even come close. In fact, folic acid deficiency is the most common vitamin deficiency in the world. Since January 1998, all U.S. manufacturers of enriched products including white flour, white bread, white rice, regular pasta, and hot cereals were required to add folic acid. This fortification adds about 100 to 200 extra mg of folic acid to your daily total. If you typically choose whole-wheat bread, whole-wheat pasta, or brown rice, check the ingredient label to see if folic acid has been added. Fortification is optional for whole-grain products.

Considering the strong evidence that folic acid helps prevent birth defects—not to mention heart disease—the U.S. Public Health Service advises every woman of childbearing age to consume 0.4 mg (or 400 mcg) each day. Most multivitamins supply that amount of folic acid, which is also available as a separate supplement.

Why you need it: Folate helps to form red blood cells, forms the genetic material (DNA and RNA) within each cell, and functions as part of coenzymes in amino acid formation.

For optimal health: 400 to 600 mcg/day of folate from a synthetic supplement, plus food sources; the higher level for any woman who might get pregnant and all pregnant women during their first trimester. Older people with reduced stomach acid have less absorption and therefore also need more.

Best natural food sources: Liver, spinach (cooked), black-eyed peas, kidney beans, pinto beans, lentils, oatmeal, asparagus, and orange juice.

Fortified foods: Bread, pasta, rice, and ready-to-eat hot and cold cereals.

Minimum toxic dose: 1,000 mcg (1 gm) or more may hide a vitamin B-12 deficiency, decrease zinc absorption, and produce damaging folacin crystals in the kidneys. Amounts over 1,500 mcg can cause decreased appetite, abdominal bloating, flatulence, nausea, and interference with anticonvulsant drugs used to prevent seizures.

SELECTED STUDIES

- An analysis of twelve randomized controlled trials studying the effects of folic acid supplements on blood homocysteine concentrations found that dietary folic acid reduced blood homocysteine concentrations in those with elevated levels by 25 percent in the range of 0.5 to 5 mg of folic acid daily. Vitamin B-12 supplementation of 0.5 mg daily produced an additional 7 percent reduction in blood homocysteine (*British Medical Journal,* 1998).

- A study of seventy-five men and women showed that folic acid intakes of 500 to 665 mcg per day increased red-cell folic acid levels and decreased harmful homocysteine blood levels, thereby reducing the risk of heart disease (*New England Journal of Medicine,* April 1998).

- A three-month study showed that women who increased their intake of foods rich in folic acid had significantly less red-cell folate levels compared to women who received supplements. Women who either took supplements or ate folate-fortified foods were the only ones who improved their folate status (*Lancet,* May 1996). It may be unreasonable to expect women of childbearing age to get the recommended amount of folate from foods alone. If you are of childbearing age, you should be taking folate supplements.

- Two studies, one of 5,000 Canadians and one of 80,000 U.S. nurses, found those who reported eating diets high in folate had a lower risk of heart disease over the following fifteen years (*Journal of the American Medical Association,* June 1996, and *Journal of the American Medical Association,* August 1998).

Biotin

Bios is the Greek word for life. Bacteria in the intestines usually produce enough *biotin* (BYE-oh-tin), but it is widely available in common foods. Biotin is best known as an essential nutrient for keeping your hair and skin healthy.

If you know someone who likes to eat raw eggs, here's some trivia to convince them to stop. In addition to risking serious food-borne disease, people who consume huge quantities of raw egg whites (fifteen or more per day) get too much of a substance called avidin that prevents the absorption of biotin. Most adults have the right mix of intestinal bacteria to produce their own biotin. But anyone on long-term anticonvulsant drugs, which can inhibit biotin uptake, are at risk for deficiency.

Why you need it: Biotin helps the release of energy from protein, carbohydrate, and fat during metabolism. It also helps strengthen hair and nails.

For optimal health: 30 to 100 mcg/day of biotin.

Best natural food sources: Peanut butter, cooked eggs, liver, and yeast breads.

Fortified foods: Ready-to-eat hot and cold cereals.

Minimum toxic dose: None known.

SELECTED STUDIES

- As many as half of pregnant women may be deficient in biotin, and this deficiency may increase the risk of birth defects, found a study reported in the June 2002 issue of the *American Journal of Clinical Nutrition. The suspected cause:* Consuming excessive amounts of raw egg white, which contains a compound that inhibits the absorption of biotin.

- At the University of Ferrara, Italy, it was discovered that biotin deficiency may be associated with epileptic and/or convulsive disorders (*Neuroreport,* May 1996). Biotin, or any other nutrient, cannot cure any disease such as epilepsy. If you are at risk for seizures, be sure you eat plenty of foods rich in this nutrient.

Pantothenic Acid (Vitamin B-5)

Pantothenic (pan-toe-THIN-ick) acid gets around, but it's not a popular nutrient. The proof is on the food label. Scan the nutrition facts panel of your favorite fortified foods and you won't find pantothenic acid listed along with the other B vitamins routinely added. That's because pantothenic acid deficiency is so rare we don't even know what it might look like. Pantos, a Greek root word, means "everywhere." Almost every food you eat contains some pantothenic acid. But that's just half the story.

If you rely on heavily processed, nutrient-fortified foods to provide your vitamin and mineral needs, you can end up with suboptimal nutrient levels. The pantothenic acid that occurs naturally in foods is significantly destroyed during food processing. If you don't eat a wide variety of unprocessed foods, you will fall short on pantothenic acid at the same time your intake of other nutrients looks good. For example, some women who eat a minimal amount of calories trying to control their weight often choose highly processed fortified foods that appear to be nutritious (like breakfast cereals and fruit-granola bars). They often have a salad or small meal and then add in fat-free chips or cookies and diet soft drinks. It's startling to see their nutrient intakes showing well over 100 percent of the RDA for popular vitamins and minerals. In contrast, they consume just 50 to 75 percent of the RDA for nutrients like pantothenic acid that are supposed to be so easy to get.

Why you need it: Pantothenic acid helps release of energy from protein, carbohydrate, and fat during metabolism; maintains blood sugar levels; aids in the forming of red blood cells, hormones, and substances needed for nerve transmission.

Pantothenic acid has been used as an "antistress" vitamin and is used to relieve fatigue and stress, through its support of the adrenal glands. It's also been used to relieve allergies, headaches, arthritis, psoriasis, insomnia and asthma.

For optimal health: 5 to 10 mg/day of pantothenic acid; athletes, those who perform vigorous manual work, and pregnant women need the higher amounts.

Best natural food sources: Almost all natural foods.

Fortified foods: Whole-grain cereals.

Minimum toxic dose: 10,000 mg/day of pantothenic acid or more may cause diarrhea or water retention.

SELECTED STUDIES

- It is hypothesized that pantothenic acid deficiency may cause the onset of acne, and that a cure for acne would be to supplement the acne sufferer with liberal amounts of pantothenic acid (*Medical Hypotheses,* June 1995). This research just identified an area for future clinical study and offers no proof at this time.

Vitamin C

Millions of people religiously swallow supplements of vitamin C (sometimes referred to as ascorbic acid) hoping to cure everything from the common cold to cancer. There's lots of fiction surrounding vitamin C. *The facts suggest that vitamin C…*

- Prevents scurvy, a disease reported to have caused the deaths of one-half to two-thirds of all sailors on extended sea voyages from the sixteenth to eighteenth centuries. Scurvy is still a common affliction in undeveloped countries with deficient food supplies.

- Stimulates antibodies that help fight infection and illness.

- Helps stop the production of cancer-causing nitrosamines in the stomach.

- Helps improve the body's ability to use folic acid and iron.

- Helps to rid the body of toxic levels of stored lead.

- Prevents free radical damage, which leads to cancer and promotes tumor growth, by working as an antioxidant.

- Is harmful to tooth enamel when chewable forms are taken daily.

- Is needed in higher than normal amounts by smokers and people who take oral contraceptives, anticoagulants, aspirin products, sulfa drugs, or tetracycline.

- In large amounts can cause false negative tests for diabetes (urine) and colon cancer (fecal occult blood).

Vitamin C is a puzzling nutrient. Only humans, monkeys, guinea pigs, a few birds, and some fish need vitamin C from foods. Every other living thing makes its own C from the sugar glucose. The same amount of vitamin C that prevents scurvy (10 mg) is not the same amount that can produce optimal health. Your body becomes saturated with vitamin C at intakes between 200 and 250 milligrams. If you take too much vitamin C, it stays in your small intestine and attracts water, which will eventually cause diarrhea.

Why you need it: Vitamin C forms collagen (connective tissue); maintains capillaries, bones, and teeth; aids wound healing; and increases iron absorption. As an antioxidant, it prevents cell damage and can help stop the production of cancer-causing nitrosamines in the stomach.

For optimal health: 200 mg/day of vitamin C (although the RDA is 60 mg).

Best natural food sources: Fruits—cantaloupe, grapefruit, grapefruit juice, honeydew, kiwi, mango, oranges, orange juice, papaya, pineapple juice, raspberries, strawberries, tangelo, tangerine, watermelon; vegetables—asparagus, broccoli, brussels sprouts, cabbage, cauliflower, kale, kohlrabi, mustard greens, peppers, plantain, potato (with skin), rutabagas, snow peas, sweet potato, tomato, tomato juice or sauce.

Fortified foods: Some juice and juice drinks and ready-to-eat cereals.

Minimum toxic dose: 500 to 1,000 mg/day of vitamin C or more may cause diarrhea, headache, and cramping. Large doses over time may cause urinary tract infection, and increase risk of kidney stones and erosion of tooth enamel (with chewable vitamin C).

SELECTED STUDIES

- While it's still unproven that vitamin C can prevent colds, recent studies suggest that people who regularly consume vitamin C supplements do get them less frequently and once infected, recover more quickly. In October 2002, researchers noted those taking 1,000 to 2,000 mg in supplement form seem to get some protective effect—getting fewer and shorter colds than people not taking supplements. However, it should be noted that other studies have found no protective effect.

- A University of California research team using data from the National Health Survey of nine thousand people aged 20 to 74 found that women with high blood levels of vitamin C developed half as many gallstones as those with moderate intakes. Vitamin C increases the enzyme activity that converts cholesterol to bile.

- A report of an expert review panel from the National Institutes of Health recommends that a new RDA value for vitamin C be updated to between 120 and 200 mg/day. They emphasized that whenever possible, the vitamin C should come from fruits and vegetables, and that people can get the recommended amount by eating five servings of these foods daily (*Journal of the American Medical Association,* April 1999). See our list of foods high in vitamin C on the preceding page. A diet rich in fruits and vegetables may also be beneficial in helping to prevent some types of cancer.

Despite many benefits, vitamin C may also cause harm. In June 2001, researchers at the University of Pennsylvania Center for Cancer Pharmacology reported in *Science* that the vitamin can also damage cells' genetic material—explaining why high-dose vitamin C has so far failed as an experimental cancer therapy.

LINK UP to *www.medem.com*, and search for Vitamin C to read *"How Much Vitamin C Do You Need?"* from the *Journal of the American Medical Association.*

Vitamin-Like Compounds

They don't have the status of a full-fledged vitamin, but the following vitamin-like compounds are important. Included are a variety of compounds that are necessary for metabolism. There are no RDA or DV for these nutrients. Most of these compounds are found in animal foods. Because vegans (who eat no animal products) have never been shown to have deficiencies, it appears

clear that your body makes all you need. Premature infants, though, may need an outside source of choline, carnitine, and taurine. Their bodies are not developed enough to make these substances on their own. Breast milk is loaded with these compounds, but many tiny premature babies aren't able to breast-feed or be given breast milk.

Healthy adults use amino acids and glucose to make these substances. If you have a debilitating disease, eating more foods high in these nutrients may be important. Here's a brief description of what we know about them.

Choline

Do you have a good memory? Perhaps you should thank choline (KO-leen). It helps your brain store memories and keeps your emotions and judgment in line. Choline may also help control fat and cholesterol buildup in the body and prevent fats from accumulating in the liver. One form of this fat, phosphatidyl choline, is the active ingredient in lecithin. Most people consume about 1,000 mg of lecithin from foods as part of a normal diet.

The Food and Nutrition Board recently set a precedent by classifying choline as a nutrient, even though it's not required by all groups of the population. The new recommendation for choline is 500 mg per day. Research suggests that only men and pregnant or breast-feeding women require a dietary source of choline.

Some forms of supplemental choline, such as choline bitartrate or choline chloride, can cause a fishy body odor. Other side effects from supplements include stomach and intestinal distress, loss of appetite, vomiting, nausea, and diarrhea. Some researchers believe that high doses of choline may increase the risk of stomach cancer. That's because choline can transform compounds in ways that cause them to develop into carcinogenic nitrosamines.

Pregnant women have lots of choline circulating around the placenta. That's the organ that passes nutrients from the mother to the developing baby. It's been suggested that since choline is important for fetal growth, it must have magic properties that are helpful in growing new tissue. No research has made the connection.

SELECTED STUDIES

- At the American Stroke Association's annual conference in 2002, researcher Jeffrey Saver, M.D., reported that an analysis of placebo-controlled clinical trials found that treating patients with choline precursors reduced stroke incidence by 10 percent and long-term death and disability rates by 12 percent.

- Choline circulating into the brain decreases with age. Because choline plays a key role in the structure and function of brain neurons, this change may contribute to the onset of brain impairments during aging (*Journal of the American Medical Association*, September 1995).

Carnitine

Acetyl L-carnitine (ah-SEE-tull el-KAR-nah-teen) is a molecule that helps transport fat into the mitochondria of your cells. Mitochondria are tiny energy factories in each living cell. Carnitine is a substance your body supplies for you, as long as you have enough vitamins B-1, B-6, iron, and lysine to make it yourself. Vegetarians might have low levels of carnitine if their diets are low in lysine. Such a deficiency is possible because lysine is found in high concentrations in muscle tissue; if you don't eat meat, you might not get enough.

Carnitine is also popular with body-builders, who believe it helps them add muscle bulk and improve endurance. No evidence for these claims has been documented. Many supplement manufacturers have jumped into the market with their own versions of carnitine. The National Organization for Rare Disorders tested twelve brands of L-carnitine to see just how truthful the label claims were. L-carnitine is a supplement critical to people with a particularly deadly form of genetic carnitine deficiency. Many of the brands tested showed a wide variation in L-carnitine among the individual pills sold in the same bottle. Pills in one brand ranged from 20 to 85 percent of the amount that was stated on the label. Two brands didn't even contain any detectable carnitine.

Inositol

If you want to keep from losing your money as well as your hair, don't buy *inositol* (in-AH-seh-tall). Touted as a treatment for everything from hair loss to weight control, inositol does have a redeeming role as a supplement. It keeps membranes healthy and shuttles needed fat from place to place. It helps keep your bone marrow, eye tissue, and intestines in good condition.

Premature infants and diabetics have the biggest chance of not having enough of this vitamin-like substance. Some research shows that diabetics with low levels of inositol in their nerve tissue may benefit from extra inositol, which might decrease the nerve damage, a complication common with diabetes.

Taurine

Taurine (TAR-een) is a sulfur-containing nutrient that helps manage your nervous system by keeping your nerves and muscles working together smoothly. Most taurine is found in your heart and other muscles, white blood cells, and central nervous system. It also is part of the bile that is used to help digest fats and absorb fat-soluble vitamins. It's surprising that little taurine is found in animal products since muscle is a main active storage site in humans. Taurine is one of the nutrients that your body can make itself if you have enough protein and vitamin B-6.

LINK UP to *http://nutrition.about. com/library/blvitamins.htm* for a complete reference to every vitamin.

Pills in Food Form

So, just how much of what do you need? Before you dash to the nearest supplement counter, take stock of what you are already adding to your foods in terms of extra vitamins and minerals. You may be swallowing a supplement without realizing it. Some foods are required by law to be enriched or fortified with additional nutrients. Milk and other dairy products have added vitamins A and D. One 8-ounce glass of milk provides 100 IU of vitamin D and 500 IU of vitamin A. Many grains like bread, rice, and pasta have added B vitamins, iron, and folate.

Food companies also voluntarily add nutrients to foods to increase their marketing appeal. Several leading cereal companies spray on between 25 and 100 percent of the DV of selected nutrients. Compare cereal nutrition fact labels the next time you are in the grocery store and you'll notice the randomness of how nutrients are added to foods. Eating a serving of cereal poured from one of these packages is like taking a supplement, but only if you drink the milk in the bottom of the bowl, since that's where

most of the added water-soluble vitamins end up. Keep in mind that there are more than forty known nutrients and only a few of these are added to any one food. The helter-skelter way nutrients are pumped into food can skew well-intentioned food choices. You might gobble up plenty of the popular nutrients that are cheap or in vogue and still be deficient in those that are too expensive or unpopular with food manufacturers.

As long as a "food" meets the minimum requirements for certain nutrients, it can replace a real fruit, vegetable, or grain, according to current USDA school lunch standards. Fortified candy and doctored-up sugary beverages are standing in for more nutritious foods in lunchrooms across the country. No matter what the guidelines say, vitamin-laced gummy candies are not the nutritional equivalent of a serving of fruit. Orange juice is far superior to an orange drink fortified with added vitamin C. Fortified beverages usually lack essentials including folic acid, vitamin A, potassium, phosphorus, and even a little fiber found in 100 percent juice.

Advertising campaigns encourage on-the-go yuppies, baby boomers, and their aging parents to get a "boost" from a can of fortified imitation milk-like beverages such as Ensure or Slim Fast. There are a wide variety of fortified candy and granola bars, milkshakes, puddings, soups, and cookies marketed as total meal replacements. Where are you supposed to get fiber? What about other nutrients? How about satisfaction from eating flavorful food? Food is more than just something to swallow on your way out the door—it's meant to be savored and enjoyed. A diet of vitamin-mineral fortified food fragments can't begin to compare with the health benefits and emotional satisfaction from eating a variety of fresh, wholesome, and delicious foods. Special nutritional supplements do have a place for individuals with severe health problems like cancer or cystic fibrosis, but they can't stand in for more healthful meals and snacks.

It's critical to keep in perspective the fact that nutrient requirements are interrelated. You need appropriate amounts of all nutrients to optimize your health. Meeting your nutrient needs by relying on the selected supplements included in fortified foods almost ensures you will not be eating well. Variety in food selection is what promotes optimal nutrition.

A daily multiple vitamin-mineral product that provides 100 percent of the RDA is a good place to start. Choose one with as many essential nutrients as possible. Some one-a-day type brands have fewer than ten nutrients; others more than two dozen.

If you have a specific lifestyle or health-related condition, your need for a particular nutrient or group of nutrients may be increased. *For example…*

- Most women and girls don't eat enough calories to be able to meet their iron needs.

- Cigarette smokers need twice the recommended amount of vitamin C, since smoking depletes C stores.

- Women on oral contraceptives have an increased need for B vitamins and vitamin C.

- Prolonged use of antibiotics can alter intestinal bacteria that normally help to manufacture B vitamins and vitamin K.

- The elderly tend to absorb less vitamin B-12, D, and C.

- Individuals with broken bones, recovering from surgery, or body burns need increased amounts of most nutrients, especially vitamin C and calcium if movement is restricted.

- Heavy alcohol users frequently have elevated nutrient losses associated with diarrhea and increased urine output and require both vitamin and mineral supplementation.

- Many medications can cause a deficiency of particular vitamins and minerals. Always ask your doctor or pharmacist for drug-nutrient interactions when you begin a new prescription or over-the-counter medication.

The Bottom Line

Carefully selected supplements may benefit most people. A multiple vitamin/mineral supplement is a good start. If you don't drink milk, you might need additional calcium. Research is confirming that vitamin E, in amounts higher than you can get from foods, offers protective benefits. But don't misinterpret the message. Popping a pill doesn't mean you can forget about selecting a variety of wholesome foods. While this book reviews the optimal amounts of vitamins and minerals, it does not suggest that supplementation is the preferred way to get them. Evidence that supplements help prevent or fight disease pales next to data that show the positive effects of eating the right foods, especially fruits and vegetables.

Eat the most healthful way you can, and then determine what might need improvement based on your individual circumstances. Remember, vitamin and mineral supplements are not magic pills; nor will they neutralize a high-fat, low-fiber diet of processed foods. Don't rely on supplements as a nutritional shortcut—you won't come out a winner. People of different ages, genders, and health statuses have different nutritional needs. What supplements should you take? We'll summarize that at the end of the next chapter on minerals. ❦

WHAT VITAMINS DO YOU NEED FOR SPECIAL SITUATIONS?

Nutrient	Highest Federal Standard (RDA or DV)	Optimal Intake	Individuals with Special Needs*
Vitamin A	1,000 RE (retinol equivalents)	5,000 IU	Diabetics and people who are exposed to toxic chemicals at work or heavy air pollution where they live
Vitamin C	60 mg	200–500 mg	Women on oral contraceptives and all smokers
Vitamin D	5–15 mcg	10–15 mcg	Sun-avoiders, people over 70, some vegetarians, and people with kidney failure
Vitamin E	8–10 mg	50–200 IU	Those over 55 and people with hyper-thyroiditis
Vitamin K	60–80 mcg	80–200 mg	People on very low-calorie diets
Thiamin	1–1.5 mg	Not known	People over 70, heavy coffee and tea drinkers, and those on very low-calorie or high-carbohydrate diets
Riboflavin	1.2–1.8 mg	Not known	People who eat lots of processed foods, very active adults, those with low calcium intakes, and individuals with low thyroid disorders
Niacin	13–20 mg	Not known	People over 55, diabetics, very active individuals, and those with hyperthyroid disorders
Vitamin B-6	1.64–2 mg	Not known	Women on oral contraceptives
Folate	200 mcg	400–600 mcg	People over 70, women on oral contraceptives, all women who could become pregnant, and people with sickle cell anemia
Vitamin B-12	2–6 mcg	Not known	Vegans
Biotin	30–100 mcg	Not known	Those on antibiotics, smokers, and women on oral contraceptives
Pantothenic Acid	7 mg	5–12 mg	People over 55, those on very low-calorie diets, and smokers

* Pregnant and breast-feeding women, alcoholics, and drug abusers have increased needs for most nutrients.

6

MINERALS

inerals are inorganic chemicals; this means that they are not attached to a carbon atom. They aid many biochemical functions necessary for growth, development, and overall health. Like vitamins, many minerals are a part of enzymes. Minerals are the catalysts that help enzymes to operate. Different minerals are critical to enzyme systems either because they are part of the enzyme itself or because they help the enzyme to work properly. An adult male stores about 5 pounds of minerals throughout his body.

There are several classifications for dietary minerals depending on the function they serve and how much you need. *They are…*

- Major minerals—minerals of which you need more than 250 mg per day. Calcium is a major mineral, needed in amounts ranging from 800 to 1,500 mg per day.

- Electrolytes—minerals that dissolve in water.

- Trace elements—minerals you need in very tiny amounts, less than 20 mg per day. Iron is a trace element; most people require just 10 to 18 mg daily.

- Heavy metals—toxic minerals that even in minute amounts can cause harm. They include aluminum, arsenic, cadmium, lead, and mercury.

Zinc, copper, iron, and other minerals are deposited in earth and rock. They find their way into foods because plant roots absorb minerals from dirt and water. Red

COLLOIDAL CONFUSION

Colloidal minerals are tiny particles suspended in a liquid with a yellow tint. It's the yellow color that indicates the presence of dissolved organic matter. Promoters of colloidal minerals claim that the suspension helps to improve absorption. However, there is absolutely no scientific proof for this hypothesis. If you choose to take the expensive colloidal preparations commonly available, beware of their potential toxic risk. Although concentrations of hazardous substances may be low, long-term exposure can result in a buildup of exotic and dangerous minerals including lead, arsenic, aluminum, mercury, iridium, and rhodium.

meat is the best food source of some minerals because an animal will consume vast amounts of plants over its lifetime. The minerals from plants are concentrated in the animal's tissues. Whole grains are the best non-meat mineral source, followed by fruits and vegetables.

GET THE LEAD OUT

What do paint, pencils, pollution, pipes, and pottery have in common? They can all contain traces of the toxic mineral lead. Too much lead in your system can lead to erratic behavior and mental retardation. In fact, some historians think the fall of the Roman empire was a result of chronic lead poisoning from drinking wine and eating food from vessels loaded with lead.

Major Minerals

Calcium

The message to get enough calcium has saturated just about every medium except our bodies. Bone is a growing tissue that is constantly being broken down and rebuilt, just like your hair and nails. About 20 percent of your skeleton is made brand new every year. Calcium intake is critical because it's the most abundant mineral in your body, and one of the most essential.

Women begin to lose bone mass in their 20s; it's one of those inevitable parts of getting older. Since it takes men's bodies longer to mature, they start depleting bone mass years later. More women die each year from hip fractures related to osteoporosis than from breast cancer, uterine cancer, and ovarian cancer combined.

Why you need it: Calcium builds bone and teeth and maintains their strength; assists in muscle contraction, blood clotting, and maintenance of cell membranes. The connection between calcium intake and osteoporosis prevention is so strong that the Food and Drug Administration (FDA) has ruled that food labels can advertise the link. Calcium is too bulky to include at high enough levels in multivitamin tablets, so separate supplements are usually required for those who need significant extra calcium. The typical American only gets about 600 mg of calcium a day; meanwhile, about 1,300 mg is recommended by the National Osteoporosis Foundation and National Academy of Sciences for those between ages 9 and 18, about 1,000 mg between ages 19 and 50, and 1,200 mg post-menopause.

For optimal health: 1,000 to 1,500 mg/day of calcium.

Best natural food sources: Cheese, milk, and yogurt.

Fortified foods: Orange juice, rice, and tofu (made with calcium sulfate).

Minimum toxic dose: 2,500 mg/day of calcium or more may cause nausea; vomiting; low blood pressure; irregular heartbeat; kidney stones; impaired absorption of iron, zinc, and magnesium.

SELECTED STUDIES

- A February 2002 study published in *Stroke* suggests that there could be too much of a good thing. In the first study of its kind, researchers from the Netherlands showed that people who get strokes typically have higher amounts of calcium in their coronary arteries.

- Two studies published in the November 1999 issue of *The American Journal of Therapeutics* suggest that calcium citrate supplements such as Citracel help stop bone loss better than calcium carbonate supplements. That's because they absorb calcium about 25 percent better, researchers found.

- An analysis of fourteen studies found that adding 300 mg of calcium daily in the form of supplements or the equivalent of one 8-ounce glass of milk decreased bone fractures in susceptible populations from 25 percent to 70 percent, reports the September 1997 issue of the *Journal of Bone Mineral Research*. These results were likely to be an underestimate of calcium's true effect because of inaccurate measurement of dietary calcium in the observational studies, said researchers.

GO FIGURE: HOW MUCH CALCIUM IN MY SUPPLEMENT?

All calcium supplements don't provide equal amounts of absorbable calcium. The lower the absorption rate, the more you need to take to get an adequate supply. Never take bone meal, oyster shell, or dolomite; these supplements can contain lead and other toxic metals.

Type of Calcium	% Absorption
Calcium citrate	74%
Calcium carbonate	40%
Calcium phosphate	32%
Calcium lactate	18%
Calcium gluconate	9%

Source: Adapted from the *Journal of Bone Mineral Research,* 1989

Magnesium

A special region in Greece, Magnesia, was frequently visited in ancient times because of the magical powers within a salty, white powder. Ever heard of "Milk of Magnesia"? Magnesium works as an antacid in small doses and as a laxative in large amounts. This multipurpose mineral is also what early photographers used to create light flashes before the days of flashcubes or electronic flashes.

Magnesium is the trigger that activates more than 300 enzymes and assists in several important metabolic functions. It plays a role in the production and transport of energy and for the contraction and relaxation of muscles. Magnesium is involved in the synthesis of protein, and it assists in the functioning of certain enzymes in the body.

It's important for heart health because it works as a signal for muscles to contract and relax; when the muscles that line major blood vessels contract, it impacts your blood pressure. Magnesium helps just about every other chemical in your body do its job.

Since the 1960s, researchers have known that people who live in areas where the water is "hard" often have lower rates of heart disease and stroke. ("Hard" water contains more calcium, magnesium, and other minerals than "soft" water.) But the amount of magnesium in hard water is typically no more than 3 to 20 mg per liter—less than 10 percent of what people get from a day's intake of food.

Why you need it: Magnesium builds bones, forms proteins, helps release energy stored in muscles, and regulates body temperature.

For optimal health: 300 to 500 mg/day of magnesium.

Best natural food sources: No food provides even 25 percent of the RDA in one serving. Foods that provide 10 to 24 percent of the RDA include whole grains, broccoli, spinach, skin-on potatoes, dry beans, dry peas, lentils, nuts, nut butters, pumpkin seeds, nonfat yogurt, and halibut.

Fortified foods: None.

Minimum toxic dose: Not known, but too much from supplements may cause nausea, vomiting, low blood pressure, muscle weakness, or irregular heartbeat.

SELECTED STUDIES

- Two studies published in *The Lancet* in 2001 helped verify what has long been suspected—magnesium plays a role in Chronic Fatigue Syndrome. The researchers found that those with CFS typically have low levels of magnesium, which may help explain how the disease originates. Other research has shown that magnesium supplementation can help those with chronic fatigue.

- A study of 16 healthy people who were placed on magnesium-deficient diets became less insulin sensitive. Their insulin became less effective at getting sugar from their blood into their cells. A high percentage of type 2 diabetics have a deficiency of magnesium inside their cells (*Hypertension*, 1993). Insulin sensitivity is one of the first steps that can lead to diabetes. No one knows which comes first—the diabetes or the magnesium deficiency. It's not clear whether magnesium supplements can help diabetes.

- The Atherosclerosis Risk in Communities Study (ARIC) has been following about 14,000 middle-aged people for up to seven years. They found that men and women with the lowest levels of magnesium in their blood at the start of the study were twice as likely to be diagnosed later with diabetes as those with the highest levels of magnesium (*Diabetes*, September 1997). Magnesium and insulin need each other. Without magnesium, your pancreas won't secrete enough insulin—or the insulin it secretes won't be efficient enough—to control your blood sugar. And without insulin, magnesium doesn't get transported from your blood into your cells, where it does most of its work.

Phosphorus

Phosphorus is second only to its mineral relative calcium in abundance in your body. Like calcium, phosphorus helps build strong bones and teeth.

Do you consume soft drinks or take antacids that contain aluminum hydroxide? Check the ingredient list. If you find it listed on the label, you might be disrupting your body's delicate calcium/phosphorus balance. Too much aluminum hydroxide may decrease your absorption of phosphorus, and that can lead to weakened bones. Processed foods are another culprit, frequently adding phosphorus-containing preservatives to your diet. Milk provides the best ratio of phosphorus to calcium.

Why you need it: Phosphorus builds bones and teeth; helps release energy from protein, fat, and carbohydrates during metabolism; forms genetic material, cell membranes, and many enzymes.

For optimal health: 800 to 1,200 mg/day of phosphorus.

Best natural food sources: Ground beef, carp, mackerel, salmon (canned), swordfish, milk, and low-fat or nonfat yogurt.

Fortified foods: None.

Minimum toxic dose: 12,000 mg/day of phosphorus or more may cause shortness of breath, irregular heartbeat, or seizures.

Electrolytes

Chloride

You may not know much about chloride alone, but it's part of a famous couple known as table salt (sodium chloride). Adults typically need a minimum of 750 mg of chloride a day. Part of that goes to form hydrochloric acid—better known as stomach acid. This caustic compound is what helps you break down food so individual nutrients can be absorbed and used by the body.

Why you need it: Chloride regulates cell fluids, aids the digestion of food, helps nutrient absorption, and helps to transmit nerve impulses.

For optimal health: 750 mg/day (the amount found in ¼ teaspoon of table salt), more if you exercise.

Best natural food sources: Table salt and salted foods.

Fortified foods: None.

Minimum toxic dose: Not known, but too much may cause weakness, confusion, increased blood pressure, or coma.

Potassium

It takes a minimum of 2,000 mg of potassium a day—the amount found in four bananas—to aid digestion and make protein. Often, leg cramps result from a potassium deficiency. When your muscles cramp they're screaming, "I'm tired, hungry, and need to rest!" Cramps actually force your muscles to remain inactive until they have a chance to recover. Potassium also affects blood pressure by relaxing the artery walls, which is why this nutrient is so important in managing high blood pressure. Relaxed walls allow blood to flow through smoothly, and that helps keep your blood pressure low.

Why you need it: Potassium helps muscles to contract; maintains fluid and electrolyte balance; helps send nerve impulses; releases energy from protein, carbohydrates, and fat during metabolism.

For optimal health: 2,000 to 6,000 mg/day of potassium.

Best natural food sources: 100 percent bran cereal, apricots (dried), bananas, orange juice, peaches (dried), prune juice, chard, plantains, potatoes, pumpkin, spinach, squash, tomatoes (cooked), tomato juice, pork, veal, carp, catfish, cod, flounder, mullet, black beans, kidney beans, lima beans, soybeans, lentils, dry peas (cooked), milk, and yogurt.

Fortified foods: None.

Minimum toxic dose: Not established; but amounts over 18,000 mg a day can lead to cardiac arrest. Even lower amounts may cause increased heart rate, low blood pressure, convulsions, or paralysis of limbs.

SELECTED STUDIES

- A 1996 Johns Hopkins and National Institutes of Health analysis of 33 clinical trials on more than 2,600 individuals found that those with high blood pressure who consumed an extra 2,000 mg or more of potassium lowered blood pressure a small but significant amount.

- In October 2000, the FDA authorized the use of health claim labeling on foods containing potassium that state: "Diets containing foods that are good sources of potassium and low in sodium may reduce the risk of high blood pressure and stroke." To qualify, a serving of these foods must contain at least 350 mg of potassium and less than 140 mg of sodium.

Sodium

If you ate only unprocessed foods and added no table salt, you'd still get enough sodium to meet normal needs. Just 400 to 500 mg of sodium is enough to keep body fluids and blood pressure in balance. Of course, if you are extremely active, or lose fluids due to fever, prolonged diarrhea, or vomiting, you need extra sodium. That's why soup, broth, and saltine crackers are frequently recommended during illness.

Sodium is the nutrient most frequently associated as a villain in blood pressure. High blood pressure, or hypertension, affects about 50 million Americans—one in four adults. It's the leading cause of stroke and contributes to heart attack, heart failure, and kidney failure. Some Americans, including smokers, the obese, people older than age 70, and African-Americans, have a particularly high risk from high blood pressure.

Sodium is just one factor that is believed to affect blood pressure. Various controlled intervention trials and observational studies show that cutting back moderately on sodium helps lower blood pressure. The catch is that some individuals have a much greater blood pressure response to salt than others. About half of those with high blood pressure are "salt sensitive." But only 10 percent of the total American population fall into this category. As yet, we can't predict if you're salt sensitive until you develop high blood pressure and reduce your intake. Since there is no harm in moderately cutting back on dietary sodium—and in fact, may be helpful in losing weight—it's generally recommended. There's also a theory that a high level of sodium over time is what causes rising blood pressure as the body ages. So if your blood pressure is normal now, cutting back to a reasonable amount of sodium may help keep it that way.

The Great Sodium Debate

Figuring out what a "reasonable" amount of sodium is has turned out to be a major public health debate. Many public and private organizations say Americans should consume no more than 2,400 mg of sodium a day. That equals about 6 grams or 1½ teaspoons of salt (sodium chloride). The most recent U.S. Dietary Guidelines for Americans

LINK UP to *http://www.nhlbi.nih. gov* for the National Heart, Lung, and Blood Institute site, for the latest information and research on blood pressure.

and the 2000 Dietary Guidelines for Healthy American Adults, from the American Heart Association, both suggest a limit of 2,400 mg.

It's hard to consume fewer than 5,000 mg of sodium if you rely on processed convenience foods and/or often eat meals away from home. Take a look at the sodium content of McDonald's items on the next page. Do you have high blood pressure? Are you at risk for high blood pressure because it runs in your family? If your answer is yes to either of these questions, it's worthwhile to consider ways to eat less sodium. However, if you have more pressing areas to work on —maintaining a healthy weight, changing your fat intake—don't make lowering sodium your primary focus.

Salt Sense

Salt is an acquired taste. The more you eat, the more you want. Savvy salt sleuths know that you can't tell the sodium content of a food by the way it tastes. Salt that is added to foods after cooking provides a huge amount of flavor. That's because the salt is placed right on your taste buds when it goes into your mouth. Salt or sodium-based seasonings that are cooked into food or added as preservatives don't have the same dramatic effect. The bottom line: If you need to add salt, do it at the table, not in cooking. *Look at these shocking comparisons...*

Why you need it: Sodium regulates fluid balance and helps keep your blood pH normal, regulates blood pressure, and helps send nerve impulses.

WHERE'S THE SALT IN YOUR FAVORITE FAST FOODS?

McDonald's Item	mg of Sodium	Fascinating Facts
French fries, regular size	135	Yes, these fries were salted after frying.
Milkshake, small chocolate or vanilla	250	The sodium in your shake is from added preservatives.
Hamburger, regular	580	The condiments—catsup and pickle—supply most of the sodium here.
Quarter Pounder	820	More condiments and more bread mean more sodium.
Bacon, Egg, and Cheese Biscuit	1,310	Yes, it's the highest-sodium item on the menu.

Source: Adapted from McDonald's Corporation, 1998

For optimal health: 2,400 mg a day—about 1 teaspoon.

Best natural food sources: All foods contain some sodium.

Fortified foods: Most processed foods have moderate to high amounts of added sodium; highly processed foods can have extremely high amounts of added sodium.

Minimum toxic dose: Not known; varies by person and health status. May cause fluid retention; swelling; and for those individuals who are sodium sensitive, may raise blood pressure.

SELECTED STUDIES

- After reviewing nearly two decades' worth of study, researchers reported in the Dec. 1, 1999 issue of the *Journal of the American Medical Association* what most experts already suspected—"high sodium intake is strongly and independently associated with an increased risk of cardiovascular disease and all cause mortality in overweight persons." *Their advice:* Cut back on salt and sodium-rich foods, especially if you're prone to overweight, hypertension, or heart disease.

- The lower the amount of sodium in your diet, the lower the blood pressure—for both people with and without hypertension, concludes a 2000 study by National Heart, Lung, and Blood Institute (NHLBI). The lowest sodium level tested, which produced the lowest blood pressure, was well below the currently recommended intake of 2,400 mg a day.

- The Dietary Approaches to Stop Hypertension (DASH), an ongoing study on how diet affects blood pressure, has consistently found that the best way for people with high blood pressure to reduce their risk is to consume a diet lower in fat and higher in vegetables, fruits, and low-fat dairy foods.

However, the greatest blood pressure reduction has occurred in those following the so-called "DASH diet" at the lowest levels of sodium.

- Researchers conducting the Trial of Non-pharmacologic Interventions in the Elderly (TONE) found that elderly patients could reduce their levels of hypertension medicine by reducing their dietary salt intake. This report, in the *American Journal of Cardiology* in December 1998, indicates that dietary measures are not effective in treating high blood pressure but can be more healthful and less expensive.

Trace Elements

Iron

Just as iron helps form the skeleton of a skyscraper, it helps support your strength and vitality. Although it was believed in the mid-1990s that excess amounts of iron might lead to heart disease, studies had not supported that belief.

But there is such a thing as iron overload—and a 1998 study in *Annals of Internal Medicine* says it is more common than previously believed. A condition called hereditary hemochromatosis, which affects about one and one-half million Americans, is a genetic defect that causes absorption and storage of iron at levels well above normal. There are no obvious side effects until iron stores in the brain, heart, liver, and pancreas begin to cause organ failure. Early symptoms usually don't appear until the age of thirty.

Still, the Centers for Disease Control estimates that 10 percent of the U.S. population is iron-deficient—especially women, who typically lose iron stores during menstruation. Statistics show that many women fall about 3 grams short of the recommended 15 mg a day. And it's almost impossible for

pregnant or breast-feeding women to meet their increased iron requirements. Before birth, a baby has just nine months to store up enough iron to last until it's time to start solid foods. Breast milk is naturally low in iron. New moms also need to replace iron stores that were depleted during pregnancy and to make up for the additional blood lost during delivery and recovery from the birthing process. Women with heavy menstrual blood losses may need the same high levels of iron (30 mg/day) as pregnant women.

Iron is found in both animal and plant foods. There's no dispute that heme sources of iron in meat are much better absorbed than nonheme plant iron. However, if you eat a food high in vitamin C with a plant food that contains iron, you can dramatically increase absorption of this mineral. For example, add some orange sections to your spinach salad or mix red or green peppers into your favorite bean dish. Lug out your old cast-iron cooking skillets. Cast-iron pots and pans add a small but significant amount of iron to the foods cooked in them. Yes, some iron (a 2 to 4 percent total increase) from the pan is deposited into your food during cooking.

Why you need it: Iron carries oxygen throughout the body in both blood and muscle tissue.

For optimal health: 10 to 30 mg/day of iron. Lower levels are for children, men, and postmenopausal women. Higher levels are for women with heavy periods or those who are pregnant or breast-feeding.

Best natural food sources: Beef, clams, oysters, and soybeans (cooked).

Fortified foods: Bread, pasta, white rice, ready-to-eat cereals, farina, and oatmeal.

Minimum toxic dose: 30 mg/day of iron or more may cause constipation, stomach upset, abdominal pain, or bloody diarrhea. In children, toxic doses can be severe enough to cause convulsions, coma, or death.

Chromium

The mineral chromium is the same stuff that makes old-fashioned car bumpers shiny. It also helps you shine—helping to regulate insulin. For a while, it was touted as a weight-loss aid, partly because a 1989 study found that college athletes who took 200 micrograms daily lost more weight than those on the same diet and exercise regimen who took a placebo. However, additional studies have not proven it offers any help in losing weight. Still, some experts recommend a daily chromium supplement of about 400 mcg for diabetics to help improve symptoms of that disease.

Borderline chromium deficiency is thought to be common, especially in older people. There seems to be a connection between chromium deficiency and the high rates of diabetes as you age. It might be linked to the fact that diets high in simple sugars tend to increase chromium losses. But that doesn't mean that high-sugar diets cause diabetes. Almost all adult-onset diabetes is caused by weight gain. Getting adequate amounts of chromium may decrease insulin injection doses and improve how certain diabetics handle glucose. If you want to know more about chromium picolinate or alternative supplements, see Chapter 7 for details.

Why you need it: Chromium works with insulin to help your body use glucose and maintain normal blood sugar levels.

For optimal health: 50 to 200 mcg/day of chromium; higher for those with diabetes.

Best natural food sources: Brewer's yeast, corn on the cob, beef, apples, sweet potato, eggs, and prunes.

Fortified foods: None.

Minimum toxic dose: None known from dietary sources. Long-term environmental exposure from electroplating, steel manufacturing, cement manufacturing, glass and jewelry making, photography, textile dyeing, and wood preserving may cause skin problems, liver and kidney damage, or cancer.

Copper

If your water pipes are made of copper, you're probably getting about 5 percent of your daily copper intake from drinking water. That means the rest must come from nutrient-rich foods. Copper's main priority is to aid breathing. It works to help regulate the absorption and release of iron. Copper and iron are good buddies; they rely on each other being there to work efficiently.

Why you need it: Copper helps form hemoglobin; keeps bones, blood vessels, and nerves healthy.

For optimal health: 2 to 3 mg/day of copper.

Best natural food sources: Barley, crab, lobster, and oysters.

Fortified foods: None.

Minimum toxic dose: 20 mg/day of copper or more may cause anemia, muscle aches, nausea, vomiting, liver damage, or coma. Wilson's disease, an inherited disorder, causes excess copper accumulation in body tissues. Treatment requires a low-copper diet and medication to bind copper before it can be absorbed.

SELECTED STUDIES

Researchers suspect that a copper deficiency may reduce your immunity. An animal study in the May 1998 issue of *American Journal of*

Clinical Nutrition found that even marginal deficiencies could make one more susceptible to disease and infection. Remember that taking too much zinc can cause a copper deficiency.

Fluoride

Do you have a mouthful of gleaming silver fillings proving you grew up without benefit of fluoridated water? For more than 60 years, the dental benefits of fluoride have been known. If you drank fluoridated water as a child, you have 50 to 70 percent fewer cavities than your peers who didn't have fluoride. Yet there are still naysayers who think fluoridated water is the cause of many cancers.

The biggest source of fluoride is usually the local water supply. Half of all U.S. water supplies are fluoridated. Those that aren't are homes that rely on well water or nonmunicipal water sources. Most bottled water does not contain fluoride. Low doses of fluoride are beneficial to the dental health of adults as well as children. If you don't know if your water is fluoridated, call your local water department to find out. A typical amount added is 0.7 to 1.2 mg per liter of water. The American Academy of Pediatrics recommends that all breast-fed infants and babies using reconstituted formula in households where the water is not fluoridated start supplements at 6 months.

Many experts recommend continuing with supplements until age 16, especially if you drink and cook exclusively with unfluoridated tap or bottled water. Unlike most nutrient supplements, fluoride is available only by prescription from your doctor or dentist.

Why you need it: Fluoride hardens tooth enamel and protects teeth from decay; strengthens bone.

For optimal health: 1.5 to 4 mg/day of fluoride.

Best natural food sources: Not widely found in foods and varies with soil content where foods are grown.

Fortified foods: Municipal drinking water (check with your local water supplier).

Minimum toxic dose: 10 mg/day of fluoride or more may cause stomach cramps, vomiting, diarrhea, and tremors. Long-term high doses cause mottled teeth, brittle bones, and increased frequency of broken bones. Toothpaste with fluoride should be spit out and not swallowed; only use a pea-size amount for children.

Iodine

Iodine is known as a micronutrient, for good reason. The average person needs only a teaspoon of it over the course of an entire lifetime. But if you don't get even that small amount, it can cause big trouble. "Lack of iodine is the world's leading cause of preventable mental retardation and can cause population-wide drops in IQ in areas where deficiency is common," according to Dr. Glen Maberly of the Rollins School of Public Health at Emory University.

However, deficiency isn't the problem for most people. The FDA estimates that most American adults consume 500 to 800 milligrams per day—more than four times the recommended amount.

Where does this iodine come from? Iodized salt is the most recognizable source, so it stands to reason that high-salt foods are big contributors. *For instance…*

- A Big Mac Value Meal has almost three times the adult RDA for iodine.

- A frozen fried chicken dinner can have from 6 to 29 times the recommended intake.

- Multivitamin supplements that use red food color #3 (which is more than 50 percent iodine) may have 100 to 150 more mg of iodine than is noted on the label. That's because when an ingredient in a product is included as an additive (a coloring agent in this example), the manufacturer isn't required to include nutrients it may add. Since two other red dyes have been banned, the use of red food color #3 has increased more than 50 percent.

- Dairy foods contribute almost 40 percent of all the iodine we eat. Cow teats, farm machinery, and processing equipment are all sanitized and cleaned with iodine-containing chemicals.

- Food processors often use iodine-based chemicals for cleaning and sanitizing. According to the FDA, significant amounts of iodine end up in foods like grains, cereals, sugars, jellies, and puddings.

This overconsumption of iodine has been blamed for the declining success in treating people with hyperthyroidism. Treatment today is only 17 percent effective, compared to 60 percent successful treatment with antithyroid medications a generation ago. People with Hashimoto's thyroiditis can have their thyroid function blocked if they get too much iodine. Iodine-containing asthma medications used by mothers during pregnancy have caused goiters in newborns.

The bottom line: If you eat a lot of processed foods, you might be better off with plain salt. If you avoid processed foods and are frugal with the salt shaker, choose iodized salt from the grocery shelf.

Why you need it: Iodine helps your body form thyroid hormones, which are vital to physical growth and development. Thyroid hormones control metabolism; improve mental functioning; and give you healthier hair, skin, nails, and teeth.

For optimal health: 150 mcg/day of iodine.

Best natural food sources: Not widely found in foods and varies with soil content where foods are grown. Saltwater fish and seafood provide modest amounts of iodine.

Fortified foods: Iodized table salt; food processors use iodized salt and sanitizing solutions that contribute iodine indirectly to foods.

Minimum toxic dose: 2 mg/day of iodine or more may cause irregular heartbeat, confusion, goiter (swollen neck or throat), and bloody or tarry stools.

Selenium

In 1979, researchers first described an association between selenium deficiency and heart-muscle disease. Often called cardiomyopathy, selenium deficiency causes enlargement of the heart and heart failure. It primarily affects women in their childbearing years and children. Today, this trace mineral is best known as being among the "antioxidants" that protect cells against the effects of free radicals that are produced during normal oxygen metabolism. Like many other minerals, it's found in plant foods, as well as meats and seafood (since animals eat selenium-containing plants).

Some studies suggest that lung, colorectal, and prostate cancer rates are lower in people with higher selenium blood levels, but the research is inconclusive. However, it's generally acknowledged that a selenium deficiency during pregnancy can have irreversible effects on your baby's development and growth.

Why you need it: Selenium works as an antioxidant with vitamin E.

For optimal health: 55 to 200 mcg/day of selenium.

Best natural food sources: Salmon and haddock. Accurate levels of selenium in cultivated foods are not available as selenium content varies with the soil levels of this mineral.

Fortified foods: None.

Minimum toxic dose: 700 mcg/day of selenium or more from inorganic sodium selenite may cause hair loss, fingernail loss, fatigue, nausea, or nerve damage.

Manganese

Manganese isn't a glamorous nutrient, but it is shrouded in mystery. We don't know much about manganese because few scientists are interested in studying it. The first reported deficiency of manganese was not noted until 1972.

Why you need it: Manganese is a vital part of many enzymes; promotes normal growth and development.

For optimal health: 2.5 to 5.0 mg/day of manganese.

Best natural food sources: Whole grains, pineapple, strawberries, lentils, kale, tea.

Fortified foods: None.

Minimum toxic dose: Not known, but large doses may cause depression, delusions, hallucinations, impotence, or insomnia and may interfere with iron absorption.

Molybdenum

If you haven't heard of molybdenum, don't worry. It's the least known of all essential minerals. It's also among one of the scarcest minerals found in the earth's crust.

Why you need it: Molybdenum promotes normal growth and development, aids in enzyme conversion of uric acid, and helps iron metabolism.

For optimal health: 75 to 250 mcg/day of molybdenum.

Best natural food sources: Leafy dark green vegetables, legumes, and milk.

Fortified foods: Breads and cold cereals.

Minimum toxic dose: 1 mg/day of molybdenum or more may cause excessive loss of copper in urine; 10 to 15 mg per day may cause gout-like symptoms.

Zinc

Your body naturally contains about the same amount of zinc as a 4-inch galvanized nail, and it's found in nearly every cell. Unlike other trace minerals, zinc is not stored in the body but acts as a functioning nutrient to stimulate the activity of about 100 different enzymes. Zinc is a party animal—it likes to circulate and doesn't take time to rest.

Zinc is needed for wound healing and supports healthy immunity—that's why it's sometimes touted as a nutrient important in protecting against colds. Even a mild zinc deficiency can increase your risk of infection. Stomach acid is important for zinc efficiency. Medications or health problems that decrease available stomach acid may limit absorption of zinc. If you have children who like to put coins in their mouths, beware of newer U.S. pennies. The zinc now added to pennies poses a new risk for stomach ulcers if a child (or anyone) swallows them.

Getting the right amount of zinc is similar to walking a tightrope. It's a fine line between too much and not enough—with hazards for any missteps. Loading up with zinc for more than a week can weaken your immune system, lower your HDL (good) cholesterol, and trigger a copper deficiency. Tumor cells demand zinc for growth, and when the supply is plentiful they thrive. If you have cancer, zinc supplements are usually not recommended. Pesky skin conditions, including dandruff flaking and psoriasis, speed up zinc losses. Since zinc is such a circulator, you lose it when your skin rubs off or you comb that "flaky white stuff" out of your hair. If you substantially increase your calcium intake, you may need more zinc. Vegetarians sometimes have a hard time getting enough zinc. That's because soy foods and whole grains are high in substances that are natural inhibitors of zinc absorption. Zinc found in animal foods, especially red meat, seafood, and eggs, is absorbed up to four times more effectively than zinc found in plant foods.

Why you need it: Zinc forms protein in the body; helps wound healing, blood formation, and general growth and maintenance of all tissues. It is part of many enzymes and is essential for most metabolic processes. Zinc also maintains normal taste and smell sensations.

For optimal health: 3 to 20 mg/day of zinc; people who take extra calcium and copper supplements need the higher levels. Don't take extra zinc without a doctor's supervision.

Best natural food sources: Beef, lamb, oysters, pork, and veal.

Fortified foods: Most fortified ready-to-eat cereals, hot and cold, contain about 10 percent of the RDA.

Minimum toxic dose: 30 mg/day of zinc or more may cause drowsiness, nausea, vomiting, diarrhea, impaired coordination, or restlessness; weaken the immune system; lower HDL (good) cholesterol; decrease copper and iron levels.

SELECTED STUDIES

Some research indicates that zinc may reduce the duration of a cold. Although not conclusively proven, one study at the Cleveland Clinic found that cold duration was halved among those who took zinc gluconate–glycine lozenges every two hours compared to those taking a placebo. That study, in the June 1998 issue of *Journal of the American Medical Association,* led to more studies, but the results have been mixed.

LINK UP to *http://nutrition.about.com/library/blmicronutrients.htm* for complete reference information on each mineral.

DUELING MINERALS

If you take too much of one vitamin or mineral, it can decrease your ability to absorb other nutrients. Here are some of the most common interactions:

If you take too much:	You might become deficient in:
Calcium	Magnesium, Iron, and Zinc
Copper	Zinc
Iron	Phosphorus and Zinc
Manganese	Iron
Molybdenum	Copper and Zinc
Phosphorus	Calcium
Zinc	Copper

MINERAL NEEDS FOR SPECIAL SITUATIONS

Nutrient	Highest Federal Standard (RDA or DV)	Optimal Intake	Individuals with Special Needs*
Calcium	1,000–1,200 mg	1,000–1,500 mg	Milk avoiders, those on very low-calorie diets, and people over 55—especially postmenopausal women
Phosphorus	700–1,200 mg	800–1,200 mg	People with kidney disease or problems of the digestive tract
Magnesium	310–420 mg	350–500 mg	People over 70, very active individuals, diabetics, and those on very low-calorie diets
Iron	15 mg	10–30 mg	Women with heavy menstrual blood losses and those on very low-calorie diets
Zinc	15 mg	15–25 mg	People over 70, some vegetarians, very active adults, and diabetics
Iodine	150 mcg	Not known	Not known
Copper	1.5–3 mg	2–3 mg	Premature babies and people who take large amounts of vitamin C or zinc from supplements
Manganese	2–5 mg	Not known	Those on very low-calorie diets
Fluoride	3.2–3.8 mg	2–4 mg	People who don't have fluoridated water, especially children 6 months to 16 years old
Chromium	50–200 mcg	50–200 mg	Those over 70 and people on very low-calorie diets
Molybdenum	75–250 mcg	Not known	Not known
Selenium	70 mcg	100–200 mg	Women in their childbearing years and children

Note: Pregnant and breast-feeding women, alcoholics, and drug abusers have increased needs for most nutrients.

Supplement Scenarios

There are a variety of ways to optimize your intake of important nutrients.

1. Don't supplement. Eat a wide variety of fruits, vegetables, and grains every day. Choose skim or low-fat milk and dairy products for adequate calcium. Eat lean red meat and seafood at least several times a week for their high mineral contents.

2. Take vitamin E and/or calcium supplements daily. It's almost impossible to get optimal amounts of vitamin E from foods. If you can't or won't drink milk or eat other calcium-rich foods, a calcium supplement is worth considering.

3. Take a multivitamin and mineral supplement daily. If you are making smart food choices, the extra amounts in a multivitamin will push you toward the optimal amounts of most nutrients.

4. Take a multivitamin and mineral supplement, along with vitamin E and calcium, if you need them. ❦

7

ALTERNATIVE SUPPLEMENTS

Many alternative supplements are drugs—they're just regulated differently. In fact, over-the-counter vitamins, herbs, and other supplements are considered "food products" by the Food and Drug Administration, and therefore don't place their manufacturers under the same rigors in proving health benefits. So even though a product has been popular and on the market for years, it doesn't mean it's safe or effective. How much do you really know about the supplements you take? People usually spend more time researching their next car or computer purchase than selecting their supplements.

Don't be afraid to call a manufacturer's toll-free number and ask questions. The National Council for Responsible Health Information (formerly the National Council Against Health Fraud) investigated performance-enhancing claims made by supplement companies. *Here's what they found...*

- Misrepresentation: Often manufacturers use information that is not 100 percent accurate. Advertising and public relations firms frequently determine what claims and slogans to use.

- Research currently underway: When asked for research data, many companies say they are in the process of conducting research. If they can't or won't give specific details or put you in touch with researchers, be wary.

- Not for public review: When you are denied access to documentation for label and marketing claims, it's likely they don't have any.

- Testimonials: Everybody loves a good story. Celebrities, sports personalities, and even politicians have been used in this popular sales technique. Testimonials are usually paid endorsements.

- Patent or patent pending: The manufacturer thinks the product is unique or special. It may be. That doesn't mean it is effective or safe.

- Inappropriately referenced material: A lengthy list of research studies looks impressive. Often studies cited are poorly designed, don't prove anything, have never been published or reviewed, don't relate to the topic, or may not even exist.

All the products in this chapter have one thing in common: They are relatively new supplements. They don't have the history of herbal products or the wealth of investigation and research supporting many of the vitamins and minerals. This doesn't make them bad; we just know less about how they may or may not act to improve or impair health.

Amino Acids

Regardless of what the supplement ads say, extra protein or amino acids—called the "building blocks of protein"—will not increase your muscle mass or improve athletic performance. Because amino acids compete with each other for absorption, too much of one substance can decrease absorption and utilization of others. In 1974, amino acid supplements were removed from the Food and Drug Administration's GRAS (Generally Recognized As Safe) list. Currently the only approved use for amino acids is as part of medical foods such as intravenous feedings for people who need special formulas because of health problems like kidney or liver disease.

Most amino acid supplements are made from egg protein or animal protein. They can be readily purchased as capsules, tablets, and powders. Small amounts of protein foods like milk, meat, or eggs can supply significantly more amino acids at a fraction of the cost of supplements.

SELECTED STUDIES
Research on U.S. Marine officer candidates showed that marines who were given amino acid supplements performed exactly the same—before, during, and after the study—as those who were given a placebo *(Medicine and Science in Sports,* April 1996). If it doesn't work for "America's best," it won't work for you.

Arginine
This amino acid has been proclaimed by its promoters as "being able to cause weight loss overnight." The stimulation of growth hormone is the supposed action that causes you to shed pounds while you dream of getting thin on *arginine* (ARE-gin-een). While it's true that arginine can stimulate the secretion of growth hormone, it must be taken in massive amounts—more than can be found in commercial supplements. But the growth hormone doesn't have anything to do with weight loss. As far back as 1978 arginine (along with cystine, treonine, tyrosine, leucine, methionine, phenylalanine, and valine to name just a few) was investigated by a scientific panel and was found to be worthless as a weight loss aid. It has also been marketed as an impotence aid, but studies don't back up these claims. And since it boosts nitric oxide, a compound that relaxes blood vessels, some marketers have promoted it as a treatment for angina and other cardiovascular problems. While it may offer some benefit, findings have been mixed.

Still, some research suggests it may offer other health benefits.

A Mayo Clinic study published in the July 1999 issue of *Circulation* found that the dietary supplement L-arginine improved chest pain symptoms in patients with early heart disease. People who took an L-arginine pill every day for six months had significantly less chest pain and improved coronary blood flow than those who took a placebo. Investigators studied 26 participants without significant heart disease and reported that improvements began after one week of use and continued for the six-month study. It's thought that L-arginine, through a series of chemical reactions, acts on the lining of blood vessels to relax the vessel wall and may inhibit the buildup of platelets and plaques. And several studies in the *Journal of Urology* from 1998 to 2000 found that oral L-arginine (1,500 mg daily) may decrease pain and urgency in some people with cystitis.

L-tryptophan

L-tryptophan (el-TRIP-toe-fan) is perhaps the most infamous of all supplements. Best known as the ingredient in turkey and milk that helps promote sleep, pills containing this amino acid were marketed as a solution for people with insomnia, because it converts into serotonin, which in turn is converted into melatonin, a sleep aid. However, despite the claims it has not been proven effective, and more than 1,200 individuals who took tryptophan developed a painful connective tissue and blood disease called eosinophilia-myalgia syndrome. At least 38 people died from exposure to a contaminant in the supplement. A variant of tryptophan is now sold as 5-HTP and may also be contaminated with an impurity known as "peak X." Contamination of supplements is common, says Roseanne Philen, an epidemiologist with the Centers for Disease Control. Some supplements have contaminants added deliberately. Herbal remedies may be laced with real drugs to give them an extra punch. For example, arthritis products spiked with painkillers, tranquilizers, or steroids have been discovered.

However, L-tryptophan is used in Canada along with other medications to treat mental depression and bipolar disorder.

PABA

What's sunscreen doing in my supplement? Para amino benzoic acid (PABA) is best known for its work as a sunscreen. It helps block out skin-damaging ultraviolet rays. It's also an ingredient used by your body to make the vitamin folic acid. Oral PABA supplements won't help you make more folic acid though; only plants and certain bacteria can do that. PABA supplements also won't make you sun-safe from the inside out. If you do take PABA supplements and sulfa antibiotics at the same time, PABA can cancel the antibiotic's effectiveness.

SAM-e

SAM-e (S-adenosyl-methionine) is one of the newest supplements to be stocked on store shelves and claims to help sufferers of osteoarthritis and depression. This compound is produced by your body from the amino acid methionine. With help from vitamin B-12 and folic acid, SAM-e helps with the maintenance of cell membranes, removal of toxic substances from the body, and the production of mood-enhancing neurotransmitters such as noradrenaline, serotonin, and possibly dopamine, according to recent marketing claims.

SAM-e has been used for two decades in Europe to treat osteoarthritis and depression. It first was discovered in the 1950s at the National Institutes of Health. In the 1970s, an Italian lab learned to produce it in cell cultures, and studied its use as an antidepressant. Some of the first patients who were given SAM-e for depression also suffered with osteoarthritis. The anti-arthritic potential of SAM-e was realized when some people reported relief from their joint pain as well as their depression. SAM-e may work by rebuilding worn-down joint cartilage through increasing production of a substance called proteoglycans. SAM-e has few, if any, known side effects. And some claim it is a faster-acting anti-depressant than prescription medications or other over-the-counter supplements such as St. John's wort.

How effective is it? According to the department of Health and Human Services, it seems promising…but more research is needed. In October 2002, researchers at the Agency for Healthcare Research and Quality (AHRQ), an arm of HHS, reviewed 102 various studies on SAM-e, including 47 depression studies, 14 osteoarthritis studies, and 41 liver disease studies. For each ailment, they found that SAM-e was statistically superior to placebo and performed similarly—not better or worse—than conventional prescription and OTC medications. *The bottom line:* It may help, but with a month's supply costing close to $100, it'll cost you more than other alternatives.

Enzymes

Enzymes are proteins that act like biological spark plugs for chemical reactions in your body. You make more than enough of your own enzymes. In fact, a single cell contains thousands of enzymes, each with a specific job. Taking enzymes in supplement form is useless because enzymes are almost all broken down into their amino acid building blocks during digestion. Enzymes can't provide any biologic benefit when they are broken down. Certain digestive enzymes, like lactase, may be taken orally if you are deficient in that particular enzyme (e.g., lactose intolerant). Digestive enzymes are the only ones that can work and survive in the digestive tract and be used effectively. People with chronic pancreas disease may need to take supplemental digestive enzymes. That's because the pancreas is where these enzymes are manufactured. Because they are protein molecules,

enzymes are inactivated by heat, often at temperatures as low as 115 to 120 degrees F.

CoQ-10

Ubiquone, or CoQ-10, is found in every cell of every plant and animal on earth. Each of your cells contains a miniature power factory called the mitochondrion. This is where the energy your body needs is made. CoQ-10 helps regulate the electrical currents that fuel this factory. Imagine a string of holiday lights. If one of the bulbs doesn't work, the others go out, too. It's CoQ-10's job to get in there and replace any defective or empty sockets to keep the system functioning.

There are many stories about how CoQ-10 can enhance athletic performance or decrease fatigue. A few athletes and coaches firmly believe that CoQ-10 supplementation benefits performance, and the result has been a virtual marketing blitz. However, credible scientific evidence to support these claims is lacking.

However, CoQ-10 is believed to have antioxidant actions similar to those of other fat-soluble antioxidants such as vitamin E, which scavenge free radicals and prevent oxidation of lipids and other molecules that are associated with "aging-related" diseases such as heart disease and cancer. In one recent study, in the October 15, 2002 issue of *Archives of Neurology*, high doses helped slow the progression of Parkinson's disease in some patients by as much as half.

Ergogenic Aids

The quest for more energy, bigger muscles, and less body fat is a popular one. *Ergogenic* (err-go-JEN-ick) aids sometimes help fuel this search. Ergogenic aids are broadly defined as techniques or substances used for enhancing athletic performance. Ergogenic aids include food, supplements, drugs, training methods, or psychological manipulation. They range from use of reasonable techniques such as carbohydrate loading to illegal and unsafe approaches like anabolic-androgenic steroid use.

Protein is the most popular and enduring ergogenic aid. The notion that massive amounts of protein are necessary during training has evolved from ancient beliefs that great strength could be obtained by eating the raw meat of lions, tigers, or other animals that displayed great fighting strength. Although few athletes consume raw meat today, the idea that "you are what you eat" is still widely promoted by food faddists. The problem is that some athletes go too far with ergogenic aids.

Chromium Picolinate

Need to slim down and bulk up at the same time? Patented, pricey, designer-labeled *chromium picolinate* (pick-OH-lin-ate) isn't a better choice than ordinary chromium that's found in food and many multivitamin and mineral supplements. It's true that picolinate is a compound that, when combined with a metal like chromium, enhances the ability of that mineral to get into the body's cells. Chromium picolinate is remarkably stable in the body, which may explain why it is more readily absorbed than chromium obtained through regular dietary sources. But this stability may also allow it to be accumulated in cells in its DNA-damaging form.

The chromium craze started in 1989 when researchers at the U.S. Department of Agriculture reported that 200 mcg of daily chromium supplements dramatically increased lean body mass in college football players during six weeks of resistance training. However, future studies have shown less promising, if any results.

Probably what piques interest in chromium picolinate is the lure of losing fat and gaining muscle tone without any effort. But the studies these claims are loosely based on used crude measures of testing body fat that were not reliable and have not been duplicated by other research. When the USDA Human Nutrition Research Center tried to replicate its own data using sophisticated, state-of-the-art techniques to measure body composition, there was no difference between those who took chromium picolinate for two months and those who did not.

Chromium picolinate does help insulin transfer glucose and other nutrients from the bloodstream to cells. If the glucose doesn't move readily into your cells after eating, it keeps your blood sugar unnecessarily high and can result in diabetes. But any modest reduction caused by chromium picolinate in your blood sugar level isn't enough to bring it back to the normal range.

SELECTED STUDIES

Dr. John Vincent, a University of Alabama researcher, reported at the American Chemical Society's annual meeting in March 1999 that the popular dietary supplement chromium picolinate may damage DNA in living cells, possibly increasing the risk of cancer. Vincent looked at the chemical reaction among vitamin C, other compounds, and chromium picolinate at 100 times less than the concentration found in human body tissue after long-term use. The researchers found that the reaction produces chromium II, which interacts with oxygen to produce hydroxyl radicals, agents known to cause mutations and other types of DNA damage. Careful investigation into the effects of long-term diet supplementation with chromium picolinate is needed. Chromium picolinate supplements that are combined with vitamin C supplements may be the most dangerous.

THE TRUTH ABOUT SPORTS BEVERAGES

Hype: Touted as the ideal replacement for water loss during exercise.

Help: You can replace lost fluids with any liquid, but water is best unless you need or want extra calories. Eating any regular foods after exercise can replace lost sodium and stimulate thirst.

Harm: Constant consumption of sports drinks or any other beverage high in sugar can promote tooth decay if you don't brush your teeth frequently.

ENERGY BARS

Hype: Advertised as instant energizers.

Help: The bars are convenient to carry, but many are only reduced-fat candy bars with some added nutrients.

Harm: None really, except that some bars have close to 500 calories. Be sure to drink plenty of water to help improve nutrient absorption. However, some energy bars now contain herbs that could cause adverse reactions in sensitive individuals.

PROTEIN POWDERS

Hype: Protein and amino acid supplements claim to enhance muscle development.

Help: None. Only physical training builds muscle.

Harm: Too much protein can be harmful and may stress your kidneys and lead to dehydration. Taking individual amino acids can also cause nutrient imbalances. Some protein powders contain added herbs and megadoses of vitamins and minerals.

GOOS AND GELS

Hype: Quick energy (calories) for endurance athletes.

Help: The tubes and packets that hold these products are convenient for long-distance runners and cyclists. Most are nutritionally equivalent to jelly or jam.

Harm: High-priced source of calories. Be sure to drink plenty of fluid when using goos or gels or you could develop cramps.

GLYCEROL

Hype: A way to "hyperhydrate" or store large amounts of water before training or competition.

Help: Glycerol, usually found in fatty foods, chemically attracts and holds water like a sponge.

Harm: May cause bloating and feelings of nausea. While glycerol does enhance fluid retention, there is no proof that this helps endurance or has a positive effect on athletic performance.

SPORT FUEL: NECESSARY OR NOT?

The explosive sports food market beckons elite athletes and everyday exercisers alike. But are these high-tech fuels really necessary for the average person? Probably not, say sports medicine experts. What most athletes need is calories and water, plain and simple.

The Creatine Craze

It's not unusual for high school and college coaches to see several student athletes before practice huddled together measuring out a small amount of a white powdery substance. No, it's not cocaine, it's the other c-word—creatine. Baseball batting demons Mark McGwire and Sammy Sosa helped fuel the creatine craze toward the end of the 1998 slug-fest season when they both admitted using this performance-enhancing potion.

Creatine is found naturally in animal muscle tissue and is named after the Greek word for flesh. Creatine monohydrate is taken up by muscle cells and converted to creatine phosphate, where it is stored until it's needed to make chemical energy. If plenty of creatine isn't available from the foods you eat, it is easily made by the liver and kidneys from a few amino acids (arginine, glycine, and methionine).

When certain athletes supplement with extra amounts of creatine, their muscles can produce more quick energy—but only in highly explosive activities or those with quick repetitive movements. If you need to bat a ball, lift heavy weights, or tackle your opponent to the ground, you might gain a competitive edge with creatine. If you're an endurance athlete such as a distance runner, swimmer, or triathlete, creatine won't help. Use of creatine by nonathletes is senseless.

According to sports nutrition expert Dr. Chris Rosenbloom, a professor at the University of Georgia, creatine supplementation…

- Appears to benefit athletes during high-intensity, intermittent exercise. Improvements are most noticeable in athletes who have low creatine stores (i.e., vegetarian athletes or those who eat little meat).

- May enhance training sessions, allowing athletes to train at higher intensity.

- Is associated with an increase in body mass, with the average weight gain of two to six pounds in as little as a week. It is unclear if the added weight is from extra water held in the muscles or from an increase in muscle mass. Most female athletes avoid this supplement like the plague. Extra pounds are a negative, undesirable side effect for many female athletes, especially those involved in endurance sports.

Most athletes take 20 to 25 grams a day during a weeklong "loading phase," in divided doses of 5 grams taken four or five times a day with food or a carbohydrate-containing beverage. The dose is tapered to 2 to 10 grams daily during the "maintenance phase." Extra water when supplementing with creatine is essential to prevent dehydration. Caffeine may diminish the ergogenic effect of creatine supplementation. Despite this, some of the commonly available powdered drink supplements contain both creatine and caffeine.

Claims of creatine's power have escalated beyond the science to support them. Athletes from a wide variety of sports are loading up with this expensive supplement. No long-term safety studies have been done, and most research is limited to just a few weeks of observation of creatine's effects on the body. That's unfortunate because more young athletes are taking creatine for longer periods of time. Reports in sports magazines and newspapers suggest as many as 25 percent of Major League Baseball players and up to 50 percent of National Football League players have tried creatine.

Some creatine users report increased muscle cramping (especially during exercise in high heat), nausea, and other gastrointestinal disturbances. Creatine supplementation, in the dosages commonly used, results in urine concentrations that are ninety times greater than normal. Since creatine is filtered by the kidneys, there is the potential for significant kidney damage or disease with long-term use.

The bottom line is that no one can confidently state that prolonged creatine supplementation is safe. Use of creatine should be avoided, especially by young athletes, until more is known.

SELECTED STUDIES

German researchers reported in a 1998 issue of *Medicine and Science in Sports & Exercise* that low doses helped boost energy and performance in endurance athletes in low doses. And results from a small crossover random test, in the July 1997 issue of the *Journal of the American Dietetic Association,* showed that after a week of supplementing with creatine monohydrate, muscular performance was increased in athletes during high-intensity resistance exercise. However, both these studies were very short and experts believe that an average person may not get the same type of results as these highly trained athletes.

Hormones

Hormones regulate overall body conditions, such as your blood sugar level (insulin

LINK UP to *http://www.ncaa.org/ sports_sciences/drugtesting/banned _list.html* for a list of all substances banned or restricted for athletes competing under the National Collegiate Athletic Association (NCAA) guidelines.

hormone) and your metabolic rate (thyroid hormone). Hormones are chemical messengers that target specific tissues or organs. Unlike enzymes, not all hormones are made from protein, and they don't start chemical reactions, they just pass messages along. Hormones are highly potent chemical change agents and should not be taken without the recommendation of a health care provider. They are safest when purchased by prescription to ensure purity and quality.

DHEA

If you want something to slow aging, burn fat, build muscle, strengthen your immune system, ward off heart disease, prevent cancer, treat diabetes, delay Alzheimer's, or invigorate your sex life, dehydroepiandrosterone (dee-HI-drow-ep-EE-an-DOS-tur-own), or DHEA, is not the answer.

The FDA banned over-the-counter sales of DHEA in 1985 because of its potentially harmful side effects. Since then, it's reappeared in exactly the same form, as a "dietary supplement," which, of course, doesn't require FDA approval.

When you wake each day, the adrenal glands nestled on top of your kidneys release a form of DHEA into your bloodstream. As it merges into body tissue, DHEA is converted into tiny amounts of the sex hormones testosterone and estrogen. Normal DHEA levels in your body increase sharply at puberty, peak during early adulthood, and then gradually diminish with age until there's practically none left. So doesn't it make sense to add some back to recapture lost youth and vigor?

If you swallow these assumptions, you are risking your health. Not one of the above claims has been proven true in humans. However, there is plenty of evidence about the damage that DHEA can cause. It has been shown to stimulate the enlargement of the prostate gland and to promote prostate cancer in men. In women, high levels of supplemental DHEA are linked to menstrual irregularities, masculinization (facial and body hair growth, deeper voices), and a higher risk of endometrial cancer. If you already have prostate or endometrial cancer, DHEA supplements can make it spread faster. However, it has been shown to help relieve some symptoms of lupus in several studies, including one by Stanford University researchers reported in the Feb 25, 1998 issue of the *Journal of Rheumatology*.

Still, the bottom line: Human hormones are powerful chemicals. Do-it-yourself DHEA hormone therapy is just plain D-U-M-B.

Melatonin Mania

Can't sleep? Have to work the night shift this week? Want a "natural" remedy for jet lag? Melatonin is a naturally occurring hormone that helps regulate sleep. Cued by nightfall, melatonin production begins at dusk and halts each morning as the sun rises. Your pineal gland (found in the brain) is the master controller of this rhythmic hormone that sets your sleeping and waking schedule. If you happen to live in a northern latitude where winter darkness extends beyond your normal wake-up time, you know melatonin's strong grip. Your body correctly senses it's still nighttime when it's dark outside and lures you to stay in bed.

Travelers may be able to decrease jet lag by taking melatonin at strategic times over a period of days and setting the body clock to a new time zone. Research seems to suggest that melatonin may decrease, but not eliminate, jet lag symptoms. Improvements such as decreased sleepiness and less morning tiredness may result.

There are preliminary data suggesting that low-dose melatonin supplements, given at specific times of day, can aid in the treatment of wintertime depression. However, the studies to date are too small and short-term to draw any conclusions.

Other Common Alternatives

A lot of strange and unusual things are taken in the quest for health. Here are some common alternative supplements and what they will and won't do for you.

Bee Pollen

Bees keep busy bringing nectar and pollen to the hive—it's their full-time, lifelong job. They collect the pollen on body hairs, place it in "pollen baskets" on their legs, and then carry it back to the hive to be deposited in the honey cells. Pollen is essential for bees, but what about you? Proponents of bee pollen suggest that it can treat ailments ranging from allergies to fatigue.

Eating "nature's most perfect food" can make you sick. Bee pollen can cause life-threatening allergic reactions in some people, even though it's often promoted as an allergy cure. Some early warning signs include numbness or tingling on the lips or in your mouth. If you have any reactions to eating bee pollen, go directly to the closest emergency room.

Chitosan

Chitosan (KITE-oh-san), like glucoasmine, is nothing more than crushed crab and lobster shells. Indigestible fiber from the shells supposedly binds and absorbs the fat you eat before it has a chance to be metabolized. Believers claim that chitosan can absorb up to six to twelve times its weight in fat, but it also decreases the absorption of the fat-soluble vitamins A, D, E, and K and carotenoids. As with other fat removers or replacers, folks who take chitosan will end up spending more time on the toilet than usual. A few studies done outside the United States show it may have some effect on weight loss, but those studies are not well respected and were not published in peer-reviewed journals. One 1999 study published in the *European Journal of Clinical Nutrition* found that people who took eight chitosan pills daily for four weeks had no more weight loss than a placebo group. No "real" studies have been done in the U.S.

Because crab and lobster shells are a natural substance that can't be patented, there is little financial incentive to conduct extensive studies. Like other products, you can label it a dietary supplement and go to market without FDA approval or review. Also, if you are allergic to shellfish, you can experience similar reactions with these supplements.

Cholestin

Cholestin (KO-less-tin), a dietary supplement introduced in 1997, blurred the already fuzzy line between food supplements and prescription drugs. Cholestin is made from red yeast that has been fermented from rice.

Its main ingredient is a naturally occurring form of lovastatin, a synthetically produced compound similar to the prescription drug Mevacor. Previously, the FDA declared Cholestin an unapproved drug because its main ingredient is identical to the lovastatin in Mevacor. A Utah processor sued in federal court and won the right to market the product as a dietary supplement.

Cholestin can be purchased without a prescription, but the price is about the same ($30 to $37/day) as Mevacor if adjusted for a similar dose of 5 mg per day. Until early 1999, the only data on Cholestin's health effects came from China, where the rice-yeast extract has been used for centuries as a spice in dishes such as Peking duck. Two studies presented at the American Heart Association's March 1999 Epidemiology and Prevention conference showed that a daily 5 mg dose (divided into 4 capsules) lowered cholesterol levels by 35 points, or about 15 percent in those study participants with elevated cholesterol levels. Mevacor, in comparison, lowers cholesterol about 60 points in people with levels above 240 mg/dl. Both studies were funded and researched by the company that successfully sued the government, and the American Heart Association continues to urge caution in using Cholestin.

Since Mevacor can cause dangerous side effects such as liver damage, it's suspected that Cholestin may also cause harm. Only about 20 percent of people with cholesterol levels above 240 mg/dl currently take drugs to lower cholesterol. That is due to fear of side effects, the high cost, and the possible risk of heart attack. Cholestin is a natural version of Mevacor. There is no reason to believe, without further study, that

Cholestin is more beneficial or less harmful than the synthetic drug.

GBL

GBL, or *gamma butyrolactone* (GAM-ah bew-TROH-lack-tone), is an ingredient in a variety of liquid and powder supplements that claim to build muscle, enhance your sex drive, reduce stress, or help you fall asleep. Some popular supplements that include GBL are Blue Nitro, Revivarant, Gamma G, and Remforce. In January 1999, the FDA asked all companies distributing or producing products with GBL to recall them. Why? At least 55 people have gotten sick from this supplement, and it's been blamed for at least one death. Symptoms include seizures, slowed breathing, and a slowed heart rate. About one-third of those who reported problems became unconscious or comatose.

Glucosamine

Glucosamine (glue-KOSE-ah-mean) is an over-the-counter dietary supplement that's gained a lot of attention as an arthritis treatment. Glucosamine sulfate comes primarily from crab, lobster, or shrimp shells. Another version, glucosamine chondroitin, is extracted primarily from cow trachea cartilage. Sports physician Jason Theodosakis led glucosamine to fame in 1997 with his book, *The Arthritis Cure.*

There's growing evidence glucosamine may improve symptoms of osteoarthritis but not rheumatoid arthritis. Osteoarthritis results when there's a gradual deterioration in joint cartilage—the smooth, rubbery stuff that acts like a shock absorber so the ends of your bones don't rub together. The "wear and tear" on the cartilage is caused by overactive enzymes that break down tissue. Traditional treatment prospects are dismal:

painkillers to ease the agony and, when that doesn't work any more, surgery is employed to install artificial joints.

Glucosamine is what gives cartilage strength and rigidity and can help prevent further breakdown. In fact, a study in the January 2001 edition of *The Lancet* even showed improvement in knee function among patients who took 1,500 mg of glucosamine sulfate over three years. This confirms earlier results that it can be helpful.

The supplements sold in stores are a processed version of the glucosamine found naturally in your body. Claims that glucosamine works by stimulating growth of new cartilage and maintaining existing cartilage are promising.

Jane Brody, health columnist for the *New York Times*, reported that after she spent eight weeks on glucosamine, the osteoarthritis in her knees improved dramatically. "I do not have pain-free knees, but I no longer have disabling discomfort," Brody said after more than a year on the treatment.

SELECTED STUDIES

Ninety-three people with osteoarthritis of the knee were recruited for a randomized placebo-controlled study of a popular glucosamine chondroitin supplement. During the six-month study, those with mild to moderate osteoarthritis showed improvement at both four and six months on the supplement (*American Academy of Osteopaedic Surgeons,* 1999 annual meeting). This study, funded by Nutramax Labs, shows possible improvement for people with less severe forms of osteoarthritis of the knee. They received 1,000 mg glucosamine hydrochloride, 800 mg sodium chondroitin sulfate, and 152 mg manganese twice daily. No information is known on which single or combination of ingredients offers the reported benefit.

Royal Jelly

The thick, milky substance that is secreted from the glands of a special group of young nurse bees between their sixth and twelfth days of life is called royal jelly. When honey and pollen are combined and refined within the young nurse bee, royal jelly is born. Royal jelly is made only for the queen bee. It has no proven benefit for humans—even those with royal bloodlines. *If you have allergies, be careful:* Royal jelly can cause highly allergic reactions in some people.

Lecithin

Lecithin is needed by every living cell in the human body. Cell membranes are made up mostly of lecithin, which keeps them from hardening or drying out. It also forms the protective covering around the brain. That makes lecithin pretty essential—so essential that it's made by your liver. You can get bonus amounts from foods including whole grains, fish, soybeans, and egg yolks. Most lecithin supplements are made from either eggs or soy products. You don't need extra lecithin and if you think you do, just eat the real thing.

Laetrile

Cyanide poison tops the ingredient list of the supplement laetrile. It's made from ground apricot pits and is still promoted as an alternative cure for cancer. Chronic cyanide intoxication from laetrile in the diet has produced thousands of cases of slowly progressive nerve damage. Common effects include muscle weakness, blindness, and loss of hearing. If you have cancer, laetrile won't help and will likely make you worse.

Fish Oil Capsules

Omega-3 fatty acids are the key to this oily sea supplement. Fish and fish oils have a great potential for the prevention and treatment of coronary artery disease. That's because eating fish or taking fish oil supplements works on many problems at the same time. Omega-3 fatty acids are most important in the prevention of arrhythmia or irregular heartbeat and can actually fend off the process that leads to many heart attacks. In addition they have an anti-inflammatory effect that *may* help to relieve the pain associated with rheumatoid arthritis and ulcerative colitis.

Growing evidence, including a study in the July 26, 2002 issue of the *American Journal of Clinical Nutrition,* shows that ischemic heart disease (IHD) and sudden cardiac deaths occur less frequently in those who habitually eat omega-3-rich fish such as mackerel and salmon. But most experts, including the American Heart Association, suggest eating fish at least once weekly, not the supplements.

If you choose fish oil capsules, remember you are also swallowing fat grams and calories. David Leonard, M.Ag., freelance nutrition/agriculture extension specialist, says, "To avoid possible contamination problems buy capsules labeled 'distilled' or 'molecularly distilled,' which assures that they are virtually free of PCBs, mercury, and lead, which tend to accumulate in some fish." A cholesterol-free designation usually indicates distillation, too. Capsules that also contain vitamin E and other antioxidants can help prevent rancidity during storage, but keep your capsules in the refrigerator for extra protection.

Pycogenol

Pine tree bark extract is the source of *pycogenol* (puh-KOJ-ee-noll). Pycogenol and other similar extracts are promoted as treatments for AIDS, arthritis, heart disease, cancer, Alzheimer's, attention deficit disorder (ADD), allergies, and aging. Literature on pycogenol has been almost exclusively written by the product manufacturer. There is no scientific proof that pycogenol is effective against any disease or that it promotes health.

Shark Cartilage

Shark cartilage supplements became popular among cancer patients based on the theory that if sharks rarely get cancer, there must be something in them that could solve the cancer mystery in humans. William Lane, author of *Sharks Don't Get Cancer*, sparked public interest in this supplement. Test-tube studies in the 1980s showed promise. Harvard scientists found that certain compounds in shark cartilage have "anti-angiogenic" properties, meaning they block the growth of the tiny blood vessels that feed tumors. But the latest study, conducted by the independent Cancer Treatment Research Foundation (CTRF), tested shark cartilage powder on advanced-stage cancer patients; it neither slowed the progression of their disease nor improved their quality of life. As a result of the CTRF's study on shark cartilage, two new anti-angiogenic drugs, angiostatin and endostatin, are currently being investigated. However, no studies have been completed to date.

William Lane's son Andrew, now president of Lane Labs, which makes a brand of shark cartilage, says that it takes sixteen to twenty weeks for the cancer-fighting agents to work. Four or five months is a long time for someone with cancer to try an alternative therapy. With a cost of up to $1,000 a

month, terminally ill patients might find a better use for their dollars.

Shark populations worldwide are now threatened because of the sudden popularity of shark cartilage. Unethical fishermen sometimes catch sharks, slice off their fins, and toss them back into the ocean to die. Sadly, it's much more lucrative to harvest sharks for fin cartilage than for meat.

SELECTED STUDIES

A clinical trial at the Cancer Treatment Research Foundation in Arlington Heights, Illinois, provided shark cartilage supplements to forty-seven people with advanced forms of various types of cancer. After three months, five of the patients died and five had to stop the shark cartilage because of the toxic side effects it was causing. Twenty-seven people had their cancer worsen. Ten people had their tumors grow more slowly than expected, but that often happens (*Journal of Clinical Oncology*, November 1998). While such poor outcomes are common in people with advanced cancer, not one person had any tumor shrink or disappear. Since the research began in 1995, all of the people in the study have died. Also in 1998, preliminary studies were presented to the American Association for Cancer Research finding that an extract from the cartilage of a small shark known as the dogfish showed anti-cancer activity.

However, in 2000, a team of Johns Hopkins researchers found that sharks do indeed get cancer—debunking the belief that the cartilage prevents cancer in sharks.

Spirulina

Spirulina is a form of freshwater blue-green algae that has been marketed as a wonder supplement. This algae has been said to help with weight loss, improve the health of those with malnutrition, cure diabetes and hypoglycemia, and treat addiction to drugs and alcohol. Those are pretty amazing claims for dried-up pond scum. The original source of Spirulina was algae from Lake Texcoco, a polluted lake outside of Mexico City. Most of the algae used in Spirulina are now cultivated in clean ponds.

Spirulina is a single-celled, waterborne algae that is rich in chlorophyll, just like all green or blue-green foods. Mainly it contains protein, which you probably don't need anyway. Spirulina also has some trace minerals, but you'd have to eat quite a few mouthfuls to get a reasonable amount. Even manufacturers readily admit there are no scientific studies that indicate Spirulina or blue-green algae has any benefit in humans. Why pay for pond scum that might be contaminated with bacteria, insect filth, and potentially toxic substances? Besides, it tastes terrible and may make you sick. "Cleansing" reactions such as headaches,

tiredness, runny nose, constipation, or diarrhea may appear. Other symptoms, such as fatigue, skin rashes, nervousness, and increased susceptibility to colds, will supposedly pass after about a week, claim manufacturers. Often, customers are told not to use any medication that suppresses these symptoms and to avoid high-protein food because it can compromise the healing process. This is not good advice.

The next time you're tempted to buy a supplement that hasn't been scientifically proven to help, take your dollars to the produce counter or farmer's market and buy some of those more exotic pricey foods like mangoes, papayas, raspberries, or red peppers that you might otherwise pass over because they're too expensive. The odds for improving health from nutritious foods are much higher than the chance that most supplements will provide a benefit. 🍒

8

HERBAL PRODUCTS

Do you occasionally drink herbal tea? Ever buy a jar of minced garlic at the grocery store? Sometimes add spices or herbs to foods you cook? Then you, too, are among the 33 percent of Americans who use herbal products. As you can see, surveys and studies that define use of herbal products use vague criteria. *Consider these claims by reputable sources…*

- Herbals are the primary source of health care treatment for 80 percent of the world's population (World Health Organization).

- One in three Americans, or about 60 million people, spends an average of $54 on herbals a year, totaling $3.24 billion (*Prevention Magazine* survey).

- Almost 70 percent of German doctors prescribe herbal supplements for their patients (Reuters News Service).

Such impressive statistics may leave those who haven't jumped onto the herbal bandwagon wondering, "What am I missing?" Statistics can be misleading, so let's probe a little deeper.

It's true that a large percentage of the world's people rely on herbal or botanical remedies. Most don't have any other choice. Basic health care and pharmaceutical drugs are simply not available in many sections of the world. If you're poor and can't afford medication, you do what you can. That includes using local roots, herbs, and potions. Herbal products can be effective for a variety of conditions if used in the proper context. For many herbal remedies it takes daily—often multiple daily—doses over the course of many weeks to gain the desired effect. Herbs, for the most part, aren't a quick or easy therapy.

If 70 percent of German doctors prescribe herbal products, that leaves 30 percent who don't prescribe them. We're given no information on how frequently this 70 percent recommend herbs over pharmaceuticals— once a year, once a day, with every patient?

Herb Appeal

Use of herbal preparations in Western cultures began to boom in the early 1990s. You can now purchase exotic herbs and combinations of botanicals in retail outlets ranging from supermarkets to superstores. In 1994 the estimated market for botanical medicines was approximately $1.6 billion; today it's twice that amount.

Time magazine's November 23, 1998, issue featured a cover story on the big business behind herbal supplements (the same year that federal National Toxicology Program urged more study on them). Wall Street investment groups are now sponsoring conferences on how to buy into lucrative botanical medicine companies, just as they did with biotechnology companies a dozen years ago. Growing herbs is big business, too. Herbs for health are grown in the United States for export to European and Asian countries. Currently, forty-three U.S. approved drugs are derived from herbs.

Many traditional pharmaceutical giants have jumped into the market with herbal products just since 1997. They include Bayer (One-A-Day), Whitehall-Robbins Healthcare Division of American Home Products (Centrum), Pfizer (Quanterra), and SmithKline Beechum (Abtei).

Herbal remedies are appealing. Plants are living, fresh, and green—the very essence of natural. They might seem safer and gentler than synthetically manufactured pills. Using "herbs to heal" sounds better than "taking drugs." Drugs are perceived as negative because of their potential for harm and abuse. Why else would pharmaceutical companies be required to print all the warnings, side effects, and negative study results when they advertise their products? As with most debates, the issues aren't so simple.

Arsenic, nicotine, heroin, salmonella, and alcohol are all 100 percent natural botanicals and can be toxic or fatal, depending on the dose. The ancient philosopher Paracelsus summarized it best: "Everything is poison. There is nothing without poison. Only the dose makes a thing a poison." As with any

TOP-SELLING HERBAL SUPPLEMENTS IN THE UNITED STATES

Retail Sales for 2001

1.	Gingko	$46,115,692
2.	Echinacea	$39,700,408
3.	Garlic	$34,834,928
4.	Ginseng	$30,964,420
5.	Soy	$27,625,944
6.	Saw Palmetto	$24,616,420
7.	St. John's wort	$24,132,972
8.	Valerian	$11,777,825
9.	Cranberry	$10,279,853
10.	Black cohosh	$ 9,639,506

Based on sales in food, drug, and mass-market retail stores.

nutritional supplement or drug, herbal products can and do have side effects. Botanicals are not inherently safer than other types of remedies. Some plants are harmless or beneficial if you use the berries or flowers, but the leaves can kill you—or vice versa!

From the dawn of history herbs have been known as medicines with the power to cure or alleviate a host of afflictions. The famous Ebers Papyrus contains an Egyptian physician's herbal remedies written over thirty-five centuries ago. The pharmacologic treatment of disease is grounded in the use of herbs. The coca shrub from the new world yielded cocaine—the prototype for modern local anesthetics. The bark of Cinchona species yielded quinine, a drug still important in the treatment of malaria. Salicylic acid from willow bark was extracted and refined into aspirin. Echinacea was listed in the U.S. drug formulary before the discovery of antibiotics.

Most herbal remedies do not provide immediate results. This can be confusing for the many Americans who seek simple solutions for health problems. Therapeutic effects from botanicals often appear only after weeks or months of continued use. When you visit the doctor for something urgent, you expect immediate relief and recovery. It's the American way—"give me something to take care of what ails me and it better work fast."

We also want easy solutions—a pill to swallow just once a day—no injections, multiple medicines, or complicated dosing schedules. People with infants or toddlers are thrilled to learn there's a new medicine for ear infections to be administered just once a day for five days. Previously the cure involved trying to get four equally spaced doses of gooey pink medicine into a squirming child on ten consecutive days. The most

common complaint from physicians is that as soon as a child starts to improve on antibiotics, parents stop the medicine. It's just too much hassle. But most herbal products don't have simple dosage regimens. Europeans and Asians are far more likely to take their herbal tonic as a tea or tincture. Multiple daily doses are common. Often it takes several weeks to notice any improvement. Herbal and botanical remedies are not simple, easy alternatives.

Herbal products are prepared in a variety of ways. Only a scant number of scientific studies have been conducted using herbal products found on American store shelves. *When research shows that a particular herb is beneficial, there are many factors to consider before you buy:*

What part of the plant was used?

What form of the herb was studied?

What was the marker or standardized ingredient?

What dose was taken?

How many times per day?

How many days did treatment last?

Is this product available in the United States?

How many people were in the study?

Who were these people and are they similar to you?

Nightmare on Herb Street

The herbal marketplace is a regulatory mess. There are no federal standards for botanicals to ensure dose, safety, or purity. Many products are standardized according to industry guidelines that differ from producer to producer. Herbal products and botanicals generally don't contain calories, fiber, vitamins, or minerals. Therefore, no RDA or Dietary Reference Intake (DRI) guidelines exist for them. Herbal remedies are usually marketed

HERBS THROUGHOUT THE AGES

AROUND 2000 B.C.

Emperor Shen Nung (2737 B.C.–2697 B.C.) published a medical treatise about the use of medicinal herbs. This was probably the first documentation on the subject.

AROUND 300 B.C.

Hippocrates, the ancient Greek physician known as the father of medicine, gave his patients St. John's wort for a variety of ills.

A.D.

Dioscorides, a Greek physician, wrote the *Codex Anicare Juliane*, an herbal formulary. He recommended St. John's wort for a number of ailments ranging from burns to recurring fevers.

Pliny, the Roman herbalist, prescribed St. John's wort in wine for snake bites (A.D. 23–79).

The Greeks and Romans believed that St. John's wort's pungent odor protected against witches' spells.

St. John the Baptist, from whom St. John's wort claims its name, was beheaded (A.D. 32). The plant's blooms are yellow with red spots, said to symbolize the blood spilled during his beheading. It also blooms on June 24, St. John the Baptist's traditional birthday.

THE MIDDLE AGES (5TH–15TH CENTURY)

The Benedictine Monastic Order became famous for its expertise and use of herbal remedies. The monastic infirmaries were host to a broad range of medicinal plants.

The Doctrine of Signatures was adopted. It stated that an herb's physical appearance revealed its healing power.

In the Middle Ages, it was common for individual villages to have herbal healers. The concoctions brewed up by these healers have since been shown to have beneficial qualities.

Christians burned St. John's wort in bonfires on St. John's Eve to purify the air, ward off evil spirits, and ensure healthy crops.

Paracelsus (1493–1541), known for revolutionizing the practice of medicine in his day, embraced the practice of using herbs to treat and prevent disease.

16TH CENTURY

Numerous books about herbs and herbal medicine began to appear with the invention of the printing press. William Turner's *The New Herbal* (1551) and John Gerard's *Herball* (1597) were the standard herb texts of the day and are still used today.

17TH CENTURY

Nicholas Culpeper, an English apothecaries, published *The Complete Herbal* in 1649. In it he wrote, "Tincture of the (St. John's wort) flowers in spirit of wine, is commended against melancholy and madness."

Early colonists introduced St. John's wort into North America but found that the Native Americans used the plant much in the same way as it was used in Europe.

19TH CENTURY

Throughout the nineteenth century, homeopathy was as popular as "traditional" medicine.

Charles Millspaugh, M.D., a nineteenth-century botanical expert, used St. John's wort on wounds during the Civil War.

20TH CENTURY

Germany's Commission E was established to test the efficacy and safety of herbs. Many in the herbal industry tout it as a model to regulate the expanding herbal supplement market in the U.S. (1978).

U.S. Congress enacted the Dietary Supplement Health Education Act, more commonly known as DSHEA (1994).

Source: Lichtwer Pharma U.S., Inc., 1997

165

HOW YOU BUY HERBS

CAPSULES: Hard gelatin shells that protect a powdered or granulated drug. They also help protect the stomach and prevent dilution before reaching the small intestines.

COATED TABLETS: Compressed tablets with a coating of sugar, dye, fat, and wax. The coating helps protect the medicinal core, extends shelf life, and can allow slow release of the medication.

GRANULES: Mix of powders held together by binders.

LOZENGES: Molded or cut shapes that can be sucked on or chewed. They permit slow release of medicine into the mouth. Often lozenges contain up to 90 percent sugar.

OILS: Fatty oils or liquid waxes that contain solutions or extracts.

SYRUPS: Thick, 60 to 65 percent sugar-based liquids used to help mask the flavor of the herb and to extend shelf life.

TINCTURES: Alcohol-based solutions with a limited shelf life. Popular "tonics" can be 50 percent or more grain alcohol.

UNCOATED TABLETS: Compressed powder or granules plus binders and color/flavor agents.

for their "acclaimed" drug effect but are not regulated as drugs.

However, in December 2002, the United States Pharmacopeia (USP), an independent agency that serves as the government's official compendium for dietary supplement standards, began to issue its "seal of approval" on herbs and other dietary supplementation in hope of notifying consumers of "quality" products.

The U.S. Dietary Supplement Health Education Act (DSHEA) uses the words "herbs" and "botanicals" when referring to herbal supplements. The more accurate term is botanical, meaning a substance derived from plants or a vegetable drug, especially in its crude state. Botanically speaking, an herb is a plant with a nonwoody stem that dies back in winter. The DSHEA laws of 1994 forbid advertising that implies herbal products treat or prevent specific illnesses. But advertising, product labeling, and news reports still claim that "St. John's wort treats depression" or say to use "echinacea to prevent colds."

Right now there are four pathways to sell herbal products in the United States. A supplier can choose any or all of these distribution channels, each with different requirements.

1. Herbs can be sold as foods. You probably have some in your kitchen right now. They include flavoring spices (parsley, sage, rosemary, and thyme), candied ginger, minced garlic, jalapeño peppers, and more. Some of these products require Nutrition Facts labeling on the package, some do not. Only those that have significant nutrient value of basic vitamins and minerals must carry this label.

2. Herbal products can be sold as dietary supplements and make claims as to their effect on the structure or function of the human body. These claims are permitted as long as the company has adequate documentation. The FDA is not permitted to request or review this evidence. *In addition, any product that makes a structure or function claim must print a disclaimer on the package:* "This statement has not been evaluated by the Food and Drug Administration. This product is not intended to diagnose, treat, cure, or prevent any disease." Search out the smallest print on the label—that's where you'll usually find this note.

3. Some herbal remedies are sold as over-the-counter medication. This permits the use of more specific therapeutic claims—similar to some drug claims. This doesn't mean that the identical product can't also be sold as a dietary supplement, but it must have different labeling.

4. The newest regulatory category available for botanicals is through the Investigational New Drug/New Drug Application (IND/NDA) process of the FDA. Until recently only the U.S. pharmaceutical industry had access to this option. According to the FDA's Center for Drug Evaluation and Research (CDER), there are fifty botanicals or botanical formulas holding active IND applications.

Some herbal companies plan to seek Food and Drug Administration approval to sell their most effective herbs as prescription drugs. That way, doctors and consumers wary of unregulated supplements could choose, for a little higher price, a fully tested and regulated medicinal version. There already are scientific data from Germany that particular herbs have beneficial drug-like effects. Germany's data prompted our National Institutes of Health to finance a study comparing St. John's wort to the prescription antidepressant Zoloft. The study is designed to determine which product will better help moderately depressed Americans. Such careful studies are new for the U.S. supplement industry, but more are planned.

Why aren't more companies running scientific trials? There's little incentive to spend up to $500 million on tests that can take ten to fifteen years to complete. That's the process new drugs must fulfill—and herbs don't have to. But unlike most prescription or over-the-counter drugs, plant material such as an herb can't be patented. Drug manufacturers profit only if they can patent the process used to create, isolate, or modify a drug. Competitors are not permitted to copy patented drugs. If a botanical

BOTANICALS AVAILABLE OVER-THE-COUNTER

Herb	Approved Use
Aloe (*Aloe ferox*)	Stimulant laxative
Cascara sagrada (*Rhamnus purshiana*)	Stimulant laxative
Peppermint oil (*Mentha x piperita*)	Antitussive
Psyllium (*Planago afra*)	Bulk laxative
Red pepper (*Capsicum spp.*)	Counterirritant
Senna (*Alexandrian*) (*Cassia senna*)	Stimulant laxative
Slippery elm (*Ulmus fulva*)	Demulcent
Witch hazel (*Hamamelis virginiana*)	Astringent

Source: OTC Drug Review Ingredient Status Report, September 1994

company finances scientific studies about the effectiveness or safety of an herb, competing brands would be able to capitalize on the results.

If healing herbs were always as effective as the spin-offs patented by the drug companies, there would be no reason to produce pharmaceutical drugs. Many herbal products are not better or safer than pharmaceuticals. A case in point is aspirin (a derivative of the active component of willow bark). Aspirin is much gentler on your stomach and easier to swallow than natural willow bark. Both products work, but aspirin has fewer negative side effects. In *Herbs of Choice*, the late Dr. Varro Tyler calculated you would need to brew ten cups of the highest-quality willow bark tea to make the equivalent of a single aspirin tablet. If you substitute ordinary white willow bark, you'd need seventy cups to substitute for one aspirin.

Almost all synthetic drugs are first tested in laboratory animals before they are tested on people. Animal experimentation greatly speeds up scientific research and points to potential harm or side effects. By contrast, herbal remedy support is often linked to casual observation of what happened to particular individuals. Convincing evidence to support mainstream herbal therapy using U.S. products has not been completed. It's difficult to draw conclusions from studies of other countries that test doses and forms of herbal products not available in the United States. Consumers should demand, at the very least, evidence that shows which options are safe and actually deliver the results they promise. According to the Food and Nutrition Science Alliance (FANSA), too few herbal products list the contraindications on their labels to warn consumers of potential ill effects. Responsible manufacturers voluntarily provide this information.

DSHEA, which went into effect in 1994, prohibits manufacturers of herbal supplements from advertising that their products treat or prevent specific illnesses. Aside from that, the industry is mostly unregulated. Given the dramatic increase in volume and variety of dietary supplement advertising in recent years, the FTC staff has issued guidelines to clarify long-standing FTC policies and enforcement practices related to dietary supplement advertising. You're left on your own to find out what herbs are used for, how much you need, and what any possible side effects might be.

Germany is often praised as the world model for successful regulations and use of botanical medicines. The German rules permit herbs and botanicals to be sold either as self-selected or prescription drugs. Their government requires absolute proof of their safety and a reasonable certainty that herbs will do what they promise. The words "reasonable certainty" are extremely important. They require that some scientific and clinical evidence be provided prior to approval. These requirements are not the same as would be necessary for a new chemical entity. "Their system is the best because it encourages research," said Tyler, a noted herb expert. "The literature is reviewed. They do trials." Because the German system is based in science, consumers are more satisfied and are guaranteed to receive a quality product with proven results.

That is not the case in the United States, where almost anyone can sell herbal supplements and claim they contain an herbal ingredient. U.S. consumers are largely dependent on the goodwill or integrity of manufacturers. Now that reputable U.S. companies and trusted German supplement companies have entered the market, more reliable, science-based products are becoming available. In late 1998, the United States Pharmacopoeia (USP) released the first voluntary U.S. standards for the potency of nine herbal products. Manufacturers that follow these standards can add the letters NF, for national formulary, to their labels. NF is like the Good Housekeeping Seal of Approval for herbal remedies.

Buying Better Botanicals

You can't rely on health food sales staff or even pharmacists for accurate information about both the risks and the benefits of the herbal remedies they sell. An informal survey at the March 1999 meeting of the American Society for Clinical Pharmacology and Therapeutics in San Antonio reported that neither pharmacists nor health food retailers provided much accurate information on herbal products. For example, almost half didn't know any of the negative side effects of St. John's wort and valerian root. *Since you are on your own when purchasing herbs, here are some tips to follow...*

Buy "standardized" preparations. Standardized means that an herb has been processed so that every pill or capsule contains the same amount of one or more chemical "markers" (not necessarily the active ingredient). It will be listed as a certain percentage of the ingredients. Look for the USP National Formulary (NF) approval on labels.

Choose products that give specific and clear information on dosing. Don't use guesswork to determine how much you need. Start with the smallest recommended dose.

Buy from a reputable company that researches its products. Check with as many sources as you can to find out which companies are good. Supplements imported from Germany tend to be high quality, as do the newer ones from U.S. pharmaceutical companies. Find out what brands are being used in U.S. clinical trials by noting the journal source of published research and going online to find details.

Don't hunt for bargains. Budget-priced herbal supplements are typically lower quality. As more mainstream companies enter the herbal marketplace, prices will come down. In the meantime, purchase name brands you can trust.

Choose solid products rather than the liquid-based tinctures. Most liquids are not standardized. Many active ingredients are less stable in liquid form. Creating a tincture is a simple process of infusing herbs in alcohol, while an extract requires heating and greater concentration of the original material.

Check expiration dates. Since herbs are plant-based, they can quickly lose potency. It has long been advised to toss out any kitchen herbs and spices after six months. Currently there are no standards for evaluating the shelf life of herbal products. Choose products with imprinted expiration dates when possible. Like other medicines, store in a cool, dry place.

Common Myths About Herbs

Herbal products have been used for their health benefits throughout history. In ancient times, people used herbals because there were few alternatives. Knowledge about herbal remedies was carefully passed down until two to three generations ago, when Western medicine became the norm. Information almost reached the vanishing point in the rush to modernize medicine. Renewed interest, which began in the 1990s and continues today, sparked a response that was more enthusiastic than knowledgeable.

WHO'S REPUTABLE AND RESPONSIVE

SELF Magazine contacted 100 of the major companies in the herb industry to determine which provided top-quality products. Of the thirty-three that responded, only a few companies produce standardized extracts, have strict quality assurance programs that include outside testing, provide complete labeling information (including contraindications and warnings), conduct clinical research on their products, and offer comprehensive customer service.

Source: Adapted from *SELF Magazine's "Ultimate Guide to Herbal Medicines,"* November 1998

HANDY HOTLINES:
For reputable herbal companies' customer service:
Enzymatic Therapy 1-800-783-2286
Lichtwer Pharma 1-800-92-PROOF
Nature's Answer 1-800-439-2324
Nature's Herbs 1-800-437-4372
Nature's Way 1-800-9NATURE

Although there are a variety of modern health care options available today, the use of herbals is growing. Herbs are now being used in conjunction with traditional pharmacological-based medicines to help maintain health. The benefits of herbals are just beginning to be verified in clinical studies, and scientists are discovering the key ingredients in herbs responsible for their beneficial effects. Nevertheless, myths persist.

Herbs can't harm, only heal. Some of the most toxic substances on earth are made from plants, for example, strychnine. The most common side effects of toxic herbs are quite vague and are similar to those acquired from drugs, the flu, or viral infections. You can develop allergic reactions, cramps, diarrhea, dry mouth, digestive system upset, headache, nausea, and vomiting from taking some herbal products. A significant portion of all currently used pharmaceutical drugs are derived, either directly or indirectly, from active ingredients that have been taken from plants. *In spite of this fact…*

- 80 percent of consumers think there is a low risk of side effects or problems with natural remedies.
- 84 percent rated synthetic drugs as having a moderate to high risk for potential side effects or harm.

Whole herbs are more effective than isolated active ingredients. Many herbs contain a variety of compounds, some helpful and some toxic. Many isolated ingredients from plants become mainstream medicines. They are sometimes safer and more effective when isolated. Penicillin is a good example. Obtained from a mold by the Department of Agriculture during World War II, all of its descendants are single chemicals made by the pharmaceutical industry. The vast majority of prescription drugs and many over-the-counter medicines are based on single chemicals. Most of these satisfy standards defined by the USP and provide the best control of dose, effect, and purity.

All herbs are the same—from my backyard or around the world. When an herb does provide some benefit, you need a standardized formula or home "recipe" that carries a consistent dose of the active ingredients that makes it work. Wine flavor and quality vary from vineyard to vineyard, and melons from one field can be sweet while those from another are tasteless. These same variations in climate and growing conditions affect the ingredients in any particular herb. Different species of the same plant may not have the same beneficial effect you desire. Some local co-ops or specialty stores may sell pure strains of herbs or seeds for home gardeners.

The Western medical establishment is trying to discredit and discourage use of herbs. There is no conspiracy here—just a lot of ignorance. Most health professionals don't have the time or energy to learn about other systems and styles of caring for your health. After many years of formal training and daily practice, today's health care workers would have to completely retool their professional skills. Not only that, they are expected to set aside the scientific foundation of their training and adopt new treatment options based on testimonials and consumer demand. Some of the first U.S.-commissioned scientific studies of botanicals are just being released in the traditional method of peer-reviewed research publications. As more scientific verification of herbal medicines is available, it will be easier for health professionals to choose them as practice options. Remember, it's hard to teach an old dog new tricks, but it can be done.

Quality Products

The cup of coffee you make might be twice as strong as your neighbor's. The mix of chemicals in your morning brew depends on many variables: the type of coffee, quality of the water, kind of pot or percolator, brewing time, and temperature. This chemical combination changes if you make a pot of coffee at 6:00 a.m. and keep it warm all morning for refills. The many variations of this theme illustrate some of the problems of self-med-

ication with botanicals. It's difficult to get a consistent dose.

The United States Pharmacopoeia (USP) Convention was established more than 175 years ago, when most medicines were obtained from the garden. Some physicians formed this alliance when they realized that the medicinal effects of extracts of plants, such as purple foxglove, varied greatly depending on how they were prepared. Differences in plant variety, garden soil, climate, method of preparation, and other factors produced a medicine that was far from uniform. The organization was founded to provide recipes and standards that would result in more uniform medicines having more predictable effects. Doses came to be better defined.

Dietary supplements are subject to looser standards of dose, efficacy, labeling, purity, and safety than required for medicines by the Food and Drug Administration. Only if harm has been proven can the FDA investigate a supplement.

Poor manufacturing practices are not unique to dietary supplements, but the growing market for supplements in a less restrictive regulatory environment creates the potential for supplements to be prone to quality-control problems. For example, the FDA has identified several problems where some manufacturers were buying herbs, plants, and other ingredients without first adequately testing them to determine whether the product they ordered was actually what they received or whether the ingredients were free from contaminants.

Safety Classifications

The American Herbal Products Association (AHPA) publishes the Botanical Safety Handbook (BSH) list of almost six hundred

PROTECT YOURSELF FROM INFERIOR OR UNSAFE HERBAL PRODUCTS

- Look for ingredients in products with the USP NF notation, which indicates the manufacturer followed national formulary standards established by the U.S. Pharmacopoeia.

- Realize that the label term "natural" doesn't guarantee that a product is safe or free from chemicals. "Think of poisonous mushrooms," says Elizabeth Yetley, Ph.D., director of the FDA's Office of Special Nutritionals. "They're natural."

- Consider the name and reputation of the manufacturer or distributor. Supplements made by a nationally known food or drug manufacturer, for example, have likely been made under tight controls because these companies already have manufacturing standards in place for their other products.

- Write or phone the supplement manufacturer for more information. Ask the company about the conditions under which its products were made.

Source: FDA Consumer, September/October 1998

herbs and botanical products sold in the U.S. market. BSH has created a standardization of the safety of these herbal products by developing four classes of herbs with a grading for their relative safety and potential toxicity.

Herb Hunter's Guide

Here's a description of the most popular herbs in the United States that haven't been deemed dangerous. Some have proven benefits, others don't. Information from the German Commission E Monographs and the advice of numerous herb experts from around the world have been integrated into this section.

Astragalus

Several small studies report that astragalus may stimulate and improve immune system function in conditions such as the common cold, blood disorders, cancer and HIV/AIDS, and help improve heart function in people with chest pain, history of heart attack, or congestive heart failure. However, these were all small trials and most dealt with injected forms—not the supplements.

The University of Texas did test-tube studies that suggested astragalus may be able to halt immune damage caused by cancer and common cancer treatments. Human studies need to be completed before it can be proved. Polysaccharides such as astragalus are thought to stimulate your production of immune cells, including interferon. Used frequently in Traditional Chinese Medicine (TCM), astragalus is often added to hot broth. In the United States it's usually sold as capsules or tinctures.

Standard Active Ingredients: Not known, but choose products that contain only astragalus root. Other species such as locoweed may be toxic.

Dose: Common TCM dose is 4 gm/day.

AHPA Safety Rating: Not rated.

Cautions: Don't use for acute problems such as high fever or inflammation. Not recommended if you have an autoimmune disease because there is some concern it may aggravate your condition. Not appropriate for the treatment of AIDS, cancer, and other life-threatening immune diseases.

SAFETY RATINGS FOR HERBS

CLASS 1: Herbs that, when used appropriately, can be safely consumed

CLASS 2: Herbs for which the following restrictions apply, unless otherwise directed by an expert qualified in the use of the described substance:

  2A: For external use only

  2B: Not to be used during pregnancy

  2C: Not to be used while breast-feeding

  2D: Other specific restrictions

CLASS 3: Herbs for which enough information is known to recommend the following labeling:

"To be used only under the supervision of an expert qualified in the appropriate use of this substance."

The label must include proper information on the dose, contraindications, potential side effects, and drug interactions and any other relevant safety information.

CLASS 4: Herbs for which insufficient data are available for classification.

Source: Botanical Safety Handbook, 1997

Black Cohosh (ko-hosh)

A forest plant from North America, black cohosh is thought to relieve symptoms of PMS and menopause, including hot flashes. In fact, in 2001, the American College of Obstetricians and Gynecologists stated—primarily on the basis of consensus and expert opinion—that black cohosh may be helpful in the short term (six months or less) for women with menopausal symptoms.

Sometimes black cohosh is also called black snakeroot. It was a main ingredient in Lydia Pinkham's Vegetable Compound—an early American "snake oil" remedy. Native Americans used it for a variety of conditions, including sore throat and rheumatism. How it works is unclear. At first black cohosh was thought to have estrogen-like properties; now that has been disputed by research.

Standard Active Ingredients: Unknown.

Dose: Common dosage is 40 mg/day for PMS and menopause-related symptoms.

AHPA Safety Reading: Class 2b (not to be used during pregnancy).

Cautions: In Europe it's not used for longer than a six-month period. Too much can cause severe headaches, dizziness, low heart rate, nausea, and vomiting. Studies suggest that black cohosh impacts hormone regulation. Toxic effects have not been studied.

Cat's Claw Bark

Cat's claw is a tropical vine from the Amazon forest in South America. It clings to trees with the help of hooks that look like cat's claws. The Indians of Peru consider "Una de Gato" to be a life-giving plant with many virtues. They use extracts of the bark for gastric and intestinal problems and for inflammation from diverse causes. It is also used against many types of infections, as both an internal and external remedy. They also claim that cat's claw can ward off diseases and cure cancers and tumors. It's also thought to normalize women's menstrual cycles and work as a contraceptive. Cat's claw is often used to treat AIDS, arthritis, cancer, and tumors because of its antioxidant and anti-inflammatory properties, but its effects have not been scientifically proven.

Standard Active Ingredients: Not known. Cat's claw is widely available in teas; tablet, capsule, and extract form are made from both the inner bark and root of the vine.

Dose: Unknown.

AHPA Safety Rating: Class 4.

Cautions: Do not use if you are pregnant or breast-feeding.

Chamomile

Bright, daisy-like *chamomile* (KAM-ee-mill) flowers have been used as medicine since ancient times. Today five thousand tons of chamomile are cultivated worldwide each year. Chamomile is so popular in Europe as a cure-all herb, it's said to be the Europeans' answer to ginseng.

Historical records reflect chamomile's soothing properties, but few controlled therapeutic studies have been completed or published that prove effectiveness. Much of the research available is based on one chamomile product, Kamillosan, sold in Germany since 1921. In 1987, German chamomile was named medicinal plant of the year.

The Commission E Monographs say chamomile is best used for "inflammations of the skin, mucous membranes, and bacterial diseases involving the skin, oral cavity, or gums."

There are no known side effects or interactions for chamomile, except for potential allergic reaction. If you are allergic to ragweed, asters, chrysanthemums, or related plants, you may also have a negative reaction to chamomile. Chamomile tea should be made from fresh herbs and should smell like apples. If your tea bag or loose chamomile smells like hay, it's too old.

Standard Active Ingredients: Three groups of active ingredients account for the known benefits of chamomile; volatile oils provide a mild anti-inflammatory action, flavonoids help as an antispasm agent, and pectinlike mucilages help soothe the lining of the stomach.

Dose: 1 cup of tea made with 3 gm or a heaping tablespoon of chamomile, 3 to 4 times a day between meals.

AHPA Safety Rating: Class 2b.

Cautions: Do not use if you are pregnant or breast-feeding.

Echinacea

Echinacea (eck-in-AY-shia) is firmly rooted in America—the Midwest prairie to be specific. Nine species of echinacea are native to the central Midwest region of the United States.

This pretty, purple, daisy-like flower is one of the top-selling herbal remedies worldwide. Echinacea gets its name from the Greek echinos meaning "hedgehog" or "sea urchin," because of the prickly scales of the dried seed head. It was first introduced into Western medicine in 1871 by H.C.F. Meyer, a Nebraska doctor who learned about its medicinal uses from Native Americans. Meyer made a "blood purifier" out of echinacea, which he used to treat everything including rheumatism, migraines, dizziness, tumors, syphilis, gangrene, typhoid, and malaria. Echinacea was a popular herbal cure in the 1920s and was added to the U.S. Formulary. Echinacea was quickly overshadowed by the introduction of sulfa drugs such as penicillin in the 1930s. In Germany today, echinacea is given by injection or applied directly to the skin. In the United States it is available in liquid or tablet form. Swallowing liquid is believed to stimulate an immune response from lymph tissue in the mouth. If that's true, powdered echinacea may not provide the desired benefits.

So much has been written on echinacea that it's challenging to separate fact from fiction. While echinacea does not kill bacteria, it does increase the number of white blood cells, which in turn can speed up destruction of invading organisms. Echinacea may also block an enzyme that helps infections spread. Its most popular uses are to help "support the immune system" and to shorten the duration and severity of common colds. As with other antibiotic-like compounds, you can develop resistance if you use it on a regular basis. Most experts who recommend echinacea advise you start taking it as soon as you notice the symptoms of a cold, and never use it for more than two weeks at a time.

However, studies have produced mixed results as a cold remedy—some show it is effective, others show no benefit. *One reason for the discrepancy:* Of the nine species, three—E. purpurea, E. angustifolia, and E. pallida—are used in varying amounts and dosages in over-the-counter products. Trying to identify the active ingredients or how they work has eluded scientists, and as a result, they have tinkered with different combinations in different studies.

The American Botanical Council reports that in twenty-one studies on 3,500 people comparing these extracted mixtures to a placebo, eighteen showed that echinacea can shorten the duration of a cold and ease its symptoms. There is no compelling evidence that it prevents colds, as some advocates maintain.

Standard Active Ingredients: E. angustifolia or pallida appears to be the most likely key, active ingredient.

Dose: Depends on the potency, but usually 8 to 9 ml of juice extracted from the aboveground parts of the plant.

AHPA Safety Rating: Class 1.

Cautions: Although it's rated a Class 1 herb, some experts discourage use of echinacea during pregnancy. Echinacea should never be used by those with autoimmune disorders like lupus, HIV, multiple sclerosis, or tuberculosis. Anyone with allergies to the ragweed family of plants may also react to echinacea. Do not use on a regular basis or you may develop resistance. Eight weeks is the longest you should use echinacea at one time, according to the German Commission E reports.

Evening Primrose Oil

Noxious weed—that's how this biennial herb is classified by many in North America. Evening primrose is one weed we transported to Europe in the early seventeenth century. The feisty, fertile seeds of evening primrose sailed uninvited across the ocean in the ballast of ships.

The special ingredient that the pressed seeds provide, called GLA or *cis-gamma-linolenic acid* (sis-GAM-ah-lyn-oh-LAY-ick), accounts for about 9 percent of this oil. A vast number of positive effects are touted, but not proven, for GLA. They include lower blood cholesterol, lower blood pressure, slowed progression of multiple sclerosis, PMS relief, and (saving the best for last) weight loss without dieting. Dr. Varro Tyler, in his book *The Honest Herbal*, makes the following analogy: If you assume that evening primrose oil works based on its GLA content, that's the same as thinking your "car will run better if the gas tank is completely full instead of only half full." If the GLA content is key, then two other plants—black current and borage—provide even higher concentrations than evening primrose.

Several studies have showed evening primrose oil had no greater effect on PMS symptoms than a placebo.

Standard Active Ingredients: Not known; some products are standardized for GLA.

Dose: One 500 mg capsule, 4 times a day.

AHPA Safety Rating: Class 1.

Cautions: If you have arthritis, asthma, epilepsy, or migraine headaches, evening primrose oil could make your symptoms worse. If you take this oil on an empty stomach, you might feel nauseated. No data are available on long-term use and toxicity.

Feverfew

Some clinical trials, most from the 1980s or early 1990s, have documented the effectiveness of feverfew in reducing the severity and frequency of migraine headaches, and more recently, a 1998 report on 70 patients in a small medical journal also found it to be beneficial. But it's not a widely studied herb. Parthenolide in feverfew is believed to act in opposition to serotonin. Serotonin is one of the most important brain chemicals; it lowers your tolerance for pain from headaches that involve blood vessels in your brain. Thus, feverfew may also help by relieving muscle spasms in those same vessels.

The most common way to ingest feverfew is to chew fresh or freeze-dried leaves. But this can cause mouth ulcers and stomach upset in up to 15 percent of chewers. Tablets or capsules are also available, and the consensus is that 250 mcg of parthenolide daily will provide relief. The problem is that U.S. feverfew products are not standardized. Numerous studies and reports show that many brands marketed are of extremely poor quality. Your guess of feverfew content in any particular product is probably just as reliable as the label.

Standard Active Ingredients: Canada guidelines recommend a minimum concentration of 0.2 percent parthenolide.

Dose: One 300 mg capsule, 2 to 4 times a day.

AHPA Safety Rating: Class 2b.

Cautions: Do not use if pregnant or breast-feeding. May interfere with the ability of blood to clot.

Ginger

Ginger is a favorite spice in many cultures. It's the base flavor of many foods from curry to gingersnaps. Ginger has also long been used as a remedy for nausea and motion sickness.

Did you ever have ginger ale to soothe an upset stomach as a child? Airlines stock it regularly to help passengers avert motion sickness. Ginger works in the stomach, not on your central nervous system. In fact, too much ginger causes the exact same symptoms it soothes at lower doses—nausea, vomiting, and gas. German health authorities have suggested that 2 to 4 gm of ginger is effective for preventing motion sickness. Ginger can also be consumed as a tea or in the form of candied ginger. How much ginger is in a ginger ale? We don't know since the most popular brands (Schweppes and Canada Dry) do not provide information on the ginger content of their beverages.

Although not often studied, most experts agree that ginger poses no real side effects, so it doesn't warrant the same warnings as other herbs. And the American Cancer Society recommends it to help relieve nausea and vomiting in cancer patients.

Standard Active Ingredients: Volatile oil (1 to 3 percent) is the substance that gives the characteristic odor to ginger; oleoresin is the component that provides the pungent flavor. Look for both on the label.

Dose: 2 to 4 gm, usually in hard-gel capsules of 500 mg each. Take 2 capsules 30 minutes before trip and then every 4 hours. A 1-inch square candied or crystal ginger is approximately 500 mg.

AHPA Safety Rating: Fresh root Class 1; dried root Class 2b.

Cautions: Do not use dried root if pregnant or breast-feeding. Those with gallstones should consult their physician.

Ginkgo Biloba

The world's best-selling herb is also one of its most versatile. Although best known as a "memory enhancer," ginkgo actually does several things. It improves blood flow, and this is how it helps prevent the breakdown in memory loss that occurs with age or Alzheimer's. Some believe it also helps relieve headaches, ringing in the ears (tinnitus), and dizziness; again some of these problems result from reduced blood flow to the brain. But its benefits are not regulated only to the brain's blood supply. Some research suggests it may also help with impotence by improving blood flow to the penis, and in preventing macular degeneration by boosting blood flow to the eyes.

If you are young or middle-aged and have no brain-related disorders, ginkgo won't do anything for you. If you're aging and suffering from short-term memory loss, dizziness, ringing in your ears, or headache caused by decreased blood flow to the brain, ginkgo might be worth a try. It usually takes up to six weeks or more to notice improvements. If no improvements are noted after two months, discontinue use.

The *Ginkgo biloba* tree is a living fossil. It has survived unchanged in China for 200 million years. In fact, it's the oldest surviving tree on earth. Ginkgo trees reach up to 100 feet tall and 20 feet wide. In the eighteenth century, a German surgeon, Englebert Kaempher, was the first Westerner to describe the tree by calling it "ginkgo," which is the phonetic pronunciation of the Japanese name. In 1870, it was brought to Europe as a decorative tree. Many American cities now plant ginkgo trees to help combat urban pollution. These hardy trees can withstand lots of environmental abuse.

The parts of the tree used in herbal supplements are the delicate, fan-shaped leaves, which are harvested when green. Since the development of standardized ginkgo extract in the past thirty years, it has become one of the most widely researched and most popular herbal extracts in the world. Ginkgo leaves are dried and ground and the active ingredients are then extracted.

SELECTED STUDIES

The *Journal of the American Medical Association* published a study in 1997—the first clinical trial in the U.S.—that found ginkgo is safe and capable of stabilizing a significant number of people with dementia (though it won't cure it). Sales of ginkgo were reported to rise more than 125 percent after the JAMA article was released and reported in the press. Lots of people dropped out of the study after twenty-six weeks. But more people on the drug continued with therapy compared to those on placebo. Researchers studied only a single dose even though previous studies indicated that some need higher doses. Improvements noted in people with Alzheimer's disease and other forms of senility included better personal and social functioning. It's also important to note that one-third of the participants in the study got worse. Ginkgo doesn't work as a memory aid for everyone. Since it's safe and there are no known side effects, it wouldn't hurt to try it for a limited number of weeks.

Standard Active Ingredients: The standard formula provides a potency of 24 percent flavonoids and 6 percent terpenes. The extract named EG6 761 is used in most research.

Dose: Usual dose is one to two 40 mg tablets 1 to 3 times/day.

AHPA Safety Rating: Class 1.

Cautions: None known.

Ginseng

Ginseng (JIN-seng) is the Oriental herbal equivalent of the U.S. one-a-day supplement in popularity. Many people take it faithfully every day to ensure good health. Based on the Doctrine of Signatures theory, the human-like form of this root suggests that it treats anything that ails you—and as an added bonus, it will spice up your sex life. But like echinacea, much depends on the species or type of ginseng.

Buying high-quality, real ginseng is difficult. A 1995 *Consumer Reports* analysis of ten brands of ginseng showed a huge variation in the amount of active ingredient in each brand. And medical studies show that some types—Siberian ginseng, for instance —have no proven benefits. But other forms have been reported—at least by devotees and product manufacturers—to boost energy and sexual potency, reduce menopause symptoms, and manage stress.

How do they fare? So-so. Most studies have been small, not controlled, and deal with subjective "how you feel" issues. However, one promising study published in

the April 9, 2000 issue of *Archive of Internal Medicine* found that taking American ginseng before a meal reduces blood sugar in people both with and without diabetes. And research continues on its effect on breast cancer cells. A 1999 study suggested that American ginseng may inhibit—and in large doses, kill—breast cancer cells, and more research is underway.

Ginseng is a low-growing, shade-loving perennial tree in the *Araliaceae* family. Ginseng grows slowly. It usually takes six years before the highly valued root can be harvested for its health benefits. Ginseng has been used for centuries in Asia for a variety of ailments. In 1714, a Jesuit missionary stationed in China, Father Petrus Jartoux, was the first Westerner to write about *Panax ginseng*. After reading Jartoux's description of ginseng, another Jesuit missionary stationed near Montreal, Joseph Francois Lafitau, began searching for the root. His discovery of American ginseng in 1716 initiated the harvest and export of American ginseng to China. In the practice of Traditional Chinese Medicine, Asian ginseng is deemed "cold" and American ginseng "hot." American ginseng is often used as a tonic for the elderly in China.

Standard Active Ingredients: Look for an extract standardized for ginsenoside content.

Dose: Capsules of 250 mg/day of whole root or one-half teaspoon prepared as tea.

AHPA Safety Rating: Asian root (*Panax ginseng*) Class 2d; Siberian root (*Eleutherocossus senticosus*) Class 1.

Cautions: Asian root should not be used by people with high blood pressure. Ginseng can cause insomnia, diarrhea, skin eruptions, and the jitters in sensitive individuals. Make sure you get what you pay for; buy only from reputable manufacturers.

Hawthorn

Hawthorn is a thorny European tree with bright red berries. Flavonoids are thought to be the main active agents found in both the leaves and the berries of this plant. Hawthorn has been used as an early treatment for heart disease in Europe, but it has not undergone serious study in the U.S. and many experts question its usefulness. It reportedly dilates blood vessels and can help lower blood pressure. As hawthorn relaxes and dilates smooth muscles in the heart vessels, it improves blood flow to the heart. Hawthorn also may increase the pumping action of the heart and help some people avoid chest pain. These actions are the result of prolonged use and are not at all helpful for sudden heart or chest pain. Heart disease is serious stuff, however, so before you try hawthorn or any other herbal product, consult with your cardiologist.

Standard Active Ingredients: A standard formula should contain between 5 mg flavone or 10 to 20 mg of total flavonoids.

Dose: 160 to 190 mg per day of the crude water and alcohol extract.

AHPA Safety Rating: Class 2d.

Cautions: This herb is not recommended in the United States because you can't buy a standardized product. Heart disease is a serious health problem; don't self-medicate with hawthorn. If you have leg swelling, radiating chest pain, or respiratory distress, see your physician.

Horse Chestnut Seed Extract

The dried seeds of the horse chestnut tree may help you improve the look and feel of those awful vericose veins. In fact, it

"represents a treatment worth considering," wrote a highly respected team of researchers in the November 1998 issue of *Archives of Dermatology.* Several studies—including theirs—find that horse chestnut seed extract may help chronic venous insufficiency (CVI), which causes leg pain, sensation of heaviness in the legs, night leg cramps, and swollen legs. Others believe it improves blood flow to the heart and the overall condition of the veins themselves. In several studies, including one in *The Lancet,* it performed as well as compression stockings.

Standard Active Ingredients: Look for standard formulas that have 5 percent saponins and 16 to 20 percent triterpene glycosides.

Dose: 600 mg of horse chestnut extract = 100 mg/day aescin, usually in a time-release form.

AHPA Safety Rating: Class 2b.

Cautions: Do not use if pregnant or breast-feeding.

Kava

This so-called "feel-good" drug can cause liver damage and has been banned in Canada, France, and the United Kingdom. The FDA has also issued safety warnings and alerted healthcare professionals about its dangers. The controversy began in late 2001, when the German government published studies on at least two dozen cases of kava-related liver damage. Before then, kava (KAH-va), enjoyed a reputation for reported anti-anxiety effects with promising but non-conclusive evidence.

Kava roots contain a fatlike compound called kavalactone, which is said to have anti-anxiety effects and may also aid muscle relaxation. Some experts believe that kava interferes with certain anesthetics. Some

German studies have shown it comparable to standard anti-anxiety drugs, without the risk of being addictive. Most studies showed it took about eight weeks of daily use to produce optimal effects, but a 1996 report in *Phytomedicine* found that after just a week of use, researchers could detect differences in anxiety relief in patients as measured on both the Hamilton Anxiety Scale (HAMA) and the Clinical Global Impression Scale (CGI).

Standard Active Ingredients: Only extract-based products are considered medicinal. Dried herb should contain 3.5 percent kavapyrones.

Dose: 60 to 120 mg of kavapyrones daily for no longer than 3 months.

AHPA Safety Rating: Class 2d.

Cautions: Do not use!

Licorice

Millions of pounds of licorice are imported to the United States each year. Even though glycyrrhizin (licorice's active ingredient) is fifty times sweeter than sugar, you won't find the bulk of it at the candy counter. Almost 90 percent of the licorice we use ends up in cigarettes, cigars, and pipe tobacco to provide flavor and aroma. The rest is used in a variety of pharmaceutical products like throat lozenges. Most licorice candy in the United States is flavored with anise oil and doesn't contain a speck of real licorice.

Medical journals warehouse a variety of colorful case reports of problems with people who overindulged in the real thing. Whether you consume licorice candy or chewing tobacco laced with licorice paste, too much is toxic. Side effects include headache, fatigue, fluid retention, high blood pressure, or heart failure. Licorice, in small doses, may be useful in the treatment of peptic ulcers, but careful medical monitoring is required. Licorice is also effective as an expectorant as it stimulates mucus secretion.

Standard Active Ingredient: 4 percent glycyrrhizin.

Dose: 1 to 2 grams dried root taken 1 to 2 times a day, 200 to 600 mg glycyrrhizin.

AHPA Safety Rating: Class 2b, 2c, and 2d.

Cautions: Do not use if pregnant or breast-feeding. People with diabetes, high blood pressure, liver disease, and kidney disease should avoid licorice-containing products.

St. John's Wort

St. John's wort is an aromatic perennial herb with golden yellow flowers. It is found in dry, gravelly soil in sunny areas and is native to Europe but is also found in the United States. Its leaves and flowers, which are both used in herbal supplements, contain glands that release a red oil when pinched.

St. John's wort has been used to improve mood since the time of the ancient Greeks and is prescribed for depression five times as often as prescription medications in Germany. Many studies show it can be effective: An overview of 23 clinical studies, published in the *British Medical Journal* in 1996, found it was as useful as and produced fewer side effects than other drugs in cases of mild to moderate depression. But a study in the April 10, 2001 issue of the *Journal of the American Medical Association* found it ineffective for treating major depression.

St. John's wort is not more effective than conventional antidepressants. The advantage is that St. John's wort appears to have fewer negative side effects than prescription antidepressants. Unlike the tricyclic antidepressants *Prozac* and *Zoloft*, only 3 percent of St. John's wort users reported side effects (decreased sex drive, lethargy) compared with 10 to 25 percent of the synthetic drug users. It takes several weeks of multiple daily doses to generate a therapeutic effect.

Standard Active Ingredients: Not known. Hypericin was believed to be an active ingredient, but that has recently been disputed. Newer formulas standardize for hyperformatum, but that hasn't been proven either.

Dose: 300 to 900 mg/day of a high-quality extract.

AHPA Safety Rating: Class 2d.

Caution: Photosensitivity in fair-skinned people.

Saw Palmetto

This herb is enjoying a growing following for its reported benefits in treating benign prostatic hyperplasia (BPH)—better known as an "enlarged prostate." With BPH, there are benign (non-cancerous) nodules that start growing in the prostate gland. This growth causes the prostate to enlarge, causing frequent urination, especially at night.

Half of all men older than age 50 have BPH, and studies suggest this herb may help with common side effects such as the sudden need to urinate, trouble getting the urine stream started, urinary dribbling, and waking one or more times at night to urinate.

A review of 18 studies published in the *Journal of the American Medical Association* in 1998 found that saw palmetto typically was more effective in slightly improving urinary flow rate than a placebo and could be comparable to *Proscar,* the leading prescription medication. It does not decrease prostate size.

Saw palmetto is one of five plant extracts that was used in 1500 B.C. in Egypt to treat urethral obstruction. Florida's Seminole Indians used saw palmetto berries for maintaining the health of their prostate glands 500 years ago. Saw palmetto was also used frequently in the early twentieth century as a mild diuretic and for healthy prostate function.

Saw palmetto is a fan palm of the family *Arecaceae*, which grows up to ten feet tall. It has clustered leaves, each with twenty or more thin-leaf blades with sharp pointy ends. The saw palmetto palm produces dark red or brown berries. The berries, fresh or partially dried, are the part of the plant used in herbal supplements. Saw palmetto grows in the wild in the United States, from South Carolina to Florida and around the Gulf of Mexico to Texas.

Active ingredients in the berries slow down the conversion of testosterone into a more active form. It's the active testosterone form that causes the prostate to enlarge. Over-the-counter drugs to treat BPH, including saw palmetto, have been banned in the United States because they were deemed to be potent drugs. Because manufacturers position saw palmetto as a supplement, it is exempt from the ban.

No long-term trials have been completed testing saw palmetto for BPH. Most men were studied for just one to three months. At this time there are no known side effects, with one dangerous exception. A newer blood test called PSA has helped increase the early detection rate of prostate cancer. Like the drug *Proscar,* if you use saw palmetto for six to twelve months or longer you can invalidate the results of the PSA test. Saw palmetto can lower PSA levels, which makes it much more difficult to make a clinical diagnosis of prostate cancer. If prostate cancer is not detected early, the prognosis is poor. See your doctor first to rule out cancer. Prostate cancer is the most commonly diagnosed cancer in American men.

Standard Active Ingredients: Fatty acids, linoleic acid, linolenic acid, lauric acid, and ethyl esters are thought to be active agents.

Dose: Most research indicates a saw palmetto extract of 320 mg/day provides relief.

AHPA Safety Rating: Class 1.

Cautions: Get a baseline PSA level before using this herbal remedy. Your doctor's ability to detect prostate cancer by PSA is diminished when you take saw palmetto.

Valerian

Need help sleeping? Imagine closing your eyes and opening a door to the odor of a closet full of old socks and pungent cheese. *Valerian* (va-LAIR-ee-in) doesn't quite qualify as aromatherapy, but it does have a mild sedating or tranquilizing effect. Like many herbs, no one has yet discovered exactly how it works. It probably depresses the brain centers and relaxes smooth muscles, which in turn helps you to relax. Traditionally taken as a tea, you can avoid the smelly scent by taking valerian in other forms.

There are more than 250 species of valerian worldwide. Most experts recommend the European form, *Valeriana officinalis,* because Mexican or Indian varieties can cause toxic side effects. Valerian appears to be so effective that it's sometimes used to break addictions to sleeping pills. The French buy more than fifty tons a year of this non-habit-forming sleep aid. It may take several weeks of continued use to help promote more natural sleep. There is no known risk of dependence or adverse side effects. Valerian does not work like a typical,

instant-acting sleep aid. This may be an advantage since instant effects promote dependency. Use it for four weeks before assessing the effects.

At least three controlled studies conducted in the U.S. showed that patients who took valerian experienced less insomnia and had improved quality of sleep compared to those taking a placebo. While promising, these studies are limited by small sample sizes and short follow-up periods. On the basis of animal studies and several clinical trials in Europe, German health officials have approved valerian as a sleep aid and mild sedative. In the U.S., officials say there is insufficient data to recommend it as an insomnia treatment.

Standard Active Ingredients: Unknown, but thought to be a combination of volatile oils found in the root portions of cut, dried plants.

Dose: 2 to 3 gm of the dried herb as a tea, once to several times a day; or 600 mg of the ethanol extract 2 hours before bedtime.

AHPA Safety Rating: Class 1.

Cautions: Only the European variety (*Valerian officinalis*) is for medicinal use; Mexican or Indian valerian can cause toxic effects. All varieties may cause mild stomach upset.

Herbal Tea Time

Herbal teas have been enjoyed for centuries throughout the world. It's only been in the last twenty years that they've become popular in America. Herbal teas are now commonly sold in supermarkets, coffee houses, and restaurants. Most are harmless, but not healing to drink.

Herbal teas are not recommended for infants and children. Both the Nutritional Committee of the German Society

LINK UP to *http://www.rt66.com/ hrbmoore/HOMEPAGE/HomePage. html* to see Michael Moore's site featuring a collection of medicinal plant images.

of Pediatrics and most major U.S. health organizations recommend no additional fluids (herbal or otherwise) for healthy breast-fed or bottle-fed infants. Water may be given as a thirst quencher during hot summer days. Fever and diarrhea are the exceptions where additional fluids are encouraged. Children's herbal tea remedies, while popular, have received stunningly little scientific review. Because children are growing and building new tissue constantly, it makes them more vulnerable to supplements.

Weak chamomile tea and weak catnip tea have been given to babies with colic and children with upset stomachs. Parents tend to think of herbal preparations as less harsh than medications. However, there are no herbal standards for dosage and no valid data indicating safe use for infants.

Beware of Diet Teas

Enjoying a warm cup of herbal tea is often soothing. However, specially designed "diet" teas that claim to promote weight loss in reality just make you sick. Diet teas can have dire consequences and would more honestly be labeled laxative teas. Herbal weight-loss teas work by causing severe

LINK UP to *http://www.fda.gov/ fdac/features/1997/597_tea.html* for more facts on dieter's tea in the article *"Dieter's Brews Make Tea Time a Dangerous Affair,"* from the *FDA Consumer*.

diarrhea and dehydration. Sure, you lose weight fast—water weight. As soon as you start eating or drinking, the pounds pile back on. Common ingredients include diuretic herbs such as dandelion leaves, juniper, and parsley. Aloe, buckthorn, rhubarb root, and senna are also potent laxatives. Side effects, other than frequent trips to the bathroom, include severe abdominal cramping, diarrhea, and dehydration that can lead to potassium deficiency. Over time too little potassium can cause heart irregularities and even heart failure.

Professional Help

When it comes to seeking advice about herbal remedies, *Prevention Magazine* says that people turn to friends and family, magazines, books, and health food stores more often than they turn to their doctors. Little wonder. Most physicians, pharmacists, and dietitians aren't well versed in the medicinal uses of herbs. According to a survey conducted at the Center for Food Marketing, St. Joseph's University, Philadelphia, every one of the more than three hundred pharmacists interviewed said they were queried about herbals by their customers but most were unable to respond to the questions posed.

Up to 25 percent of all modern pharmaceutical drugs are derived from herbs. Some of the more common include aspirin (willow bark); digitalis, a heart medication (foxglove); birth control pills (Mexican yam); and taxol for cancer treatment (Pacific yew tree). Today, few pharmacists and physicians receive any training in the medicinal use of herbs. They used to, but most schools dropped their classes about plant origins of medicine when high-tech

WARNING: HERBS THAT CAN BE HARMFUL

Herb	Possible Health Hazards
Chaparra A traditional American Indian medicine.	Rapidly developing liver disease—some liver damage may be irreversible; has caused at least six cases of acute nonviral hepatitis in North America.
Comfrey (*KUM-free*) Contains unsaturated pyrrolizidine alkaloids that have been shown to be carcinogenic, toxic, and cause mutations in animals.	May lead to death; has been linked to at least seven cases of obstructed blood flow from the liver with a potential for cirrhosis. Australia, Canada, Germany, and Great Britain ban or restrict availability of comfrey for safety reasons.
Germander	Liver disease, may be fatal.
Lobelia Indian tobacco, was used to treat asthma and bronchitis in the nineteenth century; acts like a mildly potent nicotine.	Ranges from breathing problems, sweating, rapid heartbeat, low blood pressure, and possible coma or death at higher doses.
Magnolia-Stephania Preparation.	Kidney disease that may lead to permanent kidney failure; has resulted in at least twenty people needing kidney transplants or dialysis.
Sassafras Removed from root beer production more than thirty years ago, all sassafras bark banned from food use.	Nervous system stimulant, causes cancer in laboratory rats.
Willow bark May be marketed as an aspirin-free product but it contains an ingredient that converts to the same active ingredient in aspirin.	Reye's syndrome, a potentially fatal disease associated with aspirin intake in children with chicken pox or flu-like symptoms; allergic reactions in adults.
Wormwood Contains absinthe, an addictive substance.	Can damage the nervous system and even cause paralysis. It also can lead to mental deterioration and illness. Oil of wormwood is used to flavor absinthe, a liqueur that is illegal in the United States.

(continued on next page)

WARNING: HERBS THAT CAN BE HARMFUL (continued)

Herb	Possible Health Hazards
Yohimbe From the bark of an African tree, used for impotence or as a male aphrodisiac.	Overdose can cause weakness followed by paralysis, fatigue, stomach disorders, nervous stimulation, and even death. Some states have classified it as a dangerous drug that is available only through prescription.

Source: Adapted from FDA Supplements Associated with Illness and Injuries Statement before Senate Committee on Labor and Human Resources and *FDA Consumer Magazine,* 1998

drugs became popular after World War II. Despite the pull-back from professional training, pharmaceutical companies are scouring the earth's rain forests for plants that might deliver a new wonder drug.

The pharmaceutical industry has focused on medicines that can be produced in a laboratory, under strict scientific control. This standardization helps to make each medication chemically stable and consistent. That way each and every pill in your bottle will have the same amount of active ingredients. The question is, have the real active ingredients been identified? In the case of St. John's wort, products have been standardized for hypericin content. New research shows that hypericin is not the active ingredient. That standard was rescinded by the Federal Institute for Drugs and Medical Products in Germany. Current dose recommendations in Germany are now based strictly on the total amount of extract contained in the drug product.

Some herbalists argue that standardization changes the whole essence of a plant. In the search for the active components, some lesser-known ingredients that enhance potency or effectiveness may be overlooked. Maybe some plant ingredients help buffer toxic side effects. Transforming herbs so they are more like pharmaceuticals is a problem for some herbal enthusiasts. It's harder for people to deny they are seeking druglike effects from herbs when they are popping purified pills from plastic bottles.

Weeding Through Herbal Research

The amount of information on herbal products for consumers is staggering. A proliferation of reputable scientific reference material on herbs was published in 1998 and 1999. Here's a sampling of titles targeted to both professionals and consumers.

German Commission E Monographs, Mark Blumenthal (American Botanical Council, 1998) ISBN 0-9655555-0-X.

In Germany, herbs are solidly mainstream. That's largely because the German government regulates them. A panel known as Commission E reviews the safety and efficacy of herbal treatments and regularly publishes the latest findings in an official register. Until now, U.S. physicians and consumers who wanted herbal medical guidance but didn't speak German were out of luck. In October 1998, the American Botanical Council published English translations of 300 of the Commission E reports in a large volume.

The Green Pharmacy, James A. Duke, Ph.D. (Rodale Press, 1999) ISBN 1-57954-124-0.

Written by one of America's foremost authorities in the field of herbal medicine, this book is an easy-to-use guide. Dr. Duke forgets, however, that some folks like to see references included, so they can look up information on their own.

Herbal Physician's Desk Reference (PDR) (Medical Economics, 1998) ISBN 1-56363-292-6.

From the publishers of the classic PDR for prescription and nonprescription medications, this book aims to give doctors and health care workers unbiased data to guide patients who may be taking such alternative therapies. Each herbal product listed includes a review of available information on indications, pharmacological effects, proper dosage, precautions, adverse reactions, symptoms of overdose, and recommended emergency treatment. The Herbal PDR incorporates and expands on information contained in the original *Commission E Monographs.*

Herbs of Choice, Varro E. Tyler (Haworth Press, 1994) ISBN 1-56024-895-5.

Textbook format that provides information about traditional use of herbs, active ingredients, current clinical applications, safety precautions, and dosages. A nice companion to the *Honest Herbal* and includes more scientific background and information on how herbs impact a variety of health conditions.

Honest Herbal, Varro E. Tyler (4th edition, Haworth Press, 1999) ISBN 0-78900-875-0.

This book is probably the "botanical bible" for herb enthusiasts and professionals. Its conservative approach is firmly grounded in science. Few modern herbalists have the comprehensive background in botany, chemistry, and pharmacology that Tyler has. *Honest Herbal* helps you decide for yourself, based on the most recent scientific evidence, whether an herb is useful, worthless, or hazardous for a particular condition. Start here for the basics.

Rational Phytotherapy, Volker Schulz, Rudolf Hansel, Varro E. Tyler (Springer, 1998) ISBN 3-540-62648-4.

If your doctor gives you a blank look when asked about herbs, try recommending a copy of *Rational Phytotherapy.* It offers quick insight into dosage, usage form, and effects of the most prominent herbal remedies. It may be the first comprehensive, science-based herbal reference book for physicians and health care providers written in English. It's based on scientific research including human clinical trials. Stuffy and technical, it's not an easy read.

Herb experts like the late Dr. Varro Tyler said these new resources mean that U.S. doctors now have unprecedented access to solid, clinical evidence of what herbal remedies can do as well as which ones to avoid. "American physicians will no longer have an excuse to be ignorant." That's a relief, because the FDA urges consumers to check with their doctors when they have questions on herbal supplements. Even with a base of information now available, there is still little knowledge about how botanicals interact with common food and drugs. Most studies haven't looked at effects of long-term use of herbal products. Even poison control centers can't supply needed information on most herbal products.

Scientific support can't keep pace with public demand. Two major issues facing the industry need to be resolved. *Hundreds of*

LINK UP to *http://www.herbal gram.org* for information from the American Botanical Council.

LINK UP to *http://www.herbs.org* for information from the Herb Research Foundation.

studies will not advance the science of herbal therapy unless these goals are met...

1. Admit that many botanicals are standardized on marker rather than active chemical components. We need to measure the substances that produce the desired effect, not just specific random components of a plant.

2. Develop industry-wide processes to analyze and identify the active chemical components and ensure a batch-to-batch similarity of products.

Future Focus

Up till now the major issues for herbal medicines have been acceptance and standardization. Other issues loom on the horizon.

Supplies of some plants may already be endangered due to sudden increases in demand. Most medicinal plants are harvested from the wild. Local people who hand-harvest small supplies for their immediate needs have little impact on the environment. Major corporations seeking large quantities for mass production may significantly harm fragile ecosystems.

Overharvesting of a growing number of areas is necessary to meet worldwide demands. A 1996 report showed that nearly 75 percent of the goldenseal population was vulnerable, endangered, or extinct. Pristine prairies on the Great Plains in North America are being decimated by "floral strip miners." Echinacea poachers dig out the roots of purple coneflower plants and leave the landscape pockmarked with holes and little hope for the native flower to return.

Exploitation of indigenous people's knowledge of medicines, without the appropriate compensation. Often local communities help provide information about best use and doses of botanicals. Some herbalists suggest it's unfair to exploit this intellectual property without fair payment. Even the ownership of the plant material itself could be a problem.

Potential for harmful interaction. Many clinical trials are still designed without consideration of the unique characteristics of botanicals and how they may affect other things you consume.

Insurance reimbursement by managed care organizations has been increasing. Interest in the use of botanicals and partial coverage of their expense will probably be the key to their widespread acceptance.

Unique delivery systems are also emerging; for example, a St. John's wort skin patch, yam cream for estrogen therapy, sustained-release herbal formulas, or microencapsulated herbs that promote immediate absorption. 🌿

PART III

HEALING AND HYPE

9

EATING TO HEAL

Prior to the twentieth century, the human lifespan increased only modestly. But since the 1900s, it has skyrocketed. The potential to improve health and cure disease will surely improve in the twenty-first century. On the downside, long-term research to determine side effects of new therapies can't keep pace with scientific breakthroughs. Most people don't want to wait for new "miracle cures" to go through years of scientific clinical trials. For example, Fen-phen and Redux weight-loss drugs were thought to be safe in 1997 when they were tested in small groups in short-term research studies. After these drugs were approved and marketed to the general population, their real danger for causing heart damage was learned. There are always risks—known and unknown—with any medication, supplement, herbal preparation, or other intervention.

Perhaps the best question is: Do potential benefits outweigh the risks?

The Connection Between Diet and Disease

As medical and nutrition experts discover more about the connections between food and health, dietary recommendations will continue to evolve. In this section, you will find a review of the major nutrition-related health problems today. We summarize the latest thinking and research on each condition and explain how new research has changed our understanding and treatment. We also give you selected research studies for some of these health concerns, and we offer specific recommendations for specific nutritional goals and objectives that will help you optimize your health. For your further reference, we have tried to provide contact information for the many organizations dedicated to educating and helping patients and encouraging scientific research for specific conditions.

We've also included, for each condition, suggestions for changing what you eat, what foods to focus on, and which supplements and herbal products may enhance your health and quality of life.

Alzheimer's Disease

About 4 million Americans currently have Alzheimer's disease, and the disease affects an additional one hundred thousand each year. Yet experts suggest that by 2050, Alzheimer's disease will claim three times as many Americans as it does today—and there is currently no cure and virtually no effective treatment.

Even now, the statistics are overwhelming. Worldwide, at least one in 10 people older than age sixty-five and up to half of those over eighty have Alzheimer's, which eventually completely deteriorates memory and mental functioning. Alzheimer's disease is the most common form of dementia. People with Alzheimer's have characteristic brain features that were first noted by Alois Alzheimer in 1907. The exact cause is unknown, but it is believed to result from proteins and plaques that cause healthy brain cells to die.

A new class of drugs, called cholinesterase inhibitors, help slow the progression of the disease in about half of patients, and trials are underway testing other drugs, nutrients, and herbs in hopes of delaying the onset of symptoms or slowing the rate of disease progression.

Nutrition Issues

Good nutrition protects both the mind and body. Well-nourished people fight off disease more easily, and that helps stabilize mental capability, daily function, and alertness. Studies suggest that people with Alzheimer's consume very low levels of certain nutrients—particularly vitamin A, several B vitamins, calcium, iron, and zinc. These substances are essential for the health of the body and the brain. Vitamin E can be effective in slowing the rate of brain function decline in those with mild to moderate cases of Alzheimer's disease. The mechanism by which vitamin E produces this benefit is not known for sure, but may be related to the vitamin's ability to protect nerve cell membranes from oxidative damage.

There have been some studies examining the role of ginkgo biloba, which is believed to improve blood circulation and is a popular (yet unproven) treatment in Europe. Most studies—including one highly anticipated trial published in the *Journal of the American Medical Association* in August 2002—have found that the rate of mental decline is slower among patients taking ginkgo compared to those taking a placebo. But none have documented substantial evidence that the herb offers significant memory, learning, or concentration benefits for Alzheimer's patients.

Research has also suggested a strong correlation between Alzheimer's and excessive amounts of aluminum deposited in the brain. It's not known if high levels of aluminum or any other nutrient are a cause or a result of Alzheimer's. Once-popular advice to avoid aluminum cookware is no longer suggested. More significant dietary and environmental sources of aluminum include deodorant and over-the-counter medications like antacids.

High levels of the amino acid homocysteine—already linked to increased risk of heart disease—is also associated with Alzheimer's disease. Researchers say it may be possible to ward off some cases of Alzheimer's disease through supplementation with folic acid and other B vitamins. In heart disease, the higher the level of homocysteine in the blood, the greater the risk of damage to the artery lining. That, in

LINK UP to *http://www.alz.org,* the Alzheimer's Organization, for information for both patients and caregivers.

HANDY HOTLINE:
For the Alzheimer's Association is 1-800-272-3900.

turn, leads to the buildup of plaques in the artery wall. In Alzheimer's, homocysteine may similarly damage the vessel linings—but, in this case, the lining of small blood vessels in the brain. This, in turn, decreases blood flow to certain brain areas and may predispose some people to the brain plaques that characterize Alzheimer's.

In theory, estrogen may improve brain function by raising levels of certain enzymes crucial to learning and memory, stimulating the growth of brain-cell connections, and increasing cerebral blood flow. Five of the best observational studies, all done in the past few years, suggest that older women who take replacement estrogen may have a reduced risk of developing Alzheimer's disease.

New Nutrition Recommendations For Alzheimer's Disease

The major concern is malnutrition, as Alzheimer's patients may forget to eat. This is why many experts suggest that Alzheimer's patients consume nutritionally packed foods or supplements such as Ensure to guarantee good nutrition. *This includes…*

- Eating plenty of fruits and vegetables. Experts say eating a well-balanced diet with at least five servings of fresh fruits and vegetables per day is the best way to keep homocysteine levels normal. Dark green leafy vegetables and orange juice are also good sources of folic acid.

- Choosing fortified whole grains. Since fortification of enriched cereal grains began, folic acid can be found in enriched bread, pasta, flour, cereal, rice, and other grain foods in the United States.

- Checking with your health care provider about supplements to prevent interactions with current medications. For example, folic acid and B vitamins break down homocysteine in the body, thereby reducing blood levels.

- Eating smaller, more frequent meals to help increase food intake since appetite is often diminished.

Anemia

"Iron-poor, tired blood" is a good way to describe anemia. It's a blood condition in which the number and/or size of the red blood cells is reduced. Because red blood cells move oxygen from your lungs to the tissues, any decrease in size or amount limits how much oxygen is transported. Common symptoms of anemia include weakness, tiredness, poor concentration skills, pale skin, mild depression, and an increased risk of infection.

A variety of events can cause anemia. Trauma such as surgery or an accident that results in a large loss of blood can make you anemic in a matter of minutes. Slow internal bleeding or long-term marginal nutrient deficiencies can cause anemia over time.

Nutrition Issues

There are three different types of nutritional anemias: iron, B-12, and folate. Having a low hemoglobin or hematocrit level doesn't tell you which nutritional anemia you have. A serum ferritin test is more sensitive for detecting iron-deficiency anemia, the most common type.

Women of childbearing age and young children are most susceptible to iron-deficiency anemia. It takes a long time for this type of anemia to occur. Infants whose mothers had poor iron status during pregnancy are most susceptible to anemia, as are babies who are not breast-fed and are given infant formula that is not iron fortified. Before menopause, women need almost twice as much iron as men do because of the menstrual blood they lose each month.

It's hard for women and children to get enough iron from the foods they eat. It's not that there aren't enough iron-rich foods—there are plenty. The problem is that there are many obstacles to absorbing the iron from foods. On average, only about 10 percent of the iron you eat is absorbed—and iron stores are often lost in menstruation. Still, the body is incredibly adept at hoarding iron. The less you eat, the more you absorb. That's why vegetarians do not have higher rates of anemia than meat eaters. However, this adaptation only goes so far. If you get far too little iron, you can't catch up.

There are two forms of iron: heme and nonheme. Heme iron (found in meat) is absorbed at a rate of 30 to 40 percent. Compare that to nonheme iron (from plants); only 3 to 4 percent of the available iron is absorbed. About 40 percent of the iron in meat is heme iron, but all the iron in plant foods is nonheme. Eating just a little bit of meat can significantly improve the absorption of all iron in a meal. "Meat factor" is the name of the substance believed to cause this effect. If you can't or won't eat meat, then the acidity from foods that contain vitamin C (ascorbic acid) can boost nonheme iron absorption.

Pernicious anemia is caused by a lack of the stomach chemical "intrinsic factor." You need intrinsic factor to absorb vitamin B-12. Vegetarians who eat no milk or meat eventually develop pernicious anemia unless they take supplemental B-12. Anyone who has much of the stomach or small intestines removed is usually unable to absorb B-12 and may also need supplemental injections.

Folate-deficiency anemia occurs when you don't eat enough folate-rich foods. Low folate stores during the critical first few weeks of pregnancy are linked to an increased risk of neural tube defect (NTD). NTD is a birth defect in which the skull and/or spinal column does not close properly. It's harder now to become severely deficient in folate since all enriched grain foods have added folate. Alcoholics and others with marginal food consumption are almost always deficient in folate.

New Nutrition Recommendations For Anemia

For iron-deficiency anemia...

- Choose a healthful variety of foods, focusing on iron-rich foods such as clams, organ meats like pork or calf liver, tofu, pumpkin seeds, and fortified cereals.

- Include vitamin C foods when eating foods that contain iron. The vitamin C helps absorb more of the available iron from foods or supplements. This means having broccoli with a serving of clams.

- Use cast-iron cookware. Tiny iron particles from the cookware are transferred to food and can provide a significant source of dietary iron.

- Keep all iron supplements in a locked cabinet, out of the reach of children. Accidental iron overdose is the number-one cause of fatal poisoning in young children.

    For pernicious anemia...

- Get periodic lab tests to monitor B-12 levels if you are a strict vegetarian or have had your stomach or intestines removed through surgery. Injections of B-12 are occasionally necessary when levels become too low.

    For folate-deficiency anemia...

- Start a folate supplement several months before conception if you are planning to become pregnant, to help prevent the risk of NTD.

- Choose foods rich in folate, which include organ meats and other iron-rich foods, as well as lentils and beans, asparagus and spinach.

Arthritis

Arthritis is the common name for about 100 different rheumatic diseases that cause pain, degeneration, and inflammation of the joints. Osteoarthritis, the most common form, results when the cartilage that cushions joint bones deteriorates—usually the result of a previous sports or other injury. In the less common but more debilitating rheumatoid arthritis, the immune system attacks healthy joints, causing inflammation, pain, and sometimes disfiguring joint damage. The cause of rheumatoid arthritis is unknown.

Unfortunately, there is no cure for arthritis, which affects an estimated one in three Americans. It's not surprising, then, that arthritis ranks second only to cancer in the number of bogus "miracle cures." Americans spend about $1 billion a year on unproven arthritis remedies. Though there is growing evidence that some nutrition remedies may be helpful, no one therapy can be expected to work for every type of arthritis.

Nutrition Issues

An estimated seventy million Ameri-cans have some form of arthritis, according to a study by the CDC released in October 2002. Can a nutritional approach help those who suffer chronically from the pain, swelling, and joint stiffness of arthritis? There is some evidence that it can.

The single most significant nutrition tool in managing arthritis is maintaining a healthy weight. Symptoms of osteoarthritis are aggravated by excess weight, and often subside when excess pounds are shed. Rheumatoid arthritis is linked to overall poor nutritional status. The inflammatory process of arthritis changes your intestinal lining and reduces the absorption of some nutrients. Often the long-term medications used to treat chronic pain and swelling can increase nutrient needs beyond normal requirements.

Because arthritis symptoms come and go, it's tempting to blame foods for flare-ups. There is no evidence that any food triggers arthritis symptoms. A common diet remedy is avoiding the nightshade family of vegetables (eggplant, tomatoes, peppers, and potatoes). There is no proof these foods have any effect on arthritis. However, it's easy to avoid particular foods if you think they are a problem. *But beware:* If you eliminate any category or group of foods from your diet over the long run, you risk nutritional deficiencies that, in turn, can aggravate your arthritis.

Omega-3 fatty acids found in cold-water fish such as salmon and mackerel, along with antioxidant nutrients such as vitamins C, E and beta-carotene, may have an anti-inflammatory action. Several studies have reported an easing of joint pain and morning stiffness and decreased fatigue with fish oil consumption. Symptoms reappeared when the large doses of fish oil supplements (2.5 to 5 gm a day) were stopped.

Preliminary research shows that a vegetarian diet may be effective in reducing the symptoms of rheumatoid arthritis. The research diet in one study consisted of no animal meat, more fish rich in omega-3, less fat, and more fruits and vegetables. It's not clear which component or combination of them was responsible for the positive results. If you decide to try a vegetarian diet, it is very important to make sure you are getting enough protein. People with rheumatoid arthritis tend to lose muscle mass, so those choosing a vegetarian diet must take care to get adequate dietary protein.

The omega-6 fatty acid GLA, or gamma-linolenic acid, may suppress the production of prostaglandins that trigger inflammation.

LINK UP to *http://www.arthritis. org* for the Arthritis Foundation for nutritional resources.

HANDY HOTLINE: For the Arthritis Foundation is 1-800-283-7800.

Two studies have shown promising results from using one to three grams a day. Finding a good source of GLA is more of a problem. Evening primrose oil contains some GLA, but it's quite expensive. Check the label to determine the amount of oil that provides one to three grams of GLA.

The antioxidant effect of vitamins C, D, E, and beta-carotene may offer protection from certain types of arthritis in a variety of ways. Vitamins C and D may help with osteoarthritis. One promising study showed a slowing in the progression of osteoarthritis of the knee when people had 150 mg of vitamin C (the equivalent of two 8-ounce glasses of orange juice) and 400 IU of vitamin D. Vitamin E has been shown to reduce pain and inflammation. Low beta-carotene levels have been linked to rheumatoid arthritis. Getting adequate amounts of these nutrients, except vitamin E, is easy if you follow the recommendations of the food guide pyramid.

Jason Theodoskis's controversial best-seller, *The Arthritis Cure*, recommends using the dietary supplements glucosamine and chondroitin to treat arthritis. These compounds may stimulate the growth of new cartilage. Both substances are safe to use and have been shown to provide pain relief; however, it's too early to call it a cure. Clinical trials typically used a total of 800 to 1,000 mg/day divided into two doses. Several government trials are currently underway using glucosamine.

New Nutrition Recommendations For Arthritis

- Maintain a healthy weight. If you have osteoarthritis of the knee, hip, or ankle, losing weight will reduce stress on your joints. Every additional pound of weight is equal to three pounds of pressure on your knees.

- Eat a healthful diet. Include a generous variety of fruits and vegetables, whole grains, skim or low-fat diary products, legumes, and fish.

- Get regular exercise; physical activity helps strengthen muscles, keeps joints flexible, and aids mobility. Try activities that don't strain joints, like swimming or walking. Best of all, exercise can improve functioning without increasing symptoms. A lack of exercise, on the other hand, leads to weakening and breakdown of cartilage.

- Try cayenne from hot peppers; it stimulates blood flow, loosening up any blockages associated with stiff, inflamed joints. It also functions as a pain inhibitor when applied as a cream to painful joints.

- Seek a doctor's advice. Getting prompt treatment can help to slow or prevent damage that might otherwise progress. Be sure to tell your doctor which supplements you take to prevent possible drug-nutrient interactions.

- Don't overuse nonsteroidal anti-inflammatory drugs (NSAIDs) such as aspirin and ibuprofen; they can cause severe complications like internal bleeding and liver and kidney damage. Check the package for information on the maximum recommended dose per day.

LINK UP to *http://www.arthritis. ca/home.html* for additional suggestions for coping with arthritis from the Arthritis Society.

Asthma

The causes of asthma are not clearly understood. In fact, there are probably a variety of

HANDY HOTLINE:
For the Asthma and Allergy Foundation is 1-800-7-ASTHMA.

circumstances that cause the spasms in the muscles surrounding the small branches of the lungs to occur. This constriction reduces the outward passage of stale air. Typical symptoms include coughing, wheezing, a tight chest, and difficult breathing. When the air can't pass freely to and from the tiny air sacs in the lungs, bronchial asthma occurs. These muscular spasms, along with mucus production, are brought on by histamine made by the immune system during an allergic response. Asthma often runs in families, indicating there may be a genetic link. Children who grow up exposed to cigarette smoke tend to have a higher risk for asthma than those whose parents don't smoke.

Nutrition Issues

A person who has any type of allergy may be at increased risk for asthma. Some children with asthma, who are also allergic to at least one food, may fail to respond positively to asthma treatment unless they avoid the offending foods, especially eggs, wheat, cow's milk, soy, and fish. Several sulfites in food products can also be a factor in asthma attacks. These can be found in preservatives for prepared salad greens, dips, precut or sliced fruit, coleslaw, processed potato products, and other prepared foods.

Vitamin B-6 has been studied for its effect on reducing wheezing. Those with asthma tend to have low blood levels of B-6. Supplements usually don't work to raise blood levels, but they may decrease the severity, occurrence, and length of an asthma attack. The antioxidant vitamins C and E, beta-carotene, and the mineral selenium may have a role in reducing the risk of asthma. It's interesting to note that blood levels of vitamin C temporarily drop during an asthma attack. There is no research to show why this happens or if taking additional vitamin C may prevent or lessen the severity of attack.

In both adults and children, obesity and asthma seem to go hand-in-hand. Overweight children are more likely to develop asthma than their thinner peers, according to a 1999 study of 16,862 children between the ages of nine and fourteen. Some experts suggest that excess weight pressing on the lungs may trigger the hyper-reactive response in the airways typical of asthma, while others believe that asthma leads to obesity by inhibiting physical activity (although recent studies found no difference in activity levels between people with or without asthma). Still, both asthma and obesity are on the rise.

New Nutrition Recommendations For Asthma

- Maintain a healthy weight, especially in childhood.

- Take a multivitamin and mineral supplement in addition to focusing on a healthful diet rich in antioxidant fruits and vegetables.

- Consider 100 mg/day supplement of B-6 for a short time (three to four weeks) to determine if it might lessen the intensity of your attacks.

LINK UP to *http://www.aaaai.org* for the American Academy of Allergy, Asthma, and Immunology.

Attention Deficit Hyperactivity Disorder

Between 5 and 9 percent of schoolchildren have Attention Deficit Hyperactivity Disorder (ADHD), making it among the most common disorders affecting children. Typical ADHD symptoms include fidgety behavior, inattentiveness, impulsiveness, forgetfulness, and easy distractibility. Some studies have shown that teachers rate as many as 20 to 40 percent of the children they teach as having the behaviors that define ADHD. Most children with ADHD act perfectly normal when they are involved in activities that interest them, and learn best in settings that involve high levels of stimulation. These observations prompt some researchers to suggest that it's not the kids with the problem, it's just that they clash with our traditional "worksheet—stay in your seat" style of classroom learning.

There is much debate over how nutrition influences ADHD, but so far, no evidence to support any type of food connection. The most publicity was gained by Dr. Ben Feingold, who argued that foods containing salicylates, which are present in almonds, certain fruits and vegetables, artificial flavors and colors, and preservatives, contributed to and aggravated ADHD. He advocated a strict and very restricted diet, but it's interesting that nearly 30 years later, no scientific basis for these restrictions has ever been offered.

However, a very few children do seem to improve on the Feingold diet. Two possible explanations seem likely. First, some children may have biological reactions or interactions with certain food chemicals or ingredients that can influence their behavior. Eliminating the offending substance will result in improvement. There is no harm in restricting food colors and preservatives, artificial flavors, and the few foods that contain salicylates. None of these is an essential nutrient or contain nutrients that aren't easily found in other foods. Every good scientific study of this diet says it doesn't work for almost all kids with ADHD. Your child may be one of the few who shows improvement, so it won't hurt to try, as long as you are careful to provide a variety of nutritious foods.

Since we don't know why these diet modifications work for particular children, researchers have tried to guess. The second explanation is that all the extra attention given to children on this diet is what causes the behavior change, not the change in food choices. ADHD children need much more attention from parents, teachers, and caregivers than other kids. When they get attention or are extremely interested in something, their behavior is more like that of other children. The constant involvement with food decisions may cause parents to spend more intense, attentive time with their children.

A relatively new area of research surrounds fish oils and magnesium. Some studies suggest that many children with symptoms of ADHD have low levels of omega-3 fatty acids and the mineral magnesium, and that behavior may improve with higher levels. However, these studies have all been small and most experts discount the role of diet.

New Nutrition Recommendations For ADHD

- Eat a healthful diet. Include a variety of at least five fruits and vegetables, whole grains, skim or low-fat diary products, legumes, and plenty of fish.

LINK UP to *http://www.adhdnews. com* for the Attention Deficit Hyperactivity Disorder news connection.

- Give your child a children's multivitamin and mineral supplement that includes 100 percent of the RDA of critical nutrients. Nutrients that may enhance brain function include magnesium, selenium, zinc, and vitamin B-6.

- Monitor height and weight at least every three months. Children on Ritalin or other stimulants may have delayed growth if on medication continuously. Some physicians encourage "drug holidays" during the summer to allow for catch-up growth. Experts believe that this delayed growth is not permanent. Instead of reaching full height at age eighteen or nineteen, it may take several additional years for these children to reach their full height.

Cancer

The National Cancer Institute estimates that approximately 7.4 million Americans alive today have a history of cancer. Scientists still don't really know what causes cancer to appear, much less how to make it permanently go away. When cancer does occur, it's the result of a mutated cell that multiplies out of control. When the growth progresses, it takes over vital organs and causes them to fail.

Nutrition Issues

Two of every three cancers may be prevented with diet and nutrition, say experts, and the "magic bullet" is the often-stressed eating regimen—less fat and more fruits and vegetables.

Since the 1970s, the National Cancer Institute has stressed the importance of diet, and growing research makes it even more important.

People are beginning to understand that cancer is preventable despite family histories, just as heart disease is. But cancer is a lot more complicated. Unlike heart disease, cancer is a hundred or more unique diseases that attack different organs and that have different risk factors. One thing is absolutely clear: a diet high in fruits and vegetables is associated with a lower risk of cancer at almost every site on the body. This link with fruits and vegetables was not clear before the 1990s.

Alcohol is associated with a whole spectrum of different cancers. We haven't dealt with alcohol very much as a public health issue in relation to cancer. Not all cancers are linked to alcohol but decreasing consumption is important in breast, colon, and rectal cancer prevention. Alcohol, even in small amounts, increases the risk for breast cancer.

There's no question that gaining weight after menopause raises the risk of cancer. We know that hormones and reproduction have an impact because women who start puberty early or go through menopause late have higher overall cancer risks. Women who have children at a young age have a lower cancer risk than those who never have children or start having children after age thirty.

Fiber is another component of vegetables, fruits, and grains that helps protect against cancer. Fiber does more than make stools bulkier. Fiber is fermented by the bacteria in the large intestine. It appears the colon needs some of the products of fermented fiber to function properly.

New Nutrition Recommendations For Avoiding Cancer

- Choose an eating plan that gets less than 30 percent of all calories from fat sources and no more than 9 percent from saturated fats. You should also consume at least five servings of fruits and vegetables each day, along with three to four servings of whole grains. No single food or nutrient causes or prevents cancer, but antioxidant nutrients found in many fruits are believed to have a protective effect. Meanwhile, a high-fat diet is implicated in boosting risk of breast, colon, prostate and other cancers.

- Aim for 25 to 30 grams of fiber from sources like whole-grain foods, fruits, vegetables, and dried beans. The protective effects of fiber are associated with eating fiber-rich foods and not with taking fiber supplements. A diet that's high in fiber and low in fat may protect you from colon and rectal cancer.

- Include more garlic and onion in your meals. The amyl sulfides they contain may prevent the formation or spread of various cancer cells—especially those in the breast and stomach.

HANDY HOTLINE:
For the American Cancer Society is 1-800-ACS-2345; for the American Institute for Cancer Research is 1-800-843-8114; and for the National Cancer Institute is 1-800-4-CANCER.

LINK UP to *http://www.cancer.org* for the American Cancer Society for general information on nutrition and cancer.

- Eat more vegetables from the cabbage family (broccoli, cauliflower, brussels sprouts, and kale); they contain the potent phytochemical sulforaphane. These cruciferous vegetables have been connected to a lower incidence of colon cancer, cancer of the esophagus, oral and pharyngeal cancers, breast cancer, and thyroid cancer.

- Drink a cup or two of brewed tea daily. Catechins and polyphenols in tea are powerful antioxidants.

- Seek out selenium-rich foods. Selenium is found in seafood, meats, garlic, and whole grains.

- Consider adopting a varied eating style that includes whole grains, fish, nuts, seeds, tofu, and vegetables; it's consistent with dietary recommendations for preventing cancer. However, macrobiotic diets of any kind should be avoided by people who already have cancer, because they may not provide enough calories and protein to protect against the wasting effects (cachexia) associated with the disease.

- Trim all meat, poultry, and fish of fatty deposits before cooking. This will not only reduce your fat intake, it will also decrease your exposure to harmful toxins that are stored in fatty tissue.

- Avoid foods grilled at very high temperatures or crisply blackened, especially fatty foods. The smoke produced by the burning fat produces polycyclic aromatic hydrocarbons (PAHs) that may be carcinogenic. You can reduce the negative effects of grilling by trimming as much fat as possible from meats, skinning poultry before broiling, and defrosting meats before grilling.

- Reduce your consumption of smoked foods because they tend to absorb carcinogens that are similar chemically to the cigarette tars in tobacco smoke.

- Don't eat salt-cured, pickled, and nitrite-cured foods (processed luncheon meats and bacon); these may increase the risk of stomach cancer.

- Although alcohol has a protective effect against heart disease (by raising HDL "good" cholesterol), limit alcohol intake to no more than one drink a day for women or two drinks per day for men. Too much alcohol increases your chances for liver cancer.

- Maintain a healthy weight and include regular physical activity. Obesity is linked to cancers of the breast, colon, gallbladder, and uterus.

Cataracts

The most common cause of blindness in the world today is cataracts. If you live long enough, chances are high you'll develop cataracts; in fact, two in three sixty-year-olds have them. A cataract is formed when the natural lens of the eye, which focuses light and makes images sharp, becomes cloudy and hardens, resulting in a loss of sight. A cataract is painless and usually develops gradually over several months or years. Your ophthalmologist may prescribe stronger glasses, medication, or surgery depending on your symptoms, complications, or age. But wouldn't it be better to just prevent cataracts in the first place? Cataracts may not be an inevitable consequence of aging.

HANDY HOTLINE:
For the Lighthouse National Center for Vision and Aging is 800-334-5497.

Nutrition Issues

Studies on the relationship between cataracts and nutrition began in the late 1980s. Multiple studies have shown that increased amounts of dietary or supplementary antioxidants can reduce the risk of developing cataracts by up to 50 percent. Much of the oxidation that happens to your eyes is the result of exposure to UV radiation from sunlight. We're still in the beginning stages of learning which specific food components offer the best weapon to battle oxidation in the eye. *One thing is sure:* People who eat the most fruits and vegetables have the lowest rates of cataracts.

Vitamins C and E may protect against cataracts or at least delay their onset. Something in foods high in carotene also seems to have a protective role, but it's not the beta-carotene.

SELECTED STUDIES

- Higher intakes of protein, vitamin A, niacin, thiamin, and riboflavin were associated with reduced prevalence of nuclear cataract in a study of two thousand Australians reported in the March 2000 issue of *Ophthalmology.*

- A number of epidemiological studies have suggested an association between cataract incidence and antioxidant status. In one study, reported in October 1999 in *Archives of Ophthalmology,* French researchers found that people with the highest blood levels of vitamin E had the lowest rate of cataracts.

One year earlier, the Longitudinal Study of Cataract Group that included 764 participants showed that the risk of cataracts was decreased by approximately 50 percent in subjects who regularly used vitamin E supplements and in those who had higher plasma vitamin E concentrations.

New Nutrition Recommendations For Avoiding Cataracts

- Eat plenty of fruits and vegetables. Aim for a minimum of five servings each day.

- Add blueberries to cereals, pancakes, yogurt, or just about anything. They are especially high in flavonoids that can help prevent eye damage.

- Take a multivitamin and mineral supplement that provides 100 to 150 percent of the RDA for the antioxidant nutrients vitamins C and E, and beta-carotene.

- Keep your blood sugar in tight control if you have diabetes. Fluctuating blood sugar levels can damage the lens of the eye.

- Wear a wide-brimmed hat and UVA- and UVB-protection sunglasses. While not a nutrition recommendation, eye protection is especially critical between the hours of 10 a.m. and 4 p.m. Don't forget to apply this same advice to your children; UVA and UVB light damage is cumulative.

LINK UP to *http://www.AAO.org* for the American Academy of Ophthalmology web site.

LINK UP to *http://www.ascrs.org* for the American Society of Cataract and Refractive Surgery.

Diabetes

Diabetes mellitus is a chronic disease in which the body either can't produce enough insulin or can't properly use the insulin it does produce. About seventeen million Americans have diabetes, which is a leading cause of blindness, foot and leg amputations, and advanced kidney disease and a major contributor to heart attacks and strokes. Uncontrolled diabetes can complicate pregnancy, and birth defects are more common in babies born to women with diabetes. Diabetes accounts for about one in five of every adult deaths and during the last twenty years, more people have died from diabetes than in all of the wars throughout the world in the last century.

For every two people with diagnosed diabetes, there's a third person who has the disease but doesn't know it. Because symptoms can be mild or nonexistent, many people realize they have it only when they develop one of its serious complications—blindness, nerve damage, kidney disease, heart disease, or impotence. There are three main types of diabetes.

Type 1 diabetes is thought to be an autoimmune disease in which the immune system attacks the insulin-producing beta cells in the pancreas and destroys them. The result is that the pancreas makes little or no insulin. Scientists do not know exactly what causes Type 1 but they believe that both genetic factors and viruses are involved.

Type 2 is the most common form of diabetes, accounting for 90 to 95 percent of all cases. It usually develops in adults over the age of forty, but is becoming more common in obese teens. In Type 2, the pancreas usually produces insulin, but the body cannot use it effectively.

Gestational diabetes shows up only during pregnancy. This type usually disappears when the pregnancy is over, but women who have gestational diabetes have a greater risk of developing Type 2 diabetes. Older and obese women have the highest risk for gestational diabetes. Children born to mothers with gestational diabetes tend to have higher risk rates for chronic diseases later in life.

All diabetics need to carefully monitor their blood sugar levels to prevent complications. Unless it's wildly high or low, you can't guess what your blood sugar level is; only a fingerstick test or blood draw can do that. Ideally, diabetics should check their own blood sugar level several times a day. It may not be too long before easier and less painful options are available. Several new devices are currently under review at the FDA, including an electronic inhaler that automatically delivers insulin deep into the lungs where it is absorbed into the bloodstream; glucose meters in the form of a disposable skin patch; and an infrared light scanner that painlessly interprets the wavelength of your blood and calculates your blood glucose level.

HANDY HOTLINE:
For the American Diabetes Association is 1-800-232-3472.

Nutrition Issues

Eating a well-planned, consistent diet appears to be part of managing diabetes for the foreseeable future. Diabetic diets have come a long way, and are now much more palatable and personalized. Here are the most common strategies to keep blood sugar levels in control.

The *No Added Sugar* plan has also been called the *No Concentrated Sweets* diet. It's pretty simple—no sugar, jam, jelly, syrup, honey, soda, candy, cakes, pastries, cookies, sweet fruit drinks, or any other food packed with sugar. This plan works best for people with borderline diabetes or those who simply aren't able to follow a more complicated system. It does not provide the best control of blood sugar.

Exchange Diets are perhaps the most familiar diabetic meal plan. Foods are categorized into groups that have approximately the same levels of protein, carbohydrate, and fat. With a dietitian, you plan how many of each group you may eat at meals and snacks. All foods need to be eaten in specified amounts at a designated time. It's a rigid system where food is in control.

The *Total Average Glucose* (TAG) plan is based on adjusting the amount of insulin you take to the total amount of glucose eaten in foods. "Points" are calculated from each meal according to its content of fat, protein, and carbohydrate. This approach is a good choice for very motivated people who need tight glucose control and who take insulin. The diet requires that you measure and weigh foods. It allows flexibility so that if you eat more or less than usual, you can adjust your insulin to accommodate the change.

The Carbohydrate-Counting approach focuses on the grams of carbohydrates eaten at meals and snacks, since carbohydrates have the greatest effect on blood sugar.

LINK UP to *http://www.aace.com* for the American Association of Clinical Endocrinologists.

LINK UP to *http://www.diabetes. org* for the American Diabetes Association for latest information about living with diabetes.

Carbohydrate counting is more precise, yet simpler to apply, than the exchange system. You still need to refer to or memorize a list of foods and their carbohydrate content and must adjust the foods to fit your carbohydrate limit each time you eat. This is the best option for people who are very carbohydrate-sensitive and need tight glucose control (sometimes called brittle diabetics) or pregnant women with gestational diabetes.

Exercise lowers blood sugar levels and can allow a little more dietary freedom. The best time to exercise is when your blood sugar is at its highest, which is usually about an hour after a meal. Active diabetics can have more concentrated sweets if they plan to engage in vigorous activity.

Artificial sugars have made life a whole lot sweeter for diabetics. Basically there are two types of sweeteners, those with calories and those without. The ones that do have calories—fructose, sorbitol, and mannitol—can cause severe cramping and diarrhea if you eat too much. That's your body's way of saying back off. Non-nutritive sweeteners like aspartame, saccharin, and acesulfame K don't provide calories or carbohydrates. As with all foods, moderation is the key.

Alcohol tends to lower blood sugar levels. If you consume alcohol you must carefully adjust your diet and medication. This should always be done with input from your physician or dietitian.

New Nutrition Recommendations For Diabetes

- Maintain a healthy weight; it is paramount for preventing or slowing the progression of diabetes. Excess body weight encourages insulin resistance, resulting in chronically high blood glucose. Losing as few as five to ten pounds can bring blood glucose down and sometimes prevent the need for medication.

- Find an eating plan that fits your lifestyle. Work with a dietitian to personalize how you eat to maximize glucose control and your enjoyment of food.

- Choose foods high in fiber, ideally 25 to 30 grams a day. Fiber slows digestion, which causes blood sugar to rise more slowly when you eat carbohydrates.

- Do regular moderate exercise. This helps blunt the effects of diabetes in people who already have it. For every 200 calories burned in physical activity, vigorous or not, insulin sensitivity increases by almost 2 percent. The higher your body's insulin sensitivity, the more effective insulin is at removing sugar from the blood.

- Maintain a near-normal blood sugar level that is between 70 mg/dl and 150 mg/dl and frequently check blood sugar levels throughout the day. The Diabetes Control and Complication Trial, a ten-year nationwide study, demonstrated that by keeping blood sugar as close to normal as possible, people with Type 1 diabetes were able to reduce their risk of serious long-term complications by 50 percent or more.

- Do not rely on alternative supplements or herbal aids. None of them can cure or treat diabetes. It can be life threatening to stop insulin, medication, or your diet plan for false promises. The American Diabetes

LINK UP to *http://www.eatright.org* for the American Dietetic Association.

Association predicts a cure for some types of diabetes in the next decade. There are no cures today.

- Take a multivitamin and mineral supplement. Antioxidant vitamins may help mitigate the damaging effects of high blood glucose on cells and reduce complications.

- Check your chromium intake. There is evidence that some Type 2 diabetics may be deficient in chromium. Chromium helps insulin get glucose into the cells, so a shortage can mean higher blood sugar. Most Americans get about 50 micrograms of chromium a day from foods, including legumes, leafy green vegetables, whole-wheat grains, and nuts. The recommended safe and adequate intake of chromium is 50 to 200 micrograms a day.

LINK UP to *http://www.cdc.gov/ diabetes* for the National Center For Chronic Disease Prevention.

Epilepsy

Epileptic seizures are caused by electrical disturbances in the nerve cells in the brain. These seizures vary in their severity. Petit mal seizures are mild—the person will stare into space and may twitch slightly. Grand mal seizures are more extreme—the person will fall to the ground, become unconscious, and have convulsions. Most seizures begin in childhood; just one-fourth of new epileptics are adults. Epilepsy, which stems from erratic surges in the brain's electrical rhythms, affects almost 2.5 million people. Epilepsy can be caused by infection, meningitis, rickets, malnutrition, hypoglycemia, head injuries, fever, or allergies. Most of the time the specific cause is not discovered for each person.

Nutrition Issues

Long-term use of anticonvulsant medications is the most common treatment of epilepsy. As with any medication, the absorption of vitamins and minerals can be affected. Vitamins D, E, and B-12, and folic acid are the nutrients most likely to be affected by long-term use of seizure-prevention drugs.

A ketogenic diet (very high fat/low carbohydrate) is sometimes helpful in controlling seizures in children. Ketogenic diets are difficult to manage, and all foods eaten must be precisely weighed or measured. Most children are hospitalized for several days when the diet is started so they can be carefully monitored for side effects. Following the diet results in a metabolic condition called ketosis. Your body burns fat supplied from foods when there is not enough carbohydrate available for immediate energy needs. Ketones are what are leftover in your bloodstream after fat is metabolized. It's not known why ketone production can stop seizures in some children, because ketosis is a health hazard in almost every other instance. Growing children will not receive adequate amounts of many nutrients on this type of diet and supplementation is essential. According to Cindy Moore, M.S., R.D., F.A.D.A., of the Cleveland Clinic, "one-third of our pediatric patients with epilepsy become seizure free, one-third have a reduced number of seizures, and one-third see no change or improvement on a ketogenic diet."

LINK UP to *http://www.efa.org* for the Epilepsy Foundation of America.

The ketogenic diet was originally developed at Johns Hopkins and the Mayo Clinic in the 1920s for preventing seizures. When anticonvulsant medications were later developed, ketogenic diets lost popularity. A ketogenic diet should not be the first line of treatment for children with epilepsy. It's not a program to try on your own; close medical and nutritional supervision is required.

New Nutrition Recommendations For Epilepsy

- Choose a basic low-fat, nutrient-rich eating plan that includes plenty of fruits, vegetables, and whole grains (if not on a specialized ketogenic diet).

- Take a multivitamin and mineral supplement at 100 to 150 percent of the RDA for those not on the ketogenic diet and 150 to 300 percent of the RDA for children following the specialized eating plan.

- Do not attempt to try a ketogenic diet on your own. It can be dangerous if not closely planned and monitored.

- Avoid alcohol and caffeine since they can alter the action of anticonvulsant medications.

Fibromyalgia Syndrome

Twenty years ago *fibromyalgia* (fi-bro-my-AL-ja) was almost unheard of. Today, it's the second most commonly diagnosed musculoskeletal disorder and a hot area of research and debate. Pain is the most prominent symptom of fibromyalgia—a burning, gnawing ache that affects the soft tissues of your body. Muscles and the tendons that attach them to bone are the main targets of this disease. Perhaps the best way to tell the difference between arthritis and fibromyalgia is that arthritis causes joint deformity and fibromyalgia does not. Although many with fibromyalgia syndrome are aware of pain when they are resting, it is most noticeable when they use their muscles for repetitive activities. The presence and special pattern of "tender points" of muscle pain also separate fibromyalgia from other conditions. In addition to widespread pain, other common symptoms include a decreased sense of energy, disturbances of sleep, and varying degrees of anxiety and depression related to changed physical status.

Nutrition Issues

Because fibromyalgia often occurs in people with autoimmune diseases such as lupus and rheumatoid arthritis, some researchers think it, too, has an immune system basis. If that link proves true, then the same recommendations to increase antioxidant nutrients from foods would make sense.

Aerobic exercise, such as swimming and walking, improves muscle fitness and reduces muscle pain and tenderness. Heat and massage may also give short-term relief. Antidepressant medications may help elevate mood, improve quality of sleep, and relax muscles.

HANDY HOTLINE:
For the Fibromyalgia Network is 1-800-853-2929; for the Fibromyalgia Alliance of America is 1-614-457-4222.

New Nutrition Recommendations For Fibromyalgia

- Choose a healthful diet. There is not enough information on potential links between fibromyalgia and diet to make any specific recommendations on food intake. However, some patients have reported that fatty, fried, or sugary foods seem to worsen symptoms. And many experts recommend that fibromyalgia patients give up or at least minimize caffeine intake. Generally, a diet high in fruits and vegetables is recommended to help muscles.

- Take a multivitamin and mineral supplement that provides 100 percent of the RDAs.

LINK UP to *http://www.co-cure.org* for Chronic Fatigue & Fibromyalgia Forum.

Food Allergies, Sensitivities, and Intolerances

An allergic reaction occurs when your immune system mistakes a particular food as a harmful invader. *Histamine* (HISS-ta-meen) and other chemicals are launched to attack the food in a misguided effort to protect you from harm. This is the same system that responds to insect stings. The most common symptoms of an allergic reaction include hives, swelling (especially of the lips and face), difficult breathing (because of swelling in the throat or an asthmatic reaction), vomiting, diarrhea, cramping, and a drop in blood pressure. Allergic reactions are also called *anaphylaxis* (ann-uh-fah-LAX-iss) and can sometimes lead to death if not promptly treated.

Anaphylaxis can be sudden or appear more like a slow-developing illness. Some noted allergists believe that repeated exposure to certain medicines or food ingredients can weaken the lining of your intestines. That makes it easier for allergens to pass through this barrier and come in direct contact with your immune system, provoking a reaction.

Nutrition Issues

The majority of adverse reactions to foods are not true food allergies, but rather are sensitivities or intolerances. The symptoms are similar, but these reactions—unlike allergies—either don't involve the immune system, or they involve a different part of the immune system than true allergies do.

Many people claim to be allergic to a food. But a true allergy is quite different from a food intolerance or sensitivity, which is what most people really have. Food intolerance is caused by the lack of enzymes needed for digestion, which results in food not being broken down properly. Undigested food can enter the bloodstream and cause a reaction. The symptoms are similar to those of food allergies. If you think you're allergic to whole groups of foods, have an evaluation by a board-certified allergist. Individuals most likely to have a real allergy to foods are those affected by nuts, legumes, and shellfish. Children have the highest rate of food allergies but often outgrow them. On the other hand, allergies developed in adulthood are often with you for life.

In homes, schools, and institutions around the country, people are eliminating certain foods from their diets, believing that allergic reactions to those foods are causing physical and emotional problems. Because you eat a variety of foods daily, it's easy to associate an unexplained symptom or discomfort with

HANDY HOTLINE: For the Food Allergy Network is 1-800-929-4040.

food. When you eliminate any food, you could be limiting your access to important vitamins and minerals.

The following food additives may cause adverse reactions in a few sensitive individuals: aspartame, benzoates, BHA, BHT, food colors, MSG, nitrates, parabens, and sulfites. Since there is no nutritional need for any of these substances, there is no harm in eliminating them. However, it will make food shopping much more difficult and time-consuming.

Sulfites are among the most widely used additives in prepared foods. Sulfiting agents are used to preserve foods and sanitize containers for certain beverages. When checking food labels, look for sulfur dioxide, sodium or potassium sulfite, bisulfite, and metabisulfite. Sulfites are commonly found in a variety of foods including bakery products, teas, condiments, processed seafood, jams and jellies, dried fruit, fruit juices, frozen vegetables, soup mixes, beer, wine, and wine coolers.

Until recently, the highest levels of sulfites were in restaurant salad bars. However, because of the growing rate of reaction to sulfites, the Food and Drug Administration banned their use on fruits and vegetables intended to be served raw. The agency also

LINK UP to *http://www.foodallergy. org* for the Food Allergy and Anaphylaxis Network; it provides a wealth of resources and support group information.

ALLERGIC OR NOT?

To help distinguish among foods you just don't like, a food intolerance, and a true food allergy, ask yourself the following questions:

- After eating certain foods, do you break out into a rash or have itching or swelling?

- Do symptoms appear within minutes but not more than two hours after eating the food?

- Do you have a history of asthma or allergies to other things?

- Do allergies run in your family?

If you answered yes to most of these questions, then food allergy is more likely, as opposed to food intolerance. If you know that every time you eat a certain food you have a reaction, then it makes sense to avoid that food. If you aren't sure of the offending food, try an elimination diet under a doctor's or dietitian's supervision.

GO FIGURE:
Fewer than 2 percent of all adults suffer from true food allergies. Jordan Fink, M.D., chief allergist at the Medical College of Wisconsin and past president of the American Academy of Allergy and Immunology, agrees that "perhaps 5 percent of those individuals who think they have allergies will turn out to have one."

---

mandated labeling for packaged foods that contain more than ten parts per million of any sulfiting agent, so that people sensitive to sulfites may easily identify products they should avoid.

A number of foods commonly believed to be allergenic are not. Chocolate, strawberries, tomatoes, citrus fruits, and corn are often blamed for allergic reactions, but they are rarely the cause. Sugar is not an allergenic food, although it is often thought to be.

New Nutrition Recommendations For Allergies

- Check with a board-certified allergist to determine if you have a true allergy before you eliminate foods from your diet. Immune therapy or allergy shots have not been proven to work; neither has oral desensitization helped in eliminating food allergies. *Bottom line:* if you have a true food allergy, avoid the food.

- Take a calcium supplement with vitamin D that provides 100 percent of the RDA for these nutrients if you limit milk intake because of an allergy or intolerance.

- Always specify that you have a food allergy when eating at a restaurant. Ask how a food will be prepared and see that your waitperson checks with the chef to determine if any of the offending food is included in your selection. Never taste foods before asking questions.

- Read food ingredient lists carefully when shopping at the supermarket. Become familiar with all the names used on labels; for example, sodium caseinate and casein are ingredients to avoid if you are allergic to milk protein. If you have questions about favorite foods, contact the manufacturers of the product.

Heart Disease

The most common first symptom of a heart attack may surprise you—it's death. That's right, sudden death is the first inkling that most people have signaling heart trouble.

LINK UP to *http://www.aaaai.org* and the American Academy of Allergy, Asthma, and Immunology can help you locate a board-certified allergist in your area.

If you have chest pains, shortness of breath, or any of the other common symptoms, consider yourself fortunate. Heart disease is our nation's second most common cause of death among both men and women of all racial and ethnic groups. Three health-related behaviors—smoking, lack of enough exercise, and poor nutrition—are the major risk factors. At least fifty million Americans have some form of heart disease, including high blood pressure or high cholesterol.The American Heart Association estimates that the cost of heart disease was $330 billion in 2002, nearly $100 billion more than in 1997.

The Cholesterol Connection

Cholesterol is needed for the growth and development of cells, and hormones and contributes to healthy skin and hair. But your liver manufactures enough for your body and there is no dietary requirement for cholesterol from foods—and the only foods with dietary cholesterol are animal products such as meats, milk, and cheese. Still, lifestyle factors also contribute to the development of high blood cholesterol levels, a major risk factor in heart disease. Being overweight and inactive, eating too much overall total fat, and specifically having too much saturated fat are the most significant reasons for elevated cholesterol levels (over 200 mg/dl). For every 1 percent reduction in total cholesterol, you can decrease your risk of heart disease by 2 percent. If your cholesterol is 240 mg/dl and you bring it down to 216 mg/dl, your risk decreases 20 percent. Some people have a rare genetic predisposition to high blood cholesterol that usually requires medication for effective cholesterol control.

Cholesterol is usually a fatlike substance present only in animal products such as meat, poultry, fish, milk and milk products, and egg yolks. Lower-fat foods do not contain less cholesterol than their full-fat versions. That's because cholesterol is found in almost every part of an animal or a human body.

HDL (Good) and LDL (Bad) Cholesterol

Your total cholesterol level includes different types of cholesterol in your blood. Actually, your total cholesterol is not as important as the ratio between the good and bad forms. High-density lipoproteins (HDLs) are the good guys and low-density lipoproteins (LDLs) are the bad guys.

GO FIGURE: YOUR CHOLESTEROL

High	240 or more
Borderline high	200–239
Desirable	below 200

Elevated cholesterol is a big risk factor for coronary heart disease. According to the landmark Framingham study, which tracked cholesterol levels of five thousand men and women over twenty years, men with average blood cholesterol levels of 260 mg/dl had three times more heart attacks than men with average blood cholesterol levels of 195 mg/dl.

**GO FIGURE:
YOUR HDL LEVEL**

Low	below 35
Borderline low	35–39
Desirable	60 or more

Your HDL level is a key factor in your risk of heart attack. For example, if your HDL level is low (below 35), you are at risk even if your total cholesterol is only 200. But if your HDL level is up (above 80), your risk is lower—even with total cholesterol as high as 240. The higher the HDL, the better. That's because HDLs helps "scrub" fats from your arteries.

LDL cholesterol is the bad stuff that clogs your arteries. You want low levels of the low-density lipoproteins. LDLs can be small or large; small LDLs have recently been linked to undesirable low levels of HDL (good) cholesterol and to high levels of triglycerides. One in three men and one in six postmenopausal women have more small LDLs than large ones and may therefore be at higher risk for coronary heart disease.

Triglycerides

Triglycerides are a type of fat found in the bloodstream. If your triglycerides are high,

**GO FIGURE:
YOUR LDL LEVEL**

High	160 or above
Borderline high	130–159
Desirable	below 130
Desirable for people with heart disease	below 100

you can actually see white fatty streaks in a sample of blood being drawn. Many people with elevated triglycerides either have a genetic link or consume excessive amounts of alcohol. Still, high carbohydrate foods can cause triglycerides to rise.

**GO FIGURE:
YOUR TRIGLYCERIDE LEVEL**

Very High	1,000 or more
High	400–999
Borderline high	200–399
Desirable	below 200

Lp (a)

Lp (a) (el-PEE, lit-tull a) is a form of LDL "bad" cholesterol. It is emerging as another risk factor for heart disease. An elevated level of Lp (a) in your blood is a concern. However, it is not clear how to lower a high Lp (a) level. Some preliminary findings point to aspirin, red wine, and omega-3 fatty acids from fish as possibly lowering Lp (a) levels. More research is needed before specific dietary recommendations can be made, but following a heart-healthy diet is a good start.

Nutrition Issues

Diets to prevent heart disease always begin with what you can't have or must limit. *Try a new approach:* Eat more fruits and vegetables, add in a variety of whole-grain breads and cereals, seek out lean meats, poultry, plenty of fish, and skim or low-fat dairy products. Choose foods as close to how they were grown as possible.

These are the most popular eating plans to prevent or reverse heart disease.

STEP I DIET. Designed by the National Cholesterol Education Program as

LINK UP to *http://www.nhlbi.nih. gov* or *http://www.americanheart.org* for more specifics on the step diets if you have heart disease and need guidance on this plan.

LINK UP to *www.heartcenteronline. com* for patient information guides to many topics, including the Heart Healthy Diet, tips for reducing fat intake, and the latest research news.

HANDY HOTLINE: To the American Heart Association is 1-800-AHA-USA1.

the first step in treating high blood cholesterol. This low-fat plan (30 percent of total calories) restricts saturated fat (8 to 10 percent of total calories) and dietary cholesterol (less than 300 mg), and provides enough calories to achieve or maintain a healthy weight. If blood cholesterol levels aren't lowered in three to six months, the Step II Diet should be tried.

STEP II DIET. A more restrictive version of the Step I diet. Saturated fat is kept to less than 7 percent of total calories, and dietary cholesterol is held at 200 mg. If these dietary changes don't result in lower blood cholesterol, then medications may be prescribed.

PRITIKIN DIET. Created by Nathan Pritikin in the late 1950s, this severely low-fat diet (5 to 10 percent of total calories from fat) focuses on grain, fruits, and vegetables. Such significant fat restrictions are not for everyone. However, if you're highly motivated to lower your cholesterol, it can have good results.

ORNISH DIET. In the late 1970s, Dr. Dean Ornish developed a very low-fat diet (less than 10 percent of total calories from fat), which he claims can even reverse severe heart disease without drugs or surgery. As with the Pritikin Diet, many people find the severe fat limitations a challenge to stick with.

Generally speaking, there's plenty of evidence that antioxidants may prevent clogging of the arteries by blocking the oxidation of LDL. Vitamins E and C are showing great promise, and dietary beta-carotene has also shown positive effects. Studies show mixed results on garlic supplements, but including plenty of fresh garlic may help. Evidence is stronger that drinking one to two glasses of alcohol—beer, wine, or hard liquor—can raise "good" HDL cholesterol, and possibly reduce risk.

New Nutrition Recommendations For Avoiding Heart Disease

- Choose an eating plan that will work for you and stay with it for life.
- Maintain a healthy weight through sensible eating and regular physical activity.
- Take a multivitamin and mineral supplement with 100 percent of the RDA. Extra B-6 and folic acid may help if you have elevated homocysteine levels, unless discouraged by your doctor.
- Consider taking fish oil supplements. They may have the potential for lowering the risk for blocked blood vessels and heart attacks, but their current effectiveness and proper dosage haven't been determined.

LINK UP to *http://www.american heart.org* for the American Heart Association.

High Blood Pressure

High blood pressure, or hypertension, affects nearly 60 million Americans, or one in four adults. Yet one in three hypertensives are unaware of their condition. Historically, treatment has alternated between an emphasis on diet and use of antihypertensive drugs. The use of drugs should never be the first option because of potential serious side effects. The nondrug approach is far safer and more effective. Blood pressure is considered to be elevated when readings are above 140/90. The upper number is called the systolic pressure, which is the pressure that occurs when the heart contracts and pushes blood out to the body. The bottom number is called the diastolic pressure. This is the pressure in the arteries when the heart relaxes between beats.

High blood pressure is a significant risk factor for developing heart disease. Not only does hypertension increase the risk of heart attacks, but it also increases the risk of stroke and kidney disease. Of the 60 million people with hypertension, almost half are women.

Nutrition Issues

Only about 10 percent of Americans with high blood pressure can lower blood pressure significantly with a low-sodium diet. Eating lots of fruits, vegetables, and skim or low-fat dairy products is more beneficial than cutting back on salt for most people trying to get their blood pressure in control. Potassium, calcium, and magnesium from these foods are thought to be key to blood

WHAT YOUR DOCTOR DOESN'T KNOW

A 1998 survey to determine physicians' nutrition knowledge about diet and high blood fats showed that many doctors have a lot to learn. This study, reported in the journal *Circulation,* found that of the doctors who responded...

- 82 percent did not know that a low-fat diet would decrease HDL levels. (It does.)

- 70 percent thought a low-fat diet had no more than 20 percent of calories from fat. (It's 30 percent or less.)

- 40 percent incorrectly believed that dietary fat raises blood triglyceride levels. (It doesn't.)

- 30 percent didn't identify olive oil as a monounsaturated fat. (It is.)

This is another reason to ask your doctor for a referral to a qualified dietitian. It's clear that the National Cholesterol Education Program needs to change their recommendation that diet counseling by physicians be the first treatment for management of high levels of cholesterol and blood fats.

pressure improvements. A modest weight loss of just ten pounds, especially if you have lots of tummy fat, can often reduce elevated blood pressure to normal levels.

Coenzyme Q-10 may improve hypertension, producing a decline in both systolic and diastolic blood pressure, but use of this supplement should be managed by your health care provider. Garlic has lowered blood pressure in some studies. Eating just one clove of garlic per day in foods may have some blood pressure-lowering benefits. Do not take any form of licorice. Even relatively

HANDY HOTLINE:
For the National Heart, Lung, and Blood Institute is 1-800-575-9355.

small amounts (50 grams or less) of licorice can raise blood pressure.

Regular use of nonsteroidal anti-inflammatory drugs (NSAIDs) may raise blood pressure, particularly in older people. They may also impair the action of beta-blocking medicines that lower blood pressure. NSAIDs include *ibuprofen* (Advil, Motrin) and *naproxen* (Aleve).

Several observational studies suggest that a diet low in saturated fats and high in fruits and vegetables may help lower blood pressure. A specific eating plan—called Dietary Approaches to Stop Hypertension (DASH)—has consistently been found to reduce blood pressure in those with hypertension. In addition, a study in the Aug. 22, 2000 issue of the medical journal *Circulation* found that it can also reduce levels of the amino acid homocysteine, another risk factor in heart disease, stroke, and peripheral vascular disease. For information on DASH, go to *http://www.nhlbi.nih.gov/health/public/heart/hbp/dash/index.htm*.

In addition to DASH, experts recommend that you...

• Maintain a healthy weight. The benefits of weight loss can't be overemphasized. Overweight adults are 50 percent more likely than normal-weight adults to have hypertension.

LINK UP to *http://oto.wustl.edu/men/sodium.htm* to learn about the sodium content of common foods.

• Drink less alcohol. Although regular consumption of alcohol is associated with a reduced risk of heart disease, drinking three or more alcoholic beverages a day can raise blood pressure.

• Get regular exercise. It will help keep both your weight and your blood pressure low.

• Make peace with your salt intake. If eating less salt and less foods high in sodium helps lower your blood pressure, then stay on a low-sodium diet. If you are used to lower-sodium foods, don't start eating more. Foods rich in potassium, calcium, and magnesium may help blunt the effects of sodium on your blood pressure.

HIV/AIDS

Acquired immunodeficiency syndrome (AIDS) is a viral infection that causes a harmful antibody response in your immune system. The HIV (human immunodeficiency virus) gene actually gets into your cells and multiplies. As the HIV spreads, it weakens your immune system so that you are unable to fight off many normal infections. In a healthy immune system, the white blood cells surround a virus and destroy it. With AIDS, the HIV virus is surrounded but the white cells can't kill it, and the virus reproduces unchecked.

Nutrition Issues

It can take two to ten years (or longer) after the initial infection for symptoms of the AIDS virus to appear. When the virus becomes more active, early symptoms are vague and include weight loss, fatigue, diarrhea, headaches, swollen glands, fever, and loss of appetite. A common symptom is thrush (white patches in the mouth), which indicates a suppressed immune system. When

HANDY HOTLINE:
To the National HIV and AIDS Prevention Center at the Centers for Disease Control is 1-800-342-AIDS.

LINK UP to *http://www.hivresources. com* for the HIV ReSources, Inc., site that provides a variety of nutrition education resources.

these symptoms occur, they are the signs that the body has been depleted of many nutrients and may develop full-blown deficiencies. Many trace elements such as zinc and selenium are used up before you even notice any symptoms.

Diet is an important part of the battle against HIV infection—most to keep strength and immunity strong. In general, a nutritious variety of foods provides the best combination of nutrients, with particular emphasis on antioxidant nutrients such as vitamins C and E and zinc, a known immune-booster. What you eat is especially important when taking drug therapy for HIV infection. In many instances it makes the difference between success and failure of your medications. In order for medications to get into the body, they must be absorbed by the gastrointestinal tract (through the stomach and intestines). Some drugs require stomach acid (with no food in the stomach) to be absorbed while others need to be absorbed in the presence of food. The guidance of a dietitian in meal planning and spacing can also help alleviate some drug side effects.

Malnutrition is a very serious problem for people with AIDS. Life expectancy is directly related to how much body mass you can keep. A loss of 55 percent of lean muscle weight is practically a death sentence to those with AIDS. Another source of malnutrition comes from ongoing infections, which change how all nutrients are metabolized.

Food safety is as critical as good nutrition in the management of AIDS. Suppressed immunity dramatically increases the risk of food-borne illness and the severity of complications. There are bacteria and germs lurking in almost everything we eat and drink. When levels of these contaminants get high enough, they can make you sick. It takes far less contamination to make you ill when you have AIDS. See Chapter 3 and the appendices for a complete look at necessary food safety precautions.

New Nutrition Recommendations For HIV/AIDS

- Consult a registered dietitian (RD) as soon as you are diagnosed for a complete nutritional assessment including weight, height, body fat, lean muscle mass, and BMI. Your RD should also explain your lab results from blood and urine samples. Keep as much lean body mass as possible by staying active and eating a variety of foods.

- Focus on maintaining your weight. Eating small, frequent meals can help to increase the number of calories you eat.

- Eat plenty of quality protein and antioxidant-rich fruits, vegetables, and grains to keep your immune system strong.

- Wash all fruits and vegetables with a non-soap-based produce rinse (such as Fit®) to avoid food-borne infections.

LINK UP to *http://www.cdc.gov* for the Centers for Disease Control information on HIV/AIDS data and research.

- Never eat raw or undercooked eggs or soft ripe cheeses. Be sure ground meats are cooked well done. Use a food thermometer to check temperatures.

- Avoid exposure to people with colds, flu, and other contagious diseases.

- Drink bottled water if your local water supply doesn't meet federal safety standards. (See Chapter 2 for how to check your local water quality.)

- Use bleach or an antibacterial solution (1 tablespoon to 1 gallon water) to wipe kitchen surfaces.

- Take a multivitamin/mineral supplement that provides 100 percent of the RDAs.

- Check with your health care provider if you are on antifolate drug treatment; you may need extra folic acid.

- Try to decrease caffeine to help prevent stomach irritation.

- Take additional supplements of vitamins A, D, E, and K if you develop steatorrhea (fatty diarrhea).

Inflammatory Bowel Disease

Crohn's disease and colitis are types of inflammatory bowel diseases (IBDs). They are chronic diseases without a known cause or cure. An estimated two million Americans have been diagnosed with IBDs.

Colitis is an inflammation of the inner lining of the digestive tract affecting the colon or the rectum. Crohn's disease is an inflammation of all the layers of the digestive tract affecting any part from the mouth to the anus. It's because the symptoms and complications are similar that they both are grouped under the heading of IBDs. Common symptoms include weight loss, fever, abdominal pain, and diarrhea.

Nutrition Issues

Malnutrition is a significant problem in IBDs for several reasons. First, it's pretty miserable to live in chronic pain, and that lowers the desire to eat. Second, scar tissue forms along the digestive tract as a result of inflammation. This scarring interferes with normal absorption of nutrients and decreases the available supply of nutrients and energy. This is especially important in children because high levels of calories and nutrients are essential for optimal growth.

Sometimes it's necessary to rely on liquid meal replacement supplements such as Ensure to provide enough calories and nutrients during severe bouts of symptoms. Ideally these supplements are aids to a wholesome diet and not used in place of eating real foods. Extra supplements are not typically recommended and may even cause more harm, such as an increase in diarrhea. IBD is one of the few conditions that benefits from a lower fiber intake. Too much roughage can irritate an already sensitive digestive tract.

HANDY HOTLINE:
To the Crohn's & Colitis Foundation of America, Inc., is 1-800-932-2423.

LINK UP to *http://www.ccfa.org* for the Crohn's & Colitis Foundation of America, Inc.

New Nutrition Recommendations For IBD

- Individualize your optimal nutrition plan if you have IBD. What may work for one person may not work so well for another person.

- Choose foods that are rich in nutrients whenever possible. You may need to avoid some higher-fiber foods if they cause pain or complications of your symptoms.

- Spread meals out over the course of the day. Five small meals instead of three large ones may help decrease side effects.

- Eliminate a particular food for several weeks if it seems to intensify your symptoms. Then slowly reintroduce it to see if it has any effect.

- Avoid supplemental vitamins and minerals unless they have been specifically prescribed by your gastroenterologist.

- Try substituting a liquid diet meal (Carnation Instant Breakfast, Ensure, or Boost) to provide calories and a source of nutrients when you can't eat.

- Be cautious in your consumption of herbal teas. Tannins and other compounds may irritate your digestive system.

Macular Degeneration

Macular degeneration is the deterioration and functional loss of the yellow spot on the retina, which is responsible for central vision. The more the yellow spot deteriorates, the more vision is lost. Lutein is a yellow pigment in the human eye (it also gives marigolds their golden yellow color).

Zeaxanthin is another bright yellow pigment that is almost identical in structure to lutein. Together lutein and zeaxanthin are the pigments that color the tiny spot on your eye yellow. The density of yellow color is proportional to the amount of lutein and zeaxanthin it contains. Macular density gets worse as macular degeneration progresses because of the loss of these pigments.

Macular degeneration is a leading cause of blindness in people over fifty-five years old. It can strike anyone and works slowly and silently to destroy vision. Medical research studies show that as many as one-fourth of all people over the age of sixty-five have a measurable level of macular degeneration, and there is no treatment for the disease at present. The good news is that macular degeneration can sometimes be prevented or the progressive loss of sight slowed.

A growing body of evidence suggests that the same type of arterial plaque build-up that contributes to heart disease may also affect the delicate blood vessels in the eye, leading to macular degeneration. In a large study by Harvard researchers published in the *American Journal of Clinical Nutrition* in 2001, those eating a low-fat diet were half as likely to develop macular degeneration than those consuming the "typical" high-fat diet. Therefore, eating heart-healthy may also protect your sight.

In addition, eating more dark green leafy vegetables such as collards and spinach will add extra carotenoids, lutein, and zeaxanthin.

HANDY HOTLINE: To the Lighthouse National Center for Vision and Aging is 1-800-334-5497.

New Nutrition Recommendations for Macular Degeneration

- Eat at least one or two servings daily of a dark green leafy vegetable such as spinach, kale, or collard greens. These vegetables supply a high amount of lutein and zeaxanthin, the yellow carotenoid pigments absolutely necessary for the health of the macula.

- Eat a serving of blueberries every day. Blueberries are especially high in total antioxidative activity. Fresh or frozen blueberries are equally good choices.

- Try bilberry extract if you don't like blueberries (it ranks even higher than blueberries for antioxidant capacity). However, eating whole fruit (blueberry or bilberry) may offer other beneficial substances, which may not be present in the extract.

- Eat a total of at least five servings per day of vegetables or fruits to increase the total antioxidant activity of the blood.

- Get an adequate zinc intake of 15 mg per day. This amount of zinc is readily supplied by any good multivitamin and mineral tablet.

- Take antioxidant supplements to equal 400 IU per day of all-natural vitamin E consisting of mixed tocopherols and a supplement of 250 mg per day of vitamin C. Be sure to add up the amounts in your multivitamin and mineral supplements before choosing individual products.

- Drink one glass of red or purple grape juice or red wine every day for its protective antioxidant activity.

- Do not take ginkgo biloba extract. Although it is an excellent antioxidant, its consumption carries a very small risk of hemorrhage in the brain, usually a

LINK UP to *http://www.eyesight. org* or *http://www.AAO.org* for the American Academy of Ophthalmology's Eyenet.

lethal condition. It is doubtful whether any potential benefit outweighs the risk, no matter how small.

Menopause

Menopause, also referred to as "the change of life," is the point at which women stop ovulating. Menopause affects each woman differently. For most women, menstrual cycles become less regular at about age fifty. The cycles eventually cease. Menopause is caused when the ovaries lose their ability to release hormones. The menopausal phase can last up to five years. Although estrogen levels drop during the postmenopausal period, the hormone does not entirely disappear.

Typical menopausal symptoms include hot flashes, dizziness, headache, shortness of breath, and depression. These are thought to be the result of fluctuating estrogen levels. To help control symptoms, a small amount of estrogen daily will help. Check with your doctor about the benefits and risks of hormone replacement therapy.

Nutrition Issues

Many women complain that weight gain speeds up during menopause. The slightest fluctuation in estrogen and progesterone affects metabolism and appetite. Weight gain seems to be the body's response to this major reorganization of the female hormone system. In addition, increased calorie intake

HANDY HOTLINE: For the North American Menopause Society is 1-440-442-7550.

due to the stresses of coping with such profound body changes may also contribute to weight gain.

The abrupt loss of female hormones during menopause leads to a decrease in calcium absorption and increases the rate of bone loss. It's essential to compensate for these losses through extra servings of dairy products or calcium supplementation. Anyone who takes in high levels of calcium (more than 1,000 mg/day) should aim for at least 400 mg of magnesium to keep these essential nutrients in a balanced ratio of 2:1.

Soy and flax, plants rich in estrogen-like compounds, have been heavily promoted as helping to ease the variety of symptoms that occur with the change of life. Studies have shown that fewer than a quarter of Japanese menopausal women, whose normal diet contains lots of soy protein, complain of hot flashes. While some suggest that Japanese culture may discourage women from complaining about symptoms even if they do experience them, soy has been the subject of some 2,000 studies in the past decade—most of them small—and has produced mixed results. In some, soy offered no apparent benefit; in others, symptoms were relieved by as much as 50 percent.

Less iron is required for menopausal women because they no longer have monthly blood losses. It's still important to choose high-iron foods, since most women eat so few calories.

Herbs have long been used to help control the symptoms of menopause. Ginseng may lessen the intensity of hot flashes and other symptoms, but too much can have powerful effects on the female reproductive system and may cause uterine bleeding. (For those not yet menopausal, evening primrose oil may help alleviate premenstrual symptoms.)

SELECTED STUDIES

In October 2002, Brazilian researchers reported in *Obstetrics and Gynecology* that both menopause and heart disease risks were reduced or prevented in women who consumed 100 mg of soy daily.

Meanwhile, in 1999 researchers at Wake Forest University found that giving a soy protein beverage containing 34 mg of isoflavones once a day did nothing to ease menopause symptoms, but drinking it twice daily reduced the severity—but not the number—of hot flashes by 20 percent. The soy drinks had no effect on other symptoms.

New Nutrition Recommendations For Menopause

- Maintain a healthy weight by increasing regular physical activity. Calorie needs decrease as your age increases. Since most women eat a minimal amount of calories to begin with, burning more calories is the best solution for preventing undesirable weight gain.

- Choose foods rich in calcium and magnesium to curb bone loss. If you can't or won't consume dairy products, choose a calcium carbonate or calcium citrate supplement.

- Experiment with foods like soy and flax or supplements of ginseng or evening primrose oil to determine if they help reduce menopausal symptoms. Choose only one supplement at a time so that you can effectively judge its impact.

LINK UP to *http://www.meno pause.org* for the North American Menopause Society.

HANDY HOTLINE: To the National Headache Foundation is 1-888-643-5552.

Migraines and Headaches

It starts as a hot pain behind your eye and builds to a peak until you can't stand light, noise, or even the slightest touch. You just want to lie in dark silence. Migraines are a whole dimension beyond headaches. Migraines tend to begin in your head, but as they progress they can wreak havoc on your whole body with severe head throbbing, nausea, vomiting, dizziness, cold hands, tremors, and sensitivity to light and sound.

Migraines are thought to be triggered by an electrical spasm in the back of the brain. The spasm causes blood vessels in this area to constrict, while the vessels at the top of the brain dilate. Blood goes into the arteries around your temples, causing throbbing pain and inflammation in the brain covering. Migraines can be temporary or last a day or two. The serotonin level may play a large role in the triggering of the spasm.

Migraines are largely hereditary, and women tend to develop them three times more often than men. Nearly twenty-eight million Americans suffer migraines according to the National Headache Foundation in Chicago.

Nutrition Issues

Many things can bring on an attack of migraine: changing hormone levels prior to menstruation or during ovulation, poor eating or sleeping habits, stress, chemicals in food (including additives and preservatives), or low blood sugar.

NSAIDs (nonsteroidal anti-inflammatory drugs such as aspirin, ibuprofen, and naproxen) often cause side effects, especially upset stomachs. These pain medications are called simple analgesics because they contain a single ingredient, in contrast to combined analgesics, which contain additional ingredients such as caffeine.

Magnesium may play a role in preventing or reducing the frequency of migraine headaches. Rich food sources of magnesium include cocoa, chocolate, most nuts, fish and shellfish, legumes, kelp, corn, soybean sprouts, lima beans, whole-wheat muffins, taco shells, bran flakes, toasted wheat germ, brown rice, grain and grain products, dried figs, dried pears, bananas, and dark green leafy vegetables. Feverfew is an herb that may also provide some relief for migraines.

Probably the best news for migraine sufferers is that chocolate has been taken off the list of foods that may trigger these severe headaches. Phenols in red wine and tyramine in aged cheese can increase a hormone release that constricts blood vessels. When the vessels suddenly rebound to open, a throbbing sensation results. Caffeine can temporarily prevent a headache by dilating blood vessels, but too much will cause overdilation and that can be as painful as constriction. Some people are so sensitive to caffeine that even a little will cause a headache. Others get headaches from caffeine overconsumption. Food additives, including those containing sulfites, may cause headaches

LINK UP to *http://www.migraine-help.com* for more resources and information.

in some individuals. Another source of headaches is hunger.

New Nutrition Recommendations for Migraines and Headaches

- Avoid foods that seem to trigger a reaction; common triggers include red wine (phenols) and aged cheese (tyramine). There is no particular way of eating that universally impacts the occurrence of migraine headaches.

- Include plenty of food sources of magnesium or consider a supplement if you can't regularly eat these foods.

- Eat small, more frequent meals to help prevent hunger, which can also be a headache trigger.

Obesity

If you weigh 20 percent or more above your healthy weight, you're obese (carrying an excess accumulation of fat). Being overweight is defined as excess body weight that includes muscle, bone, fat, and water. It is possible that you may be overweight, but not obese, if you're physically fit and have lots of heavy, dense muscle mass.

Obesity is an important and dangerous disease. Despite the abundance of low-calorie and fat-free foods, Americans are getting fatter. Did you know that obesity is considered a risk factor for half of the ten leading causes of death in the United States? Carrying around an excess of body fat increases a person's risk for developing many potentially fatal diseases, including coronary heart disease, stroke, hypertension, diabetes, and some types of cancer.

Nutrition Issues

Name any diet and someone's probably lost weight on it. Losing weight is relatively simple; it's keeping those extra pounds off that's difficult. Remember, diets don't work permanently. It's attitudes and lifestyle changes that determine if the pounds you shed will stay off. A sedentary lifestyle is the single most critical factor in the explosion of obesity worldwide.

New Nutrition Recommendations to Avoid Obesity

- Get regular exercise; at least thirty minutes a day of activity equivalent to brisk walking is recommended. You don't have to do it all at once; three shorter periods of ten minutes each are just as effective.

- Monitor what you eat. Focus on healthful eating, not deprivation diets. Choose foods that enhance your health such as fruits, vegetables, whole grains, lean meats, and low-fat dairy products. Seek foods for their nutrient benefits, not their calorie content.

- Lose weight slowly; losing one pound per week is considered most effective. If you are overweight, losing as little as 5 to 10 percent of your body weight can improve your health.

LINK UP to *http://www.obesity.org* for the American Obesity Association.

HANDY HOTLINE:
To the American Obesity Association is 1-800-98-OBESE.

WARNING: PITFALLS OF POPULAR DIET PROGRAMS

Americans spend more than $30 billion a year on diet programs and products in an attempt to lose weight. Unfortunately, most will fail. Here's a look at the pitfalls of popular diet programs.

Diet Method	Premise	Why It Fails	Potential Side Effects
Fasting (no solid foods for one or more days)	Quick weight loss, natural process that detoxifies your system.	Weight loss is from water, not fat. Can't be maintained over the long run. Difficult to stop eating and be able to work or be socially active.	Repeated fasting may actually decrease your metabolism, making it harder to lose weight permanently. Fasting stresses your body systems.
Liquid meal replacements (canned shakes or drinks)	Control calorie intake by replacing one or more meals with special beverage.	Not a satisfying replacement for food. No change in eating or exercise behaviors.	Doesn't promote a healthful lifestyle. Overuse may cause nutrient deficiencies.
Over-the-counter pills (variety of appetite suppressants, bulking agents)	Decreases your appetite so you feel like eating less. Usually contain phenylpropanol amine (PPA) and/or caffeine.	PPA has been repeatedly proven ineffective in controlling appetite or weight.	Caffeine may cause elevated blood pressure, irritability. Over time one may need stronger doses and develop a dependency.
Prepackaged meals (ready-to-eat meals packaged and sold by weight-loss programs or companies)	You don't have to think about choosing foods or practice portion control.	It's not reasonable to eat prepackaged meals as a lifetime weight-control method. Alienates family and friends. Often quite expensive.	Lack of variety can lead to nutritional deficiencies. Most prepackaged meals are low in fiber and don't include enough fruits, vegetables, and whole grains.

Diet Method	Premise	Why It Fails	Potential Side Effects
Surgery (stomach stapling, gastric bypass)	Quick, dramatic weight loss without dieting or exercise.	Doesn't promote change in behaviors needed to keep weight off. Most people regain weight.	Obese people are at much higher risk for surgical complications, including death. Chronic diarrhea and malabsorption are permanent side effects of these surgeries and often cause malnutrition.
Very low-calorie diets (less than 1,000 calories)	Quick weight loss due to dramatic calorie reduction.	Most people can't keep calories this low without feeling deprived. May binge eat to compensate.	Your body can adjust to needing fewer calories by lowering your metabolism. May lead to eating disorders.
High-protein, low-carbohydrate diets	Quick weight loss, able to eat lots of meat and fat.	People get bored quickly. You may feel nauseated after 4 to 5 days. Not a healthful long-term eating plan.	Constipation, dehydration, and bad breath are noticeable. This diet lacks disease-fighting nutrients and fiber.

Osteoporosis

Osteoporosis (meaning "porous bones") is a bone-thinning disease affecting one out of every three postmenopausal women, and elderly men, too. Symptomless throughout most of life, osteoporosis usually first reveals itself as a hip or spine fracture in old age. While there is no cure for osteoporosis, its debilitating effect can be prevented.

Robert Heaney, M.D., one of the leading U.S. calcium researchers, says, "Osteoporosis is an adolescent concern that doesn't express itself until old age." Osteoporosis affects 25 million people in the United States, causes 1.5 million bone fractures a year, and costs $10 billion annually in medical costs. There is no doubt that the best protection against future bone loss is to build the best skeleton possible during the growth years of nine to nineteen.

Bone is a living tissue, just like skin or muscle. In fact, 20 percent of bone tissue is replaced every year through the process called bone remodeling. Bone-eating cells called osteoclasts break down bone, creating holes; then bone-building cells called osteoblasts come along and fill up those holes with fresh new bone. The whole process can take four to six months.

Here are the main reasons that women, especially older women, are at such high risk...

- Women have less bone mass at adulthood than men do because of their typically smaller frame size. As women age, they are therefore more vulnerable to any loss of bone.

- The male hormone testosterone protects men's bones as they age into their 60s and 70s. Women, on the other hand, need the hormone estrogen for bone health and density; after menopause, estrogen levels fall.

- Younger women who have anorexia and athletes with amenorrhea also may be at risk for bone mass loss due to decreased estrogen.

- Women typically consume less calcium-rich foods than men.

Nutrition Issues

Calcium and vitamin D help in the bone-building process by contributing to increased bone density and strength. Infants have far more bone-building osteoblasts at work than bone-eating osteoclasts. That's why their milk-based diet is perfectly suited to provide so much calcium and vitamin D. During adolescence, bone development really shifts into high gear. Nearly half of all bone is formed during the teen years. This is a time when calcium is crucial to build strong bones. Unfortunately, it is also a time when teens start replacing milk with soft drinks.

By the early twenties, you are still in the prime bone-building years. Even though the length of your bones is set, they can still grow in density and strength. Bone growth through your early thirties creates a reserve supply for the future. The peak bone mass that you reach in your early thirties is the maximum amount of bone you will ever have. As you age, you will be using up bone and calcium faster than you can replace it. Between the ages of thirty-five and forty-five you begin to use up calcium faster than ever before. Exercise and continued intake of calcium are critical for maintaining bone density. By age 45, you need to protect against a net loss of bone, which occurs when you are losing more bone material than you are making.

In the United States, the recommendations for daily calcium intake are twice as high as in other countries because Americans have greater urinary losses of calcium. There are two theories that suggest why this happens. Typical American diets have a high ratio of phosphorus to calcium, about 5:1; the ideal ratio is 1:1. High levels of phosphorus reduce calcium absorption, contributing to slow, continuous demineralization of bone tissue. Most soft drinks, particularly diet versions, are high in phosphorus, further upsetting the body's balance of phosphorus and calcium. American diets also tend to be high in protein, and you lose extra calcium through urination with high-protein diets. That's because protein foods are high in phosphorus and low in calcium, adding to the imbalance.

HANDY HOTLINE:
For osteoporosis and related bone diseases, call 1-800-624-BONE.

Calcium absorption is blocked if you drink more than two alcoholic drinks a day. The caffeine in coffee, tea, and colas (at levels of about ten cups a day) also interferes with calcium absorption.

Food plans that limit dairy products and are high in protein can deplete the bones of calcium. Vegetarians who avoid milk products may be at risk unless they are careful to get enough calcium. Crash diets and fasting also contribute to accumulated bone loss.

Those with inadequate amounts of the digestive enzyme lactase may develop lactose intolerance, a condition that makes it difficult to ingest milk products without discomfort. This can result in calcium deficiencies in people who avoid dairy foods because they cannot tolerate them comfortably. Fortunately, lactose-reduced milk and dairy products are now available, as are lactase tablets (e.g., Lactaid and Dairy Ease) that can be taken with dairy products.

Too much sodium increases urinary calcium loss. If you consume a modest amount of sodium (2,000 to 3,000 mg/day), you need about 1,200 mg of calcium. If your sodium intake is higher, you probably need more calcium.

Vitamin D enables the absorption of calcium. The natural way to get vitamin D is through sun exposure (see vitamin D in Chapter 5). Otherwise, you need about 400 IU of vitamin D a day from fortified foods or supplements. Milk is fortified with vitamin D to guard against this problem.

Another beverage that may help—alcohol. A November 2000 study in the *American Journal of Clinical Nutrition* found that women who consumed moderate amounts of alcohol had significantly higher bone mineral density than did nondrinkers.

New Nutrition Recommendations For Osteoporosis

- Build the best skeleton possible during the growth years; it's the best protection against future bone problems. Eat at least 1,000 to 1,500 mg of calcium per day from foods.

- Consume three calcium-rich dairy foods a day, along with generous amounts of green leafy vegetables. Choose nondairy foods that have been fortified with extra calcium, such as orange juice and rice.

- Use calcium supplements if you need them to assist in meeting your calcium needs.

- Space calcium supplements for optimal absorption. Your body can best retain calcium in amounts of 500 mg or less. Figure out how many tablets (of 500 mg or less) you need to take through the day to get the recommended daily amount.

- Correct chronically low amounts of vitamin D and possibly magnesium; boron; fluoride; vitamins K, B-12, and B-6; and folic acid.

HANDY HOTLINE:
For the National Dairy Council is 1-800-426-8271, and the American Dietetic Association Nutrition Hot Line is 1-800-366-1655; both organizations can provide a wealth of information on calcium sources and osteoporosis prevention.

- Limit soft drinks because they are very high in phosphorus, which interferes with the ability to use calcium.

- Get the proper amount of vitamin D; the RDA is 400 IU. For days when you can't get out in the sun, good natural dietary sources of vitamin D include cod liver oil, liver, egg yolks, tuna, sardines, and salmon.

- Make regular weight-bearing exercise a part of your daily routine. Activities such as walking, jogging, bicycling, and skiing all stress the long bones of the body against the pull of gravity, thus strengthening your bones.

- Stop smoking. Smoking can be toxic to your bone cells. It can also reduce your body's absorption of calcium. Smokers also tend to maintain a lean body weight, experience menopause earlier, and show an accelerated rate of postmenopausal bone loss.

- Moderate your caffeine intake. Caffeine can increase urinary calcium excretion. Heavy intake of beverages and foods containing caffeine along with poor calcium intake could compromise bone maintenance.

- Consider using certain herbal plants like kelp and other sea vegetables, as well as dandelion root, horsetail, and oat straw; these are good sources of calcium, magnesium, and trace minerals needed for strong and healthy bones. Kelp and other sea vegetables can be used as condiments to flavor food such as soups, casseroles, and salads.

LINK UP to *http://nof.org* for the National Osteoporosis Foundation. They provide a huge variety of resources.

LINK UP to Health World Online at *www.healthy.net* and search under 'Osteoporosis' for an article on *"What You Eat Affects Your Bones"* by Alan R. Gaby, MD.

- Try a chewable lactase supplement (such as Lactaid and Dairy Ease) just before you eat dairy foods if you're lactose intolerant.

Premenstrual Syndrome (PMS)

PMS is not a disease in the classic sense. More than 200 different symptoms have been reported by women in the days or weeks before their monthly menstrual periods. The most common symptoms include breast tenderness, abdominal bloating, weight gain, headaches, irritability, and food cravings.

Nutrition Issues

Women with periodic or mild PMS may respond well to diet and vitamin regimens based on the premise that women should not be subjecting their bodies to the "highs and lows" of certain dietary substances while dealing with the naturally occurring "highs and lows" of hormone levels. Therefore, some women are advised to avoid alcohol, refined sugar and nicotine. A well-balanced diet, with several small meals each day to avoid low blood sugar, is usually the advice. Supplements may include vitamin B-6 (under a doctor's supervision, because it can be toxic in large doses) to relieve depression, and/or oil of evening primrose, magnesium (100 mg/day) and calcium (1,200 mg/day).

SELECTED STUDIES

Healthy, premenopausal women between the ages of eighteen and forty-five years who had moderate to severe, cyclically recurring premenstrual symptoms were recruited across the United States. The women were randomly assigned to receive 1,200 mg of elemental calcium per day in the form of calcium carbonate or placebo for three menstrual cycles. Of the 466 women who participated in the study, those who took the calcium supplements each day experienced a 48 percent reduction in their overall PMS symptoms, compared with a 30 percent reduction among women given dummy pills (*American Journal of Obstetrics and Gynecology,* August 1998). Calcium depletion may interact with female hormones at certain stages of the menstrual cycle, leading to the physical and emotional discomfort of PMS. But note that there was also a 30 percent reduction in symptoms in women who took the placebo.

New Nutrition Recommendations For PMS

- Get the nutrients you need from foods to compensate for the marginal deficiencies that make many women more prone to PMS.

- Break a sweat. Even moderate exercise can help reduce PMS symptoms. If you work up a sweat, the loss of water can help decrease bloating.

- Opt for high-carbohydrate foods like potatoes, whole-grain breads, or crackers instead of sweets. They'll help soothe your mood without aggravating your PMS symptoms.

- Limit consumption of alcohol, caffeine, and salt if these compounds aggravate your symptoms. Alcohol may worsen mood swings and irritability. Caffeine can increase breast tenderness and nervousness. Foods high in sodium may increase bloating and fluid retention.

Ulcers

Calming down and taking it easy isn't good advice for the prevention of ulcers. It's a myth that anxiety, anger, and type A personalities cause ulcers. Recent research shows that most ulcers are caused by the bacteria *Helicobacter pylori. There are two main types of ulcers:* duodenal and gastric. Duodenal ulcers are the more common variety and are located in the small intestine right next to the stomach. Gastric ulcers are true stomach ulcers that occur when stomach acid eats away at the stomach's lining. Esophageal ulcers are quite rare and are often a result of alcohol abuse.

It's believed that the *Helicobacter pylori* bacteria somehow change the tissue lining in the digestive tract, making it more susceptible to ulcer formation. *Helicobacter pylori* is present in 92 percent of duodenal ulcers and 73 percent of gastric ulcers. Certain drugs can also promote the growth of ulcers. Aspirin and ibuprofen can irritate the stomach or intestinal lining enough to trigger an ulcer.

Fortunately, ulcers are relatively easy to treat; in many cases they are cured with antibiotics. Still, the dangers associated with ulcers—such as anemia, hemorrhage, pancreatic problems, and stomach cancer—are serious, so ulcers should always be monitored carefully.

Nutrition Issues

Overzealous use of over-the-counter analgesics (such as aspirin, ibuprofen, and naproxen), heavy alcohol use, and smoking exacerbate and may promote the development of ulcers. In fact, research indicates that heavy smokers are more prone to developing duodenal ulcers than are nonsmokers. Those who drink alcohol are more susceptible to esophageal ulcers. If you use moderate or great amounts of aspirin for a long period of time, you are at increased risk for gastric ulcers.

Studies show that gastric ulcers are more likely to develop in elderly people. This may be because arthritis is prevalent in the elderly, and alleviating arthritis pain often includes taking daily doses of aspirin or ibuprofen. Another contributing factor may be that with advancing age, the pylorus (the valve between the stomach and duodenum) relaxes and allows excess bile to seep into the stomach and erode the stomach lining.

Vitamins A and E and the mineral zinc help increase the production of mucin, a substance your body secretes to protect the stomach lining. Choosing more high-fiber foods can also reduce your chances of developing a duodenal ulcer. Fiber also enhances mucin secretion, which protects the duodenal lining.

New Nutrition Recommendations For Ulcers

- Ban bland diets. Since it's fairly clear that bacteria, not what you eat, cause most ulcers, there is no need to have a bland diet. There is no scientific evidence that a bland diet helps ulcers heal or reduces the painful symptoms that accompany ulcers. And spicy foods do not contribute to them.

- Don't overdose on iron supplements. Although people with bleeding ulcers can develop anemia and may need to take iron as a treatment, taking too much can irritate the stomach lining and make you worse. Ask your doctor how much iron you need.

- Avoid foods that irritate your stomach. Use common sense: if it upsets your stomach when you eat it, don't. Everyone is different, but spicy foods (especially black pepper and chili powder) and fatty foods are common irritants.

- Stop smoking. Heavy smokers are more likely to develop duodenal ulcers than nonsmokers, largely because nicotine is thought to prevent the pancreas from secreting acid-neutralizing enzymes.

- Don't eat close to bedtime. Late-night eating stimulates the secretion of stomach acid while you sleep.

- Cut out alcohol. It irritates the lining of the digestive tract. If you must drink, dilute with water, soda, or juice and eat food along with alcohol to help decrease its acid-stimulating effect. ❦

10

EVALUATING NUTRITION PRODUCTS AND PURVEYORS

Accurate nutrition information is hard to obtain when your primary "scientific" source is your local newspaper, favorite magazine, Internet, or popular TV news/magazine show.

Freedom to Deceive

"Congress shall make no law abridging the freedom of speech, or of the press."
—First Amendment to the U.S. Constitution

Freedom of expression is the right of every U.S. citizen. Each individual can gather and present or publish information or opinions without fear of punishment or control by the government. These freedoms apply to all types of printed and broadcast material, including seminars, books, newspapers, magazines, pamphlets, films, radio, and television programs. Why a review on constitutional freedoms? We all have the right to say or print anything. The only exceptions are very narrowly defined. If you don't threaten to overthrow the government, slander someone, or include pornographic material, you can publish your opinions on any topic as if they were fact. Legally, it doesn't matter if what you say is true or false. You can make things up, list impressive-sounding references that don't exist, and twist someone else's ideas or research. Just browse the diet and nutrition section of your local bookstore. Most of the offerings there should be shelved in the fiction section. Do any of these claims sound familiar?

• Lose as much weight as you want without depriving yourself

• Burn fat while you sleep

• Miracle diet pill lets you lose weight instantly

Most nutrition articles are written by journalists who write about science—not by scientists. Nutrition research today includes techniques and tools unknown a decade ago. Journalists may be excellent writers, but often they don't have the scientific savvy to critically examine the research behind the stories they write. Of course there are exceptions. If you rely on newspapers, here are some of the best journalists who currently cover nutrition topics—Nanci Helmich of *USA Today*, Jane Brody of the *New York Times*, Sally Squires of the *Washington Post*, and Kathy Doheny, who writes for the *L.A. Times*.

Sizing Up Research

People often ask why we need controlled clinical studies when it's so "obvious" that something has worked for years or centuries. The best answer is to look at studies that backfired. The 1992 CAST (Cardiac Arrhythmia Suppression Trial) study showed that commonly held beliefs are not always true. Three drugs were being routinely used in the 1980s and early 1990s to prevent irregular heartbeats (arrhythmia) in people after they had already had a heart attack. Researchers set up a study to determine which of the drugs was most effective. Fortunately, they included a control group in addition to the three "experimental" groups that received the various drugs. The control group didn't receive any medications to prevent arrhythmias, just a placebo (an inactive substance that looks the same as the medicine being tested). Guess what? Each of the three drugs being studied caused more deaths than the placebo. For years, physicians had routinely prescribed drugs they felt helped patients. Based on their experience, most physicians believed the drugs were helpful. If a carefully controlled study had not been done, no one would have ever realized these drugs were harming, not helping, people.

The Power of Placebo

If you feel better after using a product or having a procedure done, it is natural to credit the new pill, potion, or treatment. It is important to remember, however, that taking action often produces temporary relief of symptoms due to a placebo effect. This effect is a beneficial change that can't be explained by the treatment given. You don't even have to believe in the power of a placebo for it to work. The placebo effect may be enhanced by impressive procedures and an enthusiastic therapist or healer.

The placebo effect is inherently misleading. It can make you think something is effective when it's not. Without controlled clinical trials, any treatment that is used could receive credit for your body's natural ability to heal. Since placebo therapy does work sometimes, it's obvious that we need to learn more about how the mind and the spirit act to heal our bodies.

Sensationalized Science

In 1975 the chances were slim that a nutrition-related study published in a scientific journal would make the evening news or appear in the headlines of your morning newspaper.

There are many ways a scientific study can be completed, but none of them is perfect. Here are some of the most popular types.

Case-control studies try to match up people with similar profiles, except one of them has the active disease or ailment being studied and the other does not. The studies follow these sets of people over time to look for similarities and differences.

Clinical trials are studies that provide different interventions to similar groups of people and compare differences or reactions.

Cohort studies start with basically healthy people and follow them over time, keeping track of their lifestyle patterns and rates of disease.

Epidemiological studies look at population trends and demographics to develop theories for noted changes or differences between people.

Prospective studies plan ahead for the variables they want to track over time and develop ways to collect that information.

Retrospective studies look at already accumulated study information and try to pull out information to reach conclusions that were not part of the original study design.

In May 1996, two studies about sodium were published in the same week. One study in the *British Medical Journal* urged cutting back on salt, but research in the *Journal of the American Medical Association* (JAMA) proclaimed no need for concern about salt intake. Then in March 1998, research papers on both sides of the ocean flip-flopped positions. Another British journal, *The Lancet*, reported that people with low sodium intakes had higher death rates and questioned the recommendation to reduce salt intake for the whole population. On the U.S. side, a major controlled trial of sodium restriction in older people with high blood pressure, in the March 1998 issue of JAMA, provided clear evidence of the benefit of decreased salt intake in this group. The *JAMA* article said that a decrease in salt intake, especially if combined with weight reduction, had definite benefits, such as preventing cardiovascular complications or reducing the need for drug treatment for hypertensive men and women ages sixty to eighty.

Confused yet? First of all, each of these studies deals with different issues. The 1998 studies were looking at different groups of people in markedly different ways. The British researchers were questioning the need to restrict salt intake for the population at large. They did suggest that one shortcoming in their research can't be overlooked—some of the people in their study who died may have been on a low-sodium diet because of existing cardiovascular disease. Their study didn't exclude such people, who have higher death rates. The second 1998 study focused on a specific subgroup—older people with

RATING MAGAZINES FOR ACCURACY

The American Council on Science and Health (ACSH) has been tracking magazine nutrition reporting for many years. Here are their most recent findings.

Magazine	Percent Accurate Nutrition Information	Magazine	Percent Accurate Nutrition Information
Consumer Reports	95	Redbook	83
Better Homes and Gardens	92	Runner's World	82
Good Housekeeping	90	Shape	81
Glamour	89	Men's Health	81
Parents	88	Fitness	79
Health	87	Reader's Digest	86
Self	77	Prevention	86
Cosmopolitan	74	Woman's Day	85
Muscle & Fitness	70	Cooking Light	85

Source: ACSH Nutrition Accuracy in Popular Magazines Special Report, 1995–1996

high blood pressure. If you are between sixty and eighty years old and have high blood pressure, a low-sodium diet is usually a good thing. Unfortunately, because of the misleading and conflicting headlines, a person with heart disease, severe high blood pressure, or certain forms of liver or kidney disease may consider dropping his/her low-salt diet. That action could be dangerous or even deadly. Never change how you eat based on just one or two studies, especially if you've only heard of them through the media.

As you wait in the check-out lane at the supermarket, tabloid papers and popular women's magazines shout dramatic claims and amazing health findings that often contradict each other. You need to look beyond the hyped-up headlines and catchy phrases for the truth.

Don't Swallow Half-Baked Nutrition Claims

First of all, never change your lifestyle habits based on a single study or report. If you've ever worked in communications, you'll realize how easy it is to get the facts wrong. Remember the "Liquid Candy" report from the Center for Science in the Public Interest (CSPI) in the fall of 1998? It announced a dramatic increase in teen consumption of soft drinks. Two weeks after the report was highlighted by nationwide media, it was discovered that a consulting firm hired by CSPI made a serious error in calculation. It failed to divide the number of cans of pop consumed over two days by two to get a daily average intake. The corrected press release listed thirty-six separate mistakes from ten different sections of the original report, including additional mistakes made by CSPI. If you never saw the corrections from this report, you are not alone.

You don't have to be a health statistician (though it would help) to objectively dissect a scientific study. There are lots of simple ways to determine if the conclusions of research are valid and if they apply to you. Using five key factors, let's size up the much-publicized *Journal of the American Medical Association* study from the Arizona Cancer Institute that suggests selenium supplements can reduce the risk of many different types of cancer.

1. Study size: 1,300.

2. Study group: men (75 percent) and women (25 percent); all people with a previous history of skin cancer who live in the southeastern United States.

3. Length of the study: 4 years.

4. Study objective: To determine if selenium supplements can help protect against skin cancer.

5. Control group protocol: Half the group took 200 mcg of selenium and the other half took placebos. Neither the subjects nor the researchers knew who had the placebo.

Size: The number of subjects in this study is too small to prove there is a cancer-reduction benefit from selenium supplements. Many impressive statistics are quoted, such as: the selenium group developed 63 percent fewer prostate cancers, 58 percent fewer colorectal cancers, and 46 percent fewer lung cancers than the placebo group. How many new cancers would you normally expect 1,300 people to be diagnosed with over four years' time? If a specific cancer commonly affects 1 in 1,000 people, then you need large numbers of people in both control and experimental groups to know if your results are significant. How many people who have already been treated for skin cancer go on to develop a completely different type of the disease? That factor increases the pool of needed test subjects even more.

Study group: Just 25 percent of the participants were women (about 325 females), not nearly enough to estimate how selenium supplements affect women in general. Also, women cannot get prostate cancer and have much lower rates of colorectal cancer than men. Don't forget that all the participants had a history of skin cancer—do you? These people live in the southeastern part of the United States, where foods are often low in selenium. That's because the soil in this part of the country is low in selenium. Do you live in the scorching southeast? If not, you're different from the study group and the results may not apply to you. Environmental conditions like sun exposure surely contributed to the risk of their initial skin cancer.

Length of the study: In an ideal world, long-term studies that span the course of generations would be used to draw scientific conclusions. Realistically, we don't want to wait that long for cures to dangerous and debilitating conditions. There needs to be a middle ground. How reasonable is it to expect that in any four-year period, someone would develop cancer? Would longer-term supplementation show the same or different effects? Most research concludes by asking more questions than it answers.

Study objective: The original clinical trial was to determine if selenium affected risk of skin cancer. The answer to the original study question—Do selenium supplements protect against skin cancer?—was no. It wasn't until the study had been underway for several years that the scientists decided to start looking at whether selenium supplements had an impact on cancers other than

skin cancer. Such unplanned searches are mathematically more likely to turn up results that occur by chance.

Control group: Controlling people isn't easy. It's important that no one involved directly in the study knows who gets the "real" medicine and who doesn't. Care must be taken to be sure that both placebo and the pills, potions, or remedies look, smell, taste, or feel identical. For example, zinc lozenges taste terrible. Placebo zinc lozenges should taste just as bad. That's because study participants often talk with each other and the study staff. They like to compare notes while waiting for appointments.

How is compliance tracked? Did the people in the study really take all the pills they were supposed to? Did they also take other products and not inform the researchers? Often, people who participate in clinical trials are paid. In addition, they may receive free medical care, in-depth laboratory tests, gain important information about their health, and receive much personal attention. Sometimes these benefits are enough to "fake" compliance. Food-related studies are even more difficult to control. How accurately and honestly do you think people estimate and record the types and amount of food they eat?

Funding sources: Everyone loves to zero in on who funded the study. It's a reasonable concern. Think of it like buying a car from a used-car salesperson. You need to approach with caution and ask lots of questions. Most research is funded by private companies. If we relied solely on federal dollars, little valuable research would occur. For many pharmaceutical companies, research is part of their business. Now that foods are being investigated for their health benefits, it makes sense that food companies and dietary supplement manufacturers will start funding research, too.

Also, beware of consumer groups that publicize opinions as fact. Just because an agency is nonprofit doesn't mean it is ethical. Nonprofit companies need money to operate just like for-profit companies. Nonprofit companies just have different tax advantages and must spend most of the money they take in instead of rewarding owners or shareholders.

Junk Science

Any combination of the following signs should raise a red flag of warning to be skeptical.

1. Recommendations that promise a quick fix.

2. Dire warnings of danger from a single product or regimen.

3. Claims that sound too good to be true.

4. Simplistic conclusions drawn from a complex study.

5. Recommendations based on a single study.

6. Dramatic statements that are refuted by reputable scientific organizations.

7. Lists of "good" and "bad" foods.

8. Recommendations made to help sell a product.

9. Recommendations based on studies published without peer review.

10. Recommendations from studies that ignore differences among individuals or groups.

Source: Food and Nutrition Science Alliance (FANSA), a partnership of The American Dietetic Association, American Society for Clinical Nutrition, American Society for Nutritional Sciences, and Institute of Food Technologists

Supplement Savvy

Have you ever ventured into a casino? Dim lights, smoky air, and a rainbow of flashy games entice you to part with your money. You might wonder if the slots are rigged or the dealers crooked; yet the seductive promise of walking away a winner can be difficult to resist. This same image comes to mind when stalking the supplement shelves. Though the lighting is better and smoking is prohibited, you usually don't know what you're getting into, but hopes are high for choosing a winner.

Although most people believe otherwise, vitamin, mineral, herbal, and other dietary supplements are some of the most loosely regulated products in America. In 1994, over two million Americans wrote or called congressional representatives and told them to back off on supplement regulations being proposed by the Dietary Supplement Health and Education Act (DSHEA). Supplement manufacturers misled people into thinking that all dietary supplements would become as regulated as prescription drugs—in other words, limited or difficult to get. The public confusion and upset led to passage of a flimsy set of regulations that fail to provide even minimum standards of safety and truthfulness. Instead of requiring that all types of supplements be proven safe and effective, as is required for foods, drugs, and additives, the Food and Drug Administration (FDA) must wait for proof that a product has caused serious harm or death before it can be pulled from the shelves.

DSHEA essentially gives dietary supplement manufacturers freedom to market more products as dietary supplements and provide information about their products' benefits on the label. No license, inspection, or quality control is mandated. There are no government specifications for scientific testing of supplements. Each manufacturer can determine what type of testing, if any, will be done. Dosages are also set by product manufacturers, not the FDA.

Supplement manufacturers aren't required to completely list the ingredients included in their products. For example, researchers at Cedars-Sinai Bone Center in Los Angeles found that 10 percent of the older people they studied were taking toxic levels of vitamin D. Two of the supplements commonly used by those in the study (which happened to contain some of the highest levels of vitamin D) didn't even list vitamin D as an ingredient!

The United States Pharmacopoeia (USP) sets standards for drug products. It recently established standards for individual and combination vitamin and mineral nutritional supplements. These standards detail quality practices for supplement manufacturers. Because the USP is a nongovernmental organization, compliance with such standards is voluntary for supplements. However, USP standards for drug products are legally enforceable by the FDA. The USP notation on supplement labels is currently the best way to ensure product quality.

There are several key measures that are important in making sure that vitamin and mineral tablets and capsules do the job you expect them to. *The following quality indicators are based on USP laboratory testing standards...*

- Disintegration measures how fast a tablet or capsule breaks into small pieces. Smaller piece size makes it easier for the ingredients to dissolve. If a tablet or capsule does not break down within a certain amount of time, it may pass through your body without being absorbed. Water-soluble vitamins should disintegrate in less than forty-five minutes (uncoated) or in less than sixty minutes (coated).

- Dissolution gauges how fast and how much of a vitamin or mineral dissolves in a fluid that is similar to your digestive tract. USP standards track pyridoxine when testing multivitamins. Its standards require that 75 percent be dissolved within sixty minutes.

- Strength is the amount of a specific vitamin or mineral substance in each tablet or capsule. To meet USP product quality standards, the amount present must be within a narrow range of the amount declared on the label.

- Purity is controlled by USP standards that set a range for acceptable impurities that can result from contamination or degradation of the product during processing or storage.

- Expiration dates must be imprinted on the package. When the date is past due, the nutrient ingredients in a bottle or package of supplements may no longer meet USP standards of purity, strength, and/or quality.

It's been widely reported that you can test your own supplements at home for disintegration. But home experiments using water or vinegar don't come close to copying the conditions in your stomach or at a laboratory.

The Claim Game

DSHEA allows all types of vitamin, mineral, herbal, and dietary supplements to carry "structure or function" claims, but not statements that imply their products can treat, diagnose, cure, or prevent disease. All structure or function claims must be based on scientific information about using supplements to maintain health. However, the term "scientific" is defined by the supplement manufacturer or the advertising agency. Thumb through magazine ads for supplements and you'll see that almost anything counts as scientific in the minds of the companies that are challenged to market these products.

Benefit claims have always been a controversial feature of dietary supplement labeling, and manufacturers rely on claims to sell products. Can you trust them? DSHEA and previous food labeling laws allow supplement manufacturers to use three types of claims. Nutrient content claims and health claims follow rules similar to those required for food products. Nutrition support claims, which include "structure-function claims," are unique to supplement products. As with food products, nutrient levels required for any claims are based on Daily Values and not Recommended Dietary Allowances.

Nutrient-content claims describe the level of a nutrient in a food or dietary supplement. For example, a supplement containing at least 200 mg of calcium per serving could carry the claim "high in calcium" since it provides at least 20 percent of the DV for calcium. A supplement with at least 12 mg per serving of vitamin C could state on its label "Excellent source of vitamin C."

Health claims indicate a link between a food or substance and a disease or health-related condition. The FDA preauthorizes these claims based on a review of the scientific evidence or authoritative statements from certain scientific bodies, such as the National Academy of Sciences, that show or describe a well-established diet-to-health link. *As of this writing, a few of the approved claims that appropriate supplements may use include…*

- Folic acid and a decreased risk of neural tube defect–affected pregnancy (if the supplement contains sufficient amounts of folic acid).

- Calcium and a lower risk of osteoporosis (if the supplement contains sufficient amounts of calcium).

- Psyllium seed husk (if the supplement contains sufficient amounts of psyllium seed husk) and a lower risk of coronary heart disease (as part of a diet low in cholesterol and saturated fat).

Examples of prohibited claims for a dietary supplement include "protects against cancer," "treats hot flashes," and "reduces nausea associated with chemotherapy." If you find dietary supplements whose labels state or imply that the product can help diagnose, treat, cure, or prevent a disease (e.g., "cures cancer" or "treats arthritis"), remember that the product is being marketed illegally as a drug and has not been evaluated for safety or effectiveness.

Nutrition support claims describe a link between a nutrient and the deficiency disease that can result if the nutrient is lacking in the diet. For example, an iron supplement label could state that iron prevents anemia. When these types of claims are used, the label must mention the prevalence of the nutrient-deficiency disease in the United States. Structure-function claims refer to the supplement's effect on the body's structure or function, including its overall effect on a person's well-being. *Examples of structure-function claims are…*

- Calcium builds strong bones.

- Antioxidants maintain cell integrity.

- Fiber maintains bowel regularity.

Manufacturers can use structure-function claims without FDA authorization.

Structure-function claims are easy to spot because the label must carry the disclaimer "This statement has not been evaluated by the Food and Drug Administration. This product is not intended to diagnose, treat, cure, or prevent any disease."

In an effort to correct problems with supplement regulations, the FDA is trying to update DSHEA. "Consumers want access to dietary supplements, but also need reliable information about the products they are consuming," announced William Schultz, the FDA's Deputy Commissioner for Policy, in explaining the proposed changes. "By clarifying for manufacturers what types of claims can and cannot be made on a dietary supplement label, this new proposal helps consumers make more informed and wiser choices."

The Federal Trade Commission (FTC), not the FDA, regulates claims made in the advertising of dietary supplements. In recent years, the FTC has taken a number of enforcement actions against companies whose advertisements contained false and misleading information. Erroneous claims that chromium picolinate was a treatment for weight loss and high blood cholesterol were removed. An action in 1997 targeted ads for an ephedrine alkaloid supplement because they understated the degree of the product's risk and featured a man falsely described as a doctor.

WHAT YOUR DIETARY SUPPLEMENT LABEL MUST TELL YOU

Statement of Identity

GINSENG
A DIETARY SUPPLEMENT

Net quantity of contents — 60 CAPSULES

Structure-function claim
Directions

"When you need to perform your best, take ginseng."
This statement has not been evaluated by the Food and Drug Administration. This Product is not intended to diagnose, treat, cure, or prevent any disease.
DIRECTIONS FOR USE: Take one capsule daily.

Supplement Facts pane

Supplement Facts
Serving Size 1 Capsule
Amount Per Capsule
Oriental Gingseng, powdered (root)   250 mcg*
*Daily value not established

Other ingredients in descending order of predominance and by common name or propriety blend.

Other Ingredients: Gelatin, water, and glycerin
ABC COMPANY
Anywhere, USA 00001

Name and place of business of manufacturer, packer, or distributor. This is the addtess to write for more product information.

Source: Food and Drug Administration—Website

HOW TO READ A SUPPLEMENT LABEL

This is the brand name of the product.

"Serving size" is the manufacturer's suggested serving expressed in the appropriate unit (tablet, capsule, softgel, packet, teaspoonful).

"Amount Per Tablet" heads the listing of nutrients contained in the supplement, followed by the quantity present in each tablet or capsule (if the serving size is one tablet).

International Unit (I.U.) is a standard unit of measurement for fat-soluble vitamins (A, D, and E).

Milligram (mg) and microgram (mcg) are units of measurement for water-soluble vitamins (C and B-complex) and minerals. A milligram is equal to 1/1,000 of a gram (a microgram is equal to 1/1,000 of a milligram).

A complete list of all ingredients will appear outside the Nutrition Facts box. This includes nutrients and other ingredients used to formulate the supplement, in decreasing order by weight.

This voluntary notation indicates the supplement has passed certain quality-control tests.

BRAND NAME

MULTIVITAMIN AND MINERAL SUPPLEMENT

DIRECTIONS: One (1) tablet daily as a dietary supplement.

Nutrition Facts

Serving Size 1 tablet

Amount Per Tablet	% Daily Value
Vitamin A 5000 I.U. 50% as Beta Carotene	100%
Vitamin C 250 mg	417%
Vitamin D 400 I.U.	100%
Vitamin E 200 I.U.	667%
Thiamin 5mg	333%
Riboflavin 5 mg	294%
Niacin 20 mg	100%
Vitamin B$_6$ 5mg	250%
Folate 0.4 mg	100%
Vitamin B$_{12}$ 6 mcg	100%
Biotin 150 mcg	50%
Pantothenic Acid 10 mg	100%
Calcium 200 mg	20%
Iron 18 mg	100%
Phosphorus 200 mg	20%
Iodine 150 mcg	100%
Magnesium 200 mcg	50%
Zinc 15 mg	100%
Selenium 25 mcg	*
Copper 2 mg	100%

* Daily Value not established

INGREDIENTS: vitamin A acetate, beta carotene, vitamin D, dl-alpha tocopherol acetate, ascorbic acid, folic acid, thiamin mononitrate, riboflavin, niacinamide, pyridoxine hydrochloride, vitamin B-12, biotin. d-calcium pantothenate, potassium chloride, dicalcium phosphate, potassium iodine. ferrous fumarate, magnesium oxide, copper sulfate, zinc oxide, manganese sulfate, sodium selenate, chromium chloride, sodium molybdate, microcrystalline cellulose, calcium carbonate, sodium carboxymethylcellulose

STORAGE Keep tightly closed in dry place; do not expose to excessive heat.

KEEP OUT OF THE REACH OF CHILDREN
EXPIRATION DATE: NOV. 2005
Manufacturer or distributor's name, address and zip code

USP

Usage recommended by the manufacturer.

"Percent Daily Value" (DV) is a new label reference term for the percentage of the recommended daily intake for each nutrient for adults and children over 4 years.

An asterisk under the "Percent Daily Value" heading indicates that a Daily Value is not established for that nutrient.

All supplements should be stored in a cool, dry place in their original containers.

All dietary supplements, particularly iron, should be kept out of the reach of children.

The product should be used before this date to assure full potency.

The manufacturer or distributor's name, address, and zip code are required to appear on the label.

According to many professional groups, including the American Dietetic Association, consumer perception of supplement claims should also be part of the decision-making process. For instance, just what does "strengthen immunity" mean to the average supplement shopper? Preliminary research by the FDA shows that current health claims lead consumers to believe that products are likely to have positive health effects well beyond those promoted on the label.

In 1999, the Federal Trade Commission released a business guide for the dietary supplement industry. It encourages the industry to use accurate information in making claims. For the first time ever, it's spelled out that anyone who "participates directly or indirectly in the marketing of dietary supplements has an obligation to make sure that claims are presented truthfully and to check the adequacy of the support." According to the FTC, the amount and type of support needed will depend on a variety of factors. These factors include consumers' expectation of what a claim means, the specific claim being made, how claims are presented in the context of the entire ad, and how statements are qualified. In evaluating the adequacy of support for a claim, the FTC expects to consult with experts in a wide variety of fields, including those with a background in botanicals and traditional medicine. The FTC's definition of dietary supplements includes vitamins, minerals, herbal products, hormones, and amino acids.

Supplement Profiteers

It's not just the claims that are sometimes fraudulent, often it's also the prices. In May 1999, the U.S. Justice Department won its largest case ever, with fines of $725 million, against several giant foreign drug and chemical companies for engaging in a worldwide conspiracy to raise and fix the prices of vitamins and other supplements. It's estimated that the inflated prices in effect since January of 1990 affected more than $5 billion of common products ranging from vitamins to enriched foods, including milk, cereal, and pet foods. The firms involved include Hoffman-LaRoche, BASF AG, and Lonza AG. More charges are expected to be filed as the case progresses.

The U.S. market for vitamins and supplements is projected to be worth between $11 billion and $20 billion. The editor of *Nutrition Business Journal* estimates that mainstream physicians directly sold about $120 million worth of supplements to their patients last year. Chiropractors, homeopaths, naturopaths, and other alternative practitioners sold $680 million in supplements from their offices.

For years the federal government has frowned upon doctors sending patients' blood and urine samples to their own labs for analysis. The concern is that extra tests will be ordered to add profits to the balance sheet. The American Medical Association Code of Medical Ethics says physicians should not let their wallets influence what they prescribe. Would you trust a doctor who recommended supplements if he or she made as much or more money from selling supplements as from an office visit?

Personal selling creates the lion's share of wealth in the supplement industry. Pyramid selling programs like Amway, Rexall, and Shaklee allow anyone to sell supplements. These salespeople benefit personally when you take their advice, as does the eager health food store employee who works on commission. If you've ever been asked to sell supplements, you are probably aware that more time and energy goes into training you to be a super salesperson than teaching you about what you sell.

If you are spending more than $10 a month on vitamin/mineral supplements, you're getting ripped off. Enough said.

Protecting Your Investment

Ads for supplements have powerful messages that play on your fears and exploit the desire to find an easy and "natural" solution to eating right. The FDA has little control over dietary supplements. This means that you have the responsibility for checking on the safety of dietary supplements and determining the truthfulness of any label claims.

Here's how to get the most for your money when purchasing vitamin/mineral supplements…

- Choose only vitamin/mineral supplements designated as meeting USP guidelines to ensure you are getting a quality product that will deliver what's listed on the label.

- Don't pay extra for "natural" supplements— they all work the same. Minerals are always natural since they can't be made from other substances. Vitamins present in food and plants are considered natural vitamins. Vitamins created in a laboratory are synthetic. There is no difference in most vitamin molecules whether they are synthetic or natural. Synthetic vitamins are usually less expensive, their potency can be better controlled, and they may be purer or less contaminated with pesticides and fertilizers. On the other hand, natural vitamins may, by default, include other food components that are beneficial to health. One notable exception to this rule is vitamin E. The natural form of vitamin

E (alpha-tocopherol) varies slightly from the synthetic versions (beta-, delta-, and gamma-tocopherol) and the nutrient is more effective in the natural form.

- Compare the labels. Generics can be a good deal. National retailers like K-Mart, Target, and Wal-Mart purchase supplements that are often identical to the higher-priced name brands.

- Don't pay extra for high-potency supplements. Since "high potency" is not legally defined, anyone can slap the term on the label of a supplement. It means nothing. Supplements work best when taken in several small doses spread throughout the day. That's because you can absorb more of a nutrient when your system isn't overloaded. When a high concentration of a nutrient enters your bloodstream, your kidneys work to quickly get rid of the excess. Taking a one-shot supplement isn't ideal, but it is convenient. Time-release supplements don't offer much of an advantage. Since vitamins and minerals are absorbed at different places in the gastrointestinal tract, it's highly unlikely that a time-release tablet will deliver each nutrient at the optimal time and place for absorption. Vitamin sprays and patches are sold in some parts of the United States and Canada. Contrary to their marketing literature, it has not been proven that you can absorb more nutrients because they have been applied to your skin or sprayed inside your mouth.

- Take your multiple vitamin and mineral supplements with food and water. You need fat and water to maximize nutrient absorption.

- Avoid frills and extras such as glandular products, hormones, and amino acids. All of these add-ons can increase the cost of a supplement without a proven benefit. Supplements that include such products often do not completely label or disclose the total amounts of nutrients they contain and may result in potentially toxic doses.

- Never purchase supplements past their expiration dates, no matter how cheap they are. In fact, if a product is within six months of expiring you can be sure it's lost some of its stability and potency.

- Never store supplements anywhere in your bathroom. The heat and moisture variations may change the action of the vitamin or speed deterioration. Store supplements tightly capped and safely out of the reach of young children. Most supplements do best in a cool, dry place away from direct sunlight. A high shelf in the kitchen—away from the oven or stove— is usually a good choice.

- If money is scarce, spend it on produce instead of supplements. Eating a variety of wholesome foods has a greater benefit than supplements to correct poor nutritional status.

Alternative to What?

In 1993, a landmark study captured attention for today's alternative medicine movement. It was published in the prestigious *New England Journal of Medicine*. News stories based on this article proclaimed everyone was jumping into alternative medicine. It made you think, "What am I missing out on?"

Dr. David Eisenberg wrote a special article (not a clinical research paper), "Unconventional Medicine in the United States, Prevalence, Costs and Patterns of Use." The paper compiled results of a random telephone survey of 1,539 consumers. The survey included only those out of 2,295 households contacted where someone actually answered all of the questions asked. People were excluded who did not speak English, were physically or mentally incapacitated, refused to participate, or hung up before finishing the survey. When the participants indicated they had a "bothersome or serious" health problem, they were asked if they had seen their doctor for this condition in the last twelve months. Next, they were asked if they had used "any other kinds of therapies and treatments." A list of sixteen unconventional therapies was read for each ailment that was noted. The person would say if he or she had tried each one. *Here's the list in order of most frequently reported therapies...*

- Relaxation techniques
- Chiropractic
- Massage
- Imagery
- Spiritual healing
- Commercial weight-loss program
- Lifestyle diets
- Herbal medicine
- Megavitamin therapy
- Self-help groups
- Energy healing
- Biofeedback
- Hypnosis
- Homeopathy
- Acupuncture
- Folk remedies

These sixteen categories included any common option for improving health, such as joining a Weight Watchers group, trying a low-fat diet, napping for relaxation, joining a support group, having a massage, trying to be positive about feeling better, or taking anything more than a one-a-day multivitamin supplement. Newspaper headlines screamed, "One in Three People Use Alternative Medicine." The fire was lit.

In fairness to Dr. Eisenberg and his colleagues, their conclusions were quite different from the media reports. The researchers summarized: "Our observation that the majority of users of unconventional therapy did not discuss this therapy with their medical doctors suggests a deficiency in current patient-doctor relations. Medical doctors should begin to ask their patients about their use of unconventional therapy whenever they obtain a history. We suggest that medical schools include information about unconventional therapies and the clinical social sciences (anthropology and sociology) in their curriculums." This conclusion isn't news. Sometimes health care providers are so focused on the disease they forget there is a human being to interact with. Have you ever heard a doctor or nurse talk about the "appendix in room 202" or the "broken arm in exam room 3"?

Perhaps physicians should begin to view diet, nutrition, relaxation, massage therapy, and referral to self-help and support groups as not only conventional but essential therapy for people with chronic health problems. There is increasing scientific support for the benefit of such changes in lifestyle.

Expert Evaluation

If you have a chronic disease, complicated eating preferences, or just like the idea of checking out your food intake, it's critical to find a reputable professional to help guide you. As with all trades or professions, there is a range of competencies among those who practice. Team up with someone who has a strong academic and practical background in food, nutrition, and health. They should be able to personalize suggestions and offer strategies right for you.

Memorizing the chemical structures of vitamins or digestive pathways doesn't make someone a nutrition expert. Many health professionals, including doctors and nurses, learn the biology of nutrition. Most don't have a clue how to translate that into what to eat in order to attain optimal health. The endorsement of special diets or nutrition products by people with a string of initials after their name should make you skeptical. Nutrition professionals shouldn't be endorsing specific products. Don't hand over your money to hucksters and celebrities; they may be great salespeople, but they are not usually great nutrition advisors.

Who's Who in Nutrition
Registered Dietitian (RD)

No doubt about it, RDs are the nutrition experts in the United States. No other group of individuals has their integrated training in the art and science of food and nutrition.

HANDY HOTLINE: For the National Center for Nutrition and Dietetics is 1-800-366-1655. You can ask to be referred to a registered dietitian in your area.

LINK UP a registered dietitian at *http://www.eatright.org* at the American Dietetic Association.

An RD separates fact from fiction. He or she can explain the latest scientific findings in an easy-to-understand way. An RD gives you personal attention and helps you create an eating pattern and nutrition program that is uniquely yours.

RDs must complete a bachelor's or master's degree in nutrition, dietetics, public health, biochemistry, medicine, or other nutrition specialty from an accredited college or university. As part of, or in addition to, this schooling, RDs must perform a rigorous, supervised internship. When the learning and practice are completed, there's a national exam to pass. Continuing professional education is mandatory for RDs. The only credible national credential for a nutrition expert is the RD.

Nutritionist

Never see a nutritionist. That's because anyone can claim this title. No credentials, no knowledge or training, no ethics required. The term "nutritionist" is not federally regulated and neither are its practitioners. If someone calls him- or herself a nutritionist, ask what other credentials he or she has. Some RDs may also refer to themselves as nutritionists. Be sure to verify the RD status.

Certified Nutritional Consultant (CNC)

The trademark designation CNC after a nutritional consultant's name indicates the person is a member of the American Association of Nutritional Consultants (AANC). Being a member or certified member of this association doesn't mean you're qualified to practice nutrition. "Membership in AANC and its predecessors has been open to anyone," according to Dr. Stephen Barrett, a leading authority on medical fraud. To prove that fact, years ago the late Victor Herbert, M.D., J.D., a prominent nutrition scientist, obtained a "professional membership" for his dog in AANC by sending $50 plus the name and address of his pet. Today's fees are higher, $150, plus you are required to take an open-book, at-home exam. But according to AANC's web site, "we realize that after looking over the tests, the candidate may feel that he or she needs to review one or more of the subjects. Therefore, we include with the examination a list of recommended textbooks. The textbooks recommended are those which will assist the candidate in successfully completing the specific portions of the examination the candidate finds troubling." Enough said.

Alternative Systems of Practice

The Office of Alternative Medicine (OAM) was initiated by congressional mandate under the 1992 National Institutes of Health (NIH) Appropriations Bill. The mission was to oversee new types of medical practices and provide grant money for their research. Questionable leadership and funding of inappropriate projects quickly eroded political and public confidence in this agency. In 1998, the OAM was reorganized as the National Center for Complementary and Alternative Medicine (NCCAM). The NCCAM's purpose is to facilitate the evaluation of alternative medicine treatment modalities and provide a public information clearinghouse. It does not serve as a referral agency for alternative medical treatment or individual practitioners.

HANDY HOTLINE: For the NCCAM is 888-644-6226 for inquiries about NCCAM research and general information about complementary and alternative medicine.

LINK UP to *http://nccam.nih.gov/* for more detailed information on research studies in progress and background on the OAM and NCCAM.

The NCCAM has funded nine Specialty Research Centers to study complementary and alternative treatments for specific health conditions. These centers form the foundation for conducting ongoing research through the NIH.

Surfing the Net

The amount of nutrition information available via computer is mind boggling. With so much data, the challenge is finding trustworthy sites to meet your needs. All of the web links listed in each chapter have been accessed just prior to publication to help ensure they are current. They have not been screened for accuracy, just for the specific web address (URL) listed. If you want to check out other sites, you might start with the Tufts University Nutrition Navigator (http://www.navigator.tufts.edu). This site evaluates the accuracy of several web sites, most of them dealing with nutritional issues, and allows you to do a keyword search or search across eight categories:

- Educators
- General nutrition
- Health professionals
- Journalists
- Kids
- Parents
- Special dietary needs
- Women

The Nutrition Navigator's reviews are based on criteria developed by an advisory board of leading U.S. and Canadian nutrition experts and conducted by RDs at Tufts. Sites are rated on a 25-point scale. Each site can score up to 10 points for accuracy, 7 points for depth of nutrition information, 3 points for frequency of updates, and 5 points for ease of use. Sites with accuracy scores below 7 are not recommended. Why? "If a site isn't based on sound science, it doesn't matter how good it is in other ways. Our goal is to help people get to the information they can trust most," says Jeanne Goldberg, Ph.D., RD, director of the Center on Nutrition Communication at the Tufts University School of Nutrition Science and Policy.

The U.S. Food and Drug Administration (FDA) is one of the main government organizations that posts nutrition and health information for both consumers and health professionals. According to William M. Rados, director of communications staff at the Office of Public Affairs at the FDA, "We're actually doing away with print distribution of many materials and relying on the Internet instead." The Electronic Freedom of Information Act Amendments of 1996 requires all federal agencies to post any

LINK UP to *http://www.fda.gov* to access a variety of food and nutrition resources from the Food and Drug Administration.

> **LINK UP** to *http://www.nlm.nih. gov* for *Healthfinder,* a gateway site to help consumers find health and human services information quickly. Healthfinder includes links to more than 1,250 web sites, including federal, state, local, nonprofit, university, and other consumer health resources. Topics are organized by subject in an index.

> **LINK UP** to *http://www.health.nih. gov* for the NIH Health Information Page, which provides access to the National Institutes of Health consumer health information resources including publications, clearinghouses, and databases.

document on the Web that would normally be posted in reading rooms or requested by more than one person.

With more than sixty central web sites on eight different domains, the Department of Health and Human Services (HHS) provides one of the richest and most reliable sources of health information on the Internet.

How to Duck the Quacks

"Americans love hogwash—in the sense that 'hogwash' is worthless, false, or ridiculous speech or writing," said Edward H. Rynearson, M.D., Emeritus Professor of Medicine of the Mayo Clinic and Mayo Foundation, at the

> **LINK UP** to *http://www.nlm.nih. gov* for *Medline,* the world's most extensive collection of published medical information, coordinated by the National Library of Medicine. Originally designed for health professionals and researchers, *Medline* is also ideal for students and those seeking more specific or technical information about health conditions and treatment. Once a fee-based service, *Medline* is now free. *PubMed* provides direct web links between *Medline* abstracts and the publishers of the original full-text articles.

Scientific Awards Dinner at a meeting of the American Medical Association on June 26, 1973. Not much has changed since then. Nutrition quackery today mimics the patent medicine craze of the 1800s. Early patent medicines were imported from Europe and sold by postmasters, goldsmiths, grocers, and tailors. Many of the patent medicine manufacturers were the first companies to seek national audiences through daily newspapers and national weeklies to get their product messages out to the public. "Lydia Pinkham's Vegetable Compound" was the most successful patent medicine of the nineteenth century. She had special cures to heal a variety of "women's ills." Grain alcohol was the largest ingredient of most patent medicines, including Pinkham's. In addition to the vegetable extracts and sugar that gave each brand its flavor and color, the remedies were sometimes laced with cocaine, caffeine, opium, or morphine. The Sears catalog sold a morphine-laced mixture intended to be slipped into a wayward husband's coffee in order to keep him home nights. Bored housewives and the homebound elderly were susceptible to becoming patent medicine addicts. Other patent medicines included "Kopp's Baby Friend," which was made of sweetened water and morphine, and was advertised as the perfect way to calm babies down. Or wives could try Dr. Winslow's Soothing Syrup on husbands who like to roam at night. It promised to "make 'em lay like the dead 'til mornin'."

Nutty Nutritionists

Adelle Davis sold more than 10 million copies of her four books, including *Let's Get Well. Much of what she said remains true:* Our diets are loaded with too much salt, sugar, and preservatives. Despite a degree in dietetics from the University of California, Berkeley, and a master's degree in biochemistry from the University of Southern California School of Medicine, Davis did make some serious errors in judgment. For example, Davis recommended raw milk and liquid potassium supplements for infants with colic. These and other unfounded recommendations resulted in numerous cases of harm and at least one death.

Horace Fletcher chewed his way to fame and fortune. Fletcher insisted that food be chewed until almost liquid—thirty to seventy chomps per mouthful.

Carlton Fredricks liked to call himself "America's Foremost Nutritionist." That's pretty impressive for someone with no nutrition or science training. In 1945 Fredricks pled guilty to practicing medicine without a license and then promptly restarted his "medical" practice. In his last years he performed nutrition consults from the offices of the late Dr. Robert Atkins.

Sylvester Graham's legacy is the graham cracker. This 1820s minister blamed refined flour for most common diseases of his day. Today's graham cracker bears little resemblance to the whole-grain brown bread he promoted. He also preached against meat because he believed it inflamed bad tempers and led to sexual excess.

John Harvey Kellogg was the first person to earn more than $1 million from health food sales—and that was more than 100 years ago. Kellogg was hired by the Seventh Day Adventist Church to run a health sanitarium in Battle Creek, Michigan. Patients were fed handfuls of sterilized bran to promote elimination after every meal. Later John's brother William started the Kellogg Toasted Corn Flake Company.

Linus Pauling earned his Nobel prizes for chemistry and peace—not nutrition. He claimed that large amounts of vitamin C could cure or prevent the common cold. Pauling himself took 12,000 mg of vitamin C daily and then upped it to 40,000 mg if he felt a cold coming on. Numerous well-designed, double-blind clinical studies have never been able to duplicate his results. Huge doses of vitamin C act similarly to antihistamines. These drugs work to stop runny noses and watery eyes. Lots of vitamin C, like any over-the-counter antihistamine (Contac, Dristan, Nyquil), can reduce your cold symptoms, but you're still sick.

Charles Post visited Kellogg's sanitarium and saw a business opportunity. He created a competing company and began producing Post Toasted Corn Flakes, Postum, and Grape Nuts, which he promoted as cures for appendicitis, malaria, and consumption. Post surpassed Kellogg and earned $1 million from his products in just one year—1901.

Lendon Smith thought he had the dietary solution for many of his pediatric patients with allergies, hyperactivity, insomnia, and a host of other ailments—avoid white sugar, white flour, pasteurized milk, and then take a variety of supplements to get what you're missing. Smith was first placed on medical probation and then permanently surrendered his medical license rather than face charges of fraud in 1987.

Web Fraud

"Operation Cure-all" is a new law enforcement and consumer education campaign that focuses on stopping Internet quacks and bogus claims for products and treatments touted as cures for various diseases. In 1997 and 1998 the Federal Trade Commission (FTC) surfed the Web and found approximately 800 health-related sites and numerous Internet user groups that contained questionable promotions for products or services. These web sites were sent e-mail messages alerting them that their claims require scientific substantiation and that disseminating unsubstantiated claims violates federal law (FTC News Release, June 1999). Only 28 percent of those sites contacted removed the illegal content or closed their sites in response to notification from the FTC. Violators may be given a civil penalty of $11,000. With soaring profits being made in the supplement industry, an $11,000 fine is no real deterrent.

Why Bogus Therapies Seem to Work

"At least ten kinds of errors and biases can convince intelligent, honest people that cures have been achieved when they have not," says Barry L. Byerstein from the Brain-Behavior Laboratory, Department of Psychology, Simon Fraser University in British Columbia, Canada. That's why anecdotal reports, testimonials, and uncontrolled observations often inappropriately conclude that some questionable therapies work.

HANDY HOTLINE:
For the FTC's consumer response center is 1-877-382-4357 to report or find out about Internet health scams.

LINK UP to *http://www.ftc.gov* for copies of complaints, proposed settlements, and more information from the Federal Trade Commission on how to safely surf the Web for health information.

Here are the top ten ways fake cures seem to work...

1. The disease may have run its natural course. Your body's own curative powers often work to restore health without any treatment at all.

2. Many diseases are cyclical. Symptoms of chronic conditions such as arthritis, allergies, and stomach complaints often vary dramatically over time. If you try a treatment at a peak time of discomfort, an improvement may just be a normal change in severity.

3. Spontaneous remissions, though quite rare, do happen for both fatal and chronic diseases.

4. The placebo effect. Through a combination of suggestion, belief, or expectancy, people do report positive improvement when given a placebo or dummy remedy.

5. Some allegedly cured symptoms are psychosomatic (just in your mind) to begin with.

6. The symptoms of your problem go away and you think you're cured—but the disease is still there.

7. Many people hedge their bets and try lots of therapies at the same time.

8. Sometimes you get misdiagnosed—you never really had what they said you did.

9. By-product benefits produce results that lead to improvement. You try a fad diet that is so low in calories you lose weight

and your arthritis improves. It's the weight loss, not the diet, that helped.

10. Some people are mentally ill and can't tell reality from make-believe.

Source: Adapted from Barry L. Beyerstein, *The Skeptical Inquirer,* September/October 1997

LINK UP to *http://www.quack watch.com* for an amusing and insightful review operated by Stephen Barrett, M.D., of hundreds of medical quacks and their bogus products and services.

If You Can't Beat 'Em—Join 'Em

Ever wonder what it would be like to be part of a scientific research trial? Now, if you have Internet access, you can log onto a survey and become part of scientific history. This type of survey is self-selected and not randomized and does have limitations, but you may learn ways to improve your health and nutrition habits. You will certainly gain valuable insight into how study data are collected and all the potential errors that can occur. 🍎

APPENDICES

GLOSSARY: A MOUTHFUL OF NUTRITION DICTION

It takes a whole new language to talk about nutrition today. Here's a collection of new nutrition terms, with pronunciations for those hard-to-say words.

acidophilus (as-uh-DAF-uh-les)—A type of beneficial lactobacillus bacteria that lives in your digestive tract. Imagine a lush, tropical rain forest teeming with life. It's a warm, wet environment where things grow wild. That's what your intestines are like, too. Acidophilus is a *probiotic* that helps keep the healthy bacteria in your gut alive.

antioxidants (an-tea-OX-i-dants)—Chemicals that help protect the body from harmful substances called "free radicals." There are two different types of antioxidants in the body: antioxidant enzymes, which prevent too many free radicals from being produced, and dietary antioxidants, which neutralize free radicals and single oxygen cells. You find antioxidants in foods that are rich in vitamins E, C and selenium.

biosource—Labeling foods by the geographic area in which they are grown.

biotechnology—The use of advanced scientific techniques to alter and ideally improve selected characteristics of animals and plants.

carcinogen (kar-SIN-oh-gin)—Anything that can potentially cause cancer. In 1958, Congressman James Delaney from New York introduced legislation to ban carcinogens in the food supply. Distraught over his wife's recent death from cancer, Delaney's proposal said that if any substance is determined to cause cancer in any animal (or human) in any amount, it can't be added to a food. Today's sophisticated technology is capable of finding such minute quantities of these substances that almost all foods could be considered carcinogenic. This was not the case when the Delaney rule was passed. Regardless, the rule is still in effect today.

carotenoid (ka-ROT-in-oid)—Pigment substances in plants that often form vitamin A. Beta-carotene is the most active form.

chemopreventive agents (keem-o-pre-VEN-tive)—Parts of food that have the potential to prevent or inhibit cancer.

flavonoids (FLAY-vuh-noyds)—Originally called vitamin P factors, flavonoids work both inside and outside your cells to protect blood vessels and connective tissue. Flavonoids bring zest to foods in the form of color and flavor. These *phytochemicals* tend to hide in difficult places, like the pith of an orange or the inside of an apple peel. Other good sources of flavonoids include berries, broccoli, celery, cranberries, citrus peel and pulp, grapes and grape juice, green tea, and red wine.

free radicals—Unstable oxygen molecules that cause problems in the body. In healthy molecules, each atom contains a pair of electrons. While your body works, some of the oxygen molecules lose one of these electrons. When this happens, the formerly stable oxygen molecules become harmful free radicals. These free radicals try to stabilize themselves by taking an electron from another healthy molecule. Some experts estimate that your body is attacked up to ten thousand times a day by free radicals. Free radicals don't usually start a disease process, but they encourage speedy progression of any damage already present. See also *antioxidants*.

functional foods—Those foods that offer a health benefit beyond their vitamin and mineral content, such as antioxidant flavonoids in fruits and vegetables.

isothiocyanates (i-so-thi-o-SI-uh-nates) —Plant chemicals that may strengthen your body's natural defenses against cancer.

lactobaccillus (LACK-toe-bah-sill-us)— A specific strain of beneficial bacteria that lives in your small and lower intestines.

lutein (lew-TEEN)—A *carotenoid* found in foods that are dark green and deep orange, plus tomatoes and red peppers. This *phytochemical* helps protect the macula (center

portion) of your eyes from oxidation, which results in macular degeneration.

lycopene (LYE-ko-peen)—A colorful red pigment found in foods that may reduce the risk of certain cancers. Tomatoes, watermelon, pink grapefruit, and berries are the best sources of lycopene. Cooking actually enhances their ability to work.

nutraceutical (new-tra-SOO-teh-kal)— A food or food ingredient designed or marketed to provide particular health benefits, including the prevention and treatment of disease. These foods are sometimes called *functional foods* or designer foods. Calcium-fortified orange juice and carrots (when their beta-carotene content is highlighted) would be examples of nutraceuticals.

olestra (Olean)—A no-calorie fat replacer made with sugar and vegetable oil. Olestra has extra molecules that makes it too large to be digested or absorbed, which is why it contains no fat or calories. Since olestra is a fat, it attracts fat-soluble vitamins A, D, E, and K and prevents their absorption in your body. A 1-ounce bag of potato chips made with Olean contains 0 grams of fat and about 70 calories, compared to 10 grams of fat and 150 calories for a 1-ounce bag of full-fat potato chips.

omega-3 (oh-MAY-ga)—A highly unsaturated family of fatty acids often referred to as linolenic acid. They are mostly found in fish and other marine plants and animals (cold water species have the highest concentrations.) They are also found in canola oil, flaxseed, leafy green vegetables, and walnuts. *Omega-3* is thought to lower "bad" cholesterol and raise "good" cholesterol levels in the blood and may ease some symptoms of rheumatoid arthritis.

omega-6—Fats most commonly found in polyunsaturated oils like corn, safflower, soybean, and sunflower. Only in the last hundred years have these oils been commonly eaten. Some estimates suggest that omega-6 fats now make up 90 percent of the polyunsaturated fats in a typical diet. Because we eat most of our unsaturated fats as omega-6 or linolenic fatty acids, we probably don't consume enough *omega-3*. Try to reduce your consumption of polyunsaturated fats. If you have to substitute another fat, choose a monounsaturated variety like olive or canola oil.

phytochemicals (fi-toe-KEM-eh-kals)—Unique plant chemicals from fruits and vegetables that may be essential in boosting health and preventing diseases. They're not vitamins or minerals. So far over four thousand phytochemicals have been identified. It's estimated that only fifty or sixty remain active enough after eating to provide benefits and include *lycopene, leutin,* and *zeaxanthin.*

phytoestrogens (fi-toe-ESS-trow-gins)—Plant chemicals that generate effects similar to the female hormone estrogen. Soy foods, yams, and some legumes are rich in phytoestrogens.

polyphenols (paul-ee-FEE-nalls)—Compounds that slow anticarcinogenic, antioxidant, antibacterial, and antiviral activity. They can also combine with iron and decrease iron absorption. Green, black, and oolong teas may offer health benefits because they contain *antioxidant* polyphenols.

prebiotics (pree-bye-OT-icks)—Substances in food that are not digestible by humans but are digestible by beneficial bacteria that reside in your body.

probiotics (pro-bye-OT-icks)—Live bacterial supplements used to support beneficial bacteria in the digestive tract.

quercetin (QUER-sa-tin)—One of the most powerful *antioxidants*. It acts like a Teflon coating in your bloodstream to prevent the deposit and buildup of sticky cholesterol plaque. Red grapes are a good food source of this antioxidant.

reductive enzymes—Toxic, cancer-causing by-products of harmful bacteria.

tyramine (TYE-ra-meen)—An ingredient in some foods that increases a hormone release that, in turn, causes blood vessels to constrict or tighten. The rebound effect that happens when the blood vessels open wide is throbbing head pain. Foods that contain tyramine include chocolate, aged cheese, and red wine.

Xenical (ZEN-ah-cal)—Known chemically as orlistat (OR-la-stat), an antifat pill that works by blocking absorption of about one-third of the fat you eat. Due to its blocking function, Xenical can cause unpleasant and embarrassing side effects including gas, oily or loose stools, oily spotting from the rectum, increased urgency to move your bowels, and intestinal cramping. Xenical can also decrease the amount of vitamins A, D, E, and K you absorb from foods.

zeaxanthin (zee-ah-ZAN-thin)—A carotenoid found in eggs, dark green leafy vegetables, and corn. This antioxidant has been shown to protect against age-related macular degeneration.

zoochemicals (zoo-KEM-eh-kals)—Substances in animal foods that help prevent disease. ❦

INGREDIENT LISTS: WHAT AM I EATING?

Ingredient lists are required on most food products sold. Food components must be listed in order by weight from the most to the least. However, individual variations of the same type of food do not have to be lumped together. For example: honey, sugar, and corn syrup can all be used in a product. Because they are listed separately, total sweeteners are much farther down on the ingredient list than if they were combined.

Lots of unusual-sounding ingredients show up on food labels. Some of the ingredients listed sound like they came from a chemical factory instead of a food plant. But they're not all as bad as they appear. For example, ascorbic acid may sound like it would eat away at the lining of your stomach. Actually, ascorbic acid is vitamin C. Of the nearly three thousand direct food additives that are used today, sugar, salt, corn syrup and dextrose account for more than 90 percent of the total weight. Other common additives in your food include modified starch, yellow mustard, sodium bicarbonate (baking soda), yeast, caramel color, citric acid, carbon dioxide and black pepper.

GUESS WHICH FOODS THESE INGREDIENTS DESCRIBE

1. Water, starches, cellulose, pectin, fructose, sucrose, glucose, malic acid, citric acid, succinic acid, anisyl propionate, amyl acetate, ascorbic acid, beta-carotene, riboflavin, thiamin, niacin, phosphorus, potassium.

2. Water, triglycerides of stearic, palmitic, oleic and linoleic acids, myosin, actin, glycogen, collagen, lecithin, cholesterol, dipotassium phosphate, myoglobin, urea.

You guessed correctly if you answered cantaloupe for the first and steak for the second.

On the following page, you'll find some quick tips to help you decipher food labels. Often you'll find familiar words on the label that may not mean what you think they do. *Here are some, with their technical definitions…*

Enriched: The vitamins thiamin, riboflavin, and niacin and the mineral iron have been added at varying levels to the

LABELING LINGO—WHAT'S REDUCED, LOW, AND FREE.

Many people get confused about what is on the food label and the subtle differences among what is reduced, low, or even free. There are simple definitions for the terms on a food label for specific nutrients and the health claim stated.

If the label says	One serving can have no more than
Calorie free	5 calories
Low calorie	40 calories
Sugar free	½ gm sugar
Fat free	½ gm fat
Low fat	3 gm fat
Sodium free	5 mg sodium
Low sodium	140 mg sodium
Cholesterol free	2 mg cholesterol and 2 gm saturated fat
Low cholesterol	20 mg cholesterol and 2 gm saturated fat
Reduced	25% less of that ingredient than the standard version of the product
Lean (meat products only)	10 g total fat and 4 g saturated fat and 95 mg cholesterol
Extra lean (meat products only)	5 g total fat and 2 g saturated fat and 95 mg cholesterol

Source: FDA Regulations, 1993, 1994, and USDA Regulations, 1994

product to replace what's lost during processing.

Fortified: Vitamins and/or minerals have been added to a product in amounts higher than 10 percent of what's normally found in that food.

Healthy: The FDA is proposing a definition of "healthy." The term would be applicable to foods that are low in fat and saturated fat and that do not contain more than 480 mg of sodium or 60 mg of cholesterol per serving.

Light or Lite: These words can mean one of three things:

1. In reference to fat or calories, a food can be altered to contain one-third fewer calories or 50 percent less fat than the regular version of that product.

2. A 50 percent reduction from the amount of sodium in the regular product is required.

3. The term "light" can also be used to describe the color and texture of a food. "Light" pancakes may just be fluffy, not low fat or low calorie. When light is used this way, it must tell you which attribute the food is light in.

Good source: One serving contains 10 to 19 percent of the Daily Value for a particular nutrient.

High or Excellent Source: One serving contains 20 percent or more of the Daily Value for a particular nutrient.

Organic: In October 2002, the U.S. Department of Agriculture put in place a set of national standards for food labeled "organic" whether it is grown in the United States or imported. This is great news for consumers and farmers alike. Previously, states could mandate their own standards and there was little consistency or enforcement of standards. There is still no evidence that organically produced food is safer or more nutritious than conventionally produced food, but it is better for the environment. Organic food differs from conventionally produced food in how it's grown, handled and processed.

Organic food is produced by farmers who use renewable resources, conserving soil and water to enhance environmental quality for future generations. Organic meat, poultry, eggs and dairy products come from animals that are not given antibiotics or growth hormones. Organic food is produced without using most conventional pesticides, fertilizers made with synthetic ingredients or sewage sludge, biotechnology or irradiation. Before a product can be labeled "organic," a Government-approved certifier inspects the farm to see that the rules necessary to meet USDA organic standards are met. Companies that handle or process organic food must be certified, too.

To find organic foods at the market, look at labels and for signs in the produce department. The USDA Organic seal tells you that a product is at least 95 percent organic.

The FDA also allows a list of nutrient-disease relationships on food labels such as:

- Calcium and osteoporosis
- Fat and cancer
- Saturated fat and cholesterol and heart disease
- Fiber-containing fruits, vegetables, and grain products and cancer
- Fiber-containing fruits, vegetables, and grain products and heart disease
- Sodium and hypertension
- Fruits and vegetables, and cancer
- Whole-grain foods and heart disease
- Whole-grain foods and cancer
- Soy and heart disease ❦

FEDERAL NUTRIENTS STANDARDS

DAILY VALUES (USED ON FOOD LABELS)
Daily Reference Values (DRVs)[a]

Food Component	DRV	Food Component	DRV
Fat	65 g[b]	Fiber	25 g
Saturated fatty acids	20 g		
Cholesterol	300 mg[c]	Potassium	3,500 mg
Total carbohydrate	300 g	Protein[d]	50 g

a Based on 2,000 calories a day for adults and children over 4 only.
b (g) grams
c (mg) milligrams
d DRV for protein does not apply to certain populations; Reference Daily Intake (RDI) for protein has been established for these groups: Children 1 to 4 years: 16 g; infants under 1 year: 14 g; pregnant women: 60 g; nursing mothers: 65 g.

Reference Daily Intakes (RDIs)[a]

Nutrient	Amount	Nutrient	Amount
Vitamin A	5,000 International Units (IU)	Folic acid	0.4 mg
Vitamin C	60 mg	Vitamin B-12	6 µg[b]
Thiamin	1.5 mg	Phosphorus	1.0 g
Riboflavin	1.7 mg	Iodine	150 µg
Niacin	20 mg	Magnesium	400 mg
Calcium	1.0 g	Zinc	15 mg
Iron	18 mg	Copper	2 mg
Vitamin D	400 IU	Biotin	0.3 mg
Vitamin E	30 IU	Panthothenic acid	10 mg
Vitamin B-6	2.0 mg		

a Formerly the U.S. RDA, based on National Academy of Sciences' 1968 Recommended Dietary Allowances.
b (µg) micrograms

Source: R. Kurtzweil, " 'Daily Values' Encourage Healthy Diet," *FDA Consumer,* May 1993, pp. 40–45

Bottom Line's Nutrition Secrets

Dietary Reference Intakes: Recommended Levels for Individual Intake[a]

Life-Stage Group	Calcium (mg/d)	Phosphorus (mg/d)	Magnesium (mg/d)	Vitamin D[b][c] (µg/d)	Fluoride (mg/d)	Thiamin (mg/d)	Riboflavin (mg/d)	Niacin[d] (mg/d)	Vitamin B-6 (mg/d)	Folate[e] (µg/d)	Vitamin B-12 (µg/d)	Pantothenic Acid (mg/d)	Biotin (µg/d)	Choline[f] (mg/d)
Infants														
0–6 mo	210*	100*	30*	5*	0.01*	0.2*	0.3*	2*	0.1*	65*	0.4*	1.7*	5*	125*
7–12 mo	270*	275*	75*	5*	0.5*	0.3*	0.4*	4*	0.3*	80*	0.5*	1.8*	6*	150*
Children														
1–3 y	500*	460	80	5*	0.7*	0.5	0.5	6	0.5	150	0.9	2*	8*	200*
4–8 y	800*	500	130	5*	1*	0.6	0.6	8	0.6	200	1.2	3*	12*	250*
Males														
9–13 y	1,300*	1,250	240	5*	2*	0.9	0.9	12	1.0	300	1.8	4*	20*	375*
14–18 y	1,300*	1,250	410	5*	3*	1.2	1.3	16	1.3	400	2.4	5*	25*	550*
19–30 y	1,000*	700	400	5*	4*	1.2	1.3	16	1.3	400	2.4	5*	30*	550*
31–50 y	1,000*	700	420	5*	4*	1.2	1.3	16	1.3	400	2.4	5*	30*	550*
51–70 y	1,200*	700	420	10*	4*	1.2	1.3	16	1.7	400	2.4[g]	5*	30*	550*
>70 y	1,200*	700	420	15*	4*	1.2	1.3	16	1.7	400	2.4[g]	5*	30*	550*
Females														
9–13 y	1,300*	1,250	240	5*	2*	0.9	0.9	12	1.0	300	1.8	4*	20*	375*
14–18 y	1,300*	1,250	360	5*	3*	1.0	1.0	14	1.2	400[h]	2.4	5*	25*	400*
19–30 y	1,000*	700	310	5*	3*	1.1	1.1	14	1.3	400[h]	.4	5*	30*	425*
31–50 y	1,000*	700	320	5*	3*	1.1	1.1	14	1.3	400[h]	.4	5*	30*	425*
51–70 y	1,200*	700	320	10*	3*	1.1	.1	14	1.5	400	2.4[g]	5*	0*	425*
>70 y	1,200*	700	320	15*	3*	1.1	1.1	14	1.5	400	2.4[g]	5*	30*	425*
Pregnancy														
≤18 y	1,300*	1,250	400	5*	3*	1.4	1.4	18	1.9	600[i]	2.6	6*	30*	450*
19–30 y	1,000*	700	350	5*	3*	1.4	1.4	18	1.9	600[i]	2.6	6*	30*	450*
31–50 y	1,000*	700	360	5*	3*	1.4	1.4	18	1.9	600[i]	2.6	6*	30*	450*
Lactation														
≤18 y	1,300*	1,250	360	5*	3*	1.5	1.6	17	2.0	500	2.8	7*	35*	550*
19–30 y	1,000*	700	310	5*	3*	1.5	1.6	17	2.0	500	2.8	7*	35*	550*
31–50 y	1,000*	700	320	5*	3*	1.5	1.6	17	2.0	500	2.8	7*	35*	550*

a   Recommended Dietary Allowances (RDAs) are presented in bold type and Adequate Intakes (AIs) in ordinary type followed by an asterisk (*). RDAs and AIs may both be used as goals for individual intake. RDAs are set to meet the needs of almost all (97% to 98%) individuals in a group. For healthy breast-fed infants, the AI is the mean intake. The AI for other life-stage and gender groups is believed to cover needs of all individuals in the group, but lack of data or uncertainty in the data prevent being able to specify with confidence the percentage of persons covered by this intake. Source: The National Academy of Science. ©1998

b   As cholecalciferol, 1 µg cholecalciferol = 40 IU vitamin D.

c   In the absence of adequate exposure to sunlight.

d   As niacin equivalents (NE). 1 mg niacin = 60 mg tryptophan; 0 to 6 mo = preformed niacin (not NE).

e   As dietary folate equivalent (DFE). 1 DFE = 1 µg food folate = 0.6 µg folic acid (from fortified food or supplement) consumed with food = 0.5 µg synthetic (supplemental) folic acid taken on an empty stomach.

f   Although AIs have been set for choline, there are few data to assess whether a dietary supply of choline is needed at all stages of the life cycle, and it may be that the choline requirement can be met by endogenous synthesis at some of these stages.

g   Because 10% to 30% of older people may malabsorb food-bound vitamin B-12, it is advisable for those older than 50 years to meet their RDA mainly by consuming foods fortified with vitamin B-12 or a supplement containing vitamin B-12.

h   In view of evidence linking folate intake with neural tube defects in the fetus, it is recommended that all women capable of becoming pregnant consume 400 µg synthetic folic acid from fortified foods and/or supplements in addition to intake of food folate from a varied diet.

i   It is assumed that women will continue consuming 400 µg folic acid until their pregnancy is confirmed and they enter prenatal care, which ordinarily occurs after the end of the periconceptional period—the critical time for formation of the neural tube.

Tolerable Upper Intake Levels[a] (ULs) for Certain Nutrients

Life-Stage Group	Calcium (g/d)	Phosphorus (g/d)	Magnesium[b] (mg/d)	Vitamin D (µg/d)	Fluoride (mg/d)	Niacin[c] (mg/d)	Vitamin B-6 (mg/d)	Synthetic folic acid (µg/d)[c]	Choline (g/d)
0–6 mo	ND[d]	ND	ND	25	0.7	ND	ND	ND	ND
7–12 mo	ND	ND	ND	25	0.9	ND	ND	ND	ND
1–3 y	2.5	3	65	50	1.3	10	30	300	1.0
4–8 y	2.5	3	110	50	2.2	15	40	400	1.0
9–13 y	2.5	4	350	50	10	20	60	600	2.0
14–18 y	2.5	4	350	50	10	30	80	800	3.0
19–70 y	2.5	4	350	50	10	35	100	1,000	3.5
>70 y	2.5	3	350	50	10	35	100	1,000	3.5
Pregnancy									
≤18 y	2.5	3.5	350	50	10	30	80	800	3.0
19–50 y	2.5	3.5	350	50	10	35	100	1,000	3.5
Lactation									
≤18 y	2.5	4	350	50	10	30	80	800	3.0
19–50 y	2.5	4	350	50	10	35	100	1,000	3.5

[a] UL = the maximum level of daily nutrient intake that is likely to pose no risk of adverse effects. Unless otherwise specified, the UL represents total intake from food, water, and supplements. Due to lack of suitable data, ULs could not be established for thiamin, riboflavin, vitamin B-12, pantothenic acid, or biotin. In the absence of ULs, extra caution may be warranted in consuming levels above recommended intakes.

[b] The UL for magnesium represents intake from a pharmacological agent only and does not include intake from food and water.

[c] The ULs for niacin and synthetic folic acid apply to forms obtained from supplements, fortified foods, or a combination of the two.

[d] ND: Not determinable due to lack of data of adverse effects in this age group and concern with regard to lack of ability to handle excess amounts. Source of intake should be from food only to prevent high levels of intake.

Food and Nutrition Board, National Academy of Sciences—National Research Council Recommended Dietary Allowances,[a] Revised 1989

Designed for the maintenance of good nutrition of practically all healthy people in the United States

Category	Age (years) or Condition	Weight[b] (kg)	Weight[b] (lb)	Height[b] (cm)	Height[b] (in)	Protein (g)	Vitamin A (µg RE)[c]	Vitamin D (µg)[d]	Vitamin E (mg α-TE)[e]	Vitamin K (µg)	Vitamin C (mg)	Thiamin (mg)	Riboflavin (mg)	Niacin (µg NE)[f]	Vitamin B-6 (mg)	Folate (µg)	Vitamin B-12 (µg)	Calcium (mg)	Phosphorus (mg)	Magnesium (µg)	Iron (mg)	Zinc (mg)	Iodine (µg)	Selenium (µg)
Infants	0.0–0.5	6	13	60	24	13	375	7.5	3	5	30	0.3	0.4	5	0.3	25	0.3	400	300	40	6	5	40	10
	0.5–1.0	9	20	71	28	14	375	10	4	10	35	0.4	0.5	6	0.6	35	0.5	600	500	60	10	5	50	15
Children	1–3	13	29	90	35	16	400	10	6	15	40	0.7	0.8	9	1.0	50	0.7	800	800	80	10	10	70	20
	4–6	20	44	112	44	24	500	10	7	20	45	0.9	1.1	12	1.1	75	1.0	800	800	120	10	10	90	20
	7–10	28	62	132	52	28	700	10	7	30	45	1.0	1.2	13	1.4	100	1.4	800	800	170	10	10	120	30
Males	11–14	45	99	157	62	45	1,000	10	10	45	50	1.3	1.5	17	1.7	150	2.0	1,200	1,200	270	12	15	150	40
	15–18	66	145	176	69	59	1,000	10	10	65	60	1.5	1.8	20	2.0	200	2.0	1,200	1,200	400	12	15	150	50
	19–24	72	160	177	70	58	1,000	10	10	70	60	1.5	1.7	19	2.0	200	2.0	1,200	1,200	350	10	15	150	70
	25–50	79	174	176	70	63	1,000	5	10	80	60	1.5	1.7	19	2.0	200	2.0	800	800	350	10	15	150	70
	51+	77	170	173	68	63	1,000	5	10	80	60	1.2	1.4	15	2.0	200	2.0	800	800	350	10	15	150	70
Females	11–14	46	101	157	62	46	800	10	8	45	50	1.1	1.3	15	1.4	150	2.0	1,200	1,200	280	15	12	150	45
	15–18	55	120	163	64	44	800	10	8	55	60	1.1	1.3	15	1.5	180	2.0	1,200	1,200	300	15	12	150	50
	19–24	58	128	164	65	46	800	10	8	60	60	1.1	1.3	15	1.6	180	2.0	1,200	1,200	280	15	12	150	55
	25–50	63	138	163	64	50	800	5	8	65	60	1.1	1.3	15	1.6	180	2.0	800	800	280	15	12	150	55
	51+	65	143	160	63	50	800	5	8	65	60	1.0	1.2	13	1.6	180	2.0	800	800	280	10	12	150	55
Pregnant						60	800	10	10	65	70	1.5	1.6	17	2.2	400	2.2	1,200	1,200	320	30	15	175	65
Lactating	1st 6 months					65	1,300	10	12	65	95	1.6	1.8	20	2.1	280	2.6	1,200	1,200	355	15	19	200	75
	2nd 6 months					62	1,200	10	11	65	90	1.6	1.7	20	2.1	260	2.6	1,200	1,200	340	15	16	200	75

a The allowances, expressed as average daily intakes over time, are intended to provide for individual variations among the most normal persons as they live in the United States under usual environmental stresses. Diets should be based on a variety of common foods in order to provide other nutrients for which human requirements have been less well defined.

b Weights and heights of Reference Adults are actual medians for the U.S. population of the designated age, as reported by NHANES II. The use of these figures does not imply that the height-to-weight ratios are ideal.

c Retinol equivalents. 1 retinol equivalent = 1 µg retinol or 6 µg ß-carotene.

d As cholecalciferol. 10 µg cholecalciferol = 400 IU of vitamin D.

e a-Tocopherol equivalents. 1 mg d-a tocopherol = 1 a-te.

f 1 ne (niacin equivalent) is equal to 1 mg of niacin or 60 mg of dietary tryptophan.

INDEX

A

Abdominal fat 21
Acesulfame K.................................204
Acetyl L-carnitine 129
Acne, pantothenic acid and..................126
Actin 34
Acupuncture 101–102
Acute toxicity 113
Adequate Intakes (AIs)...........................111
Adolescence
    nutrition for................................88–89
    vegetarian diet for 104
Age, calorie needs and..........................31
Agency for Healthcare Research
    and Quality (AHRQ) 151
Aging-related diseases 119, 151
AIDS. *See* HIV/AIDS
Alcohol dehydrogenase 83
Alcohol use
    bone mineral density and.................225
    cancer and 200
    effect on nutrients 82
    effects of 83
    thiamin deficiencies and 120
    vitamin needs and 131
Alfalfa 64
Allergic reactions.................95, 156–157
    See also Food allergies
Allergists.................................14

Allicin 61
Almonds 68
Aloe 183
Alpha-linolenic acid 60
Alternative medicine 241–242, 244–245
Alternative supplements 148–161
Aluminum 133
Alzheimer's Association............................193
Alzheimer's disease....................177, 192
    aluminum and 192
    cranberries and..............................56
    folate and.......................................124
    ginkgo biloba and.....................177–178
    nutrition issues.........................192–193
    nutrition recommendations for.........193
    vitamin E and 119
American Academy of Allergy,
    Asthma, and Immunology.........198, 210
American Academy of Ophthalmology ...202
American Association of Nutritional
    Consultants (AANC)........................243
American Botanical Council 186, 187
American Cancer Society 176, 200
American College of Sports Medicine.....104
American Council on Science
    and Health (ACSH) 45
American Dietetic
    Association........104, 205, 225, 239, 243
American Heart Association..............16, 212

American Herbal Products
Association (AHPA)...................171–172
American Institute for Cancer
Research..200
American Medical Association................239
American Obesity Association 221
American Society for Clinical
Pharmacology and Therapeutics.......169
American Society of Cataract and
Refractive Surgery..........................202
Amino acids.............................34, 149
Amyl sulfides..................................200
Anandamide..54
Anaphylaxis.....................................208
Anemia 193–195, 228
folate-deficiency....................194, 195
iron-deficiency.........................194–195
nutrition issues............................194
nutrition recommendations
for 194–195
pernicious...............................194, 195
Angiostatin 160
Anorexia 95
Antacids..82
Anthocyanins.....................................47
Antibiotics 131
Antibodies 12
Anticoagulant 118
Antihypertensive drugs 213
Antioxidants...............49, 77, 108–109, 205
Arginine.............................149–150, 154
Arsenic...
133
Arthritis 195–197
nutrition issues.......................195–196
nutrition recommendations for.196–197
osteo-.............................150, 158, 195
rheumatoid 121, 195, 196, 207
Arthritis Foundation 196
Artificial sugars 204
Ascorbic acid 126
Asian ginseng 178

Aspartame.................................204, 208
Aspirin...........................168, 183, 220
ulcers and 227
Asthma...................................197–198
nutrition issues.......................197–198
nutrition recommendations for.........198
Astragalus 172
Atherosclerosis Risk in
Communities Study (ARIC)..............136
Atkins diet 105
Atrial fibrillation.................................6
Attention Deficit Hyperactivity
Disorder (ADHD).....................198–199
nutrition recommendations for.........199
Autism 122
Australia, dietary guidelines in 90
Avocados...43
Easy Guacamole 43
Ayurveda 96–97

B

Baking chocolate 55
Barrett, Stephen...........................243, 248
BBQ lentils...67
Beans...43–44
Zesty Black Bean Salad 44
Beef...45–46
Herbed Tenderloin Steaks 46
Bee pollen 156–157
Believe-It-or-Not BBQ Sauce 62
Benign prostatic hyperplasia
(BPH)....................................181–182
Benzoates..208
Beriberi 110, 120
Beta-carotene.........49, 76, 81, 108, 114, 115
arthritis and 196
asthma and 198
Beta-glucan 69
Beverages
Strawberry Smoothie 76
Wild Blueberry Smoothie 48
BHA 208

BHT...208
Bilberry extract.............................218
Biotech, benefits of 46–47
Biotin..........................110, 125–126, 132
Bipolar disorders 150
Birth control pills 183
Bisulfite.......................................208
Bitter taste....................................13
Black cohosh (ko-hosh) 173
Black snakeroot 173
Black tea 77
Bladder cancer 28
Blood pressure 6
  See also High blood pressure
  sodium and................................138
Blueberries.................................47–48
  Wild Blueberry Smoothie 48
Blue Nitro 158
Body fat.....................................21–22
Body mass index (BMI)................20
Bogus therapies...................247–248
Bone density test 22
Bone density testing center 23
Bone loss, diagnosis of 22
Bone mineral density, alcohol use and 225
Bone remodeling 224
Botanicals 167
  buying better 169
  over-the-counter 167
Bottled water 29–30
Bowel diseases 48
Bran 48
  Heavy Duty Bran Muffins........48
Bratman, Steve.............................95
Breads. *See* Muffins
Breast cancer...........................13, 15
  fat and.......................................38
Breast milk....................................14
Broccoli 49
  Broccoli with Orange Sauce ...49
Brody, Jane 229
Broiled grapefruit with port wine 63

Brown rice 49–50
  Brown Rice and Chicken Salad 50
Buckthorn...................................183
Bulimia 95
B vitamins 130, 192

C

Cabbage 74
Cachexia.....................................201
Cadmium....................................133
Caffeine..............................77, 83–84
  diuretic effects of......................28
  headaches and 220
  metabolism and 82
Calciferol 115
Calcium 52, 108–109,
                    133, 134–135, 146
  absorption of 225
  Alzheimer's disease and............192, 236
  blood pressure and 213
  osteoporosis and......................22, 236
  vitamin D and............................115, 225
Calcium carbonate supplements.............134
Calcium channel blockers........................63
Calcium citrate supplements...................134
California Dry Bean Advisory Board.........44
Calloway, C. Wayne...............................106
Calorie Control Council..........................22
Calories...............................5, 30–33
  burning.............................32–33
  calculating need for..................33
  defined.....................................31
Canada, dietary guidelines in...................90
Cancer ....
  15–16, 48, 199–201
  alcohol use and.........................200
  bladder.....................................28
  breast 13, 15, 38
  colon....................................13, 15, 41
  fiber and 200
  nutrition issues..........................199–200

nutrition recommendations
for avoiding 200–201
prostate 78
Cancer Treatment Research
Foundation (CTRF) 160
Canola 38, 50–51
Sassy Salad Dressing..........................51
Cantaloupe 67
Capsaicin 51
Cayenne Pepper Rub 51
Capsules 166
Carbohydrate-Counting 204
Carbohydrates 33–34
complex...33, 34
simple 33
Cardiomyopathy...................................143
Carotene 51
Carotenoids 114, 115
Carrots 51–52
Carrot Mango Salsa 52
Cranberry Carrot Sauté 52
Casaba melon 67
Case-control studies 230
Casein 209
Cataracts 201–202
nutrition issues.................................202
nutrition recommendations
for avoiding 202
Catechins 77, 201
Cat's claw bark 173–174
Cayenne...197
Cayenne Pepper Rub 51
Center for Science in the Public
Interest (CSPI)...............................61
Certified Nutritional Consultant
(CNC)..................................243–244
Chamomile 174
Chaparra...184
Cheese 52–54
Cheesy Chili Rice 53–54
types of 53
Chestnuts...68

Chicken 54
free-range..54
Brown Rice and Chicken Salad 50
Pasta Stir-Fry with Chicken 54
Chitosan 157
Chloride....................................136–137
Chocolate...54–55
headaches and 220
semi-sweet 55
Cholecalciferol.....................................115
Cholesterol 16
capsaicin and.....................................51
in chicken..54
eggs and..57–58
fiber and 39
heart disease and 210–211
Cholestin 157–158
Cholestyramine (Questran)....................116
Choline 128–129
Choline bitartrate 128
Choline chloride....................................128
Cholinesterase inhibitors 192
Chromium.........................141, 146, 205
deficiency of 141
Chromium picolinate 152
Chronic diseases....................................10
Chronic Fatigue Syndrome,
magnesium in 136
Chronic pancreas disease 151
Chronic toxicity 113
Chronic venous insufficiency (CVI) 179
Cigarette smokers.................................131
Clinical Global Impression Scale (CGI)..180
Clinical trials 230
Clover honey 64
Coated tablets 166
Cobalamin (B-12)..................................123
Cocaine...164
Cocoa powder..55
Code of Medical Ethics 240
Coenzyme Q-10, blood pressure and......213
Cohort studies 230

Colds
    vitamin C and 127
    zinc and 144, 145
Coleslaw, tropical 65
Colitis 216
Colloidal minerals 133
Colon cancer 13, 15, 41
Comfrey 184
Commission E 186
Complementary proteins 34
Complex carbohydrates 33, 34
Conjugated linoleic acid (CLA) 45
Constipation 41
Control group 233
Cooper Institute for Aerobics Research .. 104
Copper 133, 141–142, 146
CoQ-10 151
Corn 79
    Summer Succotash 80
Coronary heart disease 16
Cos lettuce 74
Cotyledon 66
Couscous 55
    Southwestern 55
Cranberries 55–56
    Cranberry Carrot Sauté 52
    Cranberry Herb Tea 56
    Cranberry Salsa 56
Crash diets 225
Creatin 154–155
Creatine monohydrate 154
Crenshaw melon 67
Crohn's & Colitis Foundation
    of America, Inc. 216
Crohn's disease 216
Cruciferous vegetables 49
Cultural diversity in dietary
    guidelines 90–93
Cyanide intoxication 159
Cystic fibrosis 12
Cystine 149

D

Daily multiple vitamin-mineral
    product 131
Daily Values (DVs and %DVs) 111
Dairy Ease 225, 226
D-alpha-tocopherol 118
Dandelion leaves 183
Dates 56–57
    Sports Power Bars 57
Deficiency diseases 109
Dehydration 27–28
Dehydroepiandrosterone
    (DHEA) 155–156
Dementia 121
Denmark, dietary guidelines in 90–91
Dental caries, cheese and 52–53
Depression, SAM-e in treating 150
Deprivation 5–6
Diabetes 203–205
    gestational 16, 203, 204
    nutrition issues 203–204
    nutrition recommendations for 205
    type 1 .... 16, 203, 205
    type 2 .... 16, 203, 205
Diastolic pressure 213
Diet(s)
    Atkins 105
    connection between disease and 191
    crash 225
    Exchange 204
    Feingold 198–199
    Ketogenic 105, 206
    macrobiotic 201
    Mediterranean 70, 99–100
    Ornish 212
    pitfalls of popular 222–223
    Pritikin 105–106, 212
    very low-calorie 223
Dietary Approaches to Stop
    Hypertension (DASH) 139–140, 214
Dietary cholesterol 36
Dietary evolution 12

Dietary guidelines 89–95
    challenge of 93–95
    cultural diversity 90–93
Dietary Reference Intakes (DRIs)...........111
Dietary Supplement Health Education
    Act (DSHEA).....166, 234–235, 236, 237
Diet teas..183
Digitalis..183
Diseases. *See also* specific 184
    aging-related 119
    bowel 48
    chronic..10
    connection between diet and 191
    deficiency..109
    eating disorder...................................95
    food-borne 45, 59
    kidney...184
    liver...184
Diuretic herbs..183
Diuretics 82
    thiamin deficiency and......................120
Diverticulosis...41
D-alpha-tocopherol 118
Dopamine 122
Down's syndrome 124
DSHEA..168
Duodenal ulcers..227

E

Easy Guacamole 43
Easy Wine Marinade...................................81
Eating disorders...95
Eating out 4
Eating styles 5, 95–107
    choosing own 106–107
    options in 87–107
Echinacea 164, 174–175, 187
Edamame 75
    Herbed Edamame 75
Eggs 57–58
    allergies to 14
    Eggchilada 58

Elderly 131
Electrocardiogram 6
Electrolytes...................133, 136–140
Electronic Freedom of Information
    Act Amendments (1996)...................245
Ellagic acid 75
Endosperm 40
Endostatin 160
Energy bars...153
Enriched grains 40
Ensure...216
Environmental factors 10
Enzymes 151
Eosinophiliamyalgia syndrome 150
Epidemiological studies............................230
Epilepsy.......................126, 205–206
    nutrition issues................................206
    nutrition recommendations for.........206
Ergocalciferol...115
Ergogenic aids.................151–152, 154–155
Escherichia coli 45, 55, 64
Esophageal ulcers.....................................227
Essential amino acids 34
Estrogen..155
    Alzheimer's disease and.....................193
    menopause and..................................218
Ethyl esters 182
Evening primrose oil...............175–176, 196
Excessive Fat and Consumption
    Trends in Obesity Risk
      (X-FACTOR) survey.....................21
Exchange diets...204
Exercise...5

F

Fake foods 84
Families, eating with 87–88
Fast foods..3–4
Fasting...222
Fat(s) 34–39
    abdominal...21
    body...21–22

breast cancer and................................38
effects of 38
hydrogenated...................................36
monounsaturated 36, 38, 43, 102, 213
polyunsaturated....................36, 38, 102
rating your habits.............................37
saturated...............................36, 38–39
sources of, in American diets.............35
trans...39
types of 36
Fat-soluble vitamins........................36, 113
Fatty acids 182
Omega-3.................58–59, 60, 159, 196
Omega-6 60
Federal Institute for Drugs and
    Medical Products.........................185
Federal Trade Commission (FTC) ..239, 247
Feingold diet 198–199
Fen-phen 191
Feverfew 176
Fiber..................................39–41, 43
cancer and 200
excess...82
insoluble 40–41, 48
needs...40
soluble 40
Fibromyalgia Alliance of America...........207
Fibromyalgia Network..........................207
Fibromyalgia syndrome 206–207
nutrition issues...............................207
nutrition recommendations for.........207
Field green salad.................................74
Fink, Jordan......................................209
Fish 58–60
allergies to 14
buying...59
Green Tea Poached Salmon..................77
Grilled 59–60
Fish oil capsules................................59, 159
The 5 Day Miracle Diet 105
5-HTP 150
Flatulence 43–44

Flavonoids 179
Flax, menopause and 219
Flaxseed...60
Fluids...183
Fluoridated water 142
Fluoride...142, 146
Folate...............................123–125, 130, 132
Folate-deficiency anemia.................194, 195
Folic acid 43, 49
deficiency of 124
Foltz, John..62
Food, impact of, versus
    family genetics.............................12–13
Food additives 95
headaches and 220
Food allergies 14–15, 95, 207–209
See also Allergic reactions
nutrition issues.................................208
nutrition recommendations for.........209
Food Allergy and Anaphylaxis
    Network..208
Food and Drug Administration
    (FDA).......................234–235, 239, 245
Center for Drug Evaluation and
    Research (CDER) 167
Food and Nutrition Science Alliance
    (FANSA) 168
Food-borne diseases 45
fish and...59
Food colors.......................................208
Food intolerances....................15, 207–209
Food modifications 19
Food patterns, changes in
    American............................94–95
Food record 6–9
Foods
fake...84
fast...3–4
fortified 112, 130–131
selling herbs as 166
Food safety 215
irradiation and 64–65

Food sensitivities..........................207–209
Fortified foods..................112, 130–131
40-30-30 diet 105
Foxglove 183
Framingham study 19, 26
France, dietary guidelines in.................91
Free radicals 82, 118
Free-range chickens 54
French fries.......................................104
Fresh foods 3
Fructose..204
Fruits, servings of.............................19, 20

G

Gamma G 158
Garlic 42, 60–62
    blood pressure and..................213–214
    cancer and 200
    Garlic Spread...............................62
Gastric ulcers...........................227–228
GBL (gamma butyrolactone)...........158
Gels...153
Genes...15
Genetic diversity.................................13
Genetic factors............................4, 10
Genetics, impact of food versus 12–13
Genistein 74
Germander...184
Germany, dietary guidelines in...........91
Gestational diabetes 16, 203, 204
Ginger 176–177
Ginkgo biloba.............................177–178
    Alzheimer's disease and.............192
Ginseng 178–179
    American 178
    Asian 178
    menopause and..........................219
    Siberian....................................178
GLA (cis-gamma-linolenic acid).....175–176
Globin..34
Glucosamine....................................158
Glucosamine chondroitin..................158

Glucosamine sulfate 158
Glycine 154
Glycyrrhizin......................................180
Goldenseal 187
Grains
    enriched....................................40
    whole 40
Grand mal seizures....................205–206
Granules 166
Grapefruit...................................62–63
    Broiled Grapefruit with Port Wine......63
Grape juice 62
    Hot Spiced 62
GRAS (Generally Recognized
    As Safe) list..............................149
GRASS (Geographical Resources
    Analysis Support System)...........12
Green tea 77
    Green Tea Poached Salmon.........77
Grilled Fish.................................59–60
Grilled Portobello Mushrooms.........68
Growth hormone..............................149

H

Halcion 63
Hamilton Anxiety Scale (HAMA)...........180
Hashimoto's thyroiditis.....................143
Hawthorn..179
HDL cholesterol.............36, 38–39, 68, 213
Headaches
    See Migraines and headaches
Health claims...................................236
Healthfinder.....................................245
Heart disease....................16, 210–212, 213
    cholesterol connection 210–211
    Lp (a).......................................211
    nutrition issues........................210–211
    nutrition recommendations
        for avoiding..........................212
    omega-3 and................................58
    risk for 17–20
    triglycerides.............................211

Heavy Duty Bran Muffins...........................48
Heavy metals 133
Heme iron...194
Hemochromatosis.....................................140
Hemorrhoids......................................41, 48
Herbal Physician's Desk Reference..........186
Herbal teas 182–183
Herbed Edamame 75
Herbed Tenderloin Steaks...........................46
Herb Research Foundation.......................187
Herbs 162–187
    forms of 166
    future focus 187
    harmful...184–185
    marketing of....................164, 166–169
    myths about...................................169–171
    protecting yourself from
        inferior or unsafe.......................172
    research on 185–187
    safety ratings for 173
    throughout the ages 165
    top-selling...163
Herb tea, cranberry.....................................56

High blood cholesterol.................................12
    See also Blood pressure
High blood pressure 20, 213–214
    nutrition issues..............................213–214
    potassium in managing 137
    sodium and...138
High-carbohydrate, very
    low-fat diets...............................105–106
High-density lipoprotein
    (HDL) cholesterol 6, 45, 211
High protein 104–105
High-protein, low-carbohydrate
    diets 223
Histamine 207
Histidine 34
HIV/AIDS...................................214–216
    nutrition issues 214–215

nutrition recommendations
    for 215–216
    vitamin A in...115
Homeopathy 97
Homocysteine................................13, 214
    Alzheimer's disease and.....................192
    folate and.....................................124, 125
Honey..63–64
    Honeyed Red Fruit 64
Honeydew...67
Hormones...............................110, 155–156
Horse chestnut seed extract 179
Hot Spiced Grape Juice 62
Hungary, dietary guidelines in 91
Hydrazines...68
Hydrochloric acid.....................................136
Hydrogenated fats..36
Hypericin...181
Hypertension 213
Hyperthyroidism.......................................143

I

Ibuprofen (Advil, Motrin)..............214, 220
    ulcers and 227
Iceberg lettuce 74
Immune system 10
Indoles...49
Inflammatory bowel disease 216–217
    nutrition issues..................................216
    nutrition recommendations for........217
Inositol...129
Insoluble fiber................................40–41, 48
Insulin hormone....................................155
Insulin sensitivity 136
International Bottled Water
    Association (IBWA)......................29–30
International Congress of
    Anthropological and
        Ethnological Sciences....................12
International Food Information
    Council (IFIC) 46

Investigational New Drug/New
  Drug Application (IND/NDA)
      process of the FDA......................167
Iodine..142–143, 146
Iron...........49, 130, 133, 140–141, 146, 192
  heme..194
  lentils and...66
  menopause and...............................219
Iron-deficiency anemia..................194–195
Irradiation..64–65
Isoflavones...75
Isoleucine..34
Isothiocyanates......................................49
Israel, dietary guidelines in.....................91

J

Japan, dietary guidelines in.....................92
Jicama..65
  Tropical Coleslaw..............................65
Juniper...183
Junk science...234

K

Kamillosan...174
Kava..179–180
Kavalactone...179
Kelp...226
Keratin...34
Keratinization.....................................114
Ketogenic diets.............................105, 206
Ketones.......................................104–105, 206
Ketosis...206
Kiwi...65–66
  Spicy Kiwi Salsa.................................66
Korea, dietary guidelines in......................92
Kushi, Aveline.......................................98
Kushi, Michio..98

L

Lactaid..225, 226
Lactase..151

Lactobacillus bulgaricus.............................81
Lacto-ovo vegetarian.............................102
Lactose...81
Lactose intolerance............12, 53, 151, 225
Lacto vegetarian...................................102
Laetrile...159
Lauric acid..182
LDL cholesterol.....6, 36, 38, 45, 68, 69, 211
Lead...133
  toxicity to...134
Lecithin...128, 159
Legumes..44
Lemon basil pasta..................................72
Lentils..66–67
  BBQ Lentils..67
Lettuce..73–74
Leucine...34, 149
Licorice..180, 214
Lighthouse National Center for
  Vision and Aging................................217
Lima beans
  Summer Succotash.......................79–80
Linoleic acid..182
Linolenic acid..182
Liquid meal replacements....................222
Listeria..45
Liver disease...184
Lobelia...184
Lovastatin...157
Lozenges...166
Lp (a)...211
L-tryptophan...150
Lupus..12, 207
Lutein...........................65, 114, 217, 218
Lycopene.........................63, 70, 78, 114
Lysine..34, 47
Lysine amino acid deficency..................47

M

Macrobiotic diets................................201
Macrobiotics....................................97–99

Macular degeneration................80, 217–218
    nutrition recommendations for.........218
Magazines, rating, for accuracy..............231
Magnesium.............................135–136, 146
    blood pressure and...........................213
Magnolia-Stephania.................................184
Major minerals.......................133, 134–136
Malnutrition....................................215, 216
Manganese......................................144, 146
Mannitol..204
Margarine...39
Mashed Sweet Potatoes..............................76
Mealtime, making, quality time..........87–88
Medical records...6
Medications...131
    grapefruit juice and.............................63
Mediterranean Diet....................70, 99–100
Medline...245
Megadose...112
Melatonin.............................122, 150, 156
Melons...67
    tropical sunrise.....................................67
Menadione...119
Menaquoine...119
Menopause..218–219
    nutrition issues.........................218–219
    nutrition recommendations for.........219
Mental depression....................................150
Mercury..133
Meridians...100
Metabisulfite..208
Metabolism...12, 21
Methionine............................34, 149, 154
Mevacor..157
Mexican yam..183
Mexican yam bean.....................................65
Miacin...113
Migraines...220
    nutrition issues.........................220–221
    nutrition recommendations for.........221
Milk...74
    allergies to.....................................14, 75

Minerals..133–147
    colloidal..133
    dueling...145
    major..133, 134–136
    needs for special situations...............146
Mineral supplement.................................147
Mitochondrion...151
Moderate low-fat eating...........................105
Molybdenum...................................144, 146
Monounsaturated fat.....36, 38, 43, 102, 213
Motion sickness, ginger and....................176
MSG...208
Muffins, Heavy Duty Bran.........................48
Multivitamin supplements.......................147
Mushrooms..68
    Grilled Portobello Mushrooms............68
Myoglobin..34
Myosin...34

N

Naproxen (Aleve)............................214, 220
Naringin...63
National Cancer Institute.........................200
National Center For Chronic
    Disease Prevention............................205
National Center for Complementary
    and Alternative Medicine
        (NCCAM)..................................244
National Center for Nutrition
    and Dietetics.....................................243
National Council Against
    Health Fraud.....................................148
National Council for Responsible
    Health Information............................148
National Dairy Council............................225
National Health and Nutrition
    Examination Survey (NHANES)...........3
National HIV and AIDS Prevention
    Center...215
National Organization for Rare
    Disorders...129

National Osteoporosis
Foundation..................22, 26, 226
National Resources Defense
Council (NRDC) 29
Natural cheese 53
Netherlands
dietary guidelines in............................92
Neural tube defect (NTD).......124, 194, 236
New Zealand
dietary guidelines in.......................92–93
Niacin (B-3) 49, 110, 121–122, 132
Niacin supplements...................................108
Night blindness 109
Nightshade family of vegetables,
arthritis and..195
Nitrates 208
No Added Sugar plan 204
No Concentrated Sweets diet..................204
Nonsteroidal anti-inflammatory
drugs (NSAIDs)...............197, 214, 220
Norway, dietary guidelines in....................93
Nutrient-based eating styles....................103
Nutrient-control claims............................236
Nutrient measures and conversions........110
Nutritional health, determining your 11
Nutritionist..243
Nutrition products and purveyors,
evaluating...................................229–248
Nutrition quackery...........................245–246
Nutrition research, challenge of...............13
Nutrition support claims.........................236
Nuts...68–69
Trail Mix 69

O

Oats...69–70
Old-Fashioned Oatmeal
Porridge 70
Obesity......................20–21, 31, 221
nutrition issues...............................221
nutrition recommendations
to avoid..................................221

Obsessed eating 95
Oil-based laxatives......................................82
Oils 166
Older adults, calorie needs of....................89
Old-Fashioned Oatmeal Porridge.............70
Olean 116
Olive oil.........................36, 38, 70–71, 100
for dipping..71
Omega-3 fatty acids.................60, 159, 196
benefits of...58–59
Omega-6 fatty acids...................................60
Onion 42, 200
Oolong tea 77
Operation Cure-all 247
Oral contraceptives, vitamin
needs and...131
Ornish diet 212
Orthorexia 95
Osteoarthritis..195
glucosamine and...................................158
SAM-e in treating 150
Osteoblasts 224
Osteoclasts...224
Osteoporosis......................22–23, 223–226
calcium and................................134, 236
milk intolerance and 89
nutrition issues 224–225
nutrition recommendations
for..................................225–226
risk for.......................................22, 23
soft drinks and 74
vitamin D and.........................115, 117
Over-the-counter medications................222
herbal remedies as.............................167
Ovo vegetarian..102
Oxidation..108

P

Pacific yew tree...183
Pancreas...16
Pantothenic acid (B-5) 126, 132
Papain..71

Papaya..71–72
Papaya Chutney..............................71–72
Para amino benzoic acid (PABA) 150
Parabens 208
Parasites..59
Parkinson's disease
    CoQ-10 and....................................151
    cranberries and................................56
    vitamin E and................................119
Parsley 183
Parthenolide 176
Pasta..72
    Lemon Basil Pasta............................72
    Pasta Stir-Fry with Chicken 54
    Pasta with Red Pepper Sauce 73
Pasteurized processed cheese 53
Peanuts, allergies to..............................14
Pellagra 121–122
Penicillin..170
Peppers..72–73
    Pasta with Red Pepper Sauce 73
Pernicious anemia 194, 195
Persian melon......................................67
Personal nutritional survey..................9–10
Pesticide and insecticide reduction 46–47
Phenols 221
    headaches and 220
Phenylalamine 34, 149
Philippines, dietary guidelines in..............93
Phosphatidyl choline............................128
Phosphorus 52, 136, 146
Phylloquinone 119
Physical activity, need for more..............31
Phytochemicals..............................49, 75
Phytoestrogens 75
Pineal gland..156
Placebo 230
Placebo effect......................................248
Plantain..73
Pollution..82
Polycyclic aromatic
    hydrocarbons (PAHs)......................201

Polyphenols....................................77, 201
Polysaccharides 172
Polyunsaturated fats....................36, 38, 102
Potassium..............................65–66, 137
    blood pressure and 213
    deficiency in 183
Potassium sulfite 208
Pregnancy
    biotin deficiency in..........................125
    calorie needs of 30–31
    vitamin A in..................................115
Premenstrual syndrome
    (PMS) 122, 226–227
    nutrition issues 226–227
    nutrition recommendations
        for 227
Prepackaged meals 222
Pritikin diet............................105–106, 212
Progesterone, menopause and................218
Propolis..64
Proscar..181
Prospective studies 230
Prostate cancer 78
Protein..34, 52
    complementary................................34
    high 104–105
    in vegetarian eating........................102
    vitamin B-6 and..............................122
Protein powders 153
Proteoglycans......................................150
Prozac..181
PSA 181
Psoriasis..58
Psychosomatic 248
Psyllium..73
Psyllium seed husk disease 236
Purity..235
Purple foxglove 171
Pycogenol 159–160
Pylorus..228
Pyridoxine (vitamin B-6) 122–123

Q

Qi 100
Quinine...164

R

Radura symbol....................................65
Rapeseed 50
Recommended Dietary
      Allowances (RDAs) 3, 31, 108, 111
Redux...191
Registered Dietitian (RD) 243
Remforce...158
Retinal...114
Retinol 114
Retrospective studies 231
Reversatrol..80
Revivarant..158
Reye's syndrome 184
Rheumatoid arthritis 195, 196, 207
    riboflavin deficiency and 121
Rhubarb root 183
Riboflavin (B-2)...............52, 113, 121, 132
Rice
    brown.................................49–50
    Cheesy Chili 53–54
Ritalin 199
Royal jelly...159

S

Saccharin 204
St. John's wort 166, 167, 169,
                180–181, 185, 187
Salad dressings
    Grapefruit Yogurt 81
    Sassy 51
Salads...73–74
    Brown Rice and Chicken....................50
    Field Green....................................74
    Zesty Black Bean.............................44
Salicylic acid 164
Salmon, Green Tea Poached 77

Salmonella..64
Salsa
    Carrot Mango 52
    Cranberry 56
    Spicy Kiwi....................................66
Salt, as acquired taste 138
Sassafras..184
Sassy Salad Dressing...........................51
Saturated fat 36, 38–39
Sauces, Believe-It-or-Not BBQ.................62
Saw palmetto 181–182
Scurvy.......................109, 110, 127
Sea vegetables 226
Seldane...63
Selenium 108, 143–144, 146
Semi-sweet chocolate 55
Semolina...72
Senna 183
Serotonin.................34, 122, 150, 176
Shark cartilage 160
Shellfish, allergies to...............14, 157
Siberian ginseng 178
Simple carbohydrates 33
    examples of..................................33
Simple sugars.....................................33
Smoking...83
Sodium 137–140
Sodium caseinate...............................209
Soft drinks 74, 104
Soluble fiber 40, 66
Sorbitol 204
South Africa, dietary guidelines in...........93
Southwestern Couscous 55
Soy 74–75
    allergies to 14
    Herbed Edamame 75
    menopause and...............................219
Soybeans 75
Soymilk..75
Spicy kiwi salsa..................................66
Spina bifida.......................................124
Spirulina.................................160–161

Spontaneous remissions 248
Sports beverages 153
Sports power bars 57
Starches...33
Step I diet 212
Step II diet 212
Strawberries...............................75–76
    Strawberry Smoothie 76
Strength 235
Streptococcus thermophilus 81
Stress...83
Stroke..23
    risk for 24–26
Strychnine 170
Substance P..51
Sudden toxicity..................................113
Sugars 95
    artificial.....................................204
    simple 33
Sulfites 208
    headaches and........................220–221
Sulforaphane.....................................201
Sulfurophane 49
Summer Succotash 79–80
Supplements..............................234–240
    need for 108
    reading label on............................238
Surgery..223
Sweet potatoes.............................47, 76
    Mashed Sweet Potatoes 76
Syrups 166
Systolic pressure 213

T

Tannin 77, 217
Taurine 129–130
Taxol..183
Tea 76–77
    Cranberry Herb 56
    diet..183
    Green Tea Poached Salmon.................77
    herbal....................................182–183

Teratogenic toxicity 113
Testosterone.....................................155
Thailand, dietary guidelines in.................93
Thiamin (B-1) 49, 113, 120, 132
    deficiency in 110, 120
Thirst...27
Threonine..34
Thrush...214
Thyroid hormone 155
Tinctures..166
Tocopherol...77
Tolerable Upper Intake
    Levels (ULs) 111–112
Tomatoes.....................................46, 78
    Tomato Jubilee................................78
Total Average Glucose
    (TAG) plan 204
Total cholesterol 6
Toxicity
    acute or sudden 113
    chronic...113
    teratogenic 113
    vitamin A 115
Trace elements 133, 140–145
Traditional Chinese
    Medicine (TCM) 100–102, 172, 178
Trail Mix 69
Trans fats 39
Tree nuts, allergies to 14
Treonine...149
Trial of Nonpharmacologic
    Interventions in the Elderly
      (TONE) 140
Triglycerides 36, 211, 213
Tropical Coleslaw 65
Tropical Sunrise...................................67
Tryptophan 34, 110, 121
Type 1 diabetes............................203, 205
Type 2 diabetes.................68–69, 203, 205
Tyramine..221
Tyrosine 149

U

Ubiquone.................................151
Ulcers.............................227–228
  duodenal...........................227
  esophageal.........................227
  gastric............................227–228
  nutrition issues...................227–228
  nutrition recommendations for.....228
Uncoated tablets......................166
United Kingdom
  dietary guidelines in..............93
United States
  dietary guidelines in..............93
United States Department of
  Agriculture's (USDA's) Economic
  Research Service...................4
United States Pharmacopoeia
  (USP).............................166, 169, 235
United States Pharmacopoeia
  (USP) Convention...................171
Unsweetened chocolate.................55
Supplements, selling herbs as.........166
Urinary tract infections, cranberry
  juice for..........................55–56
USDA Dietary Guidelines...............31

V

Valerian..............................182
Valerian root.........................169
Valine................................34, 149
Vegans
  vitamin B-12 and...................123
  vitamins for.......................109
Vegetables............................78–80
  servings of........................19, 20
  Summer Succotash...................79–80
Vegetarians...........................34, 102–103
  carnitine and......................129
  lacto..............................102
  lacto-ovo..........................102
  lifestyle choices of...............45

ovo...................................102
pernicious anemia in..................194
source of foods.......................103
vitamin B-12 and......................123
zinc for..............................145
Very low-calorie diets................223
Vitamin A.............................52, 108, 109, 111, 114–115, 130, 132, 192
  deficiency of......................114
  mucin production and...............228
  toxicity of........................115
Vitamin B-1...........................49, 113, 120, 132
Vitamin B-2...........................52, 113, 121, 132
Vitamin B-3...........................49, 110, 121–122, 132
Vitamin B-5...........................126, 132
Vitamin B-6...........................13, 132
  asthma and.........................197–198
Vitamin B-12..........................13, 52, 104, 123, 132
Vitamin C.............................66, 78, 108, 110, 126–128, 130, 132
  arthritis and......................196
  asthma and.........................198
  cataracts and......................202
  deficiency of......................110
  smoking and........................83
Vitamin D.............................110, 115–118, 130, 132
  arthritis and......................196
  calcium and........................225
  deficiency of......................115, 117
Vitamin E.............................108, 118–119, 132, 192
  arthritis and......................196
  asthma and.........................198
  cataracts and......................202
  natural form of....................240
Vitamin K.............................109, 110, 119, 132
Vitamin-like compounds................128–130
Vitamins..............................108–132
  fat-soluble........................36, 113
  need for, in special situations....132
  water-soluble......................49, 120–128, 235

W

Warfarin (Coumadin)...............................119
Water 27–29
　　bottled..29–30
　　fiber and 41
　　fluoridated 142
　　nutrition actions to increase
　　　　intake of......................................29
　　safety of public drinking 29
Watermelon 67
Water-soluble vitamins 49, 120–128, 235
Web fraud 247
Wheat, allergies to 14
Wheat germ 80
White chocolate...55
Whole grains 40
Wild blueberry smoothie...........................48
Willow bark............................168, 183, 184
Willpower 21
Wilson's disease......................................141
Wine 80–81
　　Easy Wine Marinade............................81
Women, type 2 diabetes in.................68–69
Women's Sports Foundation 104
Wormwood...185

X

Xenical...116

Y

Yin and yang...97
Yogurt 81
　　Grapefruit Yogurt Salad Dressing........81
Yohimbe...185

Z

Zeaxanthin......................................217, 218
Zerophthalmia 114
Zesty Black Bean Salad 44
Zinc.................52, 104, 133, 144–145, 146
　　Alzheimer's disease and 192
　　colds and 144, 145
　　mucin production and......................228
　　for vegetarians 145
Zinc-gluconate-glycine lozenges 145
Zoloft...167, 181
Zostrix 51
Zucchini 81–82
　　Zucchini Stir Fry 82